ARGUING ABOUT LAW

Arguing About Law

An Introduction to Legal Philosophy

SECOND EDITION

ANDREW ALTMAN
The George Washington University

Wadsworth Publishing Company
I T P® An International Thomson Pulbishing Company

Australia • Canada • Mexico • Singapore • Spain
United Kingdom • United States

Philosophy Editor: Peter Adams
Assistant Editor: Kerri Abdinoor
Editorial Assistant: Mark Andrews
Marketing Manager: Dave Garrison
Print Buyer: Tandra Jorgenson
Permissions Editor: Bob Kauser

Production Service: Gustafson Graphics
Copy Editor: Linda Ireland
Cover Designer: Harry Voigt
Cover Printer: Webcom Limited
Compositor: Gustafson Graphics
Printer/Binder: Webcom Limited

For more information, contact
Wadsworth/Thomson Learning
10 Davis Drive
Belmont, CA 94002-3098
USA
http://www.wadsworth.com

International Headquarters
Thomson Learning
International Division
290 Harbor Drive, 2nd Floor
Stamford, CT 06902-7477
USA

UK/Europe/Middle East/South Africa
Thomson Learning
Berkshire House
168-173 High Holborn
London WC1V 7AA
United Kingdom

Asia
Thomson Learning
60 Albert Street, #15-01
Albert Complex
Singapore 189969

Canada
Nelson Thomson Learning
1120 Birchmount Road
Scarborough, Ontario M1K 5G4
Canada

Library of Congress
Cataloging-in-Publication Data

Altman, Andrew
　　Arguing about law: an introduction to legal philosophy / Andrew Altman.— 2nd ed.
　　　　p. cm.
　　Includes bibliographical references and index.
　　ISBN 0-534-54352-9
　　　　1. Law—Philosophy.   2. Rule of law.   3. Law and economics.   4. Law and ethics.   I. Title.
K230.A447 A74 2000
340'.l—dc21　　　　　　　　00-025236

To My Argumentative Family

Contents

Preface

first taught Philosophy of Law in 1978. At the time, the field of Philosophy was undergoing important changes. The idea was gaining acceptance that Philosophy could help illuminate important ethical, social, and political problems. More and more, philosophers were writing and teaching about issues that just a decade earlier had rarely been discussed in professional publications or course offerings: abortion, euthanasia, affirmative action, the death penalty, civil disobedience, and so on. Philosophy was becoming increasingly concerned with what the American pragmatist, John Dewey, called "the problems of men."

The more abstract and technical problems of traditional philosophers were not ignored, but they were no longer the exclusive focus of philosophical deliberation. Moreover, many thinkers came to the conclusion that there were important interconnections between the abstract problems of philosophers and the more concrete problems faced by society. Indeed, Dewey and others pointed out that the greatest philosophers of the past were, in their own way, grappling with the concrete problems of their age.

Philosophy of Law has proved to be a very fertile field for philosophical reflection on the problems faced by society. In one way or another, just about every significant social problem of the present day finds its way into the law and presents a legal issue. And over the past decade and a half, many philosophers have brought to bear on a broad range of these issues their skill at critical thinking and their understanding of the philosophical tradition.

This book presents Philosophy of Law as a field whose abstract theories and questions are tied to the practical problems of society. Some of the problems that I explicitly discuss are from the past, while others are contemporary. But it should not be forgotten that past problems have their analogues in the contemporary world and that we can learn much about our current predicaments by studying those of the past.

When I was a graduate student, I did not even so much as take a course in Philosophy of Law. I did not think that I would be interested in the topic. How wrong I was! And how much I needed to depend on the kind help of others in learning about both law and legal philosophy, when I finally realized my mistake several years after graduation. Among those to whom I owe thanks for helping to educate me about the law are Mark Tushnet, John Fellas, Joel Grossman, Morton Horwitz, Frank Michelman, Fred Kellogg, and Duncan Kennedy. Finally, I must thank the students who attended my Philosophy of Law courses over the years, especially the many bright students at the George Washington University. This book is in no small measure a product of my efforts to teach and to learn from them.

Preface to Second Edition

This second edition of *Arguing About Law* contains three major changes. First, the opening chapter has been extensively revised to include an examination of the impeachment of President Clinton. The idea of the rule of law repeatedly surfaced during the public debate over the investigation, impeachment, and trial of the president. As the central theme of this book is the rule of law, it seemed impossible to omit a discussion of the impeachment controversy. And once I began to write about the controversy it became clear that simply a brief reference to it would be unsatisfactory. A relatively extended treatment would be needed to explore even some of the many rich rule-of-law issues raised by the impeachment and surrounding events. Accordingly, I recast the first chapter to include such a treatment.

Second, a new chapter has been added on the topic of race. The first edition made only a passing reference to issues of race. But one of my aims in this book has been to treat issues that are both topical and of enduring significance. The issue of race certainly meets those criteria. The chapter, "Race and American Law," has more historical material than any of the others. That fact reflects my conviction that current issues of race in the United States need to be understood in the context of the nation's history. Even so, limitations of space and competence meant that I could not include in the chapter the important and complex legal issues surrounding the nation's relations with Native American tribes. Yet, the chapter does seek to examine in depth the role of American law in creating, reflecting, and reinforcing racial categories.

Third, I have added discussion questions to the end of each chapter. In some cases, the questions focus directly on the material examined in the chapter. In other cases, the questions introduce new material connected to the issues of the chapter.

Among the smaller changes is the relocation of the discussion of the Nuremberg Trial from the first to the second chapter. The discussion still raises the rule-of-law issues treated in the first edition, but it has been extended to include an examination of how the debate between legal positivism and natural law theory played out in the trial of the German war criminals.

In several places, I have modified my presentations of issues or theories in order to make them more understandable. For example, in Chapter 2, Dworkin's difficult distinction between internal and external skepticism is now explained in a clearer and more concise way.

I am grateful to those who read and sent me comments on the first edition or on drafts of the second. They include: Steven Lee, Mark Tushnet, Raymond Belliotti, D. M. Farrell, Laurence Houlgate, Kenneth Henley, Tim Torgerson, Michael Robins, and David DeGrazia. I also owe thanks to William Griffith and Amy Baehr who helpfully commented on earlier versions of the book.

Introduction

Legal philosophy can be one of the most exciting areas of philosophy for an undergraduate to study. It raises and examines problems of deep and abiding human concern. It intersects with history and politics, art and science. It treats questions that resonate with today's headlines but that also reach back to the roots of our civilization. And developments in the field over the past twenty years have provoked vigorous debate and controversy.

Yet, texts in legal philosophy typically fail to convey the intellectual excitement of the field. They are dry recitations about abstract problems disconnected from their context in history and society. And too many of them ignore too much of the recent controversy and debate.

I have written this text with the hope of conveying to the student the excitement that the field holds. This does not mean a relaxation of suitable analytical rigor. Indeed, part of the excitement of the field comes from following closely the arguments and counterarguments and counter-counterarguments that pervade it. But, to my mind at any rate, conveying the excitement of the field does mean connecting the issues of legal philosophy to history and to politics and to problems of abiding human concern.

I have not tried to write a history of the problems and theories of legal philosophy. My organizing scheme has been mainly conceptual. And yet there are important stories to tell that are part of the history of legal thought. I have tried to tell some of them as a way a giving significance to the conceptual debates and arguments that fill the pages of the history of legal philosophy: the story of the Nuremberg Trial of Major War Criminals to give significance to debates about the rule of law; the story of the Civil Rights Movement to show how law and civil disobedience can work together to promote legal and social justice; the story of the labor injunction to give significance to the legal realist attack on the distinction between private and public law. One of the most rewarding aspects of studying, and teaching, legal philosophy is seeing how its abstract theories and debates play out in events and episodes of historical moment.

Legal philosophy is a sprawling area, and no reasonably sized text can hope to cover all the important issues. My principle of selection revolves around the topic of the first chapter: the rule of law. Not too many years ago, Joseph Raz remarked that the rule of law was a relatively neglected topic among legal philosophers. Recent work in feminist jurisprudence and critical legal studies has revived interest in it to some extent. There is more discussion of the rule of law than there was just a few years back.

This text goes a step farther in making the idea of the rule of law the central organizing concept. It is an idea that stands between and connects the more abstract problems of legal and political philosophy, on the one side, and the more concrete questions about social and political life, on the other. This strategic location is illustrated at the very beginning of the first chapter, in the remarks of Congressman Henry Hyde at the impeachment trial of President Clinton. Congressman Hyde explicitly invokes the idea of the rule of law in order to place the events of the trial in historical and philosophical perspective.

Much recent work in legal philosophy is skeptical about the feasibility of the rule of law and even about the logical coherence of the very idea. In making the idea the central organizing concept I do not mean to dismiss those skeptical views out of hand. To the contrary, the intent is to take them all the more seriously because of the challenge they represent.

Although I am a defender of the rule of law, it is not the purpose of this text to prostelytize but rather to provoke careful thought and argument. While making my views about certain issues clear, I have tried to avoid a dogmatic style that would discourage students from further thought on the subjects. And I have tried to present the clearest and best arguments on all sides of the issues discussed. The text will have accomplished an important purpose if it persuades no student that my preferred solutions are the right ones, but it provokes many students into thinking in a more systematic and informed way about law and its connections to history, politics, science, and the other areas of human endeavor.

The traditional starting point for texts and anthologies in legal philosophy is the question, "What is law?" This text starts with a different question, "What is the rule of law and why is it important?" It postpones consideration to the second chapter of "What is law?" and the traditional theories responding to that question. Analytically, it may make more sense to start with "What is law?" But pedagogically I have found the question about the rule of law to be more effective at eliciting student interest in thinking carefully about the law. Moreover, the idea of law is one to which students already attach some meaning, and their intuitive notions of law as the enactments and rules laid down by a government is sufficient to get questions about the rule of law off the ground. The first chapter tries to engage these intuitive notions, even as it encourages students to think systematically about the law. This leads naturally to the questions, theories, and arguments of the second chapter.

The third and fourth chapters focus on questions about the the legal system of the United States: its Constitution and its private law, respectively. Traditionally, legal philosophy has abstracted from issues and questions relating to particular legal systems. That is, I think, a mistake from both a philosophical and pedagogical point of view. There is nothing wrong with abstracting from the particulars of a legal system. But there are no convincing grounds for holding that philosophical reflection stops once one begins to think about the particulars of a given system. Philosophical reflection on law needs to operate at varying levels of abstraction and to avoid giving what is more abstract an automatically privileged status over what is more concrete. In addition, focusing only on the most abstract issues robs legal philosophy of its most powerful sources of intellectual excitement for the student.

Issues in constitutional law present a wealth of material for philosophical analysis, reflection, and argument. Questions about the best approaches to legal interpretation are especially important in the constitutional context. Issues of political philosophy are never very far from the questions of constitutional law. And the idea of the rule of law plays a key role in many of the debates and controversies surrounding constitutional law.

The fifth chapter is devoted to criminal law. It examines general theories of criminal punishment, as well as specific practices, such as holding persons strictly liable for their conduct and its consequences. The difficult question of the relation of law and morality appears repeatedly in efforts to understand and justify the practice of criminal punishment. And the criminal law raises in stark form the enduring philosophical issue of the limits of the legitimate power of government.

The sixth chapter examines an approach to law that has developed over the last three decades, known as "law and economics." It seeks to use the basic principles of economics in order to clarify and critically analyze the legal rules and doctrines that make up our system of law. The approach has proved to be both influential and controversial. One of the central figures of the law and economics movement, Richard Posner, is currently chief judge on the Seventh Circuit Court of Appeals, and his judicial opinions are among the most cited of those written by circuit court judges. His books and articles have been taught in law schools, exercising an influence on the thinking of future lawyers and judges. Even those who would not go as far as Posner in applying economic principles to law still find that the law and economics approach can illuminate and guide the development of important areas of law. And yet others find the approach both logically flawed and politically objectionable. They argue that the principles of economics are of little help in describing, explaining, or guiding the development of the law. The sixth chapter examines some of these important arguments over law and economics.

Chapter 7 examines one of the most recent developments in legal theory, feminist legal philosophy. This approach is an outgrowth of the feminist movement that began in the United States in the mid–1960s. It utilizes some of the basic ideas of that movement in order to understand, criticize, and revise legal rules and doctrines that work against the interests of women. This chapter will outline the nature of feminism, describe the different branches of femininst legal philosophy, and analyze the disagreements and arguments between two of the main branches.

The eighth chapter treats issues of race in American law, including such topics of current controversy as affirmative action and racial profiling by police. But the chapter also seeks to provide the reader with historical perspective on these current controversies by examining how race and law have been intertwined from the nation's beginnings.

The ninth and final chapter examines the Critical Legal Studies movement, and with it we come full circle, returning to the main theme of the rule of law. Critical Legal Studies attacks the idea of the rule of law: it says that we do not have the rule of law, that the idea is a fiction. This attack is a challenge to those who, like Representative Hyde, believe the rule of law exists in our country, even if imperfectly, and that it is good for us that it does. The chapter explains the challenge and examines whether it can be met. By the time the student reaches this part of the book, she or he will be in a position to make a reasoned judgment on the issue.

The basic questions of legal philosophy have provoked controversy and argument from the earliest days of our civilization. Argument about law is at the center of our tradition in legal philosophy. But it is argument that seeks to persuade with the strongest reasons, not coerce with the most destructive weapons or silence with the loudest voice. In the final analysis, we can never be justifiably certain that we have discovered the strongest reasons or formulated the most persuasive argument. And that is why we must listen to those who claim to have better arguments and stronger reasons. And that is why the Western tradition in legal philosophy should and will continue as long as we think and argue about law.

1

※

The Rule of Law

IMPEACHMENT AND THE RULE OF LAW

The scandal stemming from his relationship with former White House Intern Monica Lewinsky consumed much of President Bill Clinton's second term of office. Among the arguments the scandal provoked was one over whether the president should be impeached, tried, and removed from office. Opinion polls consistently showed that about two-thirds of the public opposed his impeachment and removal, while about one-third was in favor. The House of Representatives did, in fact, impeach the president, but the Senate declined to convict and remove him.

The public debate over the impeachment process often made reference to the idea of the rule of law. The president's detractors, as well as his defenders, invoked the idea to support their side of the argument. Representative Henry Hyde (R-IL) was among the leaders of the impeachment effort. He spoke with eloquence and emotion about the rule of law as an ideal that Western civilization has long endorsed and celebrated. Addressing the Senate at the trial of the president, Mr. Hyde said:

> Let's be clear; the vote you are asked to cast is, in the final analysis, a vote about the rule of law. The rule of law is one of the greatest achievements of our civilization, for the alternative to the rule of law is the rule of raw power. We here today are heirs of 3,000 years of history, in which humanity slowly and painfully and at great cost evolved a form of politics in which law, not brute force, is the arbiter of our public destinies. . . .

The rule of law is what stands between all of us and the arbitrary exercise of power by the state. The rule of law is the safeguard of our liberties.[1]

The defenders of the president also appealed to the rule of law in order to bolster their case. One of the president's lawyers, Cheryl Mills, spoke forcefully in his defense:

The rule of law applies to the weak and the strong, the rich and the poor, the powerful and the powerless. If you love the rule of law, you must love it in all of its applications. You cannot only love it when it provides the verdict you seek; you must love it when the verdict goes against you, as well. We cannot uphold the rule of law only when it is consistent with our beliefs; we must uphold it even when it protects behavior that we don't like or is unattractive, or is not admirable, or that might even be hurtful. And we cannot say we love the rule of law but dismiss arguments that appeal to the rule of law as "legalisms" or "legal hair-splitting."[2]

This chapter will focus on a series of philosophical and practical questions about the rule of law and its relation to the investigation and impeachment of the president. What is the rule of law? Is it good for a country to have the rule of law and, if so, why? Are there undesirable aspects to the rule of law? Is it really possible to establish the rule of law? Did the investigation of the president's affair with Ms. Lewinsky and the Senate trial meet the requirements of the rule of law? Is an impeachment trial properly held to the standards of the rule of law? What role, if any, may political considerations properly play in an impeachment trial, or any other kind of trial, for that matter?

To address these questions, we need a more complete and systematic account of the idea of the rule of law than can be found in the impeachment record. Indeed, the politicians and media commentators involved in the impeachment debate sometimes exhibited a rather limited understanding of the idea. For example, while endorsing the rule of law, advocates of an aggressive investigation of the president's affair also argued that getting at the truth about the affair mattered above all else. The problem with this argument is that the truth cannot possibly matter above all else if the rule of law also matters. The fact is that the rule of law places substantial limits on acceptable ways of pursuing the truth.

Moreover, the rule of law is an ideal that cannot be easily or mechanically applied in the real world of imperfect human beings. Translating the ideal into a system of legal and political institutions that can work is a very complicated task. Politicians and media commentators showed little understanding of the complexities.

In addition, despite the broad endorsement of the rule of law among Western thinkers, some philosophers have argued that the very idea of the rule of law is fundamentally defective and that it is impossible to translate the idea into reality. Such arguments need to be confronted by those who celebrate the rule of law as an ideal to which we rightly commit our nation.

The public debate over President Clinton's impeachment brought attention to the concept of the rule of law, but it did little to clarify the subtleties of the concept or the difficulties involved in translating it into a functioning system of law and politics. In the remainder of this chapter, we will explore the meaning of the rule-of-law ideal and the problems raised by the practical task of making the ideal a reality. And we will confront some of the key arguments of the critics of the rule of law.

ARBITRARY GOVERNMENT AND THE PRINCIPLES OF LEGALITY

In this section, the idea of the rule of law will be explained in terms of *five principles*. These principles place important restrictions on how government is permitted to operate and how public and private power may be exercised. Some of these principles are of ancient origin, while others are of more recent vintage. Together, they define the way the rule of law has come to be understood over the centuries in Western civilization.

Government Under Law

At the center of the rule of law is the idea that a government should not exercise its power in an arbitrary manner. This idea does not exhaust the entire meaning of the rule of law, but it is the place to begin in order to understand its meaning. Arbitrary government operates by different methods and principles than does a government under the rule of law. To understand the rule of law we must understand those differences.

The ancient Greeks were the first to formulate the idea of the rule of law. They understood arbitrary government as a government that did whatever it pleased, unconstrained by any legal rules or principles. It is precisely this sort of government that they saw in their mortal enemy, Persia. The Persian Emperor possessed such arbitrary power over his subjects: he was "above the law." The Greeks contrasted such a system with a government under the rule of law, where no one was above the law. Even the highest officials in government were restrained from doing as they pleased, and they did only what the law authorized or permitted them to do. Thus, we may say that the *first principle* of the rule of law is that government must not act or operate above the law.

But what if there is a legal rule that says the government can do whatever it pleases? Would such a government be under the rule of law?

The answer is no. Such a government should be classified as an arbitrary one, not as a government under law. This is because we must understand the principle that government must not act above the law in light of a key purpose of the rule of law: to constrain and regulate the power of government so as to prevent it from doing whatever it pleases. This purpose presupposes that there are laws placing genuine restrictions on the actions of government. As the ancient Greeks well understood, a government that was legally authorized to act however it pleased would not be an example of the rule of law but rather a parody of it.

In real life, every government has officials or agencies that sometimes exceed their lawful authority or even commit criminal acts. Does it follow from that fact that there has never been a government under the rule of law?

There has certainly never been a *perfect* example of a government under the rule of law, and it is unreasonable to think there ever will be. In that sense, the idea of the rule of law is an ideal. Yet, it still may be possible to distinguish those governments that do a *reasonably* good job of meeting the principles of the rule of law and those governments that do not even come close to doing so.

It may be impossible to specify a precise line between these two kinds of government. But it is not important to do so, anymore than it is important to specify a precise line between people who are bald and people who are not. For both baldness and the rule of law, there are clear cases and there are borderline ones. And there is not much point in wrangling over how to sort out the borderline ones. All we need to do is recognize that they are borderline and go from there.

The idea of the rule of law is more complex than the principle that government must not act or operate above the law. There is a second principle, and it concerns the way in which governments carry out the task of maintaining social order and peace, including the job of detecting and punishing those who are a danger to society. Again, arbitrary governments carry out this task using different means and methods than do governments under the rule of law.

Government by Rules

Governments that operate by the rule of law maintain civil order and peace principally by laying down and enforcing general rules. Such rules are not addressed to specific persons but to the population generally or to certain segments of the population, who are required to abide by the rules. Specific persons are punished or sanctioned in some way if it can be shown that they have violated the authoritative rules. But if it cannot be shown that a person has done so, then a government under the rule of law will refrain from punishing the individual, no matter what else it or the rest of society may think about the person or his conduct.

Arbitrary governments refuse to rely mainly on authoritative rules in their efforts to maintain peace and order. Such governments either dispense with rules, or, even if they use rules, they also rely heavily on individual decrees and orders that sanction specific persons without any showing that an authoritative rule has been violated. An arbitrary government will often adopt such methods to punish persons who it thinks are dangerous to society or to its own control over society, regardless of whether it can be shown that they have violated any of the authoritative rules.

The *second principle* of the rule of law, then, is that government should maintain civil order and peace mainly through a system of general and authoritative rules, specifying whatever sanctions are to be imposed for violations. This principle has two important corollaries: (1) No action can be regarded by government as a crime unless there is a specific law prohibiting the action, and (2) No individual can be legitimately punished by government unless he has committed a crime, and the punishment must be limited to that which is provided for by the law. Legal thinkers often refer to these two principles by the Latin phrases expressing them: *nullum crimen sine lege* ("no crime without a law") and *nulla poena sine crimine* ("no punishment without a crime").

Governments under the rule of law do not only control criminal behavior through the use of general rules. They also regulate such civil matters as contracts and property ownership by means of such rules. Some of the general rules of civil law prohibit certain kinds of behavior, such as breach of contract and trespass. But others empower persons to accomplish goals that would otherwise not be possible, such as writing a legally valid will or entering into a legally binding contract. Both the civil and criminal law are important to the maintenance of peace and order in society.

Fair Warning and the Formal Features of Legal Rules

A little reflection will reveal that there are ways in which a government that governs through the use of general rules can easily "get around" the second principle of the rule of law and be just as arbitrary as a government that dispenses with general rules. For example, the government may enact general rules, but then keep them secret. Or it may enact rules that are so vague that it is impossible to know which actions violate them and which do not ("It shall be unlawful to engage in anti-Soviet activity"). Or it may enact rules and then apply them retrospectively, that is, to conduct that occurred before the rule was enacted.

Few people would disagree with the claim that governments which adopted such methods of controlling society would be acting arbitrarily. Those governments would not be giving individuals "fair warning," that is, a reasonable opportunity to know what the rules are and to choose to follow them. Accordingly, we need to add a *third principle* of the rule of law: The general and authoritative rules through which government maintains order and peace should give individuals fair warning.

Legal thinkers have generally agreed that fair warning requires legal rules to meet the following conditions: the rules must be (a) made public, (b) reasonably clear in meaning and specific in what they prohibit, (c) in force for a reasonable period of time, (d) applied prospectively, not retroactively, (e) applied in an impartial manner that is consistent with their meaning, (f) possible to comply with, and (g) enacted in accordance with preexisting legal rules.[3]

These features of legal rules are "formal" in that they do not prescribe any specific content that legal rules must have. The third principle does not indicate what behavior legal rules must regulate or whether the rules should permit, prohibit, or empower individuals to perform specific kinds of action. For example, the principle does not exclude a law that prohibits the practice of a certain religion. But it does demand that if there is such a law, then it must have the formal features needed to give everyone fair warning that the religion is prohibited.

Due Process

The next principle of the rule of law stems from yet another way in which governments may act arbitrarily: they may accuse an individual of violating an authoritative rule but then refuse to give the person a fair chance of showing that she is in fact innocent of the alleged violation. For example, the official body that hears and renders judgment on the charges may be biased against the defendant instead of impartial. Or it may refuse to let the defendant present her side of the story. Just as it is arbitrary for a government to punish a person whom it does not charge with violating an authoritative rule, it is arbitrary to charge an individual but not give her a fair chance to establish her innocence.

Thus, we are led to the *fourth principle* of the rule of law: Government must give all persons charged with violating the authoritative rules a fair chance to defend themselves against the charges.[4] Providing accused persons with such a chance is a major element of what lawyers call "due process of law."

The four rule-of-law principles we have thus far examined are sometimes called the principles of *legality*. They define a kind of government that abides by the requirements of law or legality. A government that abides by such principles is called a *constitutional government*. This does not necessarily mean that the government has a single, written document called a "Constitution." It does mean that, whether it has a written constitution or not, the government observes the principles of legality to a reasonable approximation and thus is to be distinguished from any arbitrary government.

The Power of the People

Thus far we have focused on the way in which the rule of law seeks to restrain and regulate the power of government and of the private organizations and individuals over whom government rules. But some political theorists have argued that there is a political power that stands above government: the power of the people. According to these theorists, the people are sovereign in the sense that it is in the hands of the people that ultimate political authority rests. Thus, John Locke argues that the legitimacy of any government is based on the consent of the people. And when a government violates the trust of the people, it loses its legitimacy and the people are entitled to reconstitute it. This was, of course, Locke's justification for political revolution against tyrannical government.

This view of the people as sovereign raises difficult and important questions. For example: Is the notion of "the people" simply a political fiction designed to rationalize a political power-grab by some particular segment of the society? The American revolutionaries of 1776 invoked Locke's ideas about the people, but a skeptic might argue that the so-called "people" turned out to be white, male, privileged people. But let us set aside such problems and, for the sake of argument, assume that the idea of the people as the ultimate holders of political authority can be accepted. The important question here is: Should the rule of law be understood to place limits, not only on government, but on the people as well? As private individuals, the people are no doubt subject to the rule of law. But what about the people in their collective identity as the holders of ultimate political authority? Are "We the People" properly held subject to the rule of law?

Table 1 The Five Principles of the Rule of Law

1. Government must operate under the law.

2. Government must regulate society through a system of general and authoritative rules.

3. The general and authoritative rules should give individuals fair warning: the rules should be (a) made public, (b) reasonably clear in meaning and specific in what they prohibit, (c) in force for a reasonable period of time, (d) applied prospectively, (e) applied impartially, (f) possible to comply with, and (g) enacted in accordance with preexisting legal rules.

4. All persons must be given due process, that is, a fair chance to defend themselves against formal charges that they have violated the rules.

5. The sovereign people ought to establish constitutional government and abide by its laws.

The central purpose of the rule of law is the restriction and regulation of both private and political power. Typically, political power is exercised by government, a set of distinct institutions within society.[5] But when political power is exercised by the people, it is also in need of regulation and restriction. The will of the people can be just as arbitrary as the will of the government.

Moreover, in democratic societies, there is no clear line between the will of government and the will of the people. The government is generally responsive to the will of the people, and the people typically have no instrument to express and carry out their will other than government. To argue that the people are above the law would be tantamount to arguing that democratic government is above the law and that would clearly contradict the fundamental principles of constitutional government. Accordingly, we are led to a *fifth principle* of the rule of law: the sovereign people ought to establish constitutional government and abide by its laws.[6]

CORRUPTION

We have seen that those thinkers who advocate the rule of law are critical of arbitrary government. For both ancient and modern philosophers, a major danger of arbitrary government is its tendency to become corrupt, promoting the private interests of the rulers rather than the common good of the community. Rulers who could do as they pleased would most likely be pleased to do things that enriched themselves at the expense of the community. The rule of law would help to prevent such corruption by restricting the rulers' powers to what was authorized by law.

Plato believed that there were certain extremely rare individuals who possessed both wisdom and integrity. Their wisdom meant that they knew the good of society. Their integrity meant that they pursued that good rather than their private good. Plato argued that such persons would be the best possible rulers: they would rule wisely and be as incorruptible as is humanly possible.

Yet, Plato realized that these philosopher-kings were not completely incorruptible, and his description of the ideal state includes rules and regulations by which even these wise and ethical rulers are bound. These rules and regulations are designed to ensure that even the philosopher-kings do not fall prey to temptation and pursue private benefits at the expense of the public good. Thus, the rulers are forbidden from owning private wealth because it is thought that any such wealth might tempt them to enrich themselves at the expense of the community.

This prohibition strikes us today as extreme and unworkable, but the belief that led Plato to introduce it is not at all foreign to our current ways of thinking: human corruptibility means that even the best and the brightest of rulers must be restricted by legal rules and regulations. Modern philosophers emphasize such corruptibility as much, or more, than did Plato, even if they would not adopt his rules for combating it.[7]

VENGEANCE

The ancient Greeks understood that the rule of law was important for more than just combating the danger of government corruption. They also saw that it helped to provide a controlled outlet for the potentially explosive human desire for vengeance, and modern defenders of the rule of law have again endorsed this insight of the ancients.

Persons who are harmed by another usually want revenge: they want to pay the individual back by inflicting harm on him. Indeed, all those who identify and sympathize with the victim—especially family and friends—typically desire to see the offender harmed in return. Yet, this desire for revenge can easily lead to an escalating cycle of retaliation in which each side seeks retribution for a harm the other side has committed.

Organized society clearly cannot tolerate such cycles of retaliation, but neither can it totally suppress the desire of victims for vengeance. The rule of law helps to resolve this dilemma by inserting the law between the offender and victim. The offender is punished or otherwise made to suffer, not by the victim or his family, but by the law and the officials who enforce it. The victim and family thus get to see the offender suffer, but they must get their satisfaction from the law's treatment of the offender and not seek to add some further punishment of their own. The law thus provides an outlet for vengeance, but it does so in a way that helps prevent that desire from generating a dangerous cycle of violence.

It was the ancient Greek dramatist, Aeschylus, who first presented the case for restraining the desire for vengeance by the rule of law. In his trilogy, *The Oresteia*, he tells the tragic story of a family destroyed by vengeance.

The father ritually sacrifices one of his daughters to gain the favor of the gods. The mother kills the father in revenge. The son, Orestes, kills the mother and her lover as revenge for his father's murder. Orestes is then hounded by the Furies, the goddesses of vengeance, who seek his death as revenge for the killing of his mother. In the end, a tribunal of deities finds Orestes not guilty and the goddess Athena convinces the Furies to give up their lust for vengeance and to live peaceably within the state and its laws. The Furies are thereby transformed into the Eumenides, the gracious goddesses, who look after hearth and home but do not seek blood vengeance on whoever harms a family member.

Aeschylus is proposing that the only reasonable way to end the cycle of revenge is through the establishment of the rule of law. The law will define which acts are crimes and the punishments for them, along with any conditions that may excuse from legal blame a person who commits such acts. An impartial tribunal will determine guilt or innocence and the punishment to be served. Individuals whose family members are victimized must learn to forgo private vengeance and accept the punishment meted out by the tribunal operating under the law.

In addition, Aeschylus sees that the rule of law has another important moral advantage over the Furies' pursuit of vengeance. The Furies' desire for revenge was blind in the sense that it drew no distinctions among different types of killing. Whether the person who did the killing was personally at fault did not enter the picture. Whether there were mitigating or excusing conditions was not asked. It was enough that the actions of the person caused the death; the person would then be pursued, tormented, and eventually killed by these goddesses of vengeance.

In contrast, the laws of ancient Greece—and of all Western societies since that time—did take account of personal fault. For example, intentional wrongdoing was distinguished from accidental wrongdoing. And doing something wrong under coercion was distinguished from doing it voluntarily. Such distinctions were lost upon the Furies. Thus, for Aeschylus, the move from private vengeance to the rule of law meant a move from a system that was morally blind to one that was capable of drawing important moral distinctions.

The desire for vengeance has been as much a part of human life in modern times as it was in Aeschylus's day. And modern advocates of the rule of law argue that, just as with the story of Orestes, private vengeance will threaten organized society unless it is restrained by law. In addition, the law in modern Western societies has continued to incorporate and develop the Greek idea that the rules governing society must take account of the idea of personal fault and the moral distinctions that go with it. The idea has become so deeply embedded in our notions of fairness that it is now understood to be an aspect of the principle that governments must give individuals a fair chance to defend themselves against charges of criminal conduct.

The rule of law aims to domesticate and restrain the desire for vengeance. Conversely, if that desire cannot be checked, it will destroy the rule of law. Restraining the desire for vengeance may not seem difficult to achieve for those of us who live under relatively stable and safe conditions. But history repeatedly shows that the Furies within us humans are not easily changed into the Eumenides. Because of this, the desire for revenge represents a continuing and important threat to the rule of law.

The powerful motive of vengeance can push people to demand that the law's operation be suspended so that they can have their revenge against those they perceive to have harmed them. In addition, this danger is not completely absent from a stable and safe system of representative democracy. When a large segment of the public insists on revenge in a way that the law does not allow, great pressure will be put on government officials to relax or ignore the principles of the rule of law. Legally innocent persons may then be made into "sacrificial lambs" to appease the public outcry for vengeance.

LIBERTY AND PROSPERITY

The concern with controlling through law both government corruption and private vengeance runs through Western history from ancient to modern times. But the modern age brings with it distinctive concerns, not found in previous eras: to protect individual liberty from government oppression and to promote economic prosperity.

Ancient Liberty

The modern view of liberty is very different from that of the ancient philosophers, even those ancients who supported the rule of law. The ancients understood liberty as the freedom to participate in the deliberations and decisions of the political community. It was not some private, individual space protected from outside interference. In addition, the ancients believed that the ultimate aim of the political community and its laws was to promote the life of virtue for all citizens.

The life of virtue, or the good life, consisted for them of a combination of intellectual activity, political participation, and leisure. Manual labor and commercial activity were largely looked down upon as unbefitting a true citizen. The "dirty work" of physical labor and commerce was to be left to those who were regarded as incapable by their nature of discharging the duties of citizenship. This included women and slaves. The laws were meant to ensure that these lower classes would do the jobs that would free citizens from the economic toil that would interfere with their pursuit of virtue. But the laws were not concerned at all to ensure that individuals would be free to develop and pursue their own conceptions of the good life.

Liberty and Prosperity in the Modern Era

In the modern age, Western society came to be characterized by many different, conflicting conceptions of what is good. In light of such social differences and a growing commitment to the idea of human equality, many modern thinkers have argued that each individual should have a wide area of liberty in which he could define and pursue without outside interference his own private ideas about what was good and meaningful in life.

An arbitrary government intent on pursuing its own vision of what was good for society would be far too likely to encroach upon, if not destroy, the domain of individual liberty. This would be true even of those governments and rulers who were sincerely seeking the public good and not merely using it as a way to hide their private corruption. Even governments that are not out for their own interests cannot be trusted with the unrestricted power to pursue their understanding of the public good. Thus, modern thinkers came to see that the rule of law could help to diminish the danger of oppression by restricting the power of government to do as it pleased, even when it pleased to pursue what it saw as the common good.

Philosophers have long debated the question of whether rules that oppress people, or otherwise treat them unjustly, can count as part of the law. Some have held that unjust rules, such as those authorizing religious persecution, could never be valid laws; others have disagreed. We will examine that debate in the next chapter. Here the important point is to realize that, even if unjust rules can count as part of the law, the rule of law is still better than arbitrary government as far as individual liberty is concerned.

An arbitrary government intent on persecuting a certain religion could punish individuals who practice the religion without first enacting a general rule against it. Such a government could also enact a rule against the religion and then apply it retroactively; or it could keep the rule secret; or it could punish the members of a certain religious group under a vague law prohibiting "socially undesirable conduct"; or it could punish violators in much more severe ways than what the law allows; and so on.

In addition, the absence of clear and public rules under an arbitrary government creates a "chilling effect" on the liberty of individuals. Since they do not know which of their activities may result in their punishment by the state, individuals restrict what they do, fearful that their next step will bring the punishing hand of government down upon them.

A government under the rule of law, on the other hand, would be prohibited from doing many of the liberty-restricting actions of an arbitrary government. It is true that a constitutional government might enact persecutory laws; the rule of law does not guarantee against that (assuming that unjust rules can count as law). But, to the extent it is observed, the rule of law does guarantee that all individuals will be able to know in advance what religious practices are punishable and what the punishments will be. That is, the law will provide fair warning to individuals about what conduct will make them liable to prosecution and punishment by the authorities. And the rule of law also guarantees any alleged violator a fair chance to establish her innocence. This will not be all the individual liberty we have a right to demand, but it does give us greater liberty than we would have under an arbitrary government bent on persecution.

The rule of law promotes liberty not only by protecting individuals against tyranny by government. It also helps to protect against the oppression of individuals by powerful private persons and organizations. The rule of law will not guarantee the elimination of private oppression, just as it does not guarantee the elimination of government tyranny. But it will require that even the wealthiest individuals and most powerful corporations abide by the law. In both the public and private spheres, the rule of law promotes liberty by restraining arbitrary power.

The rule of law also has important connections to economic prosperity. The modern capitalist economic system has proved to be the most powerful engine of economic growth ever developed. And under capitalism, growth depends on investments made by private individuals, corporations, and banks. Yet, private investors will be loath to put their money into countries where the rule of law does not operate. In such countries, any investment would be at risk from the arbitrary actions of those in political power. A factory built through private investment might be arbitrarily seized by the ruler and given as a gift to a family member.

Investors want to know what the rules of the game will be, before they put their money at risk in any given country, and they want assurance that everyone will be bound by those rules. Under arbitrary government, those in power are not bound by the rules. Under the rule of law, however, capitalists will know the rules and can be confident that everyone—including those in power—will be bound by them. The stability created by the rule of law thus establishes a climate in which capitalists will invest their money, enabling the capitalist system to work its economic magic. That is how many of the advocates of the rule of law see it, at any rate.

HOBBES AND AUSTIN: THE SOVEREIGN AS ABOVE THE LAW

The rule of law is meant to prevent corruption, restrain vengeance, protect individual liberty, and promote economic prosperity. But not all modern thinkers have believed that it can be established. Thomas Hobbes, the seventeenth-century English philosopher, argued that it is impossible to establish the rule of law and that it is politically dangerous to advocate its establishment.

The King versus Parliament

Hobbes's attack on the rule of law comes in the context of a political power struggle involving the English king and the Parliament. During the first half of the seventeenth century, Kings James I and Charles I claimed to be above the law. Members of Parliament (including the famous jurist, Sir Edward Coke) rejected this royalist view and asserted that the king was just as much subject to the law as anyone else in England and that his power was thus circumscribed by what the law allowed.

Although not all of Hobbes's philosophy was congenial to the royalist side, he did reject Parliament's view that the king was subject to the law. The idea of the rule of law, Hobbes explained, was one "of the number of pernicious errors: for they induce men, as oft as they like not their governors, to adhere to those that call them tyrants, and to think it lawful to raise war against them."[8] Hobbes thus believed that the concept of the rule of law encouraged people to rebel against their rulers, misled by rabble-rousers claiming that the rulers were tyrants on account of violating laws to which they were subject. And for Hobbes rebellion was an irrational act that engulfed society in the chaos of civil war.

Philosophical Confusions

Thus, there was a political purpose behind Hobbes's attack on the idea of the rule of law. Yet, his arguments aim to show not merely that the idea is a politically pernicious one but also that it is based on serious philosophical confusions. Hobbes suggests what those confusions are in the following passage:

And this therefore is another error of Aristotle's politics, that in a well-ordered commonwealth, not men should govern but the law. What man, that has his natural senses, though he can neither write nor read, does not find himself governed by them he fears, and believes can kill or hurt him when he obeyeth not? Or believes that law can hurt him; that is, words and paper, without the hands and swords of men?[9]

In order to understand these objections to the rule of law, we must first understand that, for Hobbes, any functioning society is divided into two parts: the sovereign and the subjects. The sovereign is the person or group that has supreme power in society. The sovereign issues commands and rules to the subjects, and threatens them with harm should they disobey. On account of its power, the sovereign's threats must be taken seriously. Thus, the sovereign keeps the subjects "in awe," that is, keeps them in a psychological state where their fear of the threat is sufficient to motivate them to follow the command. The laws of a society are the commands and rules issued by the sovereign to the subjects.

For Hobbes, it is best if the sovereign is a single person. The concentration of sovereign power in the hands of one individual makes its exercise more effective. And in Hobbes's view the dangers to peace and order are so great that the effectiveness of sovereign power is the overriding concern. He did acknowledge, though, that it was perfectly possible for the sovereign to consist of a body of persons. But the more compact the body, the better, again for reasons of effectiveness.

Those who defend the rule of law and argue that even the sovereign is bound by the law are confused in Hobbes's view. For a person (or body of persons) cannot bind himself (themselves) by means of his (their) own rules or commands: "he that is bound to himself only, is not bound."[10] For Hobbes, an individual can be bound by a command or rule only if there is somebody else who is in a position to credibly threaten the individual with harm should he disobey.

Even if the rules are written down, "words and paper, without the hands and swords of men" cannot be counted on to restrain a person's conduct. "The bonds of words are too weak to bridle men's ambition, avarice, anger, and other passions without the fear of some coercive power."[11] But there is no person or group capable of credibly threatening the sovereign: if there were such a person or group, then the alleged "sovereign" would not really be the sovereign after all. Hobbes concludes that the sovereign is necessarily above the laws that apply in its territory.

Hobbes's argument against the rule of law can be broken down into two distinct strands. The first strand will occupy us for the next few pages. We will see that it ultimately does not succeed in discrediting the idea of the rule of law. Then we will turn to the second strand in order to see if it can succeed where the first has failed.

A Round Square?

According to the *first strand* of Hobbes's argument, it is a *conceptual* impossibility for the rule of law to exist, much like it is a conceptual impossibility for a round square to exist. The very idea of a round square is self-contradictory because the concepts of roundness and squareness cannot possibly fit together. As so the actual existence of a round square is a flat-out impossibility.

For Hobbes, the idea of the rule of law is similar: it includes the idea of the sovereign binding herself by her own commands, but that is a self-contradictory and impossible idea. For a person to be bound by her own commands or rules, someone else would have to be in a position to penalize her for disobeying. But in that case, the second person would have power over the first, and so the first could not be sovereign. The chain of persons must stop with some person or body of persons having the power to punish others but who herself (or itself) cannot be punished by anyone in society's territory. That person or body is the sovereign, and it is necessarily in a position where it can ignore its own and anyone else's rules without fear of punishment.

This first strand of Hobbes's argument might appear to ignore the possibility that in a democratic society public opinion could induce the sovereign into obeying its own rules: the penalty imposed on the sovereign for noncompliance would be that people would generally think poorly of him or her and perhaps act to find a replacement. But a follower of Hobbes might reply that in such a democracy the public would be the true sovereign, for public opinion would be the ultimate arbiter of what is to be permitted and what is to be prohibited in that society.

However, some thinkers have questioned whether the diffuse and vague collection of individuals called "the public" can really be the sovereign of any society. After all, even in a democracy, society's official rules and regulations are typically not enacted or enforced by the public at large but by specific officials and the bodies on which they serve. Yet, even if one agrees that the public cannot really be sovereign in Hobbes's sense of the term, it is still possible to argue for his conclusion that the sovereign is necessarily above the law. The nineteenth-century English legal thinker John Austin did just that.

Austin's Contribution

Like Hobbes, Austin argues that the power of the sovereign is necessarily without legal limitation in that no legal sanction can attach to the sovereign's noncompliance with its own commands or rules. However, Austin claims that there can be other kinds of sanctions, and these might even be effective in making the sovereign comply with its own commands.

Thus, public opinion and popular morality might induce the sovereign to stay within the limits of its own commands or rules, but the sanctions imposed by public opinion and popular morality are not legal ones. This is because law, in the relevant sense, must come from some person or specific body of persons, not from the diffuse and undefined collection of individuals called "the public."

For Austin, then, the sovereign is necessarily above the law, though not necessarily above public opinion. If the sovereign were to ignore its own rules, then there would be no person or specific body of persons who could impose a legal sanction on the sovereign. The sovereign might be punished by the informal sanction of public opinion, but not by the law. And sovereigns who follow the law to avoid the sanction of public opinion are acting on the basis of political considerations, not legal ones.

Austin stresses that his argument applies whether the sovereign is a single person or a body of persons. But there is a complication he recognizes in the latter case. Individuals who are members of the sovereign body might be subject to legal penalty for violating the commands of the sovereign, since other members, acting for the body as a whole, could impose a sanction on the individual violator. Individual members of a sovereign body, thus, are bound by the law. Austin insists, however, that if the body as a whole decided to ignore its own commands, then there is no legal sanction available to penalize the body or its members. The body as whole, then, is not bound by the law.

The views of Hobbes and Austin pose a challenge to the defenders of the rule of law. For they suggest that all government is arbitrary government and that the crucial distinction between arbitrary and constitutional government collapses. Nonetheless, some of Austin's ideas can be accepted by those who defend the possibility of the rule of law, and their argument in defense of that possibility can cast doubt on Hobbes's claim that the very idea of the rule of law is self-contradictory. Let us see how the argument goes.

Defenders of the rule of law can agree with Austin that *if* the sovereign body as a whole decides to ignore the law, then there would be no person or group in society that could impose legal sanctions on the sovereign. But they can argue that this does not really exclude the possibility of establishing the rule of law, as they understand it. Some political systems are well-designed to ensure against the sovereign body acting as a whole to violate the law, and other systems are not well-designed to ensure against that possibility. Establishing the rule of law means setting up a system in which it will be unlikely that the possibility will comes to pass. No system can guarantee with certainty that the sovereign and the persons who are part of the sovereign body will always conform to the law. But defenders of the rule of law can argue that it is possible to establish a system for which we can have a high degree of confidence that political power will, by and large, be exercised in accordance with the law.

But is it possible, as a practical matter, to establish such a system? This is where the *second strand* of Hobbes's argument against the rule of law becomes relevant. Let us turn to it now.

Human Nature

Hobbes presents a view of human nature that suggests that it is *empirically impossible* to establish the rule of law. On that view, the strongest forces in human nature are egoism, competitiveness, distrust, and desire for glory and power. Hobbes does not believe in the existence of an elite group of humans who are immune to such impulses and who can be trusted to obey the law and pursue the common good for strictly ethical motives. Accordingly, making any human or group of humans sovereign has the necessary practical effect of putting them above the law. Acting for their own best interests and in the pursuit of power and glory, they will put themselves above their own laws. Given human nature, the rule of law cannot be established. That is one way of understanding part of Hobbes's argument against the rule of law. Is the argument sound?

In the centuries after Hobbes, a number of thinkers came to have doubts about the alleged incompatibility between human nature and the rule of law. Many of these thinkers believed that there was a good deal of truth in Hobbes's account of human nature. And they agreed that human nature made it very difficult to establish a government that would abide by the principles of legality. But they argued that a properly designed system could indeed establish and maintain the rule of law. Let us examine their positions.

THE CROOKED TIMBER OF HUMANITY

Immanuel Kant, the eighteenth-century German philosopher, is one of the foremost thinkers who argued that the rule of law is difficult to establish—but not impossible. Kant claimed that humans had a strong natural inclination to exempt themselves from rules and requirements that they were quite willing to impose on everyone else. Such an inclination clearly poses a serious obstacle in the way of establishing the rule of law. And Kant thought that creating a system that is the perfect embodiment of the rule of law was not possible: "From such crooked wood as man is made, nothing perfectly straight can be built."[12] The "crooked wood" is our human nature, our natural human inclinations, that make perfection impossible. But Kant believed the obstacle posed by our natural inclinations could be largely overcome, so that a reasonable approximation of the rule of law was possible.

Republican Government

For Kant, the key was to establish a republican form of government, and the essence of republican government was the separation of powers. Whereas Hobbes had believed that all the sovereign powers of government should be placed ultimately in a single person or compact group, many eighteenth-century thinkers came to the conclusion that such powers should be parceled out among different branches or departments, with no single department of government as the ultimate source of all political power.

Early in the eighteenth century, the French thinker Montesquieu had argued that separating the legislative and executive powers of government would help to protect against political tyranny. This was because whoever made the laws would be more likely to enact unduly harsh laws if they were also the persons charged with enforcing the laws: they could, after all, exempt themselves from the enforcement. By separating legislative and executive powers, it was believed that such situations could be avoided. Given Kant's belief that humans tend to exempt themselves from rules and requirements, Montesquieu's republican form of government seemed made to order.

The idea of dividing up the powers that Hobbes would have ultimately placed in a single person or compact group also struck the American founding fathers as a good idea. They, too, were committed to establishing the rule of law, and they, too, believed that ingenuity would be required to get the "crooked timber of humanity" to observe the rule of law. Indeed, in a passage that brings to mind Hobbes's argument against the possibility of the rule of law, James Madison points out that "a mere demarcation on parchment of the constitutional limits of the several departments is not a sufficient guard against those encroachments which lead to a tyrannical concentration of all the powers of government in the same hands."[13]

For Madison, a practical solution to the problem of securing the rule of law required one to recognize the "crooked timber" out of which human nature was made:

> If angels were to govern men, neither external nor internal controls on government would be necessary. In framing a government which is to be administered by men over men, the great difficulty lies in this: you must first enable the government to control the governed; and in the next place oblige it to control itself.[14]

Madison believed that a practical solution to the problem of obliging the government to control itself involved all of the following elements: (1) separation of the powers of government among three, independent branches: executive, legislative, and judicial; (2) representative democracy, encompassing many different classes and interests and requiring the periodic and staggered election of executive and legislative officials by an informed electorate; and (3) checks and balances, enabling each branch "to resist the encroachments of the others."[15]

A government system such as this was unprecedented in human history. The democracies that had existed up to the eighteenth century had all been relatively small affairs, where citizens directly participated in lawmaking and administration. But their study of history convinced Madison and his fellow framers that the old form of democracy was insufficient to establish the rule of law or prevent tyranny. And the other forms of government that had existed—monarchy and aristocracy—were no better. Nothing less was needed to establish the rule of law than a completely new form of government. Hobbes may have been right in denying that the rule of law was possible, given human nature *and* the forms of government that had existed up to the seventeenth century. But what Hobbes had not counted on was human ingenuity and its capacity for invention.

Hobbes versus Kant and Madison

If Kant and Madison are right, then a government that abides by the principles of legality is not incompatible with human nature. They did not adopt an excessively optimistic view of human nature in order to arrive at this conclusion. They were willing to concede that humans had a strong, natural streak of egoism and ambition. Their argument was that, despite our decidedly less than angelic nature, we could still establish and maintain constitutional government.

Hobbes might reply that Kant and Madison still underestimated the strength of our natural egoism and ambition. He might claim that even Madison's intricately designed system of constitutional government would succumb to ambition and self-seeking: there will always be some persons who find a way to avoid the checks and balances, the separation of powers, the electoral system, and who put themselves above the law.

But defenders of the rule of law can reply that history has proved Kant and Madison correct. Constitutional governments have been established. They have not been perfect, but they have abided by the principles of legality to a reasonable approximation. Moreover, there are clear differences between governments such as those found in the United States, England, and France, on the one side, and those found in North Korea and Iraq, on the other. It is perfectly sensible to describe those differences by saying that countries like the United States have a constitutional government, while Iraq and North Korea have arbitrary ones.

Perhaps this defense of the possibility of the rule of law can be persuasively countered. In the final chapter, we will examine another line of attack on the idea of the rule of law, from a group of contemporary legal thinkers. But it does not seem that anything in the work of Hobbes or Austin refutes the possibility of the rule of law. And in the meantime it would be reasonable to draw the (tentative) conclusion that the rule of law can be established and maintained.

SUBSTANTIVE VERSUS LEGAL JUSTICE

Thus far we have seen that the rule of law promises important advantages, such as helping to prevent arbitrary and corrupt government, to restrain vengeance, and to secure individual liberty and economic prosperity. We have also seen that there seems to be a workable, if not perfect, solution to the problem of establishing a government that abides by the principles of legality. But even assuming that this is correct, are there no drawbacks to the rule of law? Is following the rule of law always an unqualified good?

There certainly are drawbacks to the rule of law, and they concern the relationship of the rule of law to substantive justice. The drawbacks make the rule of law seem morally problematic to many individuals and often make it difficult for people to accept what the rule of law requires. Let us see how these difficulties come about.

The legal system is often referred to as the system of justice. We speak of the "criminal justice" and "civil justice" systems. But such talk hides an important truth: what the law requires does not always conform to what justice demands.

Doing what the law requires is doing "legal justice." Doing "substantive justice" to persons is treating them in the ways that they deserve: giving them the benefits to which they may morally lay claim or inflicting on them the punishments which morality calls to be imposed upon them. There is no guarantee that doing legal justice will always amount to doing substantive justice, especially in an imperfect world where decisions are made with much less than full information.

For example, it is inevitable that some guilty people will be acquitted and some innocent persons convicted of crimes in any real-world system of criminal law. The rule of law requires that we accept such faulty decisions unless they can be legally reversed. The rule of law demands that the procedures laid down by the law be followed in dealing with criminal defendants, and this will sometimes mean that innocent persons must remain imprisoned or that guilty persons be allowed to go free. In such cases, the desire that justice be done is in direct conflict with the demand that legal procedures be followed. We have a conflict between the rule of law and substantive justice.

Many people are convinced, for example, that O. J. Simpson did in fact commit two murders, despite his acquittal by a jury. They are even convinced that the evidence against him was beyond all reasonable doubt. Even if they are right, the rules of our legal system mean that Mr. Simpson cannot be subjected to criminal punishment for the murders and cannot be put on trial again for those crimes.[16]

If we know that O. J. Simpson is guilty of murder, wouldn't it be better if we just ignored the jury verdict and threw him in prison anyway? Why not dish out substantive justice, on a case-by-case basis, regardless of legal technicalities? That way we could be sure that criminals get what they deserve.

But exactly who is the "we"? And exactly what standards and procedures will dictate who deserves what? These questions cannot be answered without setting up some kind of system to deal with conduct potentially harmful to society. Any system will make mistakes and lead to outcomes that violate substantive justice. The issue is: What kind of system is, overall, the best? A system that condemned or acquitted individuals based on general public opinion might give O. J. Simpson what he deserves, but overall it would likely be much more unreliable than our current system.

It is easy to pick out a particular case here and there and argue persuasively that substantive justice has not been served. It is not even that difficult to come up with plausible suggestions for improving the current legal system, such as enforcing more vigorously the duty of citizens to serve on a jury. But it is difficult to see how any system that dispenses with the rule of law is going to be better in its overall operation than the current system, even with all its faults.

THE IMPEACHMENT CONTROVERSY:

BACKGROUND

We have carefully examined the idea of the rule of law, the principles that constitute it, the values that it promotes, and the obstacles to implementing it. Now we are in position to examine the impeachment of President Clinton and some of the controversies it raised. We will begin with a review of the events leading to the impeachment and trial of the president.

The formal impeachment process was triggered when Kenneth Starr handed over to the House of Representatives his report on the president's affair with Monica Lewinsky. But who was Kenneth Starr and how did he come to investigate a sexual affair by the president of the United States?

In 1994, Mr. Starr was a lawyer working in private practice and associated with the Republican Party. He had previously been a federal judge. But during 1994 a special panel of federal judges appointed him as an independent counsel to investigate a series of allegations against the president, the first lady, and some of their friends and associates. The allegations concerned a failed real estate deal from the days when the president had been governor of Arkansas. The deal came to be known as "Whitewater."

Mr. Starr's appointment to investigate Whitewater was made under a law Congress originally passed in 1978. The "independent counsel statute" was an effort to ensure that there would be an impartial investigation of possible criminal conduct by a president and others serving in the executive branch of the federal government. The executive branch is the one whose job is to enforce the law: under the Constitution, it is the branch that has the authority to investigate and prosecute crimes. But that authority raises exactly those worries about the rule of law that concerned Hobbes, Kant, and Madison. How can the executive branch be trusted to investigate fairly its own personnel and especially its head, the president? How can an attorney general—the nation's chief law enforcement officer—conduct an impartial investigation of a president when she is the president's subordinate? Wouldn't the president, the vice-president, the attorney general, and other high-ranking executive branch officials effectively be above the law?

The Watergate scandal had implicated President Nixon in illegal activities directed against his political opponents. With the threat of impeachment facing him, President Nixon decided to resign from office. But Congress worried that another president might be able to get away with serious illegalities, subverting both the rule of law and our form of government. The result of those worries was the independent counsel statute.[17]

The statute provides that the attorney general should undertake a preliminary investigation if she receives specific and credible evidence that a federal crime has been committed by the president or other listed executive officials.[18] If after the preliminary investigation the attorney general determines that there is a reasonable basis for further investigation, she is to apply to a special panel of federal judges to have a lawyer from outside of the government appointed as an independent counsel. At that point, the independent counsel takes over the investigation, and his job is to conduct an impartial inquiry. He has the full powers of a prosecutor, including the power to convene a grand jury in order to bring formal criminal charges.[19]

Mr. Starr began his investigation with Whitewater but soon expanded it to cover additional charges of wrongdoing against the president and his associates.[20] The independent counsel statute permits such expanded investigations, at the request of the attorney general to the special panel of federal judges who appoint the independent counsel.

While Mr. Starr was investigating Whitewater and related matters, President Clinton was involved in a lawsuit brought against him by Paula Jones, who had been a state employee when the president was governor of Arkansas. Ms. Jones alleged that he had sexually propositioned her and then penalized her when she refused his advances. After he became president, she commenced the lawsuit against him.[21]

In pursuing her case, Jones's lawyers sought to establish that the president had a pattern of rewarding female employees who acceded to his sexual propositions and punishing those who did not. The lawyers had received information that the president had sexual relations with Monica Lewinsky, when she was an intern working at the White House.[22] They sought to question both her and the president about the matter.

Ms. Lewinsky and the president sought to conceal the nature of their relationship. She swore in an affidavit in the Jones case that she had not had sexual relations with the president. The president also denied such a relationship when he gave his deposition in the case.[23] But their efforts to conceal the relationship began to unravel when Linda Tripp, a friend of Lewinsky's, contacted Kenneth Starr's office.

Ms. Tripp had befriended Ms. Lewinsky while they were both working at the Pentagon. During their friendship, Ms. Tripp secretly taped telephone conversations in which Ms. Lewinsky explicitly referred to her sexual activities with the president. Ms. Tripp contacted the office of the independent counsel to bring to Mr. Starr's attention the existence of the tapes. After hearing the evidence provided by Ms. Tripp, Mr. Starr requested and received permission to expand his investigation once more: to look into whether the president and Monica Lewinsky were guilty of perjury and obstruction of justice in their efforts to cover up their sexual relationship.

When the public first became aware of Mr. Starr's investigation of the Lewinsky affair and the existence of the Tripp tapes, many believed that the president would be forced to step down from office. But the president did not heed the calls for his resignation and sternly denied to the American public that he had had sexual relations with Ms. Lewinsky.

Months went by. The president did not retract his earlier denials of a sexual affair, and Mr. Starr's office pursued its investigation. In time, the independent counsel and Ms. Lewinsky worked out a deal in which she would receive immunity from prosecution in return for her testimony about the true nature of her relationship with the president. She testified in detail about their physical relationship before a grand jury that Mr. Starr had convened.

Perhaps the most compelling evidence confirming Ms. Lewinsky's testimony came from a blue dress she had worn during one sexual encounter with the president. The dress had a semen stain on it and DNA tests revealed that it was the semen of the president.[24]

Over the course of several months, Mr. Starr had been requesting that the president testify before his grand jury and had even issued a subpoena for the president's appearance. Finally, after the independent counsel received the DNA test results, the president agreed to testify.

Under oath, the president admitted having an "inappropriate intimate" relationship with Ms. Lewinsky. But he insisted that his deposition in the Jones case, in which he had denied a sexual relationship, had been "legally accurate."[25] He admitted, in effect, that Ms. Lewinsky performed oral sex on him but claimed that the definition of sexual relations approved by the judge did not cover such activity.[26] Moreover, the president denied having any other kind of sexual contact with Lewinsky.

The law provides that an independent counsel should refer to the House any "substantial and credible information . . . that may constitute grounds for an impeachment."[27] Mr. Starr was convinced that he had uncovered such information, and within a few weeks of the president's grand jury testimony, he sent a report to the House of Representatives detailing the evidence. The Starr report was based largely on Ms. Lewinsky's testimony and the corroborating evidence, and it spelled out the nature of her relationship with the president.

The report vigorously argued that evidence collected by the independent counsel's office about the Clinton-Lewinsky relationship constituted "substantial and credible information" that the president was guilty of a number of potentially impeachable offenses. According to the report, the president had committed perjury while testifying in the Jones case and before the grand jury and had obstructed justice by seeking to ensure that Ms. Lewinsky would conceal from the Jones lawyers the nature of his relationship with her. In addition, the president had obstructed justice by arranging for gifts he had given her to be hidden so that the Jones lawyers could not get access to them. And he had violated his presidential oath of office by lying to the public and to his own advisors about the nature of his relationship with Ms. Lewinsky. Such was the view of the Starr report.

The House took up the matter of impeachment, first in its Judiciary Committee and then in the full House. The Committee reported out to the House four articles of impeachment: perjury in the Jones deposition, perjury before the Starr grand jury, obstruction of justice in the Jones cases, and abuse of presidential powers. When the final tally was in, President Clinton stood impeached on two of the four counts: perjury before the grand jury and obstruction of justice.

The president's fate now lay in the hands of the Senate, the body given by the Constitution the sole power to try impeachments. The Constitution also provides that officials are to be convicted and removed should they be guilty of committing "treason, bribery, or other high crimes and misdemeanors." The Senate was to decide whether or not the president was guilty of any such offenses and should be removed from office.

POWER, PRIVACY, AND PROSECUTION

Federal prosecutors wield great power. They command the resources of law enforcement agencies such as the FBI. They can compel testimony in return for a grant of immunity. They can threaten an individual with a costly and risky criminal trial should the individual fail to cooperate in the way the prosecutor wants. But if regular federal prosecutors wield great power, there are certain respects in which independent counsels wield even more.

Federal prosecutors have many cases to pursue and a limited budget with which to pursue them. And such prosecutors are answerable to higher-ranking officials in the Justice Department. An independent counsel is focused on one case, or a handful of related cases, and has a virtually unlimited budget with which to pursue them. And although the attorney general has the authority under the law to fire an independent counsel for "good cause," in practice it has proved politically impossible for any attorney general to dismiss an independent counsel she thought may have abused his powers.

Table 2 Events Related to the Impeachment of President Clinton

May 6, 1994: Paula Jones sues President Clinton for having sexually harassed her when he was Governor of Arkansas.

August 5, 1994: Kenneth Starr is appointed as independent counsel to investigate possible criminal wrongdoing by President Clinton in connection with the "Whitewater" real estate transaction.

May 27, 1997: Supreme Court rules that the Jones lawsuit must go forward.

January 7, 1998: Monica Lewinsky signs affidavit in Jones's lawsuit, swearing that she has not had sexual relations with the president.

January 12, 1998: Linda Tripp gives to Kenneth Starr's office secret tape recordings of Monica Lewinsky talking about her sexual relations with the president.

January 16, 1998: Kenneth Starr receives permission from court to expand his investigation to cover possible criminal wrongdoing relating to Lewinsky's testimony in the Jones case.

January 17, 1998: President Clinton, in a deposition in the Jones case, denies having sexual relations with Monica Lewinsky.

January 21, 1998: *The Washington Post* breaks the story of the alleged Lewinsky affair and Starr's investigation of it.

January 26, 1998: President Clinton publicly declares, "I did not have sexual relations with that woman, Miss Lewinsky."

August 6, 1998: Monica Lewinsky testifies before the Starr grand jury about her sexual relations with President Clinton.

August 17, 1998: President Clinton testifies before the Starr grand jury that he had an "inappropriate" relationship with Monica Lewinsky but that his deposition on January 17 had been "legally accurate."

September 9, 1998: Kenneth Starr delivers his report to the House of Representatives, saying that he has found "substantial and credible information . . . that may constitute grounds for impeachment."

November 13, 1998: The president and Paula Jones settle her lawsuit for $850,000.

December 11, 1998: The House of Representatives votes to impeach President Clinton for perjury and obstruction of justice.

February 12, 1999: The United States Senate votes to acquit the president on both impeachment counts.

Kenneth Starr brought all of the considerable resources and powers of his office to bear on the investigation of the Lewinsky matter. But there is much dispute over whether he abused his powers. His defenders say that Mr. Starr vindicated the rule of law, while his critics charge that he violated it. Let us look more closely at the matter.

The most widespread criticism of the Starr investigation was that it violated the privacy rights of the president and Ms. Lewinsky.[28] There is no doubt that the investigation extracted from Ms. Lewinsky detailed information regarding her consensual sexual activities with the president and that this information was extracted under the threat of criminal prosecution. Ms. Lewinsky wanted to keep the information private, as did the president. And she desperately wanted to avoid criminal prosecution at the hands of the independent counsel.

So the Starr investigation amounted to government intrusion into intimate personal matters involving consenting adults. And Americans reasonably look askance on such intrusions. But in this case the intimate details were crucial in determining whether the president and Ms. Lewinsky had committed the crimes of perjury and obstruction of justice. While it is reasonable to hold a strong presumption against government intrusions into the intimate affairs of consenting adults, it is hard to deny that the presumption should give way if there is evidence that the persons in question have committed crimes and the information is crucial for deciding whether they are indeed guilty.

Of course, even in such cases, the parties do not entirely lose their privacy rights. For example, wiretapping their telephones without a warrant could not have been justified. The point is that even strong privacy rights are reasonably tailored to accommodate the legitimate need of government to investigate crimes.

But the alleged perjury and obstruction stemmed from questions the Jones lawyers asked the president and Ms. Lewinsky about their consensual intimate conduct. It might be argued that such conduct was none of the business of the Jones lawyers: they had no right to ask the questions and no right to get truthful answers.

The fact is, however, that the trial judge in the Jones case had ruled that her lawyers had a right to ask about any sexual relations the president had with government employees while he was in office. The questions were posed during the discovery phase of the trial, a preliminary fact-gathering stage in which lawyers are given wide latitude to uncover and examine facts that may be relevant to their case. Often, a judge will rule that facts uncovered during discovery are inadmissible at trial, because it subsequently becomes clear that they are not sufficiently relevant to the legal issue in the case. In fact, Judge Susan Weber Wright later decided that evidence about the president's sexual relations with Ms. Lewinsky would be inadmissible at trial for just that reason. But the discovery process is designed to cast a wide net and to err on the side of getting more facts than are needed, rather than on the side of getting fewer.

One might argue that Judge Weber Wright's decision about discovery was incorrect: sexual harassment is by definition conduct that is "unwelcome" to the victim, and the president's affair with Ms. Lewinsky was welcome by both parties. So it should have been obvious from the outset that the affair was not relevant to the Jones case.

But the problem is that there is no way for a court to determine whether an alleged sexual affair was welcome or not unless the facts about it are subject to discovery. At the outset, it was not clear that there was an affair between the president and Ms. Lewinsky, much less that there was one that both parties welcomed. Discovery was needed to find that out. Thus, it seems that Judge Weber Wright proceeded in a reasonable way: ruling that during discovery the Jones team could ask about the president's sexual conduct with Lewinsky but later deciding that the matter was insufficiently relevant to be presented at trial.[29]

The Jones lawyers had the legal right to ask about the affair and to receive truthful responses. And the deceitful responses given by the president and Ms. Lewinsky may have amounted to perjury. Accordingly, it seems that Mr. Starr's investigation of whether the two of them committed crimes by their testimony, though highly intrusive, did not violate any privacy rights.

The privacy criticism of the Starr investigation thus rests on shaky grounds. But it can be refocused to raise more substantial worries about whether the independent counsel's investigation abided by the rule of law.

THE REAL-WORLD RULE OF LAW

Lawbreaking violates the rule of law: that is true by definition. But in the real world, it would be foolhardy even to attempt to uncover and punish every single violation of the law. When translating the lofty ideal of the rule of law into concrete reality, we sensibly build some play into the joints of the system. We do not rigidly insist that each and every act of lawbreaking be detected and punished. For such an insistence would lead to a nightmarish society in which no one could reasonably feel safe and secure and scarce resources would be irrationally spent on detecting the slightest legal violation. Virtually everyone would stand under constant threat of arrest and punishment. The threat would be especially great in a society such as ours, with its myriad of legal rules and regulations.

Prosecutorial discretion plays a pivotal role in the real-world rule of law. Constraints on the prosecutors' resources of money and time mean that some amount of lawbreaking will go without detection and punishment. Prosecutors are reasonably charged with the responsibility of deciding where to focus their resources and, by implication, where to let potential wrongdoing go uninvestigated.

But if practicality licenses a significant degree of prosecutorial discretion in the implementation of the rule of law, such discretion must be exercised in an impartial and nonpartisan manner. Otherwise, the law will be turned into an instrument for the arbitrary exercise of power, precisely the evil that the rule of law is meant to stop. Thus, it would be wholly indefensible for a regular prosecutor deliberately to focus her resources exclusively on members of the opposing political party. The rule of law—not just the ideal, but the real-world implementation of the ideal—is aimed at limiting and regulating the use of power, especially the power of government. A regular prosector who targeted only political opponents would not be operating under a rule of law, but rather would be wielding the law as an instrument of arbitrary power to destroy the political opposition.

We can now better understand why many critics of the Starr investigation charge that it violated the rule of law. Those critics are claiming that Mr. Starr violated the standards of impartiality and evenhandedness that must be observed in the real-world implementation of the rule of law. The critics contend that his investigation of the president was not impartial but rather motivated by a political bias stemming from his ties to the Republican Party.

Among the factors critics cite to support their claims of Mr. Starr's partisan motivations are the great expense and repeated expansion of his investigation of the president. Beginning with Whitewater and extending through the Lewinsky affair, the independent counsel's office expended tens of millions of dollars. And over the years, Mr. Starr repeatedly sought to expand his jurisdiction beyond the original real estate matter, indicating that he was looking for some charge that he could hang on the president. That is how the critics see it.

His defenders construe Mr. Starr's conduct quite differently. In their view, what the critics complain about was simply a thorough investigation on his part. The independent counsel's duty was to investigate potential criminal wrongdoing by the president and his associates. Had Mr. Starr failed to use all of the resources and legal powers at his command to uncover evidence of such wrongdoing, he would not have been doing his job. That job was to use those powers and resources, to the limits of what the law permits, in order to determine whether crimes had been committed. Holding back was not a responsible option, in the view of the independent counsel's defenders.

The question of whether Mr. Starr was motivated by partisan bias or was simply conducting a thorough investigation is complicated by the narrow focus of his mandate as an independent counsel. Regular prosecutors deal with a large number of cases, and if they are guilty of systematic biases, that fact will likely be reflected in the patterns that emerge when one looks at the run of cases. Statistical patterns do not prove bias, but they can serve as prima facie evidence for or against charges of bias.

In Kenneth Starr's case, we have no statistical evidence to go by. Like every other independent counsel, his job was to investigate officials from a particular political party. He did not have the option of investigating suspect officials from the opposing party in order to demonstrate his impartiality. The result is that the appearance of bias easily arises but the reality of bias is difficult to establish.

Perhaps the strongest evidence for the allegation of partisan bias is Mr. Starr's repeated efforts to expand his jurisdiction beyond the original Whitewater affair. Those efforts lend credence to the idea that he was determined to find some criminal charge to level against the president, no matter how far he needed to stray from his original investigation.

Defenders of Mr. Starr point out that his requests to expand jurisdiction were approved by the attorney general and the special federal judicial panel. But the independent counsel law makes it very difficult for an attorney general to reject any such request: it requires that she give "great weight" to the independent counsel's request.

Moreover, the special judicial panel exercised questionable judgment in expanding Mr. Starr's jurisdiction to include the Lewinsky matter. By the time the Lewinsky matter arose, his conduct could have been plausibly construed as biased, even if it was also plausible to construe the conduct otherwise. The special court had the legal authority to appoint someone else as independent counsel to examine the Lewinsky matter. In light of the ambiguity of Mr. Starr's prior conduct, such an appointment would have been the more defensible course for the court to have taken.

Whether or not Mr. Starr abused his powers as independent counsel, another question remains: Did the statute under which he was operating leave the door open to abuse? The statute is what enabled Mr. Starr and the other independent counsels to conduct their investigations free of the limitations on time and money under which regular prosecutors labor. And a case can be made that such investigations are wide open to abuse: a biased independent counsel can too readily turn his investigation into an instrument of arbitrary power to use against political opponents. The independent counsel statute was intended to help ensure that the principles of the rule of law were followed. But it is questionable whether the statute contained sufficient safeguards against abuses that could subvert those very principles.[30]

POLITICAL TRIALS

Many commentators have observed that impeachment trials, including that of President Clinton, are invariably political, and most of the commentators have implied that there is nothing objectionable with the political character of such trials. But the commentators have neglected to address some pressing questions. If impeachment trials are invariably political, can they be consistent with the rule of law? And shouldn't impeachment trials, like other trials, be regulated by rule-of-law principles? Before examining such questions, let us first look at the nature of political trials and why they are often criticized for violating the rule of law.

A political trial is one in which political considerations, not simply the law and the facts, affect the proceedings and verdict. There are three distinct kinds of considerations that can make a trial a political one.

First, there are considerations of partisan political interest. Such considerations operate when the verdict (or some other important phase of the proceedings) is based on the belief that it promotes, or harms, the interests of a particular political party or other political group. Second are considerations of the general good of society. These considerations operate when the verdict is based on the belief that it is good for society as a whole and thus promotes social utility. Finally, there are considerations of public opinion, which operate when a verdict is based on the belief that the public generally favors it.

Political trials generally violate the rule of law. For a judge or jury to base their decision on partisan politics, social utility, or public opinion typically rides roughshod over the legal rights of the accused. Defendants generally have a right under the rule of law that their case be decided without regard to such considerations.

The very term *political trial* has come to acquire, in most contexts, a negative connotation. It is often used to criticize a trial, suggesting that it was fundamentally unfair and rigged against the accused. Some of the most well-known political trials of the twentieth century certainly fit this use. For example, the trials that Soviet dictator Joseph Stalin employed to eliminate all potential challengers to his power and all dissent from his policies were political trials and condemned by many for it. The accused had no chance of acquittal: guilty verdicts were preordained by Stalin to promote his unchallenged control of the Communist Party and his absolute power over Soviet society.

Political trials can also be found in the annals of U.S. history, though less extreme than those orchestrated by the Soviet dictator. For example, during the 1920s Sacco and Vanzetti stood trial for murder and armed robbery. The two Italian immigrants had been active in the anarchist movement in a period in which law enforcement authorities often broke the law themselves in an effort to suppress what they regarded as subversive political movements. The judge in the Sacco-Vanzetti case exhibited a manifest bias against the accused on account of their radical politics, for example, by improperly allowing prosecutors to question the defendants about their political beliefs when they testified in their own defense. And there is reason to think that the prosecutors and their witnesses had broken the law in their zeal to get a conviction. But the jury found the defendants guilty, and the judge sentenced them to death.

Worldwide protests followed the convictions of Sacco and Vanzetti. Many prominent Americans, including Felix Frankfurter—who was later to become Associate Justice of the U.S. Supreme Court—publicly criticized the trial as a violation of the rule of law and its demand for due process. Frankfurter and many others charged that the two immigrants had been denied a fair trial and had been convicted on the basis of their unpopular political beliefs, not on the basis of the law and the evidence. But such objections were to no avail. Sacco and Vanzetti were executed, after the governor refused to extend clemency to them.

So some of the infamous political trials of the last century were clear violations of the rule of law. However, we should not jump to the conclusion that political trials always and automatically violate the rule of law. There might be important exceptions. And even if one agrees that political trials always violate the rule of law, one might argue that such trials are not, for that reason, always indefensible. Perhaps, in certain situations, a political trial should not be judged by the principles of the rule of law. In the remainder of this chapter we will take up these issues in the context of the impeachment trial of President Clinton.

THE IMPEACHMENT TRIAL

The Constitution places in the Senate the sole power to try impeached officials. And it requires a two-thirds vote for conviction and removal. But the Constitution does not otherwise specify the rules and procedures for such a trial: the Senate is to work out the details.

The relation of impeachment trials to the rule of law is a complex matter. Let us begin by examining impeachment trials in general and then turn to the particular trial of President Clinton.

Should the Rule of Law Apply?

It is generally agreed that criminal trials should be governed by the principles of the rule of law. But what about impeachment trials of a president? Should such trials be regulated by the rule of law?

Some legal thinkers will answer in the negative. They will argue that a sharp contrast should be drawn between criminal and impeachment trials. Criminal trials must be regulated by rule-of-law principles because so much is at stake for the accused: their life or their liberty. Criminal punishment is one of the starkest forms in which government exercises its power over individuals, and the rule of law is needed to help ensure that such power is carefully controlled and justifiably exercised.

But impeachment trials are different, it might be said. At stake in such trials is not the individual's right to life or liberty, but simply her privilege to hold public office. Indeed, the Constitution explicitly forbids any further penalty for an impeachment conviction beyond removal and disqualification from office. Because loss of life or liberty is a more serious matter for an individual than the loss of office, one might conclude that criminal trials should be regulated by the rule of law but impeachment trials need not be.

The difference in penalties between conviction for impeachment and criminal conviction are indeed significant, and that difference makes it reasonable to conclude that the precise rules for regulating the two sorts of trials need not be identical. But it would be a mistake to conclude that rule-of-law principles are inapplicable when it comes to impeachment trials.

Removing an official from public office may not be a form of criminal punishment, but it is an important exercise of public power with serious consequences for the impeached person and potentially far-reaching consequences for society at large. If unbridled power is dangerous, and if the rule of law is essential for bringing such power under control, then it would seem a mistake to exempt impeachment trials from rule-of-law principles. Regulating through law the process of removing public officials from their office is no less important than regulating through law the process of visiting punishment upon those accused of crimes.

The Trial of the President

Did the impeachment trial of President Clinton meet the principles of the rule of law? A case can be made that the trial violated several crucial principles. For example, the rule of law demands an impartial body (that is, judge and jury) to hear a case. But "impartial" hardly seems like the right term to describe many of the senators who stood in judgment over the president. The problem went well beyond the apparent fact that some senators were aggressively partisan, more concerned with defending their own party's interests, or damaging the other's, than with dispensing impartial justice. The brother of one senator was actually one of the House managers arguing the case against the president. Imagine that you were a defendant in a criminal case and one of the jurors was a close relative of the district attorney who was prosecuting you. Such a trial would clearly violate the rule of law.

Moreover, some senators had served in the House when the articles of impeachment were voted against the president: these senators had, in effect, declared their verdict before the trial had even begun. The impartiality demanded by the rule of law clearly means that those deciding a case should not have made up their minds before the trial starts.

In addition, it seemed that many senators kept a close eye on public opinion polls, and their own prospects for re-election, as they considered whether the president should be convicted or not. It is reasonable to think that his strong support in the polls was an influential factor in the Senate's ultimate decision to find the president not guilty. In the trial of Sacco and Vanzetti, strong public opinion helped to ensure that they would be convicted regardless of the evidence and the law. That was a clear violation of the rule of law. But one might argue that it is also a violation if public opinion inclines judge and jury in the other direction: to acquit the accused.

Beyond the claim that the Senate was insufficiently impartial to satisfy the principles of rule of law is the idea that the standard of impeachment, "bribery, treason, or other high crimes and misdemeanors," is too vague to satisfy those principles. Treason and bribery are clearly defined in our law, but the meaning of "other high crimes and misdemeanors" is rather fuzzy.

One of the central debates of the Clinton impeachment controversy reflected the vagueness of the constitutional standard: whether the president's false and misleading statements under oath rose to the level of impeachable offenses. Respected scholars disagreed vehemently on this crucial matter. Some argued that the statements clearly did amount to impeachable offenses, while others just as confidently asserted that the statements fell far short of amounting to such offenses.

A criminal law that was as vague as the constitutional standard for impeachment would be a clear violation of the rule of law: it is too open-ended and not sufficiently specific about what is prohibited. Indeed, in regimes that have ignored the rule of law—such as the Soviet Union and Nazi Germany—vague statutes condemning "socially undesirable" conduct were important vehicles through which those in power destroyed freedom and security.

Despite these reasons for thinking that the impeachment trial violated the rule of law, a strong case can be made on the other side of the issue as well. The first point to note is that the trial was conducted in accord with the provisions of the Constitution—the supreme law of the land. Had the president been tried before a military tribunal or some body other than the Senate, it clearly would have violated the rule of law. The same would be true if he had been ousted from office by a military coup.

Some zealous partisans of the president, in fact, claimed that the impeachment process was akin to a coup. But such claims are unfortunate distortions. The process followed the procedures set down by the law and, as such, were quite different from an extralegal effort to run the president out of office.

It is true that the Constitution leaves the Senate a great deal of discretion in setting up the rules for an impeachment trial. And it might be argued that the constitutional provision placing the sole authority to try impeachments in the hands of the Senate is akin to a law giving some official or body arbitrary power. We have seen such a law is a parody of the rule of law.

But the constitutional provision placing the authority to try impeachments in the Senate is not a grant of absolute and arbitrary power. Senators are legally empowered only to remove an impeached official from office: they may not impose any additional punishment or sanction. Moreover, removal requires a vote of two-thirds for conviction. And each senator and his or her party will be answerable to the voters in subsequent election cycles. This is not arbitrary and absolute power, but rather power circumscribed by both legal and political safeguards.

Still, it would be naive to think that each senator approached the trial with an impartial frame of mind. Doesn't this seriously violate the rule of law? The violation may not be as severe as it first appears, especially if we keep in mind the fact that we are looking for a system that works, not perfectly, but reasonably well to restrain through law the exercise of power. Moreover, it is relevant to remember that the stakes in an impeachment trial are different from those in a criminal trial: the privilege to hold office and not the accused's life or liberty. In such a context, it is reasonable to hold that some of the stricter safeguards of a criminal trial can be relaxed, without dispensing with the principles of the rule of law.

One can certainly imagine a scenario in which the Senate would be biased to a degree that the rule of law could not tolerate. But it is plausible to think that in the case of President Clinton the various biases that the senators undoubtedly brought to the trial canceled themselves out to a substantial degree. Pro-democrat partisans helped to neutralize pro-republican ones and vice-versa. Moreover, the two-thirds requirement meant that the ultimate decision would rest in the hands of the least partisan and most impartial members of both parties: the "moderates" of both parties would hold the balance of power.

One might respond that a fair trial requires impartiality on the part of each and every one who is to stand in judgment and not a collection of individuals whose contrary biases "more or less" cancel out. Moreover, even "moderates" have strong party loyalties.

In the context of an ordinary criminal trial, it makes sense to insist on the impartiality of each and every one who stands in judgment.[31] But such a requirement seems excessive and impractical for an impeachment trial. The only individuals who could credibly claim to be strictly impartial in the case of President Clinton would be the relatively few Americans who were completely disinterested in politics and knew little or nothing about the scandal. Or perhaps foreigners from remote regions of the earth where there was little news of the scandal. It would hardly be reasonable to expect the American people to abide by the judgments of people so disconnected from the American political system.

Yet, it may trouble some that our senators seemed to weigh political considerations in making their decisions about the president's guilt or innocence. Even if many of the individual biases were canceled out in the vote of the Senate as a whole, it is plausible to think that political factors weighed heavily in the final judgment. In that sense, the trial of the president was, rather clearly, a political trial. And that fact returns us to a question we need to examine closely: Isn't *any* political trial a violation of the rule of law? And we still have the problem arising from the vagueness of the constitutional standard for impeachment. In the next two sections we will grapple with these issues.

The Role of Politics

In analyzing the political character of an impeachment trial of a president, we must be careful to distinguish among the three different kinds of political factors: partisan political advantage, social utility, and public opinion.[32] The first factor is simply an illegitimate basis for a judgment in an impeachment trial (or any other). Senators swear an oath at the start of an impeachment trial and, at a minimum, the oath must mean that partisan political calculations are to be left out of account. On the other hand, it can be argued that impeachment trials may properly take account of social utility and public opinion and that it does not violate the rule of law for such considerations to weigh in the final judgment.

A president is entrusted with the powers of his office on the condition that he will not do serious damage to the country. Impeachment is a process that permits the lawful removal of a lawfully elected president whose conduct has done or threatens to do such damage. The availability of impeachment means that we do not need to resort to the lawless act of a coup in order remove a president who poses a danger to the nation. Rather, a president who presents such a danger can be lawfully "fired."

Accordingly, the impact on overall social utility of a president's continuation in office is surely a relevant factor to consider. Marginal harms to social utility would not, of course, be sufficient to justify impeachment and removal from office. But there is some threshold, albeit difficult or impossible to specify precisely, beyond which considerations of utility would count directly in favor of a president's removal.

Social utility is not all that properly counts. Public opinion should count, too. In our constitutional system, the legal qualifications for someone to be able to serve as president are minimal: you must be at least 35 years old and a natural born citizen of the country. To get hired as a middle manager for most American companies, you need at least a college degree. To get hired as president to manage the whole country, you do not even need a high school diploma. The reason for this discrepancy is simple: our constitutional system leaves it up to the people to decide what qualities are part of the "job qualifications" for a president. If they want a highly educated president, then that is what they will get. But if they want a less well-educated one who has other qualities they want in their leader, then the Constitution lets them make that choice.

The prerogative of the people to decide what qualities they want in a president makes public opinion a relevant factor in an impeachment trial. This does not mean that a president should be removed just because the people decide that they do not like him anymore. In our system, the presumption is that elected officials have a right to serve their full term in office even if public opinion turns against them. That is why presidents, congressmen, and senators are not subject to recall elections. Moreover, under the rule of law, the power of the people must still be regulated by law: the constitutional procedures and requirements for impeachment must be followed, even if a large majority of the people would like to dispense with them in a particular case.

But the sovereign prerogative of the people to choose the job qualifications for a president does suggest that a decision to "fire" a president should take account of public opinion. The senators making such a decision should look at public opinion and the reasons behind it. If public opinion is clear and the reasons behind it sensible grounds for removing—or declining to remove—a president, the senators should count such opinion in their deliberations.[33]

In an ordinary criminal trial, social utility and public opinion would not properly serve as direct grounds for a verdict. The question at the center of such trials should be whether the accused violated some official rule that prohibited a specific kind of conduct, not the question of whether a guilty verdict would promote social utility or whether the public supports such a verdict.

Criminal trials and impeachment trials serve very different functions in our system of law. The former help to regulate behavior in society at large by punishing those who violate rules that have been formally adopted and promulgated. The latter help to protect society by removing from office those who have seriously abused their powers or otherwise shown themselves unfit to govern. Given the special purpose of impeachment trials, certain kinds of political considerations are legitimate grounds for a verdict, even though those same considerations would be illegitimate for a verdict in a criminal case.

Moreover, it is reasonable to construe the idea of the rule of law in a way that is sufficiently flexible to allow for the special purpose of an impeachment trial. The rule of law is a matter of placing reasonably effective, stable, and consistent limits on the exercise of power. An impeachment process involving trials with a political dimension is a sensible part of a democratic system that seeks to limit power in a such a way. Accordingly, we should see impeachment trials as consistent with the rule of law and as promoting its basic purpose.

The Vagueness Problem

But what about the charge that the constitutional standard for impeachment is simply too vague to meet the rule of law? That important question must be addressed if we are to vindicate the idea that impeachment trials are consistent with the rule of law.

It must be admitted that the standard for impeachment, "bribery, treason, or other high crimes and misdemeanors," is exceedingly vague and that, unlike other vague provisions of the Constitution, this one lacks any substantial body of precedent and case law to clarify its meaning.

Moreover, it is true that arbitrary governments have often used vague legal provisions to suppress any opposition to their rule. But the vagueness of the

Constitution's standard of impeachment functions in our system very differently from the way vague legal standards function in dictatorial regimes. The vague language of "other high crimes and misdemeanors" enables elected officials to incorporate considerations of social utility and public opinion into their decision about whether a president is to be removed from office. It does not enable dictators to crush any political opposition.

It is true that the vagueness of the impeachment standard means that it could potentially be used as an instrument to destroy political opponents. But the standard should not be judged in isolation from the legal and political system of which it is a part. And, unlike a dictatorial regime, our democratic system helps guard against abuses and does so rather effectively. Only two presidents have ever been impeached and neither was convicted. And the threat of impeachment against President Nixon helped remove from office a man who had seriously abused the powers of the presidency. The historical track record does not seem to lend support to the idea that the vagueness of the impeachment clause creates an excessive risk of abuse.

But there are many who would say that the impeachment clause was abused in the case of President Clinton. They argue that his impeachment was mainly motivated by illegitimate partisan considerations and that the president's misconduct in the Lewinsky matter clearly did not rise to the level of an impeachable offense. Suppose, for the sake of argument, that such people are right. Wouldn't that then show that the Constitution's vague impeachment language is too vulnerable to abuse by those who would seek to turn it into an instrument of political destruction?

I don't think so. Remember that we need to look at the impeachment standard as part of an overall system of law and government. The question is whether the system as a whole provides reasonably sufficient safeguards against the political abuse of the vague impeachment standard. In President Clinton's case, not only did the system formally acquit him: his Republican opponents emerged from the process politically damaged, while the president's job approval ratings were at their height. Even assuming that the president should never have been impeached in the first place, the system of free speech, free press, and free elections established by the Constitution provided effective safeguards against his removal for purely partisan reasons.

Impeachment trials are inescapably political trials, and the risks of the impeachment process becoming an instrument of arbitrary power cannot be entirely eliminated. But it is possible to construct reasonably effective safeguards against those risks, and impeachment trials can be conducted in accord with the rule of law.

The rule of law should not be understood as a rigid set of requirements, unresponsive to practical problems and differences of context and situation. Rather, it should be thought of as a flexible and adaptable scheme, so that the rules and procedures it demands in one kind of trial may not be required in a very different kind. Criminal trials will generally require the strictest safeguards; impeachment trials can, consistent with the rule of law, operate according to a looser set of rules.

SUMMARY

The idea of the rule of law played a prominent role in the public debate over the impeachment of President Clinton. Its prominence was well justified. As Henry Hyde suggested, establishing the rule of law has been a signal achievement of our civilization. It created a system by which humans could tame the rule of force and violence. And as Cheryl Mills suggested, the rule of law is a system that sometimes requires us to accept outcomes that we do not particularly like. Mr. Hyde would undoubtedly agree with Ms. Mills on the point.

This chapter has explored the principles by which the rule of law seeks to limit arbitrary power and the difficulties of translating those principles into a reasonably effective system of law. The difficulties are serious but not insuperable: with human ingenuity they can be overcome.

The establishment of the rule of law does not by itself guarantee liberty and justice for all. Substantive justice and legal justice do not always coincide. But the rule of law does seem to be an essential element of any defensible system of human governance.[34]

NOTES

1. http://www.nytimes.com/library/politics/011799impeachment-hhtext.html.

2. "The Rule of Law Protects the President Too, Counsel Tells Senate," *New York Times* January 21, 1999, A18. Ms. Mills was alluding to the charge that the president and his lawyers were engaged in legal hair-splitting when they argued that the president's misleading statements about his relationship with Ms. Lewinsky did not technically count as perjury.

3. The elements of this third principle come from Lon Fuller's account of the way in which lawmaking can go wrong. See *The Morality of Law,* rev. ed. (New Haven: Yale University Press, 1964), pp. 33 ff. Fuller would endorse the other principles as well.

4. This principle should be understood as extending as well to civil cases in which one private party has brought suit against another.

5. By "political power" I mean the power (a) to lay down rules and commands for society, (b) to have such rules and commands enforced, (c) to establish agencies that have the powers referred to in (a) and (b), and (d) to create, change, or eliminate rules that govern such agencies.

6. It might be said that subjecting the sovereign people to the rule of law would mean the prohibition of any political revolution by the people. Such revolutions are, after all, clear instances in which existing legal rules and procedures are violated as the people overthrow the government that rules them. But the fifth principle places no bar on a revolution that will establish constitutional government if the people are currently ruled by an arbitrary government. Also, we will see that the rule of law is not the only important value and does not by itself guarantee against government oppression and tyranny. There may be situations in which a revolt by the sovereign people against a constitutional government is justified. In such a situation, though, the fifth principle requires them to form a new constitutional regime.

7. The most famous modern statement of the corrupting effects of power is Lord Acton's: "Power tends to corrupt, and absolute power corrupts absolutely." J.E.M. Dalberg-Acton, *Essays on Freedom*

and Power, G. Himmelfarb, ed. (Boston: Beacon, 1949), p. 364.

8. Thomas Hobbes, *Leviathan,* M. Oakeshott, ed. (New York: MacMillan, 1962), p. 491.

9. *Ibid.,* pp. 490–91.

10. *Ibid.,* p. 199.

11. *Ibid.,* p. 108.

12. Immanuel Kant, "Idea of a Universal History from a Cosmopolitan Point of View," (Sixth Thesis), rpt. in *Kant: Selections,* L.W. Beck, ed. (New York: MacMillan, 1988), p. 419.

13. James Madison, Federalist #48, in *The Federalist Papers,* C. Rossiter, ed. (New York: New American Library, 1961), p. 313.

14. Madison, Federalist #51, *Federalist Papers,* p. 322.

15. *Ibid.*

16. Existing legal rules did not, however, immunize Mr. Simpson from a civil lawsuit for wrongful death. He was found liable in such a suit brought by the estate of Ronald Goldman, one of the victims of the murder.

17. 28 *United States Code* 49, 591–99 (1994) (expired 1999). The statute was challenged as an unconstitutional violation of the separation of powers but upheld by the Supreme Court in *Morrison v. Olson,* 487 U.S. 654 (1988).

18. In the event of allegations against the attorney general, the next most senior official in the Department of Justice is to carry out the responsibilities given to the attorney general by the statute.

19. A grand jury does not decide on guilt or innocence. Rather, it hears the evidence presented by a prosecutor who is seeking to bring formal criminal charges against someone and decides whether there is probable cause that the person has committed a crime. If it decides that there is probable cause, then the grand jury will return an indictment against the person.

It is an unsettled legal question whether an indictment can be brought against a sitting president. There is no doubt, however, that after he leaves office, a president can be indicted for crimes committed while he was in office.

20. The additional charges include the illegal use of confidential FBI files.

21. The president sought to have the case delayed until after he stepped down from office, arguing that it would unduly hamper the ability of any president to carry out his duties if he were subject to civil lawsuits while in office. The Supreme Court rejected his argument and ordered that the case go forward. See *Clinton v. Jones,* 520 U.S. 681 (1997). The trial court judge eventually threw out the Jones suit before it went to trial, ruling that there was insufficient evidence that she had suffered from any retaliation on the job. That decision was on appeal when the two sides in the case reached an out-of-court settlement providing that Jones would receive $850,000 from the president.

22. After her internship, Ms. Lewinsky worked in a paid job at the White House and later was transferred to the Pentagon. The president testified that in his recollection their intimate encounters began after she completed her internship. However, a fair reading of the evidence shows rather conclusively that their encounters began while she was an intern.

23. A deposition is testimony that is given under oath and outside of a courtroom.

24. Other evidence corroborating the sexual liaison between the president and Ms. Lewinsky included: the testimony of friends of Ms. Lewinsky, whom she had told of the affair, and files retrieved from her computer that allude to the affair.

25. *The Starr Report* (Pocket Books, 1998), p. 321.

26. The definition reads: "a person engages in 'sexual relations' when the person knowingly engages in or causes . . . contact with the genitalia, anus, groin, breast, inner thigh or buttocks of any person with an intent to arouse or gratify the sexual desire of any person." *The Starr Report,* p. 202. When asked during his grand jury testimony the direct question of whether Ms. Lewinsky had performed oral sex on him, the president

declined to affirm or deny it. But he did say that, on his understanding of the definition, if Ms. Lewinsky had given him oral sex, such activity by itself would not have been covered by the definition.

27. 28 *United States Code* 595(c).

28. Among the other criticisms were: Mr. Starr's team of prosecutors and FBI agents had exerted undue pressure on Ms. Lewinsky when they first questioned her about her relations with the president; Mr. Starr's office had questionable contacts with Ms. Jones's lawyers prior to his Lewinsky investigation and had improperly failed to disclose those contacts when the office applied for an expansion of jurisdiction to investigate the Lewinsky affair; Mr. Starr's office illegally leaked to the press secret grand jury material and improperly prosecuted individuals who did not agree to confirm stories of the president's sexual indiscretions. Also, critics claimed that Mr. Starr improperly took an adversarial position in favor of impeachment when he testified before the House Judiciary Committee. Samuel Dash, Mr. Starr's ethics advisor, quit over this last issue, arguing that Starr should simply have presented in a neutral manner the facts that his investigation had uncovered.

29. It could be cogently argued that it would have been better for Judge Weber Wright to have required the Jones lawyers to make some preliminary showing that the Lewinsky relationship was "unwelcome" before allowing them to question her and the president about it. But even granting the point, the judge's ruling did legally entitle the Jones lawyers to ask their questions and receive truthful answers.

Judge Weber Wright eventually found the president guilty of civil contempt for his testimony in the Jones case and fined him. She described the testimony as demonstrably false and intended to obstruct the legal process.

30. The statute expired on June 30, 1999. Most lawmakers and commentators agreed that it did not contain sufficient safeguards against abuse, but there was deep disagreement over whether a revised version of the statute could correct its inadequacies. Some advocated a revised statute, while others argued that the current way of handling allegations against high executive-branch officials is better than any independent counsel law. Under the current way, the attorney general has the authority to appoint a special prosecutor to investigate such allegations. The special prosecutor is not subject to the oversight of any judicial panel but rather is a kind of outside contractor working for the Department of Justice and can be fired by the attorney general. Proponents of this approach argue that ordinary political processes will help ensure that an impartial investigation is conducted, without the risks of abuse that go with an independent counsel.

31. We will examine in the next chapter an extraordinary criminal trial and its relation to the rule of law: the Nuremberg Trial of Major Nazi War Criminals.

32. Not all of the officials subject to impeachment are elected officials. For example, federal judges are subject to impeachment. My analysis in this section is directed at impeachment trials of a president. One of the issues raised during the trial of President Clinton was whether the same standards for impeachment apply to a president as apply to a federal judge. I believe that the same standards do not apply, in part due to the elective character of the presidential office.

33. In such a situation, senators who disagree with public opinion should be hesitant to vote against it, although that hesitancy should reflect a presumption rather than a decisive consideration against the senator's own considered judgment.

The decision to remove the leader of a democratic country before his term has expired is one of profound significance. It would be naive to think that there is some simple formula for making the right decision or that all sensible reasons will line up on one side of a case or the other.

34. In Chapter 9 we will examine a contemporary challenge to the rule of law, posed by the Critical Legal Studies movement.

DISCUSSION QUESTIONS

1. Perhaps the central debate of the controversy surrounding President Clinton's impeachment was over the question of whether his false and misleading statements under oath rose to the level of impeachable offenses. The key question was: Did the statements meet the constitutional standard of "high crimes and misdemeanors"?

In the public debate over this question, there seemed to be a high correlation between a person's political views and her/his answer to the question. Liberals and moderates tended to think that the president's statements did not rise to the level of impeachable offenses, while conservatives thought that they did.

Do these correlations show that the constitutional standard is simply an "empty vessel" into which individuals can pour the meaning that is most congenial to them politically? Do they indicate that the standard is too vague to meet rule-of-law standards? How can the standard impose an independent legal constraint when people consistently interpret it to reflect their own political views?

2. The Republican Party suffered political damage from the impeachment process because much of the public viewed Republican efforts to remove the president as strictly partisan politics. The political damage has led some commentators to say that it will be more difficult to impeach a future president, as politicians will conclude that it is politically too hazardous to seek the impeachment and removal of another president. In effect, the Republicans played with the fire of impeachment and were burned, so future politicians of both parties will stay away from the fire.

Other commentators say that the impeachment of President Clinton has made it easier to impeach a future president. They argue that he was impeached for relatively minor misconduct, not the major abuses of power for which impeachment should be reserved. In effect, the bar for impeaching a president has been lowered, and so future politicians of both parties will take advantage of the lower bar to threaten future presidents with impeachment.

Has the impeachment of President Clinton made future impeachments of a president more difficult or less difficult? Or has it had no effect either way? Which is the greater danger for the future: that a president will be impeached for insufficient reasons or that Congress will be too scared of the charge of partisan politics to impeach a president who has seriously abused his powers?

ADDITIONAL READING

Aeschylus. *The Oresteia.* H. Lloyd-Jones, trans. University of California, 1993.

Aristotle. *Politics.* T. A. Sinclair, trans. Penguin, 1951.

Black, Charles. *Impeachment: A Handbook.* Yale University Press, 1998.

Dicey, A. V. *An Introduction to the Study of the Law of the Constitution.* Macmillan, 1902.

Dworkin, Ronald. "A Kind of Coup." *New York Review of Books* XLVI: 1 (January 14, 1999), p. 61.

———. "The Wounded Constitution." *New York Review of Books* XLVI: 5 (March 18, 1999), pp. 8–10.

Fuller, Lon L. *The Morality of Law*, rev. ed. Yale University Press, 1964.

Gormley, Ken. "An Original Model of the Independent Counsel Statute." *Michigan Law Review* 97 (December 1998), 601–95.

Hayek, Friedrich. *The Road to Serfdom.* University of Chicago, 1944.

Hobbes, Thomas. *Leviathan.* Macmillan, 1962.

Kant, Immanuel. "Idea for a Universal History from a Cosmopolitan Point of View." *Kant: Selections,* L. W. Beck, ed. Macmillan, 1988.

Kirchheimer, Otto. *Political Justice: The Use of Legal Procedure for Political Ends.* Princeton University Press, 1961.

Locke, John. *Second Treatise of Government.* Hackett, 1980.

MacCormick, Neil. *Legal Right and Social Democracy.* Oxford University Press, 1982.

Madison, James, John Jay, and Alexander Hamilton. *The Federalist Papers.* New American Library, 1961.

Montesquieu. *The Spirit of the Laws.* Hafner, 1949.

Neumann, Franz. *The Rule of Law.* Berg, 1986.

Plato. *The Republic.* F. M. Cornford, trans. Oxford University Press, 1973.

Posner, Richard A. *An Affair of State: The Investigation, Impeachment, and Trial of President Clinton.* Harvard University Press, 1999.

Raz, Joseph. *The Authority of Law.* Oxford University Press, 1979.

Scalia, Antonin. "The Rule of Law as the Law of Rules." *University of Chicago Law Review* 56 (Fall 1989), 1175–1188.

Shapiro, Ian, ed. *The Rule of Law.* New York University Press, 1994.

Sklar, Judith N. *Legalism: Law, Morals, and Political Trials.* Harvard University Press, 1986.

Starr, Kenneth. *The Starr Report.* New York: Pocket Books, 1998.

Summers, Robert. "The Rule of Law." *Ratio Juris* 6: 2 (July 1993), 127–142.

"Symposium: The Independent Counsel Act: From Watergate to Whitewater and Beyond." *Georgetown Law Journal* 86 (July 1998).

2

Law and Morality

A COMMON SAYING

"You can't legislate morality." So goes the common saying. But what does it mean? Every country legislates against murder, assault, rape, theft, and other immoral actions. Such laws are not completely effective, but they do a reasonably good job in keeping the rates of murder and other immoral conduct much lower than those rates would be in the absence of any legal prohibitions. Unless the common saying is palpably false, then, it cannot mean that legislating against immoral conduct is impossible, impractical, or undesirable.

Perhaps we can make some headway in understanding the saying if we distinguish among four different elements of morality. First are the moral rules that obligate us to act in certain ways: to keep our promises, to refrain from committing murder, and so on. These rules concern the way we are to act but not the motives behind the actions. Keeping a promise purely for reasons of self-interest is just as much in accordance with the moral rule of promise-keeping as is keeping the promise out of a concern for the person to whom the promise was made.

The second part of morality concerns conduct that is "above and beyond the call of duty." Such conduct typically requires a considerable sacrifice by the agent or a substantial risk to her well-being. Indeed, the sacrifice or risk is so large that it seems unreasonable to require the agent to undertake the conduct. Those individuals who go ahead despite the sacrifice or risk have acted in an especially praiseworthy way.

The third part of morality concerns the motives from which a morally good person acts. For traditional morality, at least, a good person acts out of a concern for the well-being of others (altruism). In many situations, a person motivated by self-interest may act in the same way as one motivated by altruism. For example, both may reliably keep their promises. But traditional morality would not accord the two the same esteem: acting from altruism merits moral esteem, while acting from self-interest does not. That is the way traditional morality sees it, at any rate.

A fourth part of morality concerns the qualities of character that help a person act in ways that are obligatory or praiseworthy. Such qualities are called "virtues" and include courage, temperance, and perseverance. These virtues seem particularly important for praiseworthy conduct, as a person who lacks the virtues will be unlikely to accept the risks that such conduct carries. Yet, in some cases, virtues such as courage may also be needed to do one's duty, as in a case where it is one's duty to fight in a war against an invading enemy.

Having distinguished some of the different aspects of morality, we are now in better position to understand the saying, "You can't legislate morality." It is best construed as focusing on the second, third, and fourth parts of morality. The first part of morality—the rules that obligate us to act in certain ways— can and ought to be legislated. The laws against murder and rape show that at least some of morality's rules of obligation can and should be translated into the law. But the saying seeks to cast doubt on the justifiability and practicality of legislating those parts of morality that concern motives, praiseworthy conduct, and the virtues. What grounds are there for such doubts?

Consider actions that are above and beyond the call of duty.[1] It seems problematic for the law to require such actions. Conduct that is especially praiseworthy calls for a degree of sacrifice, or potential sacrifice, that goes beyond what society can reasonably demand of an individual. So even if we could increase the number of praiseworthy actions in society by legally requiring them, it would seem unfair to do so.

Now consider the motives from which individuals act. It seems impossible for laws to make individuals act from morally commendable motives. The law influences action mainly by making it in a person's interest to act in a certain way: you will get punished or otherwise fail to get something you want if you do not do as the law requires. So law uses our natural self-interest as a kind of lever to affect our conduct. But self-interest is not a motive that morality ranks high. Altruism rather than self-interest is the motive that morality rates as commendable. And it seems that there is no way, at least no direct way, in which law could make us act from such morally commendable motives.[2]

Now consider the moral virtues. Again, it seems impossible for laws to make a person virtuous. The law appeals to our preexisting self-interest: it takes us as we are and seeks to channel our behavior. The law seemingly lacks the capacity to get into our hearts and minds and change our basic moral character.

So the claim that you cannot legislate morality comes down to the claim that it is unfair for laws to require acts that go beyond the call of duty and impossible for laws to make us virtuous or lead us to act from morally commendable motives. The claim is quite plausible, though not obviously correct.

For example, laws might promote good character by helping to teach people the difference between right and wrong. The ancient Greek philosophers often looked upon the law as a potential moral teacher in that respect.

Yet, even if one accepts that "you can't legislate morality," important questions remain about the relation of law to morality. For example: Assuming that morality requires people to help those in need, should the law require us to give such help? In Chapter 4, we will examine arguments over the extent to which the law should require us to aid others.

In this chapter, our main concern will be on another aspect of the relation of law to morality. The focus will be on the part of morality that everyone agrees can be legislated: the moral rules that impose obligations on us. That part of morality is sometimes called *natural law* because it is sometimes considered to constitute a system of law in its own right, consisting of rules that can be known by our natural powers of reasoning.

Natural law is distinguished from *positive law,* which refers to any system of laws created by humans and enforced within a given territory. While natural law claims to be universally valid, imposing obligations on every individual in every country and historical era, positive law only claims validity over a particular territory and its inhabitants.

The distinction between natural and positive law raises a number of questions, among them:

1. Is the rule of law best understood as (a) the rule of positive law alone, or (b) the rule of natural law and of positive law only insofar as it is consistent with natural law?

2. Is any rule of positive law that is in conflict with natural law invalid and incapable of imposing any obligation on us?

3. Are acts contrary to natural law crimes even if there is no specific positive law that makes them criminal?

Such questions are often summarized by asking, "Is there a *necessary* connection between law and morality?" *Law* here refers to positive law, while *morality* denotes the natural law part of morality. The fact that positive laws against murder and rape should and do exist shows that there are some connections between positive and natural law: it is possible for positive law to enforce the obligations of natural law, and in many cases positive law ought to enforce those obligations and does so in a reasonably effective way.

So there is no disagreement over whether there are certain important connections between law and morality. However, there is considerable dispute over the kinds of connections at issue in the three questions enumerated earlier. And those connections involve an element of necessity. To bring out that element, the questions can be rephrased:

1. Does the concept of the rule of law necessarily include the idea of natural law?

2. Are positive laws necessarily lacking in validity whenever they conflict with natural law?

3. Are acts that violate the obligations of natural law necessarily crimes, regardless of how the positive law regards them?

The term *natural law theory* is used to refer to those theories that answer these questions in the affirmative: they assert that a necessary connection does exist between (positive) law and morality. The term *legal positivism* refers to those theories that answer these questions in the negative: they deny any such necessary connections between law and morality. We will see that both natural law theory and legal positivism come in different versions and that both types of theories have changed and developed over the years. But before we examine these philosophical disputes and developments, let us examine a trial that brought the philosophical issues down to earth in a dramatic way. It was perhaps the most important trial of the twentieth century, and it took place in Nuremberg, Germany, shortly after the end of World War II.

JUDGMENT AT NUREMBERG

Historical Background

The Nuremberg Trial was conducted by the victorious Allied Powers (the United States, Great Britain, France, and the Soviet Union) after the conclusion of World War II. The ground rules for the trial were set out in a charter agreed to by the Allies at the conclusion of the war in Europe. The judges and prosecutors all came from the Allied side. Put on trial were high-ranking officials in the Nazi Party and government, as well as German military leaders. In all, there were twenty-one defendants. Included among them were: Herrmann Goering, second-in-command to Adolf Hitler and commander-in-chief of the Air Force; Alfred Rosenberg, chief ideologist of the Nazi Party and government Minister; Albert Speer, Minister of War Production; Hjalmar Schacht, Minister for Economics; Rudolf Hess, deputy to Hitler; and Karl Doenitz, commander-in-chief of the Navy.

The men were charged with crimes against peace, including the waging of a war of aggression; war crimes, including the murder of prisoners of war and civilians; and crimes against humanity, including genocide and mass murder. In addition, the defendants were charged with conspiracy to commit the aforementioned crimes insofar as they formulated a common plan to carry out them out. Under this charge, the defendants were responsible for all of the actions committed by anyone carrying out the plan.

Three of the defendants were acquitted on all charges; the remainder were each convicted on at least one charge. Eleven received the death sentence, while the remainder of the guilty received prison sentences.

The trial documented in detail the Nazi campaign to wage war against its European neighbors and to exterminate Jews, Gypsies, and others they regarded as undesirables. The moral horrors committed by the Nazis and their collaborators were unprecedented in the annals of history. No one familiar with the facts proved at the trial could doubt that many, if not all, of the defendants bore a staggering degree of moral guilt.

Many people believed that, after the war, the top Nazi officials who were captured should have been summarily executed, taken out and shot on the spot. After all, that was a time-honored way for victors to treat their defeated enemy's leaders. The British, in fact, initially favored such summary execution of top Nazi officials, but the Americans argued vigorously for a trial, and the British eventually agreed.

A trial is a legal proceeding, and the implication of holding one is that the accused are not merely morally guilty but legally guilty as well. This entailed that the prosecutors needed some legal basis for the prosecution. It was not enough to declare that the defendants were evil men who committed evil deeds. It had to be argued that they violated the law.

The Allies argued that it was international law that the Nazi leaders had violated. International law is not enacted by any legislative body. Rather, it is defined by the treaties and customs accepted by the international community. The Allies charged that those treaties and customs made criminal the actions with which the Nuremberg defendants were charged.

The legal prosecution of the defendants also presupposed that the judicial tribunal hearing the cases had the legal authority to do so. Not just any group of persons is legally authorized to hear cases and mete out punishment. The Allies agreed to documents establishing the tribunal and authorizing it to decide the guilt or innocence of anyone who had acted on the side of the Axis powers and who was charged with the crimes against peace, war crimes, or crimes against humanity.

Criticisms of the Trial

Although it is now widely celebrated as a great achievement, the Nuremberg Trial was controversial in its time. Criticism came not only from those Germans who believed that placing their leaders on trial humiliated the whole nation. It also came from legal thinkers whose criticisms rested on philosophical theories of law.

There are two distinct lines of argument against the prosecution and conviction of the Nuremberg defendants. The first rests on the contention that any trial should follow the rule of law but that the Nuremberg proceedings seriously violated it. The second revolves around the view that law consists of the commands of a sovereign state and that the only laws applicable to the German defendants were the commands of the German sovereign, Adolf Hitler. Let us examine each line of argument, beginning with the argument based on the rule of law.

Many critics of the trial argued that, like any another trial, the legitimacy of the Nuremberg proceedings should be judged in terms of the principles of the rule of law and that, on such a basis, the trial should be deemed illegitimate. In the eyes of these critics, summary execution would have been preferable. Although summary execution would have violated the rule of law as well, the point is that a trial is a proceeding purporting to conform to the rule of law, while summary execution involves no such pretense.

The critics pointed to several ways in which the Nuremberg proceedings violated the rule of law. First, they claimed that there were no valid legal rules in effect at the time of the defendants' actions that outlawed "crimes against humanity." With respect to that count of the indictment, the principle of "no crime without a law" was violated.

The Nuremberg Charter did outlaw crimes against humanity, but that charter was adopted after the alleged crimes took place. Prosecutions based on that provision of the charter thus violated as well the principle against the retroactive application of the law.

International treaties that preexisted World War II did outlaw wars of aggression, but they had never been enforced, thus casting serious doubt on their continued legal validity. The rule of law requires consistent enforcement of the law.

Moreover, the critics pointed out, the international treaties in question did not make individuals criminally liable for their conduct and provided no specific punishments for violations. Although these treaties declared or implied that aggressive war was a crime, they did not go on to say that individual political leaders would be held legally responsible or to indicate the sanctions that would be applied. At best, the international community could punish the guilty nation through economic and diplomatic measures, even though that too was problematic without any prior authoritative specification of sanctions. And punishing nations diplomatically or economically is a far cry from executing or imprisoning political and military leaders.

The critics went on to claim that the only legal document that made individuals criminally liable for such acts as waging a war of aggression was the charter that set the ground rules for the trial and that the charter was not written until after the "crimes" had been committed. Again, there seems to be a violation of the prohibition against retroactive laws.

Similarly, the critics rejected the legitimacy of the conspiracy charge against the defendants. Prior to the Nuremberg Charter, no international treaties or agreements criminalized conspiracy. In fact, the Charter's broad view of conspiracy, making every conspirator responsible for every act carried out in furtherance of the plan, was foreign to the domestic law of Germany and many other countries.

Critics also charged that the makeup of the tribunal violated the principle that those accused of crimes have a right to defend themselves before an impartial body. Though the defendants all had lawyers to assist in their defense, the tribunal could not be regarded as an impartial one, since its judges came from the very countries against whom Nazi Germany had just fought a terribly destructive war.

In addition, the critics claimed that the newly invented legal rules being enforced against the defendants were not being consistently and impartially applied. Allied forces were also guilty of acts that could be seen as war crimes. Indeed, the dropping of atomic bombs on Hiroshima and Nagasaki and the

Allied firebombing that destroyed Dresden were viewed that way by many people, even among the Allies themselves. And the Soviet Union, one of the Allied powers making up the tribunal, was itself clearly guilty of aggression, for example, in its takeover of the Baltic states. Yet, no one among the Allies was being prosecuted for any of these crimes, and the charter that established the ground rules at Nuremberg did not even allow the tribunal to consider criminal charges against anyone on the Allied side.

Finally, some critics argued that the concept of a war of aggression was not defined with sufficient legal precision, and they doubted that it ever could be. The charter that established the Nuremberg tribunal made it a crime to wage, or conspire to wage, a war of aggression, but it did not define what such a war consisted of. In addition, any adequate definition would have to make relevant the history that lay behind a given war and the justice of the historical claims that different groups have made. This would bog any court down in a morass of historical and moral questions that could not be answered with the objectivity required for the rule of law.

In sum, this first line of argument contends that the proceedings should have complied with the rule of law but failed to do so. The trial did not administer legal justice, as it claimed to do, but rather "victor's justice." Though it was presented as a legal proceeding, Nuremberg was in fact a political trial in which the victors used their superior power to get revenge against their enemies.

The second line of criticism proceeds from the idea that the sovereign of each nation creates the law that applies within the territory it controls. Reflecting the views of Hobbes and Austin, this argument holds that law is the command of the sovereign power who rules over a given territory and that the sovereign power cannot be legally limited by any superior power, or else it would not be truly sovereign.

This understanding of law and sovereignty casts doubt on the very idea of international law. Because there is no global sovereign who enforces international treaties and agreements, so-called "international law" cannot really be authoritative and binding law at all. Accordingly, argue these critics, international law cannot serve as a legal basis for prosecution.

With international law out of the picture, all that is left is the law of each country. And critics of the Nuremberg prosecutions argued that under German law as it existed during the Nazi regime, the defendants had not acted illegally. Sovereign power lay in the hands of Hitler, and the defendants who allegedly committed the crimes simply carried out his commands. Accordingly, their actions cannot be considered crimes.

This second line of argument was reflected in two of the defenses offered by the lawyers for the accused Germans: acts of state and superior orders. Acts of state are acts of the sovereign. Defense counsel argued that such acts cannot be illegal because the sovereign dictates what is legal and illegal. Insofar as the defendants were government officials, their acts were acts of the sovereign German state. And insofar as the defendants were subjects of the sovereign state, their actions complied with orders coming from their political superiors and ultimately from Hitler. Complying with the commands that come from the sovereign cannot be a crime because those commands dictate what counts as a crime.

Justifying the Trial

The arguments of the critics were countered by those who contended that the trial and convictions were fully justified. The counterarguments emphasized that several international treaties and agreements renounced aggressive war and declared it to be criminal. Germany was itself party to some of these agreements. The charter that established the tribunal did not create new crimes in this regard but simply declared what the international community had previously agreed were crimes.

Proponents of the trial also pointed out that the international community had long recognized war crimes as a violation of international law. In fact, the Nuremberg Charter based its definition of war crimes on the Hague Convention of 1907 and the Geneva Convention of 1927.

The charge of crimes against humanity was admitted to be something of an innovation in international law, but defenders of the trial argued that such crimes could be legitimately prosecuted to the extent that they were part and parcel of the Nazi plans to wage aggressive war and commit war crimes. The extermination of Jews, Gypsies, and other "undesirables" was inextricably linked to conduct declared criminal by international law and was thereby subject to prosecution as well.

As for the alleged partiality of the tribunal, the trial's proponents argued that what counts is not what country a judge comes from but his independence and his willingness to listen to both sides and render a verdict supported by the law and the evidence. The Nuremberg judges were dedicated and independent jurists, not prone to rubber-stamp the prosecution's case, and they proved this by their verdicts. Three of the defendants were acquitted on all counts, and several other defendants were declared innocent on some of the counts. And the judges did not impose the harshest penalty on all the convicted defendants, reserving the death sentence for those most culpable and giving prison sentences to the others.

Advocates of the trial also pointed to the importance of establishing for history the deeds that had been committed by the Nazis. The trial made public massive amounts of documentary evidence establishing the plans and policies of the Nazi government. It produced personal diaries of Nazi leaders, letters, and official government documents revealing the scope and nature of the atrocities. After the trial, no reasonable person could doubt the fact that Germany had pursued a horrifying campaign of aggression and genocide.

But were the actions of the defendants truly crimes? Defense counsel had argued that the actions could not be criminal because they were undertaken as acts of a sovereign state and in compliance with the commands of the sovereign. But advocates for the prosecution rejected the premise upon which those arguments rested. Sovereign states were not above the law but were obligated by international law. And international law obligated states and their subjects to refrain from aggression, genocide, and the other conduct enumerated in the four counts of the indictment.

For its advocates, then, the trial was an example of the rule of law in action. While the rule of law had existed within certain nations, Nuremberg extended it to the international community and relations among nations. For its critics, though, the trial violated basic principles that define the rule of law. Let us turn to the question of which view is more accurate.

Assessing the Trial

Despite the best efforts of its advocates, it is difficult to think that the trial met all of the requirements of the rule of law. It seems more than a mild stretch to argue, for example, that the tribunal of judges was a truly impartial one. The Soviet judge was selected by the totalitarian dictator, Joseph Stalin, who was determined that every defendant be found guilty and sentenced to death. And it is psychologically implausible to think that any of the judges could put aside their national sentiments against Germany and render an impartial judgment.

Moreover, prior to the Nuremberg Charter, there simply was no international agreement that outlawed crimes against humanity. That count of the indictment certainly appears to be a violation of the principle against retroactive application of criminal laws. And the treaties that did outlaw wars of aggression were not enforced despite acts of aggression by other nations before Germany embarked on its campaign against its neighbors. Nor were the treaties enforced against the Soviet Union's aggression after the outbreak of the war. It is not easy to see how this lack of consistent enforcement is compatible with the requirements of the rule of law.

Defenders of the trial might concede that it had serious imperfections from the perspective of legality but argue that, nonetheless, the trial did a better job of promoting the rule of law over the long run than any of the feasible alternatives would have done. One alternative, summary execution, would not have allowed the accused their day in court. Another alternative, letting the accused go free without any trial, may well have led to widespread, violent vigilante action. Holding the trial showed that in a context where the desire for vengeance runs high, legal procedures can both restrain and satisfy that desire, while giving the accused a *relatively* fair chance to defend themselves. This was an important lesson to teach for the creation of an effective international rule of law and for the restoration of the rule of law to Germany, after a decade of arbitrary government.

However, many critics of the trial will insist that the prosecution of the German defendants rested on a fundamentally mistaken conception of the nature of law and crime. Only a law can make an act a crime, and law consists of the commands issued and enforced by a sovereign state in the territory it controls. Nazi Germany was such a state. Its law may have been grossly immoral, but it was the law nonetheless. Law derives from the power of the sovereign, not from the sovereign's moral virtue. And Nazi law did not make the actions of the defendants crimes. The trial and conviction of the defendants simply obscured the true nature of law and crime.

This conception of the nature of law and crime is a form of legal positivism that understands law in terms of the power of a sovereign to issue and enforce commands. There are other forms of positivism, ones that can be used to argue for the trial and the convictions of the defendants. Indeed, the argument based on international law is consistent with the positivist idea that there is no necessary connection between law and morality: international law can be seen as a form of positive law having no necessary connection to basic principles of moral obligation.

But it is also possible to make a natural law argument in favor of the trial and convictions. Such an argument does not simply claim that the defendants committed crimes under international law. It contends that they committed crimes under natural law by violating fundamental moral obligations. And it rejects the defenses of act of state and superior orders: no act of state or command of any sovereign can have legal validity if it is inconsistent with natural law.

The Nuremberg Trial thus presented a dramatic example in which opposing theories of the nature of law came into collision. Both natural law theory and legal positivism were part of the debate over Nuremberg. We will now turn to a closer examination of natural law theory and its different versions and then consider legal positivism. The aim is not to resolve the long-standing philosophical disagreement between the two theories. Rather, it is to gain a clear understanding of the dispute, its practical implications, and the arguments on each side.

NATURAL LAW THEORY: OVERVIEW

Natural law theory claims that a necessary connection exists between positive law and morality. This necessary connection is said to exist by virtue of the very concept of law. But what is the precise nature of that connection? There are different versions of natural law theory, each giving a different answer to that question. In this chapter, we will examine three versions.

According to the first version, rules of positive law that conflict with principles of natural law are invalid. Such rules are legally null and void and impose no obligations on anyone. The higher obligations imposed by natural law cancel out any contrary obligation that an immoral positive law may seek to impose. We will call this version of natural law thinking the "traditional" version. Its most prominent proponent is the medieval philosopher Thomas Aquinas.

The second version of natural law theory sees a different kind of necessary connection between positive law and morality. It does not claim that each rule of positive law must be consistent with natural law principles in order to have legal validity. Rather, it claims that there are certain moral principles that are applicable specifically to law and that any genuine system of law must generally respect those principles. The most prominent proponent of this approach is the American legal thinker Lon Fuller, who says that the principles amount to an "inner morality of law" and argues that the law of regimes such as Nazi Germany pervasively violates this inner morality.

The third version sees yet a different form of necessary connection between positive law and morality. It does not claim that a legal rule must be consistent with natural law to be legally valid. Rather, it claims that the positive law cannot be properly interpreted and applied without the introduction of moral judgments. We will call this the "interpretive" version of natural law theory. The most prominent proponent of this theory is the American legal theorist Ronald Dworkin, and his view will be the final version of natural law theory we examine.

TRADITIONAL NATURAL LAW THEORY: BACKGROUND

The idea that there are universal principles of right and wrong that can be discovered by human reason goes back to the days of ancient Greece. These natural law principles were seen as providing standards by which the rules of positive law could be judged. Previously, it had been accepted dogma that the laws of a state were sacred and beyond all criticism, but the ancient philosophers rejected such a dogma and claimed that the rules of positive law were subject to evaluation on the basis of the principles of natural law. These principles represented a "higher law" by which the goodness or badness of positive law could be determined.

These early ideas about natural law provided the starting points from which traditional natural law theory developed. During the Middle Ages, some natural law thinkers took the crucial step in that development and argued that the rules of positive law must be consistent with the obligations imposed on everyone by natural law in order to be legally valid. In this way, natural law was not merely a set of standards to judge the goodness or badness of the rules laid down by a state. It was a system of supreme obligations that would cancel out the legal authority of any incompatible rule of positive law. Unless it was consistent with natural law, a rule of positive law was null and void. Such a rule was like counterfeit money—though it might appear on the surface to be a valid law, it really was no law at all.[3] The medieval philosopher St. Augustine gave a succinct statement of the traditional view: "a law that is not just is not a law."[4]

It is important to recognize the difference between saying that natural law should be used to evaluate positive laws as good or bad and saying that natural law should be used to declare positive laws as legally valid or invalid. The former statement implies that even when positive laws are inconsistent with natural law, they can still be legally valid. A bad law can still be a genuine law, one that people are legally obligated to observe. In this view, being bad does not make a law null and void.

In contrast, when principles of natural law are taken as standards of legal validity, any inconsistency with those principles makes a rule legally null and void. The rule can no more impose an obligation than can a robber's threat to his victim, "Your money or your life." This is the view of traditional natural law theory.

The medieval philosopher St. Thomas Aquinas is commonly regarded as the most important proponent of traditional natural law theory. He gives the most comprehensive and systematic presentation of the traditional version. We will shortly be examining Aquinas's views in more detail. Before we do, it is important to realize that the traditional natural law view is by no means restricted to the Middle Ages, despite the fact that Augustine and Aquinas are two of its main proponents.

The most influential English legal theorist of the eighteenth century, William Blackstone, advocated traditional natural law theory. And Blackstone's ideas about law had influence in the United States well into the nineteenth century, even though his natural law approach was never generally accepted. In addition, natural law theory was part of the movement to abolish slavery in the United States. Leading abolitionists declared that the rules supporting slavery were unjust and that what was unjust could not have real legal authority and so should not be enforced by courts. An unmistakable echo is apparent in abolitionist statements of Augustine's thesis that an unjust law is no law at all.

And as we have seen, in the twentieth century, traditional natural law theory was invoked by some to argue that the Nazi decrees leading to the persecution and extermination of millions did not have the status of law and were legally invalid due to their inconsistency with natural law. The German legal philosopher Gustav Radbruch was alluding to Nazi laws when he wrote, "[T]here can be laws that are so unjust, so socially detrimental that their very character as laws, must be denied. There are, therefore, principles of law that are stronger than any statute, so that a law conflicting with these principles is devoid of validity. One calls these principles natural law."[5] Since the Nazi decrees were legally invalid, courts should have refused to enforce them, and anyone involved in implementing the decrees lacked the excuse that they were acting lawfully, if not morally.

The traditional version of natural law theory is also endorsed by legal thinkers who are writing today. Thus, Michael Moore has recently claimed, "For something to be a law at all it must necessarily not be unjust."[6] And the legal theorists Beyleveld and Brownsword have argued that there is a fundamental principle of morality that renders legally invalid any rule inconsistent with it.[7]

Let us now turn to one of the great natural law thinkers in the Western tradition, Thomas Aquinas. His ideas had a great influence on natural law theory for hundreds of years and continue to do so today.

AQUINAS'S THEORY OF LAW

Law and the Good

Aquinas's version of traditional natural law theory remains one of the most systematic and comprehensive legal philosophies ever developed. It rests on his vision of the universe as governed by a single, self-consistent, and overarching system of law. The entire system is under the direction and authority of the supreme lawgiver and judge, God. Human law occupies the lower tier of this system. Above it are eternal law, natural law, and divine law.

Eternal law consists of those principles of action and motion that God implanted in things in order to enable each thing to perform its proper function in the overall order of the universe. The proper function of a thing determines what is good and bad for it: the good consists of performing its function; the bad consists of failing to perform it.

Natural law consists of those principles of eternal law specific to human beings. Such principles are knowable by our natural powers of reason, and they guide us toward what is good for humans. Thus, it is good for humans to live peaceably with one another in society, and so natural law principles entail the prohibition of actions such as murder and theft that harm society. In general, obedience to natural law is obligatory for any human being because that is how we achieve the human good; disobedience is wrong because that is how we fail to achieve it.

For Aquinas, humans will not reach the ultimate good simply by following natural law. The principles of natural law help us reach the good that is achievable in this world. Yet, beyond this world there is the ultimate human good: eternal salvation. A type of law exists over and above natural law, guiding us to that ultimate goal. That is divine law.

Human law—Aquinas's term for positive law—consists of rules framed by the head of the political community for the common good of its members. In some cases, such rules are simply logically deduced from natural law principles. For example, the positive law against murder is logically entailed by the more general natural law that prohibits a person from wrongfully harming someone else. Once we agree that murder is a form of wrongful harm, the law against murder logically follows from the natural law principle.

In other cases, the rules of positive law make more concrete and specific the relatively vague provisions contained within natural law. For example, criminal laws specify a particular punishment (or range of punishments) for each crime, while natural law only says that criminal punishment should be proportional to the seriousness of the crime.

What happens if a rule of positive law mandates an action that is contrary to natural law? Aquinas cites Augustine's thesis that an unjust law is no law. He goes on to claim, "[E]very human law has just so much of the nature of law as it is derived from the law of nature. But if in any point it deflects from the law of nature, it is no longer a law but a perversion of law."[8] Unjust rules are without legal authority, "acts of violence rather than laws."[9] They are the moral and legal equivalent of the robber's threat "Your money or your life."

For Aquinas, an unjust rule as such cannot create any obligation to obey its terms. It may happen that, in certain circumstances, disobedience to the rule would produce "scandal or disturbance."[10] Aquinas seems to have in mind here cases in which disobedience would threaten to cause social disorder, and he is saying that we are obligated to follow an unjust rule in such cases in order to avoid the disorder. But such an obligation would not be based on any authority possessed by the rule. We would be obligated to follow the rule despite the fact that it was legally invalid. That obligation would derive directly from a natural law principle prohibiting actions that threaten scandal or disturbance.

Aquinas describes unjust rules framed by the ruler as unjust laws. Why does he do so, if he really believes that such rules are not real laws and have no legal authority? He seems to be using the term *unjust laws* in a way that is analogous to the way we use the term *counterfeit money*. We call what counterfeiters make "money," even though we recognize that it is not really money but only pretends to be. In the same way, an unjust rule enacted by a ruler poses as a real law in that the ruler will claim that the rule promotes the common good. In making such a claim, the unscrupulous ruler hopes to fool people into going along with the rule without protest. But the claim does not make the rule legally valid; at best, it only makes the rule appear to be valid. Like counterfeit money, the rule is passed off as something it really is not.

Aquinas's reasons for accepting Augustine's thesis that unjust laws are no laws at all can be concisely stated as follows. The purpose of human law is to promote the common good of the members of the political community. The common good is not promoted, however, by rules that go contrary to natural law. After all, it is the natural law that guides human beings toward the good. Thus, rules that run counter to natural law are in opposition to the very purpose of human law and so are "perversions" of law. In other words, such rules represent the misuse of the power to frame rules for the political community. As such, unjust rules are without legal authority.

Assessing Aquinas

Is Aquinas's argument for a traditional natural law approach a convincing one? There are some reasons for questioning its cogency. The most important reasons revolve around Aquinas's key claim that the purpose of human law is to promote the common good of the community. He is confident of the claim because he is confident that he knows that (1) God exists; (2) God has ordained that those in charge of political communities frame laws serving the common good; and (3) the natural reasoning powers of humans lead all reasonable persons to agree on the basic principles that determine good and bad, right and wrong.

Many current legal and political philosophers do not have Aquinas's confidence in these matters. They would argue that (1) there is no God; (2) even if there is, God's existence is not something that we can know but only believe in; (3) even if we can know that God exists, we cannot know what, if anything, God intends those in charge of political communities to do; and (4) reasonable people can disagree over fundamental principles of human good and obligation. These philosophers would, in short, expel God from consideration in developing a legal and political philosophy and argue that basic disagreements about morality and justice cannot be definitively settled by reason.

If God is expelled, the only purposes that we can attribute to the positive law are human purposes, not divine ones. And this is where the trouble for Aquinas's traditional version of natural law theory starts to become obvious. The purposes to which humans have put positive law have not always been especially moral or just. As the examples of slavery and Nazism show, oppression, exploitation, and even genocide have been among such purposes.

Contemporary defenders of the traditional natural law approach might seek to mount a secular defense of Aquinas's notion that the purpose of law is to promote the common good. They may point out that practices we understand as violations of basic moral obligations, Nazis and slaveowners regarded as just and right. The point is not to endorse the relativist notion that something is made right by the simple fact that some people think it is right. The traditional natural law view clearly rejects any such relativism in favor of the idea that there are objective moral obligations. Rather, the point is to suggest that in enacting laws people are trying to do what is right, however flawed their notions of right and wrong may be. If this is what people are trying to do, then we can still say that the purpose of law is to promote morality and justice. This is the human aim of law, regardless of whether it is God's aim as well. And unjust laws will run contrary to that aim.

Even if we accept that humans are always trying to promote justice when enacting laws, it does not follow that unjust rules cannot be genuine laws. If a philosopher is trying to write a book that answers all the basic questions of legal philosophy, we would not say that her writing cannot amount to a genuine book unless it actually answers all such questions. The book simply would not be as good as the one she had been aiming to write. Critics of the traditional natural law approach will say something similar about an unjust rule: it still can be a genuine law even if it is not as good as its authors had been aiming to make it.

Moreover, it is dubious that humans are always trying to promote justice when they enact laws. Some rather cynical political leaders throughout human history were probably not even trying to do justice. They ruled for the personal advantages they could extract using their political power, not to promote justice in their community. Of course, such cynical leaders claim publicly that their laws promote justice, but such an assertion is meant to hide, not reveal, their true purposes.

Traditional natural law theory thus seems to be on shaky grounds in claiming that unjust rules cannot have legal authority. If the claim is to be vindicated, a more persuasive approach than Aquinas's must be developed. Perhaps it can be. But even if it cannot, a necessary connection of another kind between positive law and morality is still possible. Let us explore that possibility.

FULLER AND FIDELITY TO LAW

The Inner Morality of Law

Lon Fuller argues that any genuine system of law necessarily abides by certain moral principles. He calls these principles the "inner morality of the law." A government can control and regulate the conduct of those in society in different ways. But a system of regulation and control is not a system of law, according to Fuller, unless these principles are satisfied.

What are the principles that make up the inner morality of law? Fuller derives them from the idea that law is something intended to regulate and control conduct by means of general rules that are addressed to humans as agents capable of deliberation and choice. Modes of regulation and control that do not rely on general rules or that bypass the human capacity for deliberation and choice are excluded. Accordingly, legal rules must be applied prospectively, rather than retroactively, because only prospective rules address humans as agents capable of choice. Similarly, legal rules must be relatively clear in meaning, possible to comply with, adopted in accord with existing rules, and so forth. In other words, for Fuller, a government must give individuals fair warning and abide by the other principles of legality if it is to show respect for humans as agents capable of choosing their own conduct.

Because the principles of legality embody this respect, they represent an inner morality that is part of any genuine legal system. On account of this inner morality, Fuller contends that there is a prima facie obligation to obey the rules of any genuine system of positive law. A prima facie obligation is one that can be overridden if it conflicts with a more important obligation. Nonetheless, a prima facie obligation imposes a real moral requirement on individuals. Fuller puts this point by saying that there is a duty of fidelity to the law.

The inner morality of law does not guarantee that every genuine law is a just law. And if a law is seriously unjust, the prima facie obligation to obey it may be overridden. After all, a law might be so unjust that fundamental moral obligations require disobedience.

Fuller thus believes that the basic idea behind natural law theory can be vindicated: there is a necessary connection between positive law and morality, and that connection stems from the nature of law itself. The necessary connection is not as strong as traditional natural law thinkers had postulated, for it is possible that particular positive laws are unjust and morally ought to be disobeyed. But for Fuller those possibilities do not eliminate the fact that every genuine legal system has an inner morality that imposes a prima facie obligation to obey its rules.

Fuller concedes that in real-world legal systems, the inner morality of the law is not perfectly observed. For example, it is not unusual even for a country like the United States or England to have some laws that are very vague. But some departure from the law's inner morality is, for Fuller, compatible with the existence of a legal system. He sensibly points out that having a legal system is a matter of degree and that it is a mistake to regard the existence of a system of law as an all-or-nothing affair.

Yet, Fuller also argues that at some point the violation of rule-of-law principles becomes so pervasive and serious that we are no longer dealing with a system under the rule of law but rather with arbitrary government or some similar mode of regulating behavior. He believes, for example, that Nazi Germany went past that point with its pervasive and blatant disregard of the principles of legality. Nazi Germany did not regulate behavior through a system of law but rather through an arbitrary system of terror organized and implemented by the Nazi Party and the agencies it controlled. This terror operated outside and above the law. So serious was the disregard for legality that the system of social control could not be said to treat humans as responsible moral agents. Instead, it treated them as objects to be manipulated by violence rather than as subjects capable of deliberation and decision.

What does Fuller's theory entail for the issues raised by the Nuremberg Trial? The theory seems to nullify at least one of the arguments made by the defendants, namely, that their actions were legal under the existing system of Nazi law. For Fuller, there was no system of law in Nazi Germany, only a system of lawless terror. But that leaves the question of whether there was some genuine system of law under which the acts of the defendants could be considered crimes.

The prosecution's appeal to international law would seem to be problematic from the perspective of Fuller's theory. With its lack of consistent and impartial enforcement, vague provisions, and retroactive enforcement, international law fell seriously short of meeting Fuller's inner morality and arguably did not constitute a genuine system of law.

The appeal to natural law is even more problematic from Fuller's perspective. The inner morality of law requires functioning institutions to implement, interpret, and enforce the provisions of the law. Rules of obligations that are not brought down to earth in that way do not count as a legal system.

Yet, Fuller could argue that, despite the serious flaws of international law, the trial and conviction of the defendants did a better job than any feasible alternative of promoting the inner morality of law in both the international area and Germany itself. Fuller's insight that the rule of law is a matter of degree suggests that it may need to be built over time. The initial phase of that building process may fall far short of the inner morality of the law. But it may nonetheless be justified if, under the circumstances, it is the best first step that one can take.

Assessing Fuller's Inner Morality

Fuller's approach avoids the key problem of traditional natural law theory. He does not try to show that every unjust rule of positive law is legally nullified by the higher authority of natural law. His focus is not on particular laws one by one, but rather on the kind of system by which the ruling authorities in a country seek to regulate and control society. And Fuller's central claim is that a system of law, unlike a system of lawless terror, imposes on individuals a prima facie obligation of obedience due to the respect that the inner morality of law accords to us as responsible agents.

Fuller is on safe ground in thinking that systems of lawless terror impose no obligation of obedience, not even a prima facie obligation. However, his claim that a system of law always imposes a prima facie obligation is problematic. The rules of a system that fully abides by Fuller's inner morality can be as unjust and dehumanizing as the regime of the Nazis.

Fuller argues that the inner morality of law puts significant constraints on a government bent on evildoing and injustice. Those who commit evil and injustice typically do not want others to know about it and do not want to be restricted by rules and regulations. The principles of legality, on the other hand, require that official action be authorized by rules that are made public and can be generally known. Hitler may have ordered the extermination of Jews, and many Germans no doubt were aware that exterminations were occurring on a large scale. But the extermination policy was not made public in a way that legality requires: even the Nazis were not so brazen as to advertise all of their atrocities to the world. And many of the Nazi atrocities simply ignored existing rules and regulations.

Fuller seems to be on solid ground in arguing that rule-of-law principles tend to constrain government injustice and evildoing. Certainly, all of those thinkers in Western history who have defended the rule of law would agree with him on that score. But even granting the point, it does not follow that there is always a prima facie moral obligation to be faithful to the rules of any system of law. Some systems of law may be so oppressive and unjust that there is no moral obligation whatsoever to be faithful to them.

There are many examples of terribly unjust Nazi laws that were duly promulgated and met the other requirements of the inner morality of the law. The most infamous, perhaps, were the Nuremberg laws prohibiting marriage and sexual intercourse between Jews and persons of "German blood." It would be difficult to argue that there was a prima facie obligation to be faithful to such laws just because any system of positive law as such puts certain constraints on government evildoing. In certain cases, those constraints are woefully short of what morality can tolerate, and the only reason for being faithful to such laws is fear of the awful consequences of disobedience.

Fuller would claim that the example of the Nuremberg laws does not really refute his position. He denies that Nazi Germany had a true system of law: it violated so many of the principles of legality in such an egregious way that it was a system of terror not law. Accordingly, Fuller would say that there was no moral obligation to obey the Nuremberg laws or other oppressive Nazi enactments.

Yet, granting Fuller's claim that no true system of law existed in Nazi Germany, his reply still misses the basic point: even if the Nazis had conformed to the principles of legality, they would still have been able to enact and enforce laws so draconian and unjust that the people of Germany would have had no moral obligation at all to obey those laws. Respect for the rule of law and the values it promotes might impose on us an obligation to obey laws that are in some degree unjust or unfair. But we are expecting too much from the rule of law if we think it can ground a prima facie moral obligation to obey any law, no matter how oppressive or unjust, as long as the law in question is part of a system that generally conforms to the principles of legality. The barbaric laws of the Nazis could not have been morally salvaged in any degree even if they had been enacted and enforced in a system that had observed the rule of law.

Law and Social Purpose

Fuller claims that positive law and morality are connected in another way, providing an additional moral basis to be faithful to the positive law. This alleged connection concerns the way in which laws should be interpreted and stems from the fact the function of positive law is to regulate the conduct of the members of society. Because of this function, there are social purposes that lie behind the rules of positive law. Fuller says that the rules should be interpreted so as to promote those social purposes. Doing so would (presumably) promote the good of society—something that morality commends us to do.

Consider a rule prohibiting vehicles from entering the park. Does that rule exclude an ambulance that is about to enter the park in order to go to the rescue of someone who has had a heart attack? If one just looked at the words of the rule and ignored any consideration of social purpose, then one would have to exclude the ambulance. A literalist application of the rule would lead to a situation in which medical emergencies in the park could not be effectively treated. But it seems clear that the purpose of the rule is not to interfere with emergency medical treatment but rather to promote the safe enjoyment of the park. Refusing entry to ambulances in an emergency situation would not promote that purpose but rather interfere with it.

Critics of Fuller point out that interpreting laws in terms of their underlying social purposes does not necessarily promote what is morally good, simply because social purposes can be grossly immoral or unjust. Laws establishing slavery or condemning Jews to a second-class status illustrate this point. In no sense can morality be said to be promoted by interpreting such laws in terms of their underlying social purposes.

Purposive interpretation may better promote morality than a literalist application of the law, if the laws have morally acceptable purposes behind them. But nothing in the idea of law or the idea of a legal system guarantees the law's purposes will be morally acceptable. And when the purposes are immoral or unjust, purposive interpretation could actually be worse than literalist application of the law. This possibility is again illustrated by the laws of Nazi Germany.

Nazi judges often used purposive interpretation in order to impose extra hardships on Jews and others regarded as politically and morally undesirable. For example, they interpreted the law forbidding sexual intercourse between Jews and non-Jewish Germans as also applying against sexual activities other than intercourse. Their reasoning was that the purpose of the law was to discourage intimate relations between Jews and non-Jews, and that purpose would be better served by interpreting the law broadly to include any kind of sexual activity.

Fuller's efforts to establish a necessary connection between positive law and morality thus appear to fail. But his idea that there is such a connection and that it stems from the way laws should be interpreted was picked up and developed in a different direction by the legal philosopher Ronald Dworkin. Let us turn to Dworkin's interpretive version of natural law theory.

DWORKIN'S INTERPRETIVE THEORY

Rules and Principles: The Idea of Fit

Dworkin believes that legal interpretation, when properly carried out, requires the making of moral judgments. This does not mean that rules of positive law will be declared invalid when they are judged to be immoral or unjust. But it does mean that morality will exercise some significant influence over the way those rules are to be understood and will thereby be inextricably intertwined with the positive law.

For Dworkin, the law includes more than those rules that are explicitly adopted as authoritative by the political community. Such rules can be found in statutory codes, judicial decisions, and other official documents. But it is a mistake to stop with the explicit rules in considering what belongs to the law. This is because those rules should be understood not as some miscellaneous collection of norms or a mere product of power politics but rather as the expression of an underlying philosophy of government.

Such a philosophy would consist of moral principles specifying the fundamental purposes of government and the proper relation between government and the individual. The law consists of the explicitly adopted rules plus the best moral principles that can be understood to lie behind those rules. In a country such as the United States, such principles concern the moral rights of individuals, rights that the government must respect and protect. The principles serve as legitimate bases of legal decisions, as well as help guide the interpretation of legal rules in hard cases in which the right legal answer is unclear.

How does one determine which are the best moral principles that can be seen as lying behind the rules explicitly adopted by the political community? The beginning of Dworkin's answer is that one must judge the degree of "fit" between some proposed principle and the rules. There are two aspects of fit.

First, fit is a matter of logical consistency: any viable candidate for an underlying principle must be logically consistent with most of the rules. Total consistency is not required, since it is not to be expected that any set of explicitly adopted rules will perfectly express some underlying philosophy of government. But unless there is a high degree of consistency, it will not be plausible to think that the rules of a certain legal system are an expression of the philosophy of government in question.

In addition, a proposed underlying principle must help explain why (most of) the rules explicitly adopted are good ones. This is the second aspect of fit: an underlying principle must help to justify, or provide a rationale for, the rules. Thus, the two aspects of fit are logical consistency and the power to help provide a rationale.

Fitting the Fourth Amendment: Privacy

Dworkin's idea of fit can be illustrated by using the Fourth Amendment to the U.S. Constitution. One provision in that Amendment guarantees "the right of people to be secure in their persons, houses, papers, and effects, against unreasonable searches and seizures" by government. Traditionally, this entailed that, as a general rule, government investigators could not search your home for evidence of a crime without a search warrant and that a warrant could be obtained only after persuading a judge that there was "probable cause" that the home contained evidence of a crime. In other words, unless a law enforcement agency could convince an independent court that there was probably evidence of a crime in person's home, the agency would not be legally permitted to enter the home in search of evidence without the owner's consent.

Dworkin's method of interpretation asks us to determine which moral principle fits this constitutional rule against unreasonable searches and seizures. We are to look for a principle that would be logically consistent with the rule and also help explain why the rule is a good one to have. Accordingly, a principle stating that government should do whatever it regards as useful in detecting and punishing criminal activity does not fit the rule. This is because the rule clearly places restrictions on what the government may do, refusing to give it a free hand in its criminal enforcement activities.

In contrast, a principle that mandates the protection of privacy does seem to fit the bill. If we understand privacy in terms of a certain physical space associated with an individual, where others may not intrude without that person's consent, then we can say that people have a moral right to privacy in their homes and that this right helps provide the rationale for the Fourth Amendment rule. Of course, the right to privacy cannot be considered absolute, or else effectively prosecuting crimes would be too difficult a task. But the Fourth Amendment rule against unreasonable searches and seizures in one's house is a good one, on this rationale, because it allows crimes to be effectively prosecuted while at the same time protecting to a significant degree the right to privacy.

We cannot assume, however, that the moral right to privacy is limited to the protection of physical spaces. It can also be said to include control over information concerning one's life, including information that could be used by others to harm the person. The right to privacy in this sense is a right to control the disclosure of such information to others. Without such a right, we are rendered much more vulnerable to others who may wish to harm us.

In addition, this informational aspect of the right to privacy helps provide a further rationale for the Fourth Amendment rule. If government were able to invade an individual's home at will, then it could collect virtually any information about her and use that information to harm her, whether she were guilty of a crime or simply a lawful critic of the government. Again, the right of informational privacy cannot be seen as absolute, and the Fourth Amendment can be interpreted as allowing effective law enforcement investigations to proceed while at the same time protecting to a significant degree this second aspect of privacy.

Olmstead and Beyond

Once we see the Fourth Amendment rule as the expression of a more basic moral principle about the individual right to privacy, then it becomes clear how the Amendment should be interpreted in cases that involve new technologies, unknown to those who wrote and ratified the Amendment in the eighteenth century. The 1928 case of *Olmstead v. United States* illustrates the power of Dworkin's approach. That case involved wiretapping of a suspected criminal's telephone by the government without a warrant.

Telephones and wiretaps were, of course, unknown in the eighteenth century. Government collected evidence from a person's home then by physically entering the property and taking what it found there. Thus, the Amendment speaks of "searches and seizures," acts of physical intrusion and confiscation. In

Olmstead, the Supreme Court decided that because wiretapping was not an act of physical intrusion and confiscation, the Fourth Amendment rule did not apply to it, and so it was not legally required for government investigators to obtain a search warrant before they could place a wiretap.

Dworkin's method of interpretation provides a very different approach to a case like *Olmstead.* It would look to a moral principle that fits the Fourth Amendment rule against unreasonable searches and seizures. Assuming that the principle is one that protects the right of privacy and that the preceding analysis of privacy is accurate, then we cannot simply say that wiretapping is not covered by the Amendment because it is not a physical intrusion. The analysis of privacy maintains that there are at least two aspects of privacy: a physical space aspect and an informational aspect. The problem with the Supreme Court's decision in *Olmstead* is that it ignores the informational aspect. Wiretaps are not physical invasions, but they are informational invasions. Using Dworkin's method, we must interpret the Amendment so as to promote both aspects of privacy. The correct legal result would then seem to be clear: wiretapping without probable cause is a violation of the Fourth Amendment.

The concept of privacy is complex, and different people are likely to understand it differently. Even people who agree that the right of privacy protects people against wiretaps without probable cause might disagree over whether it protects employees against random drug testing by their employers. Some will include that protection in the idea of privacy, but others will exclude it.

In addition, some people will understand the right of privacy as extending beyond protection for physical spaces and informational control. They will argue that it also protects from government intrusion certain kinds of intimate choices that persons make—for example, the choice to use contraceptives or have an abortion. Others will deny that the moral right of privacy protects such choices. The upshot is that even people who agree that a privacy principle fits the Fourth Amendment will disagree over what that principle protects. One person's privacy principle will be relatively narrow, and another's will be relatively broad. This reflects the different moral and political viewpoints people have, including differences in their philosophy of government and society. And these different privacy principles can all fit the Fourth Amendment rule: they are logically consistent with it and provide a rationale for it.

This point shows that Dworkin's method of interpretation must involve more than simply deciding which moral principles fit the community's explicitly adopted legal rules. If several competing privacy principles fit the Fourth Amendment rule, then we must decide which of them is part of the law and can be a legitimate basis for legal decision making. How can we decide?

The Role of Morality

Dworkin's solution is to look to morality: the privacy principle on which legal decisions should be made is the one, from among those that fit the explicit legal rules, that is morally best. If the best privacy principle is one that covers a person's intimate choices, such as the choice to use contraceptives or obtain an abortion, then that is the privacy principle that dictates the right legal answer in hard cases that involve the constitutional right of privacy. A more restricted privacy principle may fit the explicit legal rules, but if the correct moral judgment is that the restricted principle is not as good as the broader one, then the broader privacy principle is the one that is part of the law.

For Dworkin, then, the law consists of the rules explicitly adopted by the political community plus the best principles that fit those rules. *Best* here means morally best. Dworkin contends that this way of understanding the law enables us to find the right legal answers to cases in which the explicit rules do not provide a single, clear answer. By looking to the best principles that fit the explicit rules, we come up with an answer that the explicit rules by themselves fail to provide.

Thus, the explicit rules of the Constitution do not provide a clear answer to whether persons have a right to use contraceptives. The Constitution protects "liberty," but does that include the liberty to practice contraception? Dworkin's response is that we must examine the principles that fit the law's explicit rules and ask which is morally best.

Persons will, of course, disagree over what is morally best. Moral judgments are notoriously controversial. What is a judge, or anyone else, to do in the face of such disagreement? Dworkin grabs the bull by the horns: each person must decide for him- or herself what is morally best. For example, if a judge determines that a very broad privacy principle is best, then that is the one she should use in deciding the outcome of a case. She may not arrive at the correct legal outcome; after all, she may be mistaken in her moral judgment. But a judge who follows Dworkin's method of legal interpretation will make a good-faith effort to determine what is morally best. And such a judge is, in Dworkin's view, fully authorized to make her legal decision on the basis of what she regards as the correct moral judgment.

Dworkin says that, on his view, law has "integrity." He means, in part, that law is more than merely a miscellaneous collection of rules laid down by the most powerful institutions in society. For Dworkin, might does not make right, but neither does it make law. The idea that the law has integrity is the idea that the law consists of the rules the community has authoritatively decided to adopt *plus* the best moral principles that fit those rules. The *plus* helps raise law above the level of sheer power into the moral domain. It helps give judicial decisions in hard cases their authority. And it gives moral force to the legal obligations that members of the community have.[11]

The Challenge of Skepticism

Dworkin is well aware that his method of interpretation invites significant disagreement over the best interpretation of the law and the correct decision in specific legal cases. Under his method, the moral disagreements people have will reverberate in the arena of legal interpretation, producing disputes over what the law means and what the right answers are in hard cases. This might invite a deep skepticism about the law. After all, moral disagreements are notorious for being resistant to any definitive resolution. One might argue that

Dworkin's appeal to morality defeats his own purpose: instead of producing right answers to legal cases, the appeal to morality ensures that there are no such answers, because there are no right answers to moral questions.

Dworkin counters this sort of skepticism by criticizing one of the premises on which it rests, namely, that the existence of disagreement about some matter means that there is no right answer to it. He argues that disagreement does not by itself entail the absence of a right answer. When people disagreed over whether the earth was stationary or moved around the sun, it did not mean that there was no correct answer to the question. People disagree on many moral issues, but that does not prove that there is no right answer.

Dworkin distinguishes two distinct types of skepticism and argues that neither provides good grounds for rejecting his theory. He calls them "external" and "internal" skepticism. External skepticism seeks to cast doubt on the idea that there are right answers when it comes to basic moral questions about our obligations and rights. Internal skepticism does not challenge the existence of right answers in morality, but rather argues that Dworkin's theory is nonetheless insufficient to show that law is more than the mere exercise of power by those who control society.

External Skepticism External skepticism holds there is nothing objective in the world that can make a statement about our moral obligations true or false. When I say, "Michael Jordan is over 6 feet tall," there is something objective and perceivable to which the statement corresponds that makes it true. But consider: "There is a basic moral obligation to respect a woman's choice to have an abortion." There seems to be no similarly objective and perceivable fact in the world to which the latter statement corresponds.

The concept of height derives from a feature of the world that we can perceive, and the concept is used to describe things we see in terms of that feature. If we disagree over someone's height, the dispute can be settled empirically, by measuring the person.

In contrast, the concept of moral obligation does not seem to refer to any empirical feature of the world, and an empirical method for settling disputes about moral obligations does not appear to exist. Moral obligations cannot be perceived by our ordinary senses, and statements about them cannot be confirmed or disconfirmed by empirical means. Unlike statements about height, nothing in the empirical world corresponds to statements about moral obligations.

External skepticism can be understood as arguing that questions about moral obligations have no right answer because nothing in the empirical world makes them true or false. From such a perspective, it would seem a serious mistake to make legal questions depend on the answers to moral questions. For the implication would be that legal questions have no right answers either.

Dworkin counters the argument of external skepticism by claiming that it rests on the false premise that moral judgments must correspond to perceivable facts in order for us to reasonably assert that some such judgments are right and others are wrong. And it is equally wrong to think that disagreements over moral obligations require some empirical method for resolving them.

Underlying Dworkin's position is a view that rejects the idea that all statements need to be about perceivable states of affairs in order to be both meaningful and subject to reasoned argument. Surely, if I say "Torturing babies is wrong," I have made a meaningful statement, defensible by good reasons, even though it corresponds to no objective, perceivable state of affairs analogous to someone's height. The wrongness of torture cannot be literally perceived in the way that height can be, but that does not stop us from meaningfully asserting that it is wrong to torture babies and giving good reasons as to why it is wrong. In short, making moral judgments is a practice with its own standards of good reasoning and should not be confused with the practice of making empirical judgments.

Dworkin is certainly right in thinking that reasoning and arguing about moral questions is different from reasoning and arguing about empirical questions. But he fails to come to grips with the fact that there are many different, conflicting ways of conducting moral argument. There is not one practice of moral argument but many such practices. For some modes of moral argument, sacred texts such as the Bible or Koran provide authoritative guidance; for others, secular principles and worldly considerations are decisive. And within each category—sacred and secular—there are many conflicting versions.

External skepticism need not rest its "no right answer" thesis on the failure of moral judgments to correspond to any empirical facts. Rather, it can rest its case on the existence of conflicting modes of moral argument and on the assertion that there is no way to establish which mode is correct. And if there is some way to establish the correct method of moral reasoning, Dworkin has not told us what it is.

One of the most profound problems of philosophy is to explain how it is possible for there to be moral obligations when the world seems to be composed strictly of empirical facts. From where do such obligations come? What is the source of their authority to obligate us? How can we figure out which obligations are real?

It would be fair to say that, despite centuries of effort by philosophers and the firm conviction of most people that moral obligations are real, no thinker has yet come up with fully persuasive answers to such questions. So perhaps it is unfair to criticize Dworkin for having failed to develop the answers. But he should have admitted that an adequate refutation of external skepticism does not exist and conceded that his theory proceeded on the "unproven" assumption that there are right answers to moral questions. Such an approach would be entirely sensible. After all, the assumption of right answers does seem reasonable when we think about cases like torture and genocide, and external skeptics certainly have not proven that there are no such answers.

Internal Skepticism　Internal skepticism does not seek to cast doubt on the existence of right answers to moral questions. And it can accept Dworkin's claim that law consists of the rules explicitly adopted by the community *plus* the best moral principles that fit those rules. The problem, according to internal skepticism, is that such principles may be insufficient to give the law an integrity that raises it out of the domain of mere power politics.

According to internal skepticism, our legal system is fundamentally unjust and oppressive: the system promotes the interests of the wealthy and privileged at the expense of the rest of society. In this view, the best moral principles that fit the explicit rules of the system are insufficient to raise the law above the realm of power politics. Such principles essentially reflect and reinforce the interests of the powerful. Thus, contrary to Dworkin, the law has no integrity: it is strictly a matter of might and not of right.

Moreover, internal skepticism holds that there is no consistent set of moral principles that underlies our laws. Rather, different legal rules and doctrines reflect incompatible moral viewpoints. The result is that the law is so riddled with moral contradictions and inconsistencies that it is implausible to understand it as reflecting any coherent underlying philosophy.

Internal skepticism is associated with the view known as "Critical Legal Studies." Dworkin does not accept Critical Legal Studies' skepticism because he believes neither that the law is riddled with contradiction nor that it is unjust and oppressive. The dispute over these points will be examined in Chapter 9.

Assessing Dworkin

Dworkin's interpretive version of natural law theory seems to be the strongest of those considered. It posits an important and necessary connection between law and morality but avoids the problems afflicting the approaches of Aquinas and Fuller. Unlike Aquinas's traditional version of natural law theory, Dworkin's does not hold that unjust rules are invalid as laws. Unlike Fuller's version, Dworkin's does not hold that the principles of legality are by themselves sufficient to create a prima facie moral obligation to obey the rules of any system of positive law.

Dworkin seems to agree with Fuller that legal obligations have some moral force: there is some moral reason to abide by such obligations. But Dworkin locates the source of that moral force not merely in the principles of legality, but in the integrity of law. In other words, for Dworkin the inner morality of law is more extensive than for Fuller: it consists not only of the principles of legality but also of the best moral principles that underlie the settled law. Nonetheless, Dworkin's theory has some problems of its own.

Dworkin emphasizes that decisions in hard cases, in which the law does not have a clear answer, require moral judgments. And on his theory, judges are authorized to rely on their own moral judgments in deciding such cases. Moreover, the correct legal answers in these cases depend on what the correct moral judgments are.

Let us grant for the sake of argument that Dworkin is right in claiming that hard cases require moral judgments. It does not follow that judges are authorized to decide a case on the basis of their own moral judgments or that the correct moral judgments determine the correct legal answers. There are alternatives to Dworkin's theory even if we acknowledge the necessity of moral judgment in legal decision making.

One alternative holds that, in our system of law, judges must not rely on their own moral judgments but rather must defer to judgments that are widely accepted in society. And it is society's moral judgments, regardless of whether they are morally correct, that determine the right legal answer in a hard case. Dworkin moves too quickly from the claim that moral judgments are needed to resolve hard cases to the conclusion that the correct moral judgments determine the correct legal answers and that judges should rely on their own beliefs about which moral judgments are correct.

Dworkin might reply that the law must have integrity and that integrity is a function of the correct morality. Integrity does not guarantee the justice of law, but it does guarantee that morality determines to some degree what the law is. Thus, law necessarily has a moral dimension that raises it out of the arena of pure power politics.

Yet, Dworkin never clearly explains why law necessarily has such a dimension.[12] Granted, only a moral dimension would make law more than the mere product of power politics. But why must law be more than that? Dworkin does not tell us.

Moreover, his critics will follow up on this gap in Dworkin's theory to argue that it is a fundamental mistake to explain the nature of law in terms of morality at all, even the attenuated morality of Dworkinian integrity. These critics will argue that a superior approach to understanding law lies in the tradition of legal positivism and its rejection of a necessary connection between law and morality. Let us now turn to the positivist understanding of law.

LEGAL POSITIVISM: OVERVIEW

Critics of natural law theory have developed alternative approaches to understanding the nature of positive law and its relationship to morality. These approaches are examples of what is known as legal positivism. They reject the traditional natural law idea that genuine law is necessarily just law. But positivism goes further and rejects the necessary links between positive law and morality posited by Fuller and Dworkin. Thus, legal positivism rejects each of the versions of natural law theory examined in this chapter.

Like natural law theory, different versions of positivism have emerged. We will begin with the version formulated in the nineteenth century by John Austin. Austin explicitly develops his theory as a superior alternative to the traditional natural law approach of such thinkers as Blackstone and Aquinas. We will then turn to the version of positivism formulated in the twentieth century by H. L. A. Hart. Hart argued that Austin's theory was flawed in important respects. The remedy was not to switch back to natural law thinking but rather to develop a new and improved version of positivism. Whether, and in what respects, Hart's theory is an advance over Austin's is an issue we will examine at some length.

AUSTIN'S THEORY OF LAW

Law as Command

One of the first thinkers to formulate legal positivism in a systematic way was the English theorist John Austin. For Austin, laws are rules laid down by superiors to guide the actions of those under them. Rules are a species of command. Some commands require (or prohibit) the performance of a specific action on a specific occasion. Others require (or prohibit) a general kind of action, not limited to any specific occasion. The command "Drink milk every day" is an example of the latter kind, while "Drink milk now" illustrates the former. Laws are general commands like "Drink milk every day," not limited to a specific action on a specific occasion.

Since they are commands, Austin explains, laws impose obligations on those to whom they are addressed. Being under an obligation means that a person is liable to have undesirable consequences ("sanctions") inflicted on him or her for acting contrary to the command. Since laws are general commands, they impose continuing obligations to act in certain ways, not simply an obligation to do a specific thing at a specific time.

For Austin, then, laws are general commands laid down by superiors to guide the actions of those under them. The general commands laid down by God for humans constitute divine law and impose moral obligations. Those who act contrary to such rules are liable to punishment at the hands of God. The general commands laid down by political rulers constitute positive law and impose legal obligations. Those who act contrary to such rules are liable to punishment at the hands of the political rulers (or their designated agents).

Some of the rules found in society are not laid down or enforced by the political rulers. Certain of these rules are laid down by superiors in a private organization, for example, in a club. Others are not laid down by anyone at all and are enforced by general opinion. They consist of informal standards of behavior that society expects individuals to abide by. Even though the political rulers will not punish persons for violating these informal standards as such, people in general have a low opinion of anyone who does violate them. An example would be the rule "Give help to those in need." Neither the rule about helping those in need nor the rules of private clubs are part of the positive law. Austin places them in the category "positive morality," that is, the moral values and rules informally accepted by a given society.

Positive law consists of general commands laid down and enforced by political rulers; more exactly, it is laid down and enforced by the sovereign of an independent political society. The sovereign is the supreme power of such a society: its commands are generally obeyed by the people in the society, while it does not generally obey any other earthly power.

It is crucial to Austin's view of law that the sovereign is defined solely in terms of power, not in terms of justice or any other moral concept. Austin does not believe that might makes right; but he does believe that might makes sovereignty, and since sovereignty makes positive law, might also makes positive law. The sovereign need not even claim to be ruling justly or for the common good, much less actually doing so. The power that makes some person or group sovereign has no moral qualifications whatsoever attached to it.

In Austin's view, clear thinking about law requires that one must keep in mind certain distinctions. One crucial distinction is between the question of whether a certain rule is part of the positive law and the question of whether it is a good or just rule. These two questions must not be confused. "What is the law?" is one question; "What ought the law be?" is a separate one. In a famous formulation of his view, Austin writes, "The existence of law is one thing; its merit or demerit is another. Whether it be or be not is one inquiry; whether it be or be not conformable to an assumed standard, is a different inquiry."[13]

It is also a consequence of Austin's theory that there is no necessary connection between legal and moral obligation. Whether a general command imposes a legal obligation depends only on whether the sovereign issued it and credibly threatens to enforce it. And the fact that a sovereign issues and enforces a command does not by itself mean that there is any moral obligation for anyone to obey it. For Austin, the concepts of law and legal obligation are purely "power concepts" and not in any respect moral ones. And the source of our legal obligations is not some higher authority beyond the empirical world: it is the sovereign that governs the territory we inhabit. To have a legal obligation simply means that one is liable to undesirable consequences at the hands of the sovereign for acting contrary to its command.

Austin proceeds to condemn the traditional natural law view as "an abuse of language" and "mischievous." It is an abuse of language because "to say that human laws which conflict with the Divine law are not binding, that is to say, are not laws, is to talk nonsense. The most pernicious laws have been and are continually enforced as laws by judicial tribunals."[14] If a person thinks otherwise and acts contrary to some rule she does not regard as a positive law, then the judicial system will "demonstrate the inconclusiveness of [her] reasoning" by inflicting punishment.[15]

Traditional natural law theory is also "mischievous" because advocating that unjust laws are void "is to preach anarchy, hostile and perilous as much to wise and benign rule as to stupid and galling tyranny."[16] Austin does not claim that there is no connection between positive law and morality. He says, for example, that positive morality is an important source of positive law: the general commands of the sovereign often reflect the rules of positive morality. In addition, everything humans do stands under divine law, the ultimate standard for judging human conduct. For Austin, no human can legitimately claim to be exempt from God's law and the moral obligations it imposes, whether one is a subject deciding to obey the sovereign or a judge called on to apply the sovereign's commands or even the sovereign himself. Nonetheless, the moral obligations imposed by God's commands must not be confused with the legal obligations imposed by the commands of a political sovereign.

It was the Austinian theory of law to which the defendants at Nuremberg appealed when they asserted their legal innocence. Austin rejects the idea that "international law" is properly understood as law. The absence of a global sovereign to issue and enforce commands means that, at best, the rules of international law simply amount to a kind of positive morality for the international community, imposing no legal obligations. And one of the lawyers for the Nuremberg defendants, Hermann Jahrreis, argued for the Austinian point that the sovereign power of the state is not compatible with permitting individuals to judge the legal validity of the sovereign's commands on the basis of their views about some alleged higher law.[17] The legal obligation of the individual is to obey the dictates of the sovereign, notwithstanding international or natural law.

Assessing Austin

One of the great virtues of Austin's theory is the clarity with which it explains, distinguishes, and relates the various concepts he uses in analyzing the phenomenon of law. His positivism presents a truly clear and systematic alternative to the natural law approach. Nonetheless, the direct arguments he makes against traditional natural law theory are unpersuasive as they stand. For example, his claim that pernicious laws are enforced by courts as laws is not a claim that natural law theorists would reject. But his conclusion that, therefore, such rules are valid and genuine laws simply avoids the question that the natural law theorist would raise: Is a rule enforced as a law by the courts a valid law if it is contrary to natural law or morality? Austin thinks the answer is obviously yes, but that does not amount to a reasoned argument against someone who thinks that the answer is no.

Moreover, Austin scores no points against natural law theory in claiming that the judicial system will disabuse someone of the notion that an unjust law is not a genuine law by punishing the person for an infraction of it. A traditional natural law theorist will simply interpret such punishment as the illegal employment of brute force, not as the enforcement of a genuine legal obligation.

In addition, Austin's argument that traditional natural law theory invites anarchy is questionable. The argument assumes that a theory about the nature of law should be judged (in part) by the practical consequences of having it adopted in a society, and many legal theorists would reject such a practical test. But even if such theorists are wrong, Austin's argument still raises questions.

It is possible to point to a very desirable consequence that might ensue from the adoption of traditional natural law theory, namely, the moral progress achieved by the rejection of unjust laws and the refusal to enforce them. Such progress could, in some situations at least, outweigh the social disorder that might be caused. Austin's response to this point would likely be that so many different, conflicting ideas about justice and injustice prevail in modern society that the practical effect of traditional natural law theory would not be moral progress but moral and social confusion.

This response points to an important difference between the medieval society in which Aquinas developed his natural law theory and the modern society in which Austin developed his positivism. Medieval society was dominated by a single Church and a single value system. There was fundamental agreement about justice, obligation, and goodness. Modern society, in contrast, is fragmented into competing creeds and conflicting ideas about morality. In the context of such fragmentation, it seems that a traditional natural law approach would generate substantial disagreement, disobedience, and conflict. Yet, it should be noted that such disobedience and conflict may sometimes help generate genuine moral progress, as we will see in Chapter 8 when we examine Martin Luther King and the civil rights movement.

In addition, Austin's own theory claims that all human actions are covered by divine law. In the context of the different religious beliefs held in modern society, there will undoubtedly be a significant amount of conflict over when divine law requires disobedience to the general commands of the sovereign. And it is not at all clear that there would be more disobedience and conflict under Aquinas's theory than under Austin's.

Austin's version of positivism has also been criticized by other positivists. Such positivists agree with Austin in rejecting the existence of the kinds of necessary connection between law and morality posited by natural law thinkers. But they believe that Austin's account of law in terms of the general commands of the sovereign is fundamentally mistaken. In the next section, we examine the theory of one of the most prominent positivist critics of Austin, H. L. A. Hart.

HART: LAW AS PRIMARY AND SECONDARY RULES

Types of Legal Rules

Austin's theory provided the starting point for many positivist thinkers who came after him. But not all agreed that his version of the positivist approach was adequate. The most influential critique of Austin's theory by another positivist was developed by H. L. A. Hart. According to Hart, Austin's command theory of law fails to account for important aspects of a legal system.

Hart argues that certain types of legal rules cannot be adequately understood as commands. The rules of criminal law fit the command model fairly well, since they prohibit (or require, as in tax laws) particular kinds of conduct and provide for penalties for those who violate the prohibitions (or requirements). But Hart claims that there are legal rules very different in nature from the rules of criminal law. Thus, some legal rules do not prohibit or require but rather *empower* individuals to do things that would otherwise be impossible for them to do.

For instance, the rules of contract law empower individuals to enter into legally binding agreements. Without them, individuals would be powerless to enter such agreements, just as without the rules of baseball individuals would be powerless to hit home runs. Of course, individuals could still use sticks of wood to hit small, hard, round objects a long distance; but the point is that such actions would not count as home runs without the rules of baseball. Similarly, individuals could agree with one another to do certain things, but those agreements would not count as legally binding contracts without the rules of contract law.

Hart calls the legal rules that empower individuals "power-conferring rules." Such rules empower not only private persons but public officials as well. Thus, power-conferring rules give judges the power to officially interpret and apply the law, legislators the power to make and alter it, and executive officials the power to enforce it.

Does the existence of power-conferring rules demonstrate the inadequacy of Austin's theory? Hart seems right in suggesting that power-conferring rules cannot be properly understood as commands. Yet, such rules are like commands in an important way: the point of each is to alter the world in some way, rather than simply to describe the world as it is. A command seeks to alter the world by getting someone to do something. A power-conferring rule seeks to alter it by empowering persons to do things that they would otherwise be unable to do.

Moreover, defenders of Austin can argue that, like the prohibitions of the criminal law, power-conferring legal rules must also issue from the sovereign. Such rules are *declarations* of the sovereign, and only the "say so" of the sovereign determines whether and how individuals can enter contracts, write wills, and so forth. Austin may have failed to draw a relevant distinction between the commands of the sovereign and the declarations of the sovereign. But his theory can easily modified to take account of the distinction without relinquishing the central idea that law and legal obligations are concepts to be explained in terms of the power of a political sovereign.

Legal Obligation: Government and Gunman

Hart has more fundamental criticisms of Austin's theory to make. These criticisms revolve around Austin's conception of legal obligation. Hart believes that the conception is seriously defective and that correcting the defects necessarily involves major departures from the basic ideas of Austin's theory. Austin's positivist separation of morality and positive law will remain intact, but his understanding of positive law will require radical revision. Or so Hart argues.

What does it mean for a person to have a legal obligation to do (or refrain from doing) something? Austin's answer is that it means that he stands under some general command of the sovereign and risks having some sanction inflicted on him should he fail to comply. Hart argues that this analysis makes it impossible to correctly distinguish a government from a gunman.

The gunman's threat "Your money or your life" creates a situation in which a person is likely to experience undesirable consequences unless he complies with the order. Yet, nobody would say that the gunman's victim has any kind of obligation to fork over his money. The fact that the gunman's command is particular and not general is irrelevant, since there would still be no obligation even if the gunman ordered his victim to pay over a certain percentage of his paycheck every payday. The victim may be obliged to hand over the money in that he has a very strong incentive to do so in light of the harsh consequences he will likely suffer should he refuse. But, Hart points out, being obliged to do something is not the same as being obligated to do it.

If governments can create obligations by enacting laws, Hart reasons, governments must be different from gunmen, and their laws must be different from the commands and threats of gunmen. This is because gunmen, through their threats and orders, cannot create any obligation—moral, legal, or any other kind.

A natural law approach would seek the difference between the government's laws and the gunman's orders in some necessary connection between law and morality, a connection obviously absent from the gunman's orders. But Hart rejects the natural law approach, explicitly criticizing the views of Aquinas, Fuller, and Dworkin. Thus, he must find some alternative way of explaining the difference or else accept the implication of Austin's theory that there really is no essential difference and that government is simply the gunman who is habitually obeyed and who does not habitually obey any more powerful gunman. Since Hart does not believe that government can be understood as essentially the strongest gunman on the block, he develops an alternative to the natural law approach.

According to Hart, the idea of an obligation is to be explained in terms of the idea of a rule. A rule exists when people generally (1) act in a certain way and (2) regard deviations from that way of acting as something to be criticized. Condition (1) is external in that it involves outward behavior. In contrast, condition (2) is internal in that it involves the attitude people take: they think that violation of the rule is a reason for criticizing the violator. Hart insists that this internal perspective is essential to the existence of a rule: without it, the actions of people may follow certain patterns or regularities, but there is no rule that they are following.

For Hart, a person has an obligation when a certain kind of rule applies to her. There must be a great deal of social pressure to conform to the rule; the rule must help maintain an aspect of society that is regarded as important and valuable, and it sometimes must require persons to act contrary to their individual self-interest.

All societies have rules that impose obligations. But not all societies have rules that impose *legal* obligations because not all societies have legal systems. In order to have a legal system, a society must have certain special kinds of rules over and above the rules that impose obligations.

Primary and Secondary Rules

First, a society with a legal system must have a rule that singles out the rules that actually do impose obligations in that society. Hart calls this the "rule of recognition" because it helps people recognize the rules under which they will be officially held accountable. A rule of recognition serves a valuable function in helping diminish uncertainty over what the obligations of people in the society are. The rules singled out by the rule of recognition are the legally valid rules of that society.

Second, a society must have rules that specify how the legally valid rules can be changed. These rules help society adapt to changing conditions by making it possible to eliminate old rules and enact new ones.

Third, a society must have rules that empower specific individuals to enforce and apply society's legally valid rules. These rules help society ensure more effectively that the obligations it imposes on its members are met.

Hart calls these three special kinds of rules "secondary rules." They are secondary, not in the sense of being unimportant, but rather in the sense that they could not exist unless there were other kinds of rules, namely, rules that impose obligations. Accordingly, he calls the rules imposing obligations "primary rules." For Hart, then, a legal system is a system that brings together both primary and secondary rules.

In any functioning legal system, the people must generally comply with the legally valid primary rules, and public officials must accept the secondary rules and the primary rules identified by the rule of recognition. This means that the officials must adopt an internal perspective on the primary and secondary rules: they must regard departures from those rules as something to be criticized. But, according to Hart, the rest of the people do not need to have an *dissimilar* internal perspective on the primary rules that apply to them: they need to *morals* comply with those rules, but they might do so only from fear of the punishment that might be inflicted on them.

In such a case, people generally will perceive the legally valid primary rules merely as commands backed by the threat of force, and they will not regard violations as something to be criticized. Hart says that only in an extreme case would a legal system's primary rules be complied with by most people solely out of fear of the consequences, but he insists that even such an extreme case can count as a genuine legal system.

Hart's conception of a legal system as a union of primary and secondary rules makes it questionable whether international law, at least at the time the Nuremberg defendants committed their atrocities, constituted a genuine legal system. It is unclear whether there was any rule of recognition specifying the primary rules that obligated nations. But even if there was a generally accepted rule to the effect that the norms of international treaties counted as binding international law, clearly lacking were secondary rules authorizing particular agencies to enforce those binding rules.

Like Fuller, Hart sensibly insists that the existence of a legal system is a matter of degree, not an all-or-nothing affair. But the absence of secondary rules covering the enforcement of the primary rules seems to be a rather large gap. Rather than claiming that prior to World War II international law amounted to a legal system, albeit an incomplete one, Hart would be on firmer ground to argue that the trial of the Nuremberg defendants was the best feasible way to promote the establishment of an international rule of law. Interestingly, that is the very same argument that seems to fit best with Lon Fuller's version of natural law theory. The practical differences between Hart and Fuller may well be considerably less than their theoretical disagreements would suggest.

Assessing Hart

Some critics of Hart question whether his account of obligation is essentially different from Austin's. Hart criticizes Austin on the grounds that Austin's theory cannot distinguish the laws of a government from the coercive commands of a gunman. Unlike laws, the commands of a gunman clearly do not create any obligations. Yet, Hart's extreme case scenario—in which the people comply with the legally valid primary rules solely out of fear—does not seem essentially different from the gunman situation.

In that scenario, most people comply with the laws for the same reason a person complies with a gunman: fear of the consequences of disobedience. If a gunman's command cannot create an obligation of any kind, it seems that a government in Hart's extreme scenario cannot do so either. On the other hand, if the extreme scenario can create obligations, then so can the general commands of Austin's sovereign. It thus appears that Hart is faced with a dilemma: he must concede either that his own theory is inadequate or that his criticism of Austin's theory of legal obligation is unsound.

A natural law theorist would insist that Hart's criticism of Austin is sound and that the only way out of the dilemma is for Hart to concede that his own theory is inadequate. The natural law thinker would then press the point that Hart's distinction between a government and a gunman can be maintained only by giving up on the positivist separation of positive law and morality. The laws of a government are essentially different from the orders of a gunman because the former have a necessary connection to morality but the latter do not. Or so the natural law approach would have it.

However, Hart can escape the dilemma without giving up the positivist separation of positive law and morality or his desire to distinguish his version of positivism from Austin's. The key is for Hart to distinguish a government under the rule of law from an arbitrary government that uses law to control society as it pleases. Hart's theory applies to the former, Austin's to the latter. The former is unlike a gunman, who can command whatever he pleases without restriction. The latter is like the gunman.

For both Hart and Austin, positive law ultimately stems from the exercise of power by some human agency (or agencies) in society, and moral considerations do not necessarily regulate and control that agency in its exercise of power. Where Hart and Austin differ is over whether *legal* considerations regulate and control the source of positive law. Hart's answer is affirmative: the rules of positive law themselves empower specific individuals to make, enforce, and apply the law and direct those individuals as to how those tasks are to be carried out. That is the crucial function of Hart's secondary rules. Austin's answer, in contrast, is a negative one: the source of positive law is a sovereign power standing above any and all rules of positive laws.

Certainly society can have a sovereign that stands above the law and is free to act arbitrarily. But it is also possible for society to have a very different kind of government: one that generally abides by the rules and regulations of the positive law. Such a society would have a government under the rule of law, and it is the legal system of that kind of government that Hart is describing in his account of law as a system that brings together primary and secondary rules.

Hart can argue that his government of laws is unlike a gunman in that its exercise of power is regulated and controlled by secondary rules. In contrast, an Austinian sovereign that is above the law is in an important respect like a gunman: both exercise arbitrary power. But what about Hart's contention that his government of primary and secondary rules can impose legal obligations, while an Austinian sovereign and a gunman cannot impose any obligations at all?

Hart uses the idea of legal obligation to draw a line that has governments operating by secondary rules on the one side, and both gunmen and arbitrary governments on the other. But his positivist critics will question whether Hart has drawn the line in the right place. They will argue that the proper place to draw the line is between governments of any and all types on one side, and gunmen on the other. The difference lies simply in the location of sovereign power: governments have such power and gunmen do not, which is why the former can impose legal obligations and the latter cannot.

Hart's response would be that the gunman and the arbitrary government belong on the same side of the line because they both exercise arbitrary power. But his positivist critics would dismiss the importance, for an analysis of legal obligation, of whether power is exercised in an arbitrary or rule-governed way. For these critics, the important fact is that government—whether arbitrary or regulated by rules—has sovereign power, while the gunman lacks it. According to these positivists, whether some agent or agency can impose legal obligations is not a matter of how its power is exercised—justly or unjustly, regulated by secondary rules or unregulated. Rather, it is a matter of whether the agent or agency has the sovereign power to rule society.

Hart's problem is that he never clearly explains why the existence of a legal obligation depends not simply on whose power is imposing it but on how that power is being exercised. Fuller has an answer, but it is not one that Hart accepts. Fuller's answer is that genuine legal obligations necessarily have prima facie moral force, and they gain that force from the inner morality to which any legal system must conform. Only by following the principles of that inner morality can a government impose obligations of any kind. And sufficiently pervasive and severe violations of that inner morality turn a government into the equivalent of a gunman.

Hart's secondary rules are very much like Fuller's inner morality of law: both Hart and Fuller are providing accounts of what it is for a government to operate under the rule of law. But Fuller goes on to contend that a government abiding by his inner morality creates a prima facie moral obligation to obey its laws, while Hart resists the conclusion that a government ruling through a system of primary and secondary rules necessarily creates any such obligation.

Hart explicitly rejects Fuller's contention, taking the positivist position that legal obligations do not necessarily have any moral force at all. Yet, if there is such a separation of legal and moral obligation, the question arises as to why an absolute Austinian sovereign cannot impose legal obligations with its commands and declarations. The Austinian sovereign may rule by sheer force, with no moral justification or basis for its commands. And as we have seen in Chapter 1, governments under the rule of law generally tend to be morally much preferable to arbitrary ones. But the point of positivism is that law does not need to meet any moral test in order to possess validity or authority.

Hart might insist that, morality aside, there are good reasons to distinguish between arbitrary Austinian sovereigns and governments that operate through a system of secondary and primacy rules. For example, historians and sociologists might find the distinction useful in understanding different societies, eras, and historical trends. But the question remains as to why the distinction is to be drawn in terms of the idea of legal obligation. It is possible to agree that there are important differences—moral, sociological, historical—without claiming that Austinian sovereigns cannot impose legal obligations. Perhaps Hart would have been better off to describe the differences between arbitrary and rule-governed political systems without insisting that only the latter can impose legal obligations.

SUMMARY: NATURAL LAW
VERSUS POSITIVISM

The dividing line between positivism and natural law theory runs right through the concept of legal obligation. Do legal obligations necessarily have some moral force? Is there necessarily a moral dimension to any genuine legal obligation? Positivists insist on negative answers to these questions, arguing that the ideas of law and legal obligation can and should be explained in terms of power, coercion, control, and/or rules but not in terms of moral right and wrong. Natural law thinkers insist on affirmative answers, arguing that the ideas of power, coercion, control, and rules cannot adequately explain the nature of legal obligation: moral right and wrong are essential ingredients as well.

This chapter has not sought to resolve the dispute. Instead, it has tried to explain and critically analyze the positions and arguments on both sides. The reader must take things from there.

NOTES

1. Philosophers often use the term *super-erogatory* to describe actions that are above and beyond the call of duty.

2. Some philosophers have argued that law has a teaching function: it shows us what is right and wrong. In this view, it may be possible for law to foster virtue indirectly by letting us know the difference between right and wrong. Of course, we must then do what is right for reasons other than the law's threats in order to act from good motives.

3. The analogy to counterfeit money comes from David Lyons, *Ethics and the Rule of Law* (New York: Cambridge University Press, 1984), p. 62.

4. St. Augustine, *On Free Choice of the Will* (New York: Library of Liberal Arts, 1964), p. 11.

5. Gustav Radbruch, "Five Minutes of Legal Philosophy," rpt. in *Philosophy of Law*, 4th ed., ed. J. Feinberg and H. Gross (Belmont, CA: Wadsworth, 1991), pp. 103–104.

6. Michael Moore, "Law as a Functional Kind," in *Natural Law Theory*, ed. R. P. George (Oxford: Clarendon, 1992), p. 189.

7. Deryck Beyleveld and Roger Brownsword, *Law as a Moral Judgment* (London: Sweet & Maxwell, 1986).

8. St. Thomas Aquinas, *Summa Theologica*, Question 95, Second Article, rpt. *The Political Ideas of St. Thomas Aquinas*, ed. D. Bigongiari (New York: Hafner, 1969), p. 58.

9. *Ibid.*, p. 72.

10. *Ibid.*

11. Dworkin argues that more than integrity is needed for citizens to have an actual moral obligation to obey the law. For example, the law must also operate in the equal interests of all citizens. But Dworkin does appear to hold that legal obligations as such have some moral force and that law's integrity explains why that is so.

12. In Chapter 9, it is suggested that Dworkin defend his theory by appealing to the distinction between arbitrary government and government under the rule of law.

13. John Austin, *The Austinian Theory of Law,* ed. J. W. Brown (Littleton, CO: Rothman, 1983), p. 71.

14. *Ibid.*

15. *Ibid.,* p. 73

16. *Ibid.,* p. 74.

17. Stanley Paulson, "Classical Legal Positivism at Nuremberg," *Philosophy and Public Affairs* 4:2 (Winter 1975), 147.

DISCUSSION QUESTIONS

1. How would Dworkin's theory of law deal with the issues surrounding the trial and convictions of the defendants at Nuremberg? Could the trial and convictions be justified from the perspective of his theory? Does Dworkin's theory provide a convincing approach to the issues raised by the trial?

2. Prior to the Civil War, a number of abolitionists argued that state and federal laws upholding slavery were invalid because they were unjust. Judges and ordinary citizens alike had no obligation at all to abide by them. Rather, the abolitionists argued, everyone had an obligation to reject, subvert, and destroy the institutions of slavery. Do you agree with these abolitionists? What if you were a judge who had sworn an oath to uphold the Constitution and laws of the land? What if you were an ordinary citizen who had been asked to help an escaped slave make her way to freedom through the "underground railroad"?

ADDITIONAL READING

Aquinas, Thomas. *The Political Ideas of St. Thomas Aquinas.* D. Bigongiari, ed. Hafner, 1969.

Austin, John. *The Province of Jurisprudence Determined.* Noonday, 1954.

Bentham, Jeremy. *Of Laws in General.* Athlone, 1970.

Cohen, Marshall, ed. *Ronald Dworkin and Contemporary Jurisprudence.* Rowman and Allanheld, 1984.

Cover, Robert. *Justice Accused: Antislavery and the Judicial Process.* Yale University Press, 1975.

Dworkin, Ronald. *Law's Empire.* Harvard University Press, 1986.

_____. *A Matter of Principle.* Harvard University Press, 1985.

_____. *Taking Rights Seriously.* Harvard University Press, 1977.

Finnis, John. *Natural Law and Natural Rights.* Oxford University Press, 1980.

Fuller, Lon. *The Morality of Law,* rev. ed. Yale University Press, 1964.

_____. "Positivism and Fidelity to Law: A Reply to Professor Hart." *Harvard Law Review* 71 (1958), 630–672.

George, Robert P., ed. *Natural Law Theory: Contemporary Essays.* Oxford University Press, 1992.

Harding, Arthur L., ed. *Origins of the Natural Law Tradition.* Kennikat, 1954.

Hart, H. L. A. *The Concept of Law,* 2d ed. Oxford University Press, 1997.

_____. *Essays in Jurisprudence and Philosophy.* Clarendon, 1983.

_____. "Positivism and the Separation of Law and Morals." *Harvard Law Review* 71 (1958), 593–629.

Kelsen, Hans. *Pure Theory of the Law.* M. Knight, trans. University of California, 1967.

_____. *General Theory of Law and State.* A. Wedberg, trans. Harvard University Press, 1946.

Lyons, David. *Ethics and the Rule of Law.* Cambridge University Press, 1984.

Moles, Robert. *Definition and Rule in Legal Theory.* Blackwell, 1987.

Shiner, Roger. *Norm and Nature.* Oxford University Press, 1992.

Soper, Phillip. *A Theory of Law.* Harvard University Press, 1984.

Weinreb, Lloyd. *Natural Law and Natural Rights.* Clarendon, 1980.

3

The Constitution

POPULAR GOVERNMENT
AND THE RULE OF LAW

The Undisciplined Public

For many centuries, Western legal and political thinkers held that popular government was incompatible with the rule of law. In this respect, they followed the lead of Plato and Aristotle, both of whom believed that governments responsive to the will of the people had a dangerous and ultimately irresistible tendency to flout the rule of law. That was the lesson they saw in the outcome of the trial of their philosophical predecessor, Socrates. He had violated no laws, but his persistent philosophical questioning of his fellow citizens of Athens angered and disturbed many of them. When the jury of 501 Athenian men gathered to decide his guilt or innocence, the majority voted on the basis of their personal dislike of Socrates and convicted him.

For Plato and Aristotle, the unjust conviction of Socrates was symptomatic of a deep flaw in government responsive to the will of the people. The public does not have the discipline and patience to abide by the procedures and requirements of the law. It wants what it wants when it wants it. And government under the sway of public opinion will flout the rule of law when it gets in the way of something the public wants. In other words, popular government was incompatible with the rule of law. That was the view of Plato and Aristotle, at any rate.

Subsequent history appeared amply to confirm their view. Popular governments proved exceedingly vulnerable to factional conflict and domestic strife

79

that destroyed the rule of law and rendered them unstable and tumultuous. It seemed that you could have popular government or the rule of law, but not both. That was the situation that faced the men who met in Philadelphia in 1787 to draft a document to establish a new form of government for the United States.

The Constitution of the United States represents an effort to render popular government compatible with the rule of law. Indeed, the astounding premise behind the design of the Constitution is that it is possible to make the two mutually reinforcing: popular government could be designed to support the rule of law, and the rule of law could be arranged to support popular government.

Before the eighteenth century, popular government had been restricted to relatively compact political communities, much smaller in geographic area and population than the United States and much more homogeneous in the interests and viewpoints they encompassed. But one of the main framers of the Constitution, James Madison, argued that the size and heterogeneity of the country could be turned into an advantage over previous experiments in popular government. The diversity of interests and viewpoints meant that no one group would constitute a permanent majority and that each group would need to bargain and compromise with the others in order to exercise effective political power.

In previous popular governments, a permanent majority confronted a permanent minority. Such a situation was dangerous and destabilizing. The majority would be sorely tempted to tyrannize over the minority, and the minority would be tempted to strike preemptively to prevent such tyranny.

The United States would be different, Madison and his fellow framers believed. Any majority would actually be a shifting coalition of minorities, given the diversity of interests and viewpoints. The sharp and inflexible divisions that had brought down previous experiments in popular government could be averted. Popular government under the rule of law would be possible with a properly designed system of political and legal institutions. But what kind of design was called for? In a sense, the entire Constitution is the framers' answer to that question. But here we can focus on a few of the fundamental principles that guided their design.

The Constitutional Design

First, there should be a written constitution establishing a basic framework of government and serving as the supreme law of the land. Such a constitution would make the rule of law more secure, in the eyes of the framers. With the framework of government laid out in black and white, there would be much less room for doubt about the lawful powers and activities of government.

Second, political power must be dispersed among different branches and departments of government. For the framers, the very essence of tyranny was the concentration of power in the hands of a single person or faction. The Constitution they drafted sought to avert any such concentration by dividing power in two ways. The power of the national government was divided among three distinct branches: legislative, executive, and judicial. This approach is the famous doctrine of the separation of powers. In addition, political power was divided among the national government and the state governments, in an arrangement called "federalism."

Third, the Constitution must establish limited government. This meant that the powers legitimately held by each branch or department of government must be restricted to those powers granted it by the Constitution. The limits of the government's legitimate authority were the limits of its lawful authority, as specified in the supreme law of the land.

Fourth, each branch of the national government should have powers enabling it to check the other branches if they sought to exceed the limits of their lawful authority. Thus, the Constitution established a system of checks and balances. It did not trust each branch to restrain itself. Madison and the other framers realized that self-restraint would fail: humans have too strong a tendency to go beyond the limits of their legitimate powers unless someone else stops them from doing so. Thus, the Constitution granted each branch powers that would help stop the usurpations of the others. For example, the president was given the power to veto legislation passed by Congress, and Congress was given the power to impeach and remove from office those in the executive or judicial branches who acted unlawfully.

Fifth, the Constitution should establish representative government. The president and members of Congress should be elected by the people in periodic elections. Elections were needed to make government responsive to the will of the people. Moreover, the framers believed that such a system of elections would serve as another important check on government officials who might seek to exceed their lawful authority. The public would be unlikely to return to office those who had flouted the Constitution.

Yet, the framers also believed that representative government needed to be insulated to a substantial degree from the often momentary and sometimes destructive passions of the public. Government must be responsive to the will of the people, but that did not mean that it should be controlled by every whim and fancy that moved the masses. Indeed, previous experiments in popular government ended in the destruction of the rule of law precisely because they had been controlled by the whims, fears, and fancies of the masses.

In order to ensure that the American experiment in popular government would not meet that same end, the framers built in certain safeguards. Elections would be staggered: in each election year only a portion of the seats in Congress would be contested. That would make it more difficult for momentary popular passions to rule Congress. And Congress would be divided into an upper house—the Senate, whose members would serve six-year terms and would be chosen by state legislatures, and a lower house—the House of Representatives, whose members would be directly elected by the people and serve two-year terms. The lower house would register in a more immediate way the desires of the public, but the Senate would serve as a brake, demanding due reflection and deliberation before acting. Moreover, the president would be elected indirectly, through the electoral college, another device designed to ensure that popular government would not fall sway to the sometimes destructive passions of the people.

Sixth, the adoption of the Constitution should be ultimately left up to the people, who would select delegates to gather in special constitutional conventions in each state. The establishment of these conventions would make it clear to the public that it was their will as citizens of the nation that dictated the form of government under which the nation was to be ruled.

Seventh, the Constitution should contain an explicit procedure for its own amendment. That procedure would require a supermajority—far more than a simple majority of the country—for alteration of the supreme law of the land. This would allow for the lawful change of the nation's basic system of government, thus making it unnecessary for the people to put themselves above the law and resort to political revolution if they found the existing system to be seriously defective.

This amendment process has proved very important in American history. It is through the process that the Bill of Rights—the first ten amendments—was added to the Constitution. It was through the process that slavery was abolished and women were granted the right to vote. Despite the fact that such changes in our basic framework of government were radical ones, they were accomplished not by political revolution, but by the lawful processes of government.

The framers of the Constitution did not refer to the form of government it established as "democracy." For them, the term *democracy* referred to the previous, failed experiments in popular government, in which the passions, whims, and fancies of the people were not sufficiently filtered and moderated by political institutions. In contrast, the American government would be a *republican* form of government. By this term, the framers meant to mark the political system they were creating as a new form of popular government, one which would abide by the rule of law.

The amendment process has made the American political system much more directly responsive to the will of the people than the framers originally had in mind. While the framers would not have called the form of government they established "democratic," we can legitimately describe the current political system in those terms. Through constitutional amendment, the right to vote has been extended, first, to African-American men, then to women, and then to those between the ages of eighteen and twenty-one years. In addition, the election of senators has been taken out of the hands of state legislatures and put directly in the hands of the people. Yet, the Constitution still retains most of the arrangements and provisions designed to ensure that in the United States, popular government abides by the rule of law.

THE "TROUBLESOME" PROVISIONS

Many of the provisions of the Constitution are quite clear in their meaning. Each state is to have two senators, for example. A person must be at least thirty-five years of age to be eligible to serve as president. There is no doubt about what these provisions require.

Yet, other provisions are more troublesome in the sense that their meaning is not immediately clear and certain. There are three main sources of this uncertainty.

First, some provisions incorporate abstract philosophical concepts that can be understood in conflicting ways, and nothing in the Constitution clearly shows which understanding is the best. For example, the Fifth and Fourteenth Amendments prohibit the government from depriving persons of "life, liberty, or property without due process of law." The idea of due process is related to the notion of fair treatment by the law, but the concept of fairness is one that can be understood in very different ways. In addition, the concept of liberty is a philosophical one that can be interpreted in conflicting ways depending on one's political and moral viewpoint. The debate over abortion is just one instance in which the meanings of liberty and due process are hotly disputed.

Another important example of a provision that is unclear because it incorporates an abstract philosophical concept is in the Fourteenth Amendment: no state may deny anyone "the equal protection of the laws." This provision rests on the concept of equality. Yet, the meaning of equality is hotly contested, as contemporary debates over affirmative action show.

A second source of uncertainty in the meaning of the Constitution is the fact that some provisions make sweeping and unqualified pronouncements that cannot be taken literally. For example, the First Amendment says that Congress shall make "no law abridging the freedom of speech, or of the press." Taking such a provision literally would entail that Congress could not enact laws prohibiting the public disclosure military secrets—an absurd implication. Yet, once one agrees that the Free Speech Clause cannot be taken literally, its exact meaning becomes unclear. Does it protect obscene speech? Pornographic speech? Hate speech? Harassing speech? It is far from obvious what the answers are to such questions.

A third source of uncertainty stems from use of terms that do not refer to philosophical abstractions like liberty and equality, but whose legal meanings are nonetheless vague and controversial. Consider the term *speech*, which has a relatively clear and literal meaning in the context of ordinary discourse. But in the Free Speech Clause, the term seems to cover more than just verbal communication. Nonverbal modes of communication—such as wearing armbands and waving flags—are surely covered. But what about burning a draft card to express antiwar views? Or burning a cross to express racist ones? Or blocking the entrance to an abortion clinic as part of a pro-life demonstration? The borders of constitutional speech are fuzzy in a way that raises crucial legal questions, and significant legal and political disputes arise from those fuzzy borders.

Another example of a constitutional phrase with fuzzy and controversial borders is the standard for impeachment, "high crimes and misdemeanors." The disputes swirling around the impeachment of President Clinton revealed the existence of substantial disagreement over the crucial question of which forms of misconduct reach the level of that standard and which forms do not. Some people argued that even if the president had committed perjury in his testimony about Monica Lewinsky, such misconduct would not have been sufficiently serious to count as a "high crime or misdemeanor." The subject matter of the perjury—a private, consensual sexual affair—did not make it fit grounds for impeaching a president. Others countered that perjury—no matter what it is about—does sufficient harm to the integrity of the legal process to qualify as grounds for impeachment.

The presence in the Constitution of important provisions whose meaning is unclear and uncertain raises two crucial issues for the American legal and political system: (1) Who should have the ultimate say about the meaning of the Constitution? and (2) What approach to interpreting the Constitution is best?

There is widespread agreement these days on the answer to the first issue. Most people believe that the justices of the Supreme Court should have the final say about the meaning of the Constitution, although a growing number of legal thinkers have begun to question the conventional wisdom in that regard. Indeed, there are reasonable arguments against the idea that the Supreme Court should have the last word on what the supreme law of the land means, and those arguments have been voiced from the very beginnings of the nation's history.[1]

The second issue is more widely debated by contemporary thinkers than the first. Many theories of constitutional interpretation have been advanced, and there is little agreement on which is best.

Both issues raise serious questions about the rule of law and its relation to democratic government in the United States. The framers sought to draft a document that would establish popular government operating under the rule of law. Whether the Constitution can accomplish what the framers intended depends to a substantial degree on who has the final say on its meaning and on how that meaning is to be discerned.

THE SUPREME COURT
AND JUDICIAL REVIEW

Jefferson's View

The idea that the Supreme Court should be the final judge of what the supreme law of the land means is relatively noncontroverisal now, but it was hotly disputed during important parts of our nation's history.[2] Nothing in the Constitution itself explicitly says that the Supreme Court is the final arbiter of its meaning, and some notable individuals from the early history of the nation, such as Thomas Jefferson, argued that each branch of the federal government had the final authority to interpret the Constitution as it applied to its own sphere of government. That was the only way to ensure that the three branches—executive, legislative, and judicial—were in fact equal in their powers. And some argued that equal powers were needed to prevent one branch from tyrannizing over the other branches and over society itself.

Thus, Jefferson wrote in a letter to Abigail Adams, "[T]he opinion which gives to judges the right to decide what laws are constitutional, and what not,

not only for themselves in their own sphere of action, but for the Legislature and Executive also, would make the judiciary a despotic branch."[3]

Early in its history, the Court rejected the Jeffersonian view and claimed the legal power to declare unconstitutional state and federal laws, as well as actions undertaken by the executive branch. This power is known as "judicial review," and the Court has never relinquished it since those early days. In its more aggressive forms, the power of judicial review involves the idea that the Court's interpretation of the Constitution legally supersedes any interpretation given by the other branches or departments of government. When it comes to the meaning of the Constitution, what the Court says, goes.[4]

Judicial Review as Antidemocratic

One of the persistent claims made by critics of judicial review, from Jefferson forward, is that it is fundamentally incompatible with popular government. In contemporary terms, the charge is that judicial review is antidemocratic. Let us look more closely at this charge.

Congress and the president are accountable to the people through the electoral process. At present, senators and representatives are directly elected and must regularly face the voters. Although the president is officially chosen by the electoral college, for practical purposes the power to choose the president lies with the electorate every four years.

It is very different with the justices of the Supreme Court. They do not face the voters in election campaigns but rather are appointed for life terms and can be removed only through the impeachment process. Moreover, once they have declared a law unconstitutional, judicial review means that the elected branches of government are legally required to accept the decision: the Supreme Court's word on the meaning of the Constitution trumps what the other branches of government say about the supreme law of the land.

Since the essence of democracy is the accountability of government officials to the people by means of the election process, the simple fact that the justices of the Court—like all other federal judges in this country—are unelected seems to run contrary to democratic principles. Judicial review adds insult to injury by then making these unelected officials the ultimate arbiters of what the supreme law of the land means.

Notice that this argument for the antidemocratic character of judicial review crucially depends on the fact that federal judges are not elected. The argument would dissolve if all such judges, including the justices of the Supreme Court, were made accountable to the electorate by requiring them to periodically run for their offices.

There is nothing inherently impossible about making judges run in elections. Some state court judges must do so, for example, the justices on the California Supreme Court. Although it is often said that judicial review itself is antidemocratic, what is really meant is that the combination of judicial review with a judiciary that is not electorally accountable is what is antidemocratic. It is this combination that will be referred to from here on when the term *judicial review* is used.

The Historical Record

The debate over judicial review in the United States has been decisively shaped by the historical experience of the nation. In the nineteenth century, judicial review was used sparingly by the Supreme Court, but when it was used, it provoked great political controversy. In the infamous pre–Civil War case of *Dred Scott v. Sandford,* the Supreme Court declared unconstitutional congressional efforts to deal with the problem of slavery by outlawing it in certain of the territories of the United States. And ten years after the war, in the *Civil Rights Cases,* the Court struck down federal laws designed to ensure equality for the recently freed African Americans.

During the twentieth century, the Court used judicial review more frequently, but no less controversially. Starting at around the beginning of the century, it declared unconstitutional many efforts by Congress and state governments to regulate economic affairs. These efforts were taken in response to the harmful effects of industrialization on the working classes. The federal government and a number of states enacted laws prohibiting child labor and establishing minimum wages, maximum hours, and requirements for healthy working conditions. But many of these laws were declared by a majority on the Court to violate the Constitution. The Court said that the laws illegally infringed on economic liberties and property rights that were protected by the Constitution. Although it was strongly criticized for its view, the Court continued to hold it for several decades.

The dispute over judicial review of economic legislation came to a head during the Great Depression of the 1930s, when the national government enacted many laws designed to revive and regulate the economy. At first, the Court declared a number of these laws unconstitutional in the face of widespread popular support for the laws. But as the Depression wore on, the Court dramatically changed its position and began to let the laws stand. Since that time, the national government has had a free hand at regulating the economy with virtually no interference from the Supreme Court.

Although the Court has stepped back from the judicial review of national economic legislation, the last fifty years have seen many instances of judicial review striking down laws that were racially discriminatory or that infringed on personal liberties such as the freedom to use contraceptives and obtain an abortion. Thus judicial review has continued to play a vital role in the American legal system. Can it be justified?

Judicial Self-Restraint

Some legal thinkers who concede that judicial review is antidemocratic contend that it can be justified if judges exercise self-restraint. These advocates of "judicial self-restraint" claim that it would be illegitimate for courts to use judicial review to substitute their own idea of good policy or morality for those of the elected representatives of the people. Such substitution would not just bend but break our nation's commitment to democratic government. It would illegitimately make the Supreme Court a "superlegislature" empowered to determine the wisdom of what the other branches do. On the other hand, judicial review is legitimate if it is restricted to striking down laws and other government acts that exceed the constitutional authority of the branch taking the action. That is the position of the advocates of judicial self-restraint.

However, invoking judicial self-restraint is by itself unhelpful in showing why judicial review is legitimate. It fails to explain why the courts should have the ultimate authority to decide for the other branches of government what the Constitution means and what those branches may therefore legally do. Once that is explained, then it will follow noncontroversially that the Supreme Court should restrict itself to enforcing the Constitution and should not turn itself into a superlegislature. What we need is an argument for why the Court's interpretation of the Constitution should trump the interpretations given by the other branches of the government, and talk of judicial self-restraint does not help in providing such an argument.

Legal thinkers have developed two kinds of arguments in support of the legitimacy of judicial review. The first hinges on the claim that judicial review is required to ensure that democratic government operates under the rule of law. The second contends that judicial review, when combined with the correct approach to interpreting the Constitution, will promote a more democratic political system. Let us examine each of these lines of argument in turn.

JUDICIAL REVIEW AND THE RULE OF LAW

The Judiciary as Policeman

As a government of limited powers, each branch of the government of the United States has only those lawful powers granted it by the Constitution. The powers of Congress, for example, are enumerated in Article I, Section 8, and include the power to impose taxes and regulate interstate commerce. But can Congress be trusted to stay within the limits of those enumerated powers by policing itself? The proponents of judicial review say no. It is necessary for the courts to police Congress and declare its laws unconstitutional when it exceeds the limits of what the Constitution allows. Otherwise the risk is too great that Congress will overstep its legal boundaries and tyrannize over the country. The courts must also police the executive branch for the same reason. And for the judiciary to police the legislative and executive branches, its interpretation of the Constitution must supersede theirs.

But why can the courts be trusted to stay within the powers granted to them by the Constitution and to fairly police the other branches? The proponents of judicial review cite various reasons. One reason is that the judiciary is the weakest of the three branches and thus the branch least capable of tyrannizing over the country. This argument was made by Alexander Hamilton, one of the founding fathers.

Hamilton claimed that the judiciary was the "least dangerous" branch of the national government. Unlike Congress, it did not have the power to impose taxes. Unlike the presidency, it did not command an army. Thus, the judiciary was dependent on Congress for money to operate and on the presidency for the armed might to enforce its decisions. Being in such a dependent condition, Hamilton thought there was little danger of the federal courts turning themselves into instruments of tyranny. Although the danger may not be nonexistent, it is less dangerous to entrust the judiciary with the job of saying what the Constitution means than it is to entrust that vital task to either of the other branches of the government.

One problem with this argument for judicial review is that it ignores the fact that, unlike Congress or the president, there are few democratic controls on a Court that is abusing its power. Since democracy is the principal means by which political tyranny is thwarted in our system of government, a Court bent on the illegitimate extension of its powers would seem to be at least as dangerous as the other branches.

The legislature has the authority to impeach and remove justices who are guilty of abusing their power, but that is a drastic remedy that can be effectively used in only the most extreme of circumstances. Moreover, the executive's command of military power will be useless in many cases in keeping the Court in line. President Franklin D. Roosevelt did not find that being commander-in-chief helped him at all when a recalcitrant Court kept declaring unconstitutional key parts of his New Deal program.

The Judiciary as Expert Interpreter

Another argument made by proponents of judicial review is based on the contention that the job of interpreting and applying the laws is the job of courts, not the job of the other branches of government. Judges are experienced in figuring out how the law applies to the cases and controversies they decide. Courts are designed to examine and answer questions about the law's meaning. The Constitution is law, and so the judicial role applies just as much to the question of whether legislative and executive action is consistent with the Constitution as it does to any other kind of legal question. Thus, the practice of judicial review is a natural consequence of the role that courts play in the legal system and the Constitution's status as law.

Critics of this argument for judicial review might claim that it neglects the special significance that the Constitution has in our political system. Among all our laws, the Constitution is special in being the expression of the will of "we the people" of the United States and in establishing the fundamental features of our democratic form of government. Other laws become so by being enacted by elected representatives. But the Constitution is law because the people of the United States adopted it and the representative form of government it establishes. In light of this special status of the Constitution, the critics may continue, it is more appropriate for the democratically elected bodies of government to say what the document means than for a body insulated from the very people whose will the document expresses.

Defenders of judicial review can respond that the special status of the Constitution makes it all the more important for the Constitution to be interpreted and applied by the branch of the government whose regular job is to interpret and apply law. The Constitution takes precedence over every other law in our nation. Accordingly, its interpretation is a task for experts, not amateurs.

Yet, critics of judicial review can argue that for interpreting the Constitution what is needed are not experts in legal doctrines and technicalities but rather individuals who understand the will of the people. The insulation of judges from the political process puts them in a poor position to comprehend the people's will.

The arguments we have thus far examined in favor of judicial review have tried to show that it is needed in order to ensure that our democratic government remains a government under the rule of law. Those who make these arguments can concede to the critics of judicial review that the practice represents an antidemocratic element of our political system. But they contend that such an element is essential in helping prevent popular government from putting itself above the law.

However, there is a very different line of argument designed to defend judicial review. The argument aims to show what seems at first blush impossible: that judicial review actually helps promote democracy.

JUDICIAL REVIEW AND DEMOCRACY

Ely's Argument: Perfecting Democracy

The legal theorist John Hart Ely has developed one influential version of the argument that judicial review is justified because it can promote democracy. Ely regards the Constitution as a charter for a democratic form of government, but he sees that throughout American history, the actual political process has fallen well short of an ideal democracy. Equally important, for Ely the political process actually resists changes that would make the system a more democratic one.

Judicial review has helped overcome that resistance. This has been possible only because federal judges are insulated from the political process and need not stand for election. They have had the political independence needed to overcome the obstacles that politics has thrown in the path of the democratic promises of the Constitution. Thus, the very feature of judicial review that critics invoke to condemn it as antidemocratic—the absence of electoral accountability on the part of federal judges—Ely uses to help explain why it can be democratic after all.

Let us examine an example to illustrate Ely's theory. The example concerns one of the most important democratic rights, the right to vote. Over the course of the twentieth century, there was a dramatic shift in the distribution of our nation's population from rural to urban areas. Yet, in many states, the election districts drawn at the beginning of the century were unchanged half a century later. This meant that urban districts had fewer representatives in the state legislature than rural districts having a much lower population.

Since election districts are drawn by state legislatures and any significant changes in election districts could make it more difficult for incumbents to get reelected, the legislatures refused to redraw the districts. The urban voters, of course, could not vote these intransigent state legislators out of office, since they came from rural districts. And the voters of those districts would clearly not vote for candidates who would propose diluting their political power by giving urban districts greater representation. The result was that the electoral process was frozen in a situation that was unfair to urban voters and grossly undemocratic in that it allowed a small minority of the state's voters to control a majority of the state's legislators.

This undemocratic situation lasted until the Supreme Court stepped in to correct it. Precisely because it was insulated from the political process, the Court was able to force a change to make it more democratic. The Court ordered states to reapportion their election districts according to the principle of one person, one vote. Any other arrangement would be inimical to a fair democratic process, the Court reasoned, for it would in effect dilute the voting strength of certain citizens and magnify the voting strength of others. Whether this reasoning is sound or not, these reapportionment cases illustrate one of Ely's basic contentions: the political process cannot always be counted on to reform itself, and judicial review enables the courts to step in and compel reforms that democratic principles require.

Ely is well aware that judicial review has not always been used to promote a more fair and open democracy. It has been abused, as it was during the Great Depression when it was used to thwart the consistent will of the majority rather than make the political process more democratic. Ely is very critical of Supreme Court decisions that run contrary to his theory of judicial review, and there are many of them. But he does not see such abuse as a reason for eliminating judicial review, presumably because eliminating it would be a blow to further democratic progress and perhaps even create a risk of backsliding.

For Ely, the Court abuses the power of judicial review when it goes beyond the task of improving the democratic process and begins to impose its own idea of good or wise public policy on the country. This was the problem, in Ely's view, with the Court during the first three decades of the twentieth century: it thought that laissez-faire economics was good policy and so declared illegal the efforts by government to regulate the economy. The result was that laws expressing the democratic will of the people were effectively vetoed by a group of nine, unelected men. That was a wholly illegitimate exercise of judicial review, in Ely's eyes.

Such abuse can be avoided only if the Court refuses to impose its own ideas of wise public policy. Judges are not "philosopher-kings" who can legitimately dictate the values and policies that society must adopt. In a democracy, complicated and messy questions about the best policy are left to the representatives of the people. Thus, judicial review can legitimately aim to make the political process a more democratic one, but it cannot legitimately aim to impose on the country the Supreme Court's ideas of what political outcomes or policies are best.

Criticisms of Ely: The Political Process

The idea that the crucial job of judicial review is to improve the democratic process is an attractive one. But Ely's approach seems insufficient to guarantee the legitimacy of judicial review. Consider the following example.

Suppose a federal judge reasons that a recently conducted presidential election was fundamentally unfair. She believes that wealthy individuals and corporations had too great of an influence on the election. She says that she does not really care who wins the election, but she judges the political process by which that outcome was reached to be seriously flawed by democratic standards. She therefore declares the election null and void and orders a new round of elections in which the influence of wealthy individuals and corporations is reduced dramatically.

Such a judge would be following Ely's reasoning perfectly. Yet, most people would see her ruling as a gross abuse of the power of judicial review. Notice that people who agree with the judge that the wealthy have too much influence on the political process could still maintain that the ruling is an abuse of judicial review. If the wealthy have too much influence, the legally proper remedy seems to be a political one: Congress should reform the process. Everyone recognizes that such reforms are difficult and take a long time to enact. But the proper response seems to be "That's our democracy; it's not perfect or quick, but it is capable of eventually correcting its own serious flaws."

In fact, historical evidence suggests that a very imperfect political process is still capable of self-correction and is not nearly as resistant to change as Ely assumes. For example, the right to vote was extended to women via the political process. And the legal accomplishments of the civil rights movement were mostly won through the political process rather than through judicial review.

Ely could respond that the self-correcting political processes of an imperfect democracy operate too slowly and need a boost from time to time from judicial review. This view may well be right. But it erases any neat, clean line between legitimate and illegitimate judicial review. This is because judges will have to use their experience and judgment to determine when it is time to use judicial review to improve the political process and when it is not. This approach will require determining the likelihood that the process will reform itself, how long it might take for the reform to come, how important the reform is, and so on. This may be an intelligent and defensible approach to judicial review, but it entangles judges in complicated political and philosophical questions of the very sort that Ely wants judges to avoid.

Ackerman's Argument: The Sovereign People

Another defense of the democratic legitimacy of judicial review comes from the legal and political philosopher Bruce Ackerman. His approach rests on the idea that in the United States the people are the sovereign and the ultimate source of political legitimacy. The Constitution is the supreme law because it has been accepted by the sovereign people, and the sovereign people also have the final say on what it means and how it can be changed.

According to Ackerman, politics in our system takes two distinct forms. In periods of "normal" politics, we the sovereign people are mostly silent: we do not think and act as a people but rather as private individuals pursuing our separate concerns and projects. During these times, most individuals are politically apathetic, turning the tasks of government over to elected representatives. To the extent that some individuals are politically involved, their main motives are self-interest: they attempt to use government to get more for themselves.

Other times, however, the people are politically active and mobilized: they turn from their absorption in private affairs and address public issues and controversies. Their main motive is not self-interest but a desire to promote the common good and see justice done. In these times of "constitutional politics," we the people discuss and debate political issues of fundamental importance for the nation and eventually arrive at some decision on these issues. Those decisions have ultimate authority. They supersede any conflicting decision made by private individuals or by some branch of government. For it is not government that is the sovereign; it is the people. That means that when the people have spoken, the government must follow.

Ackerman claims that during the 1930s, when the Supreme Court struck down as illegal the efforts of the Congress and the president to deal with the Great Depression, the people of the United States made their sovereign voice heard: the Supreme Court must desist. Ackerman concedes that the Court had a strong argument in saying that those efforts were unconstitutional because they went beyond specific powers that the Constitution gave to Congress and the president. Nowhere in the document does it grant the national government the power to regulate the economy as extensively as the New Deal programs sought to do.

But Ackerman argues that the sovereign people, in effect, amended the Constitution during this period to allow for such regulation. They amended the Constitution in essentially a two-step process: first, by electing a president and a Congress committed to a fundamentally new and greatly expanded role for government in regulating the economy; and second, by reelecting the president and the other supporters of the New Deal, despite the resistance of the Supreme Court to the program. By declaring New Deal legislation unconstitutional, the Court crystallized the issue for the people: they could continue to vote for those supporting the New Deal, or they could vote them out of office and so reject their plans for fundamental change. By continuing to vote for the New Deal supporters, the people made the former choice and sent a message to the Supreme Court: we, the sovereign people, hereby change the Constitution to allow for New Deal programs, and you, the Supreme Court, must cease in your resistance to them. According to Ackerman, when the Supreme Court suddenly shifted direction and began to uphold New Deal legislation, it was doing exactly what it should: responding to the decision of the sovereign people.

It is true that Article V of the Constitution lays out a specific process by which amendments are to be added and that during the New Deal period no amendments extending government powers of economic regulation were enacted through that process. But in Ackerman's view, the people are sovereign, which for him means that they are not restricted to following their earlier decisions. Just as the people can change the Constitution, they can change how the Constitution is to be changed. In the 1930s, the people simply exercised their sovereign power to decide how the Constitution can be changed and proceeded to alter it in a manner different from what had been decided at an earlier stage in the nation's history.

The importance of judicial review for Ackerman stems from his distinction between normal and constitutional politics. The people cannot be mobilized and focused on political issues all the time. They need and want periods in which they can focus on private affairs. But during those periods it is especially important that some branch of government enforce the decisions that the sovereign people made during earlier periods of constitutional politics. This is because special interests and self-interest have a great influence on the political process during periods of normal politics. Pressured by those special interests, elected officials will be prone to overstep the boundaries set by the previous decisions of the sovereign people. For Ackerman, the judiciary is the branch of government best situated to resist special interest pressure and ensure that elected officials abide by the previous decisions of the sovereign people.

In Ackerman's view, then, American democracy is to be understood as combining two key ideas. The first is that the people are sovereign and thus have the sole authority to make the ultimate decisions about what the Constitution is and means. The second is that, for much of the time, the sovereign people are inactive and so need some branch of government to ensure that their previous decisions are respected and enforced. In light of these two ideas and the fact that special interests tend to dominate when the sovereign people are politically inactive, judicial review becomes the best way to enforce the decisions of the sovereign people. To that extent, it is not antidemocratic; rather, judicial review reinforces a fundamental element of American democracy: the sovereignty of the people.

Criticisms of Ackerman: The Rule of Law

Proponents of the rule of law should find Ackerman's theory of American democracy problematic. Even if we accept the dubious distinction between normal and constitutional politics, Ackerman's theory treats the sovereign people as above the law. Like the absolute sovereigns of Hobbes and Austin, the people exercise arbitrary power in Ackerman's model. The only difference is that Ackerman's "people" only occasionally awaken from their nonpolitical slumbers to exercise such power, whereas the sovereigns of Hobbes and Austin are ruling continuously. But when the people do awake and decide to address some political issue, Ackerman's theory places no legal restraints whatsoever on their decisions or the process by which they arrive at the decisions. The rule of law may exist during normal politics, but it is suspended during Ackerman's constitutional politics.

Critics of Ackerman will argue that an essential and desirable feature of the system of government established by the Constitution is a commitment to the rule of law, even during times of constitutional politics. That commitment entails that the law should not get suspended just because the population has become politically mobilized and has begun to address fundamental political issues. The Constitution should not cease to apply to the people just because they have begun to turn their attention from private concerns to public issues.

Ackerman points out that the Constitution does not "entrench" any of the basic rights it protects: nothing in the Constitution prohibits it from being amended so as to abolish such fundamental rights as freedom of speech and religion. He infers from the failure to entrench such rights that the Constitution regards the people as a sovereign power above even the Constitution itself. But even if the Constitution allows the sovereign people lawfully to abolish every fundamental constitutional right, it does not follow that it authorizes them to disregard the process of amending the Constitution contained in Article V.

Ackerman's view overlooks the rationale for including an explicit amendment process in the Constitution. The whole point of Article V is to enable the people to change the basic system of government lawfully, without recourse to political revolution. By ratifying a constitution that included an explicit amendment process, the sovereign people committed themselves to following the rule of law, even when they wished to make changes in the basic system of government. The political theorist John Agresto has put the point eloquently:

> Through constitutionalism we placed limits on both our political institutions and ourselves, hoping that democracies, historically always turbulent, chaotic, and even despotic, might now become restrained, principled, thoughtful and just. So we bound ourselves over to a law that we made and promised to keep. And though a government of laws did not displace governance by men, it did mean that now men, democratic men, would try to live by their word.[5]

CONSTITUTIONAL INTERPRETATION: IMPLICIT RIGHTS?

We now turn to the question of which approach to interpreting the Constitution is best. This question is distinct from the one of who should have the final word in interpreting the Constitution, although we will see that some of the same considerations are relevant to both questions. The ideas of democracy and the rule of law play an important role in debates over interpretation, just as they played in the disputes over judicial review. Nonetheless, the question of how the Constitution should be interpreted is different from the question of who should have the final word on its interpretation.

One of the more persistent questions that arises in connection with the interpretation of the Constitution is whether there are constitutional rights that are not explicitly mentioned in the text of the document and, if so, how it is possible to determine what those implicit rights are. We will first examine a crucial case addressing this question. Then we will turn to some of the major theories of constitutional interpretation defended by contemporary legal thinkers.

The Right to Privacy: *Griswold v. Connecticut*

Many people assume that the Constitution protects their right to privacy. Yet, nowhere in the document is the term *privacy* or any equivalent term used. In fact, the Supreme Court did not hold that there was a constitutional right to privacy until 1965, in the case of *Griswold v. Connecticut.*

The state of Connecticut had a law criminalizing the use of any drug, medicinal article, or instrument for purposes of preventing conception. For many decades, Planned Parenthood and other organizations fought for the repeal of the law by the state legislature, but the political power of the Roman Catholic Church defeated their efforts. It was—and still is—official Church doctrine that contraception is immoral, interfering with the purpose for which God has given us our sexuality.

Connecticut's anticontraception statute was not used to prosecute couples who practiced birth control. Women who could afford a private physician could be fitted for a diaphragm and use it without fear of legal prosecution. But the law had been used to close down birth control clinics that served indigent women. Planned Parenthood of Connecticut decided to test the legality of the statute by opening a new birth control clinic that would serve indigent, married women.

When the clinic was opened, Estelle Griswold, executive director of the state's Planned Parenthood, and Lee Buxton, a physician and medical professor who worked for the group, were charged, prosecuted, and convicted for being accessories to the crime of using articles for the purpose of preventing conception. Griswold and Buxton argued that the anticontraception statute was unconstitutional, and their case wound up before the Supreme Court.

Connecticut argued that its law served legitimate government purposes, namely, discouraging the illicit sexual acts of adultery and fornication, and so should be upheld. But the Supreme Court rejected their arguments and found the anticontraception law unconstitutional.

Writing for the Court majority, Justice Douglas claimed that (1) in addition to the rights explicitly protected by the Constitution, there are implicit constitutional rights; (2) one of those implicit rights is the right to privacy; and (3) the right to privacy protects from state interference a married couple's decision to use contraception.

Douglas's argument began by insisting that there are good grounds for asserting the existence of implicit constitutional rights. First, the Ninth Amendment suggests that there are more constitutional rights than the ones explicitly laid out in the document: "The enumeration in the Constitution of certain rights shall not be construed to deny or disparage others retained by the people."

Second, legal precedents recognized specific, implicit constitutional rights. For example, in *Pierce v. Society of Sisters,* the Court declared unconstitutional a state law that required children to attend public school but did not allow private school attendance as a substitute. The Court in effect ruled that parents have an implicit constitutional right to send their children to private school as an alternative to public school. In *Meyer v. Nebraska,* the Court declared unconstitutional a state law prohibiting the teaching of foreign languages in public schools. The Court in effect held that parents had an implicit right to have their children study foreign languages in public school. If there are such implicit rights in the Constitution, then it is possible that the right to privacy is also one.

Douglas proceeded to argue that the right to privacy is indeed implicit in the Constitution. He claimed that the right was a "penumbral emanation" from those provisions of the Bill of Rights that protect various aspects of privacy, such as the Fourth Amendment's ban on unreasonable searches and seizures and the Third Amendment's ban on the quartering of soldiers in homes during peacetime.

A penumbra is a halo of light surrounding an object, such as the halo that emanates from and surrounds the sun during an eclipse. Douglas was suggesting that the Bill of Rights also has a kind of halo that emanates from and surrounds it. The difference is that with the Bill of Rights, the halo is not one of light but rather one of implicit rights. And among the rights in the halo is the right of privacy.

Douglas then argued that the privacy right protects a married couple's decision to use contraceptives. He claimed that such a decision was at least as important to a couple as the decision to send their children to private school or put them in a foreign language class. After all, having children is a critical decision for any couple, and the marital bedroom was a "sacred precinct" of privacy that had been recognized for ages by our civilization. Since the decisions to send one's children to private school and to study German are constitutionally protected, the decision to use contraceptives must be protected as well.

Criticisms of *Griswold*

The most obvious weakness in Douglas's reasoning is his reliance on the metaphor of a "penumbra" of implicit rights that surrounds the Bill of Rights. He never gives a convincing argument for the existence of such a "halo" or for why the right to privacy is part of it.

The best Douglas can muster is the claim that specific provisions of the Bill of Rights concern aspects of privacy, such as the Fourth Amendment's ban on unreasonable searches and seizures. But he never explains how the Bill of Rights creates a right to privacy that covers more than the particular aspects of privacy protected by its specific provisions.

Justice Goldberg sought to avoid these problems by suggesting in his concurring opinion that the right of privacy was part of the concept of liberty referred to by the Due Process Clause of the Fourteenth Amendment. Such a right was a fundamental liberty that lay at the basis of our social and political institutions and, as such, was to be included among the liberties protected from state interference by the Fourteenth Amendment.

As a fundamental liberty, the right to privacy could not be legitimately infringed upon by the state, unless such infringement was necessary to serve some compelling state purpose or interest. To be compelling, a state interest had to be of the highest importance, and even then, a law restricting a fundamental liberty had to be necessary in the sense that no alternative, less intrusive means of serving the compelling interest was available.

Goldberg argued that Connecticut's law flunked the "compelling interest" test: discouraging adultery and fornication was an important state purpose, but it was not necessary to outlaw contraceptive use by all couples, including faithfully married ones, in order to accomplish that purpose. The laws prohibiting adultery and fornication were the constitutionally valid way of accomplishing the purpose. The anticontraception law was not, in Goldberg's view.

Goldberg's opinion avoids reliance on the unexplained penumbra metaphor. Yet, it fails to provide any clear explanation of the basis for determining what counts as a fundamental liberty.

In Goldberg's view, such a liberty need not be enumerated in the text of the Constitution. As long as the liberty is rooted in our nation's traditions, it can count as fundamental. But the various strands that make up our nation's traditions are conflicting and ambiguous when it comes to questions about the extent of the state's authority to regulate the lives of individuals.

One strand is represented by the federal and state laws that, in the name of morality, imposed restrictions on the sexual liberties of adults. The most notorious of these were the Comstock laws, enacted in the late nineteenth century. A conflicting strand is represented by the Planned Parenthood Association, which has been very successful in promoting the practice of birth control. What is needed is some criterion for determining which elements within our traditions can serve as the basis for fundamental liberties, and Goldberg's opinion fails to provide it.

The Court in *Griswold* may well have been right in finding a constitutional right of privacy more general in scope than any of the specific provisions of the Bill of Rights. But it failed to articulate clearly a general theory of constitutional interpretation that could provide a convincing justification for its view. It is to general theories of constitutional interpretation that we now turn.

FRAMERS' INTENT

One of the most popular ideas about constitutional interpretation is that the meanings of the various provisions of the Constitution should be dictated by what the framers of those provisions intended. In the case of the original Constitution, the framers are those who participated in the convention that came up with the document. In the case of the amendments, the framers are those who formulated them.

According to the framers' intent approach, the proper way to clarify what the various unclear parts of the document mean is to appeal to how these men specifically intended that their words be taken. Thus, if they intended that the First Amendment's protection of freedom of speech not apply to a law prohibiting the disclosure of military secrets, then we should interpret that amendment to allow Congress to enact such a law. This is true even though on the face of it the amendment declares that Congress shall make no law restricting freedom of speech. The language of the amendment mentions no exceptions to the prohibition, but the framers never intended that it be applied in a perfectly literal way. Their intentions about how it should be applied govern how we should interpret the Constitution, according to this approach.

Most legal theorists today would agree that the intentions of the framers are relevant to how the Constitution should be interpreted. But many theorists reject the idea that the framers' intentions should be the sole determinant of what the best interpretation of a constitutional provision is. Critics point to many difficulties with an approach that relies exclusively on framers' intent.

First, an intention is a subjective state of affairs, a psychological state within the mind of a person. It is often very difficult to determine what someone's intentions were, especially when he lived in a very different historical era. The problem of discovering the intentions of long-deceased men is compounded by the fact that the framing of the Constitution was a group effort. Different framers undoubtedly had very different and even conflicting intentions with respect to many of the provisions that require interpretation.

Even when we can say with some confidence what the specific intentions of the framers were, there are serious complications. Consider the Eighth Amendment ban on cruel and unusual punishments. It is fairly certain that the framers specifically intended to ban physical torture, such as the rack and screw. But it is very uncertain whether they also had the higher-level intention that only punishments they specifically intended to prohibit be declared illegal.

A plausible argument holds that the framers did not intend that future generations be bound by their specific intentions but rather be free to go beyond those intentions. The argument rests on the fact that the language of the Eighth Amendment is general, not specific. There is no reason why the amendment could not have listed the exact forms of punishment the framers intended to bar. Instead, they chose general language that allows for changing applications and interpretations. The argument is that this choice of general language is evidence that the framers intended that their specific intentions not always be decisive in what the Constitution means. Moreover, the evidence is found in all of the provisions that call for interpretation. And if the framers' specific intentions are not always decisive, then those intentions cannot possibly be the exclusive determinant of the meanings of the provisions of the Constitution.

Perhaps the biggest problem with the framers' intent theory is that there seems to be no good answer to the question of why those intentions should determine constitutional meaning to the exclusion of other factors. It does not seem to be a universal truth that written documents mean only what their authors intended. Words can have meanings that those who write them may not be intending to convey. More importantly, the framers' intent theory appears to ignore the fact that the Constitution became our supreme law only after it was ratified by the people. It would seem to be more in keeping with our democratic heritage to say that the way the people generally understood it is what determines the meaning of the Constitution. And that point suggests a different approach to interpretation.[6]

ORIGINAL UNDERSTANDING

Bork's Theory

Robert Bork has developed a theory revolving around the idea that the meaning of the Constitution is essentially determined by how it was generally understood in society at the time of its adoption. There is no need to delve in the minds of the framers and decipher what they may have intended by various provisions. Instead, we ask a simpler question: "How were these provisions generally understood by people at the time of adoption?"

Thus, in Bork's view, the Cruel and Unusual Punishment Clause bans torture because that is how it was generally understood at the time. But it does not ban the death penalty because people understood the clause as leaving that form of punishment (which was common at the time) untouched. Similarly, the Equal Protection Clause of the Fourteenth Amendment essentially means that states may not provide to whites legal rights and privileges they deny to blacks. This is because the Amendment was enacted after the Civil War and was understood as ensuring that newly freed blacks would not be discriminated against by state laws. But the Equal Protection Clause does not give women the same protections against discrimination because it was not understood in that way when adopted.

Bork argues that the original understanding theory is the only one compatible with a democratic form of government under the rule of law. When properly applied, the theory prevents judges from imposing their own values and preferences on society. Our form of government does not authorize judges to make value judgments for society. The proper role for judges is to enforce and apply the value judgments embodied in the laws enacted by the elected representatives of the people and in the Constitution ratified by the people.

Departure from the original understanding model undercuts the legitimacy of the Supreme Court and interferes with the proper operation of democratic government, according to Bork. The Court becomes a "naked power organ," exercising might but not right. The dangers of departing from original understanding are well illustrated, according to Bork, by the infamous 1857 case of *Dred Scott v. Sandford.*

Congress had outlawed slavery in some United States territories as part of its efforts to hold the Union together by political compromise. In *Dred Scott,* the Court said that such compromises were an unconstitutional violation of the slave owner's right to property, protected by the Fifth Amendment's Due Process Clause. That clause prohibits the government from taking "life, liberty or property without due process of law." In *Dred Scott* the Court interpreted the clause to mean whites have a constitutional right to own slaves, and that right cannot be interfered with by government.

Bork rejects this interpretation of the Due Process Clause. He says that the original understanding of the clause was that it barred government from taking away life, liberty, or property without first going through a fair legal process. In a criminal setting, this meant that government could not summarily punish a person for a crime but had to give him a trial at which he had a reasonable opportunity to establish his innocence. Yet, once the trial had determined guilt, the government could punish the person without a violation of due process.

In a legislative setting, due process meant that any new law had to be enacted in accordance with the preexisting laws governing legislation: it had to be duly enacted. But, Bork argues, due process did not mean that government was directly and substantively barred from enacting particular laws.

In short, the original understanding of due process was that it did not directly bar particular outcomes that government may wish to pursue but only placed restrictions on how the government could go about reaching those outcomes. Due process regulated the procedures government had to follow, not the substance of what government could do. *Dred Scott* twists the meaning of the Due Process Clause to bar substantive legislative outcomes, even when the laws are duly enacted. And by ignoring original understanding, Bork claims, the *Dred Scott* decision helped to discredit the Supreme Court and intensify the political crisis over slavery. The court turned itself into a "naked power organ," exercising might without right and illegitimately imposing its views on society.

Bork levels essentially the same criticism at the Court's decision in the *Griswold* contraception case. The original understanding of the Constitution's provisions did not include any right to privacy more general than the specific rights enumerated in the document. By finding a right to practice contraception, the Court was imposing the substantive values of the justices on society. We may agree with those values, but they were no part of original understanding. According to Bork, from a legal point of view, *Griswold* was as illegitimate as *Dred Scott*.

Criticisms of Bork: Naked Power Organs

Critics of Bork's theory of original understanding argue that it fails to consider the implications of the fact that courts are not the only government bodies that can exercise might without right. Legislatures can also act as "naked power organs," even when they are not violating the original understanding of any constitutional provision. Bork's theory requires that courts refrain from invalidating such legislative acts of naked power, if there is no constitutional provision whose original understanding prohibits the acts. But what if the original understanding was based on faulty moral ideas? How is right, as opposed to might, promoted if courts allow such legislative acts to stand?

Bork might argue that when legislative acts conform to the terms of original understanding, it is too dangerous to allow courts to strike down the acts, even if those acts are thought unjust. Giving courts the power to strike down legislative acts regarded as unjust would be tantamount to giving them a blank check to invalidate any act contrary to the moral or political values of the judges who serve on them.

Bork may concede that legislatures can sometimes act as naked power organs, even when not violating the requirements imposed on them by the Constitution as originally understood. But he would argue that, when they do act in that way, they are at least subject to the electoral process: their members can be voted out of office and the laws changed democratically. Democracy, not an imperial judiciary, is what should keep legislative (and executive) tyranny in check.

Yet, Bork's argument ignores the fact that a tyrannical or oppressive majority (or even a majority that is simply inattentive to injustice) cannot be voted down by the minorities whose rights are violated. If the courts do not vindicate those rights, then no one will, at least until the minorities are able to awaken the majority to the injustice. It is reasonable to suggest that broad constitutional provisions, such as the Equal Protection Clause and the Due Process Clause, can be legitimately interpreted in ways that vindicate individual rights, even when an interpretation according to the canons of original understanding would leave those rights unprotected.

But Bork will have none of this. He points out that such "revisionist" approaches to constitutional interpretation (as he calls them) all rest, at least implicitly, on some moral philosophy. For it is only from moral philosophy, or something like it, that one could determine what the extra rights are that need protection. In Bork's view, this is where the problem arises: no moral philosophy has proved so convincing that all reasonable, intellectually honest persons must accept it. Without such a philosophy, a judge has no legitimate authority to impose his or her own favored but controversial moral philosophy on the country.

But Bork's argument backfires. What he says about moral philosophy is certainly sound. But the same can be said about legal philosophy in general and the philosophy of constitutional interpretation in particular. There is no philosophy of constitutional interpretation so convincing that all reasonable, intellectually honest persons must accept it. Bork might beg to differ, claiming that the philosophy of original understanding fits the bill. But such a claim would require Bork to argue that everyone who disagrees with his theory—every Supreme Court justice, every judge, every legal thinker, every lawyer—is unreasonable or intellectually dishonest.

It is simply not plausible to suggest that the theory of original understanding is so compelling that one disagrees with it on pain of being unreasonable or dishonest. To suggest that the theory does not afford sufficient protection for individual rights may be wrong, but it is certainly reasonable. And if reasonable dissent from original understanding is possible, then by Bork's own criterion, judges do not have the authority to impose it on the country.

Bork has set the standards for the justification of authority too high. Neither his theory nor any other could meet them. Moreover, Bork has failed to address the very questions that are fundamental to determining when the exercise of judicial authority under the Constitution is legitimate and when it is a naked act of power. Those questions are the questions of moral philosophy that Bork breezily dismisses: What moral rights do we have as individuals against the government, and what is the line that distinguishes rule by might from rule by right? At best, Bork simply begs these questions by assuming that original understanding draws the correct line between might and right. He needs to take them more seriously.

DWORKIN AND THE CONSTITUTION

Ronald Dworkin's approach to constitutional interpretation stems from his general theory of legal interpretation. As we saw in Chapter 2, his theory claims that the law consists of more than the rules and decisions officially adopted by society. It also consists of the best philosophy of government that could justify those rules and decisions: the strongest principles of political philosophy that could be seen as underlying the official rules and decisions.

Accordingly, in deciding a hard constitutional case, a Dworkinian judge would not only consider the explicit words of the Constitution and the legal precedents relevant to the case. Such a judge would regard the Constitution and precedents as expressions of some underlying philosophy of government and would ask him- or herself, "What is the strongest philosophy of government that could justify the constitutional provisions and precedents?" The judge would rest a decision in the case ultimately on the principles of that philosophy.

Justice Douglas's talk of "penumbral emanations" from the Bill of Rights can be seen as a very unclear and inchoate explanation of what is, in essence, Dworkin's theory of constitutional interpretation. Douglas asserted the existence of a right of privacy more general in scope than the mere sum of the specific rights enumerated in the Bill of Rights. He said it emanated from the specific rights. But what exactly is the nature of this emanation?

Dworkin's theory provides an answer: the general right of privacy is part of the strongest justification for the specific, enumerated rights. In other words, the best philosophy of government underlying the Bill of Rights is one that incorporates a general right of privacy, and for that reason, Dworkin claims, the right to privacy is a genuine constitutional right. More generally, our constitutional rights go beyond those rights explicitly enumerated in the text and include whatever rights are part of the strongest philosophy of government underlying the explicit provisions of the Constitution and the relevant precedents.

Dworkin recognizes that morality determines what the strongest philosophy of government is, and so moral judgments will be needed to implement his theory. And it is certainly possible for someone to reject the idea that the strongest philosophy of government that could justify the Bill of Rights is one that protects a more general right of privacy. Dworkin's point is that anyone who wishes to reject that idea must enter into substantive moral argument: he or she must propose an alternative philosophy of government and argue that morality really favors the alternative. For it is "true morality" that determines what the strongest philosophy of government is, not simply whatever morality some person or group may happen to hold. And psychological claims about the specific intentions of the framers or historical claims about how people generally understood the Constitution's provisions are essentially irrelevant to the question of what "true morality" says.

Dworkin elaborates on the shortcomings of appealing to the framers' intentions or to the people's original understanding by drawing an important distinction, that between concepts and conceptions. The distinction can be illustrated by considering the Equal Protection Clause of the Fourteenth Amendment.

Dworkin argues that we must distinguish the conception of equality generally held by those who wrote and ratified the Fourteenth Amendment from the concept of equality. A conception of equality consists of the specific ideas some individual or group has about what counts as treating persons with equal concern and respect. It incorporates and reflects their moral and political beliefs about how persons ought to be treated. Persons will disagree with one another insofar as they hold conflicting conceptions of equality.

But any such disagreement assumes that there is some shared concept of equality about which they are disagreeing. That is because people who are talking about totally different things cannot be disagreeing with one another. The concept of equality consists of those very abstract ideas about equality that everyone can agree on, such as the formal principle that equality requires similar cases to be treated similarly. Conceptions of equality will fill in that formal principle by specifying what kinds of cases are similar and what kinds are not.

Dworkin thinks that some conceptions of a given concept, like equality or liberty, are better than other conceptions of that same concept. And central to his theory is the idea that, when a constitutional provision refers to an abstract concept such as equality or liberty, the provision should be interpreted in light of the best conception of that concept. The best conception is the one for which the strongest moral justification can be given: it is the most sound conception, from the moral point of view.

Dworkin tells us that the Fourteenth Amendment should be construed as enshrining the best conception of equality, even if that conception was not held by people in the middle of the nineteenth century. The original understanding of equality does not bind subsequent generations. If it did, we would be forced to interpret the Fourteenth Amendment in light of a philosophy of government inferior to the philosophy we have evolved over the past century and a half. Yet, we have developed a better understanding of the meaning of equality, especially when it comes to matters of race and gender. And Dworkin's theory entails that the best approach to understanding the Equal Protection Clause should rely on the most advanced moral understanding we have been able to develop of the meaning of equality.

In the famous school desegregation case from 1954, *Brown v. Board of Education,* the Supreme Court held that state-supported racial segregation in public schools was a violation of the Equal Protection Clause. The fact was that public school segregation existed when the Fourteenth Amendment was adopted, and no one suggested that the amendment would affect such segregation in any way. Schooling for blacks was inferior to schooling for whites, but most people at the time believed that it was no affront to equality to give blacks an inferior education.

By 1954, it had become clear to many Americans that the original understanding of equality was seriously flawed: the fact that blacks received inferior educational opportunities because of segregation was in fact a deep affront to equality. For Dworkin, then, the Supreme Court was exactly right in striking down public school segregation as a violation of the Equal Protection Clause. Though the framers and the ratifiers of the Fourteenth Amendment saw no problem with giving blacks an inferior education, a more advanced understanding of racial equality had developed, and the Constitution was rightly interpreted in light of this more advanced understanding.

CRITICISMS OF DWORKIN

Bork versus Dworkin

Critics of Dworkin, including Bork, argue that his approach to the Constitution ends up destroying the rule of law. They claim that the approach gives judges a blank check to impose their own values on society.

Bork contends that the problems with Dworkin's theory are highlighted by how it applies to the question of whether the death penalty violates the Eighth Amendment ban on cruel and unusual punishment. Several places in the Constitution, Bork says, clearly imply that the death penalty is permissible. For example, the Due Process Clauses say that persons may not be denied "life, liberty or property without due process of law." This implies that people may be deprived of life if there is due process of law, which is how the clauses were originally understood. But Dworkin's approach would authorize judges to ignore that understanding (it is just a mistaken "conception") and to decide a capital case based on whether they thought a superior conception of cruelty covered the death penalty. For Bork, this simply amounts to a license for judges to ignore what the Constitution says and impose on everyone else their own ideas about how society should be run. This may be appealing to those who share the values held by certain judges. But it is not the rule of law; it is the rule of judges.

Dworkin replies that his theory gives judges no such power or license. They are still required to interpret the Constitution; they are not licensed to write a new one. An interpretation of the Constitution must appeal to the best principles that fit its explicit provisions, while writing a new one need not worry about fit at all and can start with those principles regarded as morally best.[7] Thus, there is a line between interpreting the meaning of a provision and creating meaning for a provision. The proper approach to saying what the meaning of the Constitution is involves interpreting, not creating, meaning.

Whose Morality?

Yet, Dworkin's account of constitutional interpretation faces difficulties similar to those of his general theory of legal interpretation. Even if we grant that the Constitution should be understood in terms of some underlying philosophy of government, we still need to know why the best conception of the Constitution's moral concepts should dictate the meaning of the document. Why not the conceptions generally accepted in society at the current time, whether or not some philosophers have better ones?

And even given that the best conceptions determine constitutional meanings, we still need to know why judges are authorized to interpret the Constitution on the basis of their own view of the best conceptions. Again, why are they not required to defer to society's current conceptions when it comes to equality, liberty, and the like?

Following his general theory of law, Dworkin might reply that it is essential for the Constitution to be more than a mere expression of power politics; it must have integrity, or else it cannot be law, much less the supreme law of the land. And integrity requires that constitutional meanings be determined by the best conceptions of the Constitution's moral concepts.

Moreover, Dworkin appears to think that the most reliable way to ensure that such meanings are determined by the best moral conceptions is if we charge each citizen with the responsibility of grappling in the forum of his or her own conscience with the question of what philosophy of government does reflect the best moral conceptions of equality and liberty. This charge should be given not merely to private citizens but to judges in their official capacity as well. That is the best way to ensure that the Constitution rises above the realm of mere power politics and has the integrity that, as Dworkin sees it, is essential to law.

Judgment and Action

Leaving aside the validity of Dworkin's view that integrity is essential to law, his argument rests on two big assumptions. First, it assumes that the best moral conceptions are most reliably obtained when persons refuse to defer in their individual moral judgments to the collective judgment of the community and instead decide an issue in the forum of their own conscience. Second, it assumes that our institutions will more fully and reliably embody the best moral conceptions if persons are licensed to act on their individual judgments, even when they conflict with those of the community.

The first assumption has a great deal to be said for it. Independence of individual thought and judgment has been an essential element in the progress of humankind's moral thinking. It was one of the great principles of the Enlightenment, captured by Kant in the words "Have the courage to use your own intelligence." But, as Kant well realized, it is important to distinguish issues of free thought and judgment from issues relating to action on one's thoughts and judgments.[8] What is Dworkin's view on how individuals may act on their judgments about constitutional meaning?

One point that is clear is this: Dworkin is not arguing here that individuals should be free to act on whatever their considered moral judgments are, even when they contradict what the Constitution says. The issue is not whether a person is justified in breaking the law because her conscience says that obedience is intolerable. Rather, the issue is whether a person is justified in acting on her (Dworkinian) interpretation of the Constitution when most others in society would, on account of their different moral judgments, give a conflicting (Dworkinian) interpretation.

Dworkin seems to suggest that an individual would be justified in acting so, whether the person is a judge acting in an official capacity or a private citizen. Dworkin certainly seems to think that judges have that license, but he has not worked out his view on the matter very clearly and has failed to provide any argument for why judges—and perhaps everyone else—are justified in acting on their own Dworkinian interpretation of the Constitution, regardless of the interpretations of others.

Dworkin needs to distinguish more clearly the following two questions: (1) What is the best approach to interpreting the Constitution? and (2) When is an individual (judge, other official, or private citizen) justified in acting on her interpretation, given that she has followed the best approach?

If we assume for the sake of argument that the Dworkinian approach is best, we are still left with the second question. The reason is simple: as Dworkin himself readily points out, persons who use his approach will still often disagree over the meaning of the Constitution, and those disagreements will be rooted in conflicting moral conceptions. This raises the question of whether a given individual ought to defer to the Dworkinian interpretation of some other person or group, when there is conflict. Consider the following hypothetical scenario to illustrate one aspect of this problem.

The Supreme Court versus Society

Suppose that the justices of the Supreme Court (or at least a majority of them) understand and follow Dworkin's approach. In such a scenario, the justices would know that others who also use Dworkin's approach could arrive at very different interpretations of the Constitution, on account of their different moral conceptions. Now suppose that in a certain case, the justices know that most of society would arrive at an interpretation different from, and incompatible with, theirs on account of the justices' disagreement with some widely accepted moral conception. Should the justices make their ruling based on their Dworkinian interpretation or on the Dworkinian interpretation that would follow from society's moral conceptions?

Dworkin appears to support the former alternative: the justices should rule based on their own interpretation. In some cases this might well be the most justifiable approach: if society's moral judgment is seriously wrong and leads to the systematic violation of important rights and if the ruling can in fact be enforced, then a strong case can be made for overriding society's Dworkinian interpretation.

What is more questionable is the view that it would always be the most justifiable course of action for the justices to override society's Dworkinian interpretation with their own. Yet, Dworkin appears to take just that view: in his eyes, it is a matter of principle that the interpretation of the justices should take precedence. Yet, it is difficult to understand what principle would dictate that result.

Democratic principles would seem to argue in the other direction: letting society's interpretation prevail. Of course, society is not always right, but neither are Supreme Court justices, as *Dred Scott* and the *Civil Rights Cases* from the nineteenth century, and the cases involving economic legislation from the early part of the twentieth century, amply confirm. In these cases, the justices' faulty moral conceptions dealt serious setbacks to the causes of racial equality and fair treatment of workers. Dworkin fails to explain why, as a matter of principle, it was better for the Court to act on its morally flawed interpretation of the Constitution than for it to defer to an interpretation based on society's sounder moral judgments.

A more reasonable approach would suggest that no single answer emerges to the question of whether the Court should defer to society: sometimes it should, and sometimes it should not. The best answer for any given case will require moral wisdom and political insight, and it is difficult, perhaps impossible, to codify such insight and wisdom in a philosophical theory. Philosophy might provide some help in grappling with the problem in a given case, but we may be expecting too much if we think it will give us the answer.

SUMMARY

The Constitution of the United States is the supreme law of the land. It is the outcome of a daring experiment in political history, an effort to reconcile popular government with the rule of law. Yet, the Constitution contains provisions that invoke abstract and contested concepts and that make sweeping pronouncements. These provisions stand in need of interpretation. Who is to provide the authoritative interpretations by which everyone else must abide, and how are those interpretations to be arrived at? Those are two of the main philosophical questions raised by the Constitution's status as the supreme law.

This chapter has focused on the work of contemporary thinkers who have grappled with these questions. It has found that the questions implicate fundamental issues of political philosophy. But they also implicate more practical issues that require us to draw lessons about the different branches of government from the nation's historical experience. In our diverse society, general agreement on the basic issues of political philosophy or on the lessons of history cannot be expected, and our arguments over the Constitution are as much a part of the character of the nation as the document itself.

NOTES

1. Contemporary critics of judicial review include Mark Tushnet, *Taking the Constitution Away from the Courts* (Princeton, NJ: Princeton University Press, 1999), and Michael J. Klarman, "What's So Great About Constitutionalism?," *Northwestern University Law Review* 93 (Fall 1998), pp. 145–194.

2. It should be mentioned that the Court has long left the meaning of some constitutional provisions largely up to the elected branches of government. For example, the meaning of the impeachment standard of "high crimes and misdemeanors" is one that the Court has left largely for Congress to decide. The Court has also refrained from specifying the meaning of the provision that guarantees to each state a republican form of government. And under the related idea that not all claims under the Constitution are justiciable (that is, appropriate for resolution by a court), the Supreme Court has refused to hear some constitutional cases, including ones challenging the president's legal authority to commit U.S. military forces to combat situations. The view that the Supreme Court should be the final judge of the Constitution's meaning must either reject these long-standing practices of the Court or at least concede that in some limited range of cases, the Court may leave it up to the other branches to decide on the meaning of certain constitutional provisions.

3. Quoted in Gerald Gunther, *Constitutional Law* (Westbury, CT: Foundation Press, 1991), p. 22.

4. In this chapter, we will focus on the most aggressive form of judicial review. An alternative form is presented and defended in John Agresto, *The Supreme Court and Constitutional Democracy* (Ithaca, NY: Cornell University Press, 1984).

5. John Agresto, *The Supreme Court and Constitutional Democracy*, p. 96.

6. Some versions of the framers' intent theory incorporate the ratifiers in their approach to understanding the meaning of the Constitution. See, for example, the approach outlined by Edwin Meese, attorney general under President Ronald Reagan, in "The Battle for the Constitution," *Policy Review* 35 (Winter 1986), 32–35.

7. See the section on Dworkin's interpretive version of natural law theory in Chapter 2.

8. Immanuel Kant, "What Is Enlightenment?" in C. J. Friedrich, *The Philosophy of Kant* (New York: Modern Library, 1977), p. 132. Kant himself went overboard by declaring that the authorities must always be obeyed. See p. 139.

DISCUSSION QUESTIONS

1. In some countries that have judicial review, the constitutional decisions of their supreme courts can be nullified by a vote of the legislature. Some American legal thinkers have proposed that we amend the Constitution to allow a two-thirds vote in the senate to override any constitutional decision of our Supreme Court. What are the pros and cons of such a proposal? Would you support the proposal?

2. In the recent case *Washington v. Glucksberg* (1997), the Supreme Court considered the question of whether the constitutional right of privacy protects the choice of a terminally ill, mentally competent adult to commit suicide with the assistance of a physician. The Court refused to find any general right to physician-assisted suicide, suggesting that the issue was best settled in the arena of democratic politics by the states and their elected officials.

The Court did leave open the possibility that in some narrow range of cases involving intolerable pain that could not be alleviated, the choice of a dying, mentally competent patient to end her life with a physician's aid might be constitutionally protected. But the essence of the Court's position was that physician-assisted suicide was an issue to be dealt with by the democractic process and not by the dictates of judges. Do you agree with the Court?

ADDITIONAL READING

Ackerman, Bruce. *We the People: Foundations* (Vol. I). Harvard University Press, 1991.

Agresto, John. *The Supreme Court and Constitutional Democracy.* Cornell University Press, 1984.

Amar, Akhil Reed. *The Bill of Rights.* Yale University Press, 1998.

Arthur, John. *Words That Bind: Judicial Review and the Grounds of Modern Constitutional Theory.* Westview, 1995.

Bassham, Gregory. *Original Intent and the Constitution.* Rowman and Littlefield, 1992.

Berger, Raoul. *Government by Judiciary.* Harvard University Press, 1977.

Bickel, Alexander. *The Least Dangerous Branch.* Yale University Press, 1986.

———. *The Morality of Consent.* Yale University Press, 1975.

———. *The Supreme Court and the Idea of Progress.* Yale University Press, 1978.

Bobbitt, Philip. *Constitutional Interpretation.* Blackwell, 1991.

Bork, Robert. *The Tempting of America.* Free Press, 1990.

Brennan, William J., Jr. "Interpreting the Constitution." *Social Policy* 18 (1987), 24–28.

Corwin, Edward. "The 'Higher Law' Background of American Constitutional Law." *Harvard Law Review* 42 (1928–29), 149–185 and 365–409.

Dworkin, Ronald. *Freedom's Law.* Harvard University Press, 1996.

Ely, John Hart. *Democracy and Distrust.* Harvard University Press, 1980.

Freeman, Samuel. "Original Meaning, Democratic Interpretation, and the Constitution." *Philosophy and Public Affairs* 21 (1992), 3–42.

Hall, Kermit, ed. *The Oxford Companion to the Supreme Court.* Oxford University Press, 1992.

Hamilton, Alexander, James Madison, and John Jay. *The Federalist Papers.* New American Library, 1961.

Hand, Learned. *The Bill of Rights.* Harvard University Press, 1958.

Lyons, David. "Constitutional Interpretation and Original Meaning." *Moral Aspects of Legal Theory.* Cambridge University Press, 1993.

Meese, Edmund. "The Battleground for the Constitution." *Policy Review* 35 (Winter 1986), 32–35.

Parent, W. A. "Privacy, Morality, and the Law." *Philosophy and Public Affairs* 12 (1983), 269–288.

Rehnquist, William. "The Notion of a Living Constitution." *Texas Law Review* 54 (1976), 693–706.

Richards, David. *Foundations of American Constitutionalism.* Oxford University Press, 1989.

Sunstein, Cass. *One Case at a Time: Judicial Minimalism on the Supreme Court.* Harvard University Press, 1999.

Thayer, James. "The Origin and Scope of the American Doctrine of Constitutional Law." *Harvard Law Review* 7 (1893), 129–156.

Tribe, Laurence, and Michael Dorf. *On Reading the Constitution.* Harvard University Press, 1991.

Tushnet, Mark V. *Taking the Constitution Away from the Courts.* Princeton University Press, 1999.

Walzer, Michael. "Philosophy and Democracy." *Political Theory* 9 (1981), 379–399.

Wechsler, Herbert. "Toward Neutral Principles of Constitutional Law." *Harvard Law Review* 73 (1959), 1-35.

4

Private Law: Torts, Contracts, and Property

THE FUNCTIONS OF PRIVATE LAW

Human beings are vulnerable to harm. In the course of pursuing their daily activities, inevitably many in society will suffer harm in the sense that they will suffer some kind of setback to their interests or their plans.[1] Some will suffer physical harm; others will suffer financial or professional or personal setback; some will have their plans upset by those they were counting on to help them; others will have their plans upset by persons they have never met or conditions over which they have no control. Every legal system must address the question of how to deal with the various setbacks from which people suffer.

It is not possible for all setbacks to be legally prohibited and all interests and plans to be legally protected. The law must be selective, in part because only limited resources are available for the operation of any legal system, and also because people's interests often conflict in such a way that it is impossible to protect certain interests without harming others. My interest in peace and quiet conflicts with my neighbor's interest in playing her stereo at a high volume. If the law protects me, it causes a setback for her, and vice versa.

Once the law has selected which harms to protect people against, it must then decide how to protect them. Our legal system is based on the idea that such protection necessarily involves holding persons responsible for causing harm. The law operates on the premise that the harms it targets are brought about by the actions (or inactions) of persons and that the individuals who cause such harms are to be held liable. Holding an individual liable involves subjecting him to punishment and/or requiring him to pay compensation to those harmed.

111

According to a traditional view, our system of law looks at legally prohibited harms in two distinct ways. In the first way, the law is concerned
with harms insofar as they are setbacks to the interests of society as a whole.
These public harms are defined mainly by the criminal law, and government
officials, acting on behalf of society, seek out and prosecute those who commit such harms. Murder, theft, arson, and rape are some common examples
of conduct prohibited by the criminal law on account of the harm caused
to society.

According to the second way of looking at harms, the law sees prohibited harms as a private matter between the individuals involved. The government leaves it up to the aggrieved individual to bring a lawsuit for damages against the party she believes harmed her.[2] It will provide a neutral
forum and an impartial judge to decide the case. But the government's
function is not to act as an advocate on one side or the other. Rather, its
function is to be a fair umpire to determine who is in the right and who
is in the wrong.

The legal rules that define prohibited private harms are part of what is
called the "private law." Legally prohibited private harms, excluding breach of
contract, are called torts. Examples of torts include medical malpractice,
defamation, and trespass.

Some overlap is apparent between the harms of criminal law and those of
the private law. For example, battery is both a crime and a tort. As a harm to
society, battery is a crime subject to prosecution by the government. As a private harm, it is a tort for which the injured party may bring a lawsuit in order
to collect compensation.

The private law does more than define and prohibit private harms. It also
facilitates interaction and exchange between individuals. The law of contracts
and property is central to this facilitative function. The law of property defines
the rights of ownership, while the law of contracts governs the binding agreements private individuals make. Such private-law rules enable individuals to
work out arrangements that are mutually beneficial. These legally backed
arrangements make it easier for individuals effectively to plan their lives and
pursue their best interests. Accordingly, private law is a means for facilitating
the private choices of individuals.[3]

Historically, the legal rules covering contracts, torts, and property
stemmed from the system of law known as the common law. Over the course
of many centuries, judges in England developed a system of legal rules that
were generally applicable across the country. These rules stood in contrast to
legal rules that applied only within a certain part of the country; accordingly,
they were called the "common law," meaning that they were common to the
whole nation.

In this chapter, we will explore the traditional view of private law and
the criticisms that have been made against it. The traditional view was developed during the nineteenth century and became dominant during the latter
part of that century. Beginning in the early part of the twentieth century, the
traditional view came under heavy criticism. Those criticisms have had a

substantial impact on the way judges, lawyers, and legal theorists think about the law. Yet, it would be an exaggeration to say that the traditional view is dead. It is still influential in some quarters, while critics and proponents continue to debate it.

Two distinctions lie at the heart of the traditional view of private law. The first is the distinction between public law and private law. The second is a distinction within private law itself, between contract and tort law. Let us examine each of these distinctions.

THE TRADITIONAL
PUBLIC-PRIVATE DISTINCTION

According to the traditional view, the legal rules governing certain areas should reflect the political will of the people, but the rules covering other areas should not be dictated by politics. In the former category belong the rules that establish the basic framework of government (constitutional law), as well as the rules that define what counts as a harm to society as a whole and how those accused of such harm are to be dealt with (criminal law).

But the traditional view holds that in some areas the law should not be responsive to politics. In particular, the legal rules covering torts, contracts, and property should be apolitical. Each of these areas of law is defined in terms of certain basic concepts and is governed by legal rules that follow necessarily from those concepts. For example, contract law is based on the idea that in a contract each individual imposes a certain obligation on herself. From this idea of a self-imposed obligation follows the legal rule that there is no contract between two parties unless there is a "meeting of the minds." In other words, each party to a contract must understand which obligation the other is imposing on herself, or else there is no true agreement.

Similarly, the fundamental concept of tort law is the idea of a wrongful harm committed against the person or property of an individual. Traditionalists argue that wrongful harm implies that the wrongdoer is at fault, and so they conclude that a basic principle of tort law should be that individuals are liable for the harm they cause only if they are at fault. Some exceptions to this principle exist, in which liability is imposed regardless of personal fault. But traditionalists regard these "strict liability" exceptions as the illegitimate intrusion of legal principles foreign to the essence of tort.

The correct rules of private law are thus determined not by political will but by the concepts that are fundamental to each area of private law. Traditionalists argue that their view of private law entails that legislators should not be involved in formulating or modifying such rules. This is because the political pressures that make legislators responsive to the will of the majority also make it likely that they will not abide by the correct legal rules when those rules stand in the way of the majority getting what it wants. So the traditional view hands over to judges the task of formulating the rules of contract, tort, and property. Judges can better resist political pressures to deviate from the rules that are required by the basic concepts of each area of private law.

This distinction between areas of law that should be responsive to the political will of the people and areas that should not be is the essence of the distinction between public and private law. Criminal law and constitutional law are public because their rules should reflect the political will of the people; tort, contract, and property law are private because their rules have some deeper source than the political will of the people or their elected representatives. That deeper source is not responsive to what the majority wants. It is as fixed and as apolitical as the rules of mathematics. Unlike public law, private law represents, in the minds of the traditionalists, an area of law that should be separate from politics.

The traditional view of private law is illustrated in the 1901 case of *Hurley v. Eddingfield*. This case involved a claim of wrongful death against a physician. Those representing the dead person's estate made the following allegations: the deceased had become ill and had a messenger sent to the family doctor to inform him and request his assistance; despite being offered his usual fee, the doctor refused, for no reason; the deceased died as a result of lack of medical attention.

The court decided that, even if all of the allegations were true, there was no legally valid claim of wrongful death against the physician. They reasoned that the basic idea of a contract as a self-imposed obligation left individuals free to decide whether to enter into a contract or not. The physician had simply exercised this freedom. There was thus no fault on his part, and so no wrongdoing.

The court dismissed arguments to the effect that medicine was a profession of such vital public importance that physicians had a legal duty to attend to those who were in need of medical assistance. It suggested that a physician's decision to offer medical help or not was his alone, and the law did not impose on him a duty to offer the help to one who was willing to pay. Arguments based on the public good or social need were deemed inapplicable.

Traditionalists of the late nineteenth and early twentieth century held that the common law of their time generally incorporated the correct, apolitical rules of contract, tort, and property. Moreover, public law in the form of statutes generally did not attempt to alter the common-law rules. In the view of traditionalists, then, the law was as it should be, with private law carefully separated from politics and from public law.

Contemporary traditionalists are not so happy with the current state of the law. For one, legislation has in many cases preempted common-law rules. And even within the common law itself, the influence of what traditionalists would regard as illegitimate political factors has been felt. For example, the scope of strict liability in tort law has expanded dramatically in the past fifty years. These developments, unfortunate from the viewpoint of traditionalists, were in part the result of the criticisms of the public-private distinction that began to be voiced in the early part of the twentieth century. Let us turn to those criticisms. Later, we will examine the traditional distinction within private law between tort and contract.

CRITICISMS OF THE PUBLIC-PRIVATE DISTINCTION

Legal Realism and the Politics of Private Law

Criticisms of the traditional public-private law distinction are based on eight key ideas:

1. Private law is not some domain separate from politics, but rather its rules and principles are the product of the political choices of judges.

2. The choices made by the judges who fashioned private-law rules during the nineteenth century reflected a conservative political viewpoint.

3. Different private-law rules create different distributions of wealth and power in society.

4. No distribution of wealth and power is natural or neutral: it is always the creation of legal rules that reflect political choices.

5. The only way to evaluate any system of private-law rules is on the basis of some political position or ideology.

6. The government does not in fact treat obedience to private-law rules on the part of individuals as a purely private matter, since it plays a role in the enforcement of the rules.

7. The rights protected by private-law rules are merely creations of the rules themselves, not some independent basis for the rules.

8. Because of points 3 through 7, there is no way to eliminate politics from private law: it is irretrievably political.

These criticisms were initially leveled by a group of thinkers known as the legal realists and their allies in the early decades of the twentieth century. In contemporary legal thought, the criticisms are associated most closely with the scholars in the Critical Legal Studies movement. The realists and their allies were largely concerned with demonstrating that the existing private-law rules were politically biased in favor of the wealthy. But their deeper philosophical point was that any set of private-law rules would be politically biased in some way. There was no way to escape the essentially political nature of private law. To that extent, the traditional private-public distinction was bogus.

Contemporary critics of the distinction contend that it is an effort to hide the political nature of private law. Judges who think in terms of the distinction can rationalize their decisions as apolitical and neutral, even though those decisions in fact reflect particular political values and choices.

For both the legal realists and contemporary critics, the attack on the traditional distinction is part of a broader effort to promote progressive values through the law. Their aim is to use the legal system to reduce inequalities of wealth and power in society. In the final chapter of this book, we will examine the kinds of changes called for by the Critical Legal Studies movement. Here it will be helpful to examine the political agenda of the realists and their allies and to explore how that agenda was promoted by the attack on the traditional view of private law.

Property and Progress: The Labor Injunction

For the realists and their allies, using the law for progressive social change meant, first and foremost, using the legal system to assist wage-workers in their struggles with their capitalist bosses. During the second part of the nineteenth century, the industrial system had produced a large but impoverished working class and a small but extremely wealthy owning class. By the time the realists came on the scene in the early decades of the twentieth century, the private law had long been used by capitalist owners to promote their own economic interests at the expense of the workers. The realists aimed to turn the tables by reshaping the private law. In more general terms, they aimed to create a system of private law that would spread the benefits and burdens of life more evenly throughout the different levels of society. But the first step in this process of reshaping the private law was to expose the fact that the rules and principles of private law were political through and through and that the politics was of a decidedly conservative form. Then, the realists hoped, judges with a more progressive frame of thought could begin the job of refashioning the private law according to the progressive agenda.

A major target of the realists and their progressive allies were the legal rules that courts used to help capitalist owners resist actions by workers seeking to win higher wages and better working conditions. During the late nineteenth and early twentieth centuries, owners frequently went to court in order to obtain legal orders curtailing or stopping strike actions by workers. Courts repeatedly granted these orders, known as labor injunctions. The labor injunction was a powerful tool that owners could use in their struggles with workers. It seemed clear to the realists that courts were not acting neutrally or apolitically in these disputes; rather, by granting such injunctions, they were throwing the weight of the government on to the side of the owners and against the workers.

Courts saw the matter differently. Adopting a traditionalist view, they argued that the legal principles inherent in the very idea of property meant that strike actions were wrongfully interfering with the owners' legal right to use their property as they saw fit. If you are a worker who is picketing my factory and the picketing is deterring other potential workers from coming to work for me, then you are illegally harming my interest in running my factory. That was the traditionalist reasoning of courts. On the surface, political factors did not enter into the reasoning; rather, the legal conclusions were presented as ones dictated by necessary principles of law, not by a political choice.

The realists and their allies sought to debunk this traditionalist reasoning. Such realists as Wesley Hohfeld and Walter Wheeler Cook suggested that courts granted labor injunctions not because they were forced to do so by the concept of property but on account of their pro-business political values. Labor injunctions were not apolitical or neutral but rather strengthened the hand of owners in their efforts to get as much as they could of society's wealth and power.

According to the realists and their allies, property rights—and all other rights—are the creations of government and the legal rules it lays down and enforces. If a property owner has the right to curtail the activities of workers striking his factory, that is only because government has, in effect, delegated to the owner the legal power to go to court and obtain an injunction. But government can just as well choose legal rules that do not give that power to owners. Property rights thus derive from the rules laid down and enforced by government, and the realists insisted that there is no necessary, natural, or neutral way of laying down the rules. The decision to have one set of rules or another is a political choice.

For the realists and their allies, the ultimate test of any political choice was the good of society as a whole. The judges who granted labor injunctions were making political choices that obstructed rather than promoted the good of society. These judges represented the desires of the elite minority of capitalist owners. What was needed were judges who represented the desires of the working masses. Such judges would refashion the rules of private law and deny the requests of owners for labor injunctions.

The private law was necessarily political. The question was whether it would represent the politics of the wealthy minority or the politics of the working masses. The realists hoped that making clear this stark choice would at least defeat the idea that the existing rules of private law were necessary, natural, or neutral.

Once private law was seen as political, there was no reason to limit the battle against the labor injunction to the courts. It made perfect sense to fight as well in the legislative arena for laws that would override the traditionalist interpretation of property law and sharply limit the authority of courts to issue labor injunctions. The realists and their progressive allies did precisely that, and their efforts were rewarded in 1932 when Congress enacted landmark legislation, the Norris-LaGuardia Act. The act dramatically limited the authority of federal courts to issue injunctions in labor disputes. Traditionalists saw this as blatant and illegitimate political interference with the operation of the private law. But for the realists and their allies, the private law had been political all along.

Assessing the Realist Challenge

It is difficult to deny the accuracy of much of the realist challenge to the traditional public-private distinction. Private-law rules are political in some important ways: government does play a key role in their enforcement; the rules do deeply affect the distribution of wealth and power in society; and during the nineteenth century, their formulation by judges likely did reflect conservative political values.

Yet, the critics of the traditional distinction go too far when they claim that the rights protected by private-law rules are nothing but creations of the rules themselves. The critics reject the idea that there are any rights that preexist legal rules, often called "natural rights." They are especially vehement in their rejection of a natural right to private property, but they do not stop there. In their view, there are no natural rights—period.

The critics take this position for essentially three reasons. First, they believe that cases such as those involving labor injunctions show that a person's rights depend on which legal rules the government enforces. Second, they regard the whole idea of natural rights, especially the right to property, as creating a major obstacle to their efforts to make the distribution of power and privilege in society more equal. Third, they believe that the so-called natural rights cannot be defined in any but the vaguest and most general of ways, which robs them of all practical significance. Only the rights that follow from legal rules and decisions are specific enough to have practical significance.

None of these reasons seems sufficient to conclude that, as a general matter, rights are merely creations of legal rules. Even if one agrees that property rights are simply such creations, it does not follow that all other rights are as well. Thus, it is invalid to generalize from the labor injunction cases, since they concerned only property rights. The right to religious liberty, for example, could still be a natural right even if the right to property were not.

In addition, even if one accepts the legitimacy of a progressive political agenda, the critics' own arguments cast doubt on their claim that the idea of a natural right to property necessarily reflects a conservative political viewpoint. Everything depends on how that right to property is defined. If it is defined in the way that judges who granted labor injunctions did, then it will obstruct the progressive agenda. But it could also be defined in ways that promote that agenda.

For example, the right to property could be defined in terms of a worker's fair claim to the value of what he or she labors to produce. One could then argue that workers should receive more than they do under current capitalist arrangements. The critics' own argument that the legal right to property can be specified in any number of incompatible ways undercuts the idea that a natural right to property is necessarily a conservative one. For if a legal right to property can be defined in various ways, some helpful to the wealthy and some helpful to the working masses, then so can a natural right to property.

Finally, even vaguely defined natural rights can have practical importance. Consider the individual's right to religious liberty. The law must make this very general and vague right more specific because it must deal with the particular controversies over religious liberty that arise in society. Should an Air Force psychologist who is Jewish be allowed to wear a skullcap even though it is contrary to military dress regulations? May a city outlaw the practice of animal sacrifice when it is part of the rituals of some church? Should Native Americans have the right to ingest peyote as part of their religious rituals even when the state has enacted criminal prohibitions against possession of the drug?

These are questions that cannot be answered simply by stating that individuals have a natural right to religious liberty. But that does not make the idea of such a right practically meaningless. Its great practical importance can be seen in the fact that political systems committed to the idea operate very differently from ones committed to enforcing a single, orthodox religion for everyone. The former tolerate a great deal of religious diversity, while the latter suppress those who dissent from the officially endorsed religion.

To assert the existence of a natural right to religious liberty does not in itself tell us how that right is to be specified in a host of particular situations in which the right might be claimed. But it is wrong to conclude from this that the assertion of the right's existence is a meaningless exercise. To the contrary, such an assertion was one of the great achievements of modern Western civilization and formed the basis of the system of religious toleration that we still enjoy today.

THE TRADITIONAL
CONTRACT-TORT DISTINCTION

Just as the traditional view of private law distinguishes it from public law, it also distinguishes two categories within private law: tort and contract. Two main features are said to differentiate tort from contract. First, the duties that persons have under tort law are imposed by society, while the duties persons have under contract law are self-imposed. Second, tort law aims to compensate the victim for the harm suffered as a result of another's tortious conduct, while contract law aims to give the victim of a breach of contract the equivalent of what she would have had if the contract were honored. Let us look at these two alleged differences more closely.

The tort law says that, among other duties, individuals have a duty to exercise due care in their relations with other people. Violating that duty amounts to negligence. Thus, a property owner who fails to exercise due care in cutting down a tree on her property, with the result that harm is done to her neighbor's property, is liable for that harm. This is so even if the property owner never agreed to compensate her neighbor should her failure to exercise due care cause harm. Rather, as the traditional view sees it, society imposes on her and on others the duty to exercise due care.

The traditional view interprets the legal duties arising under contract law in a very different way. Those duties are self-imposed by individuals. Contract law enables individuals to place themselves under an obligation to act in a certain way, if they so choose. It does not impose that obligation on them irrespective of their own choice to accept it. Thus, contract law does not impose on a person the duty to give his automobile to his neighbor. But that person can impose the duty on himself by entering into a legally binding contract.

Why would anyone choose to impose a legal obligation on himself? One reason is that it is a very effective way of getting others to impose obligations on themselves in return. And it is often easier for people to carry out their plans, counting on the cooperation of others, when they have agreed to self-imposed, mutual obligations.

In the traditional view, then, contract law facilitates the private arrangements and plans that individuals make. It does not impose standards of behavior on them but rather enables them to choose their own standards of behavior to impose on themselves. Under contract law, I do not have any obligations I did not accept for myself. For the traditionalist, this stands in contrast to tort law, which sets the standards by which individuals must abide, whether they have agreed to them or not.

This first aspect of the traditional distinction between tort and contract leads naturally to the second. Traditionalists hold that the rules for recovery are essentially different in the two areas of private law. In tort law, the rule for recovery is that the victim of tortious conduct is entitled to an amount that reflects the harm done to him. Thus, if my negligence toward you causes $1,000 worth of damage to your property, then you are entitled to recover that amount from me.

In contract law, according to the traditionalists, the rule for recovery is not harm-based but expectancy-based. This means that if I breach a binding contract with you, then you are entitled to an amount that puts you in a position as good as the position you would have been in had I kept the contract.

Suppose, for example, that I agree to buy your car for $1,000, and you accept the offer. You go home and drive it back to my place. In the meantime, I change my mind. As a result, you end up having to sell it to your Aunt Minnie for $750. The expectancy rule would entitle you to recover $250 from me, because that is the amount that puts you in the position you would have been in had I kept my end of the bargain ($750 plus $250 equals $1,000).

Traditionalists see the expectancy rule as a logical consequence of the idea of a contractual obligation as a self-imposed obligation. Since I obligated myself to buy your car and then reneged on the obligation, it is natural that I should be required to pay you an amount that would leave you as well off as if I had not reneged.

CRITICISMS OF THE
CONTRACT-TORT DISTINCTION

Many legal thinkers have attacked the traditional distinction between tort and contract. Both aspects of the distinction have been challenged: the idea that contractual obligations are essentially different from tort duties and the idea that the rule for recovery in contracts is necessarily different from the rule in torts. The critics have argued that the duties arising under contract law are not self-imposed but rather are imposed by society through the judges who fashion and enforce the common law of contracts. They have also argued that recovery in contract cases is dictated by basic principles that come from tort law.

These criticisms link up with the criticisms of the public–private distinction. Like tort law, contract law is seen as embodying standards for individuals that are set by society through the legal system. But standards set by society are presumably not apolitical: they reflect political choices and political ideologies, and they help determine the distribution of power and privilege in society. Thus, even contract law fails to be an apolitical island in a sea of political choices, according to critics of the traditional view. Let us now examine these criticisms more closely.

In the traditional view, there is no legally binding contract unless there is a "meeting of the minds." Since each party is imposing an obligation on herself, there is no genuine agreement without each party understanding the obligation the other understands herself to have undertaken. In a legally binding contract, the obligation each party intends to accept is the precise obligation the other party expects the first party to fulfill. And the contractual obligation of each party is limited to the obligation that she intends to accept and the other person expects her to fulfill.

Critics of the traditional view argue that common-law rules often disregard what is in the mind of a party to a contract. For example, if a certain contract calls for the delivery of grade A eggs, then courts will not try to determine what the parties understood by *grade A;* rather, they will rely on the generally accepted meaning of the term. If one of the parties happens to attach an unusual meaning to the term, then it is too bad for her. The law will impose the standard meaning in its interpretation of the terms of the contract, and the person will be legally bound by that standard meaning. The jurist Learned Hand put this point in vivid terms by saying that the parties would be bound by the usual meaning of the words in their contract even if "it were proved by twenty bishops that either party, when he used the words, intended something else."[4]

According to the critics, courts are prepared to override a person's subjective interpretation of the terms of her contract because they see the legal imposition of standard meanings as good public policy. Imposing a standard meaning on the parties to a contract helps establish uniformity and predictability in the law and in people's contractual dealings with one another. When entering into contracts, individuals need not fear that their expectations will be disappointed because of some idiosyncratic interpretation the other party attaches to a key term in the contract. It is good policy to foster such conditions, and so society, through the courts, adopts rules of contract law suitable to such a policy. As a result, considerations of public policy take precedence over the obligations people may think they are imposing on themselves. Critics of the tort-contract distinction thus conclude that self-imposed obligations are not at the basis of contract law. Obligations imposed by society are.

The critics provide a similar analysis of the rules regarding damages. They claim that the damages owed to someone who is the victim of a breach are typically not determined by the will of the parties to the contract but are imposed by courts based on considerations of social policy. Most contracts do not have terms that specify what damages are to be paid in case of breach. And the rule of expectancy-based damages is only one possible measure that courts use in determining the amount that must be paid to the victim.

Consider the following case. Suppose I agree to buy your bedroom set for $1,000, and you accept the offer. You go home, clean and polish the set, and rent a van to bring it to my place. In the meantime, I change my mind. You sue me for breach of contract. What should your damages be?

Under the expectancy rule, I would owe you $1,000 minus the lowest amount you would have been willing to take for the bedroom set. The lowest amount you would have taken represents the value you place on retaining the set. Since you retain the set as a result of my breach, that amount must be deducted from the $1,000 in order to put you in the same position you would have been in without the breach.

But courts sometimes use a different approach in determining the appropriate damages: they do not try to put you in the position you would have been in if not for the breach; rather, they try to restore you to the position you were in before the breach. In the bedroom set case, this would involve assessing damages on me amounting to the costs you incurred in cleaning and polishing the set and renting the van. As a result of relying on an agreement that I later breached, you incurred costs that you would not have otherwise incurred. Courts sometimes set damages to reflect the costs or the harm suffered by the victim of the breach as a result of his reliance on the agreement. Such reliance-based damages are aimed at restoring the victim to his condition prior to the agreement, and in that respect they are like the damages given the victim of tortious conduct such as negligence.

If courts sometimes use an expectancy-based measure of damages and sometimes a reliance-based measure, then what determines the choice? The critics of the traditional view claim that considerations of social policy and substantive justice play determining roles. The choice is not an apolitical one but rather reflects the views of the judge about good public policy and what the victim of a breach deserves as a matter of substantive justice. The self-imposed obligations of the parties again take a back seat.

DEFENSES OF THE CONTRACT-TORT DISTINCTION

Defenders of the traditional view deny that the contract rules governing interpretation and recovery collapse the distinction between contract and tort. Using standard meanings rather than idiosyncratic ones to construe a contract does not refute the idea that contractual obligations are self-imposed. Rather, it simply represents the most practical and feasible way of answering the question: How can the courts determine which obligations the parties imposed on themselves?

There is no way to peer directly into the mind of a person and figure out what obligation she understood herself to be accepting when she entered into a contract. As a general rule, the standard meanings of the words used in the contract provide the most reliable evidence of what she understood herself to be doing. Thus the move to standard meanings is a good practical solution to a problem about getting evidence of which obligation was self-imposed; it is not a refutation of the idea of a self-imposed obligation.

In addition, defenders of the traditional view can argue that once a "standard meaning" rule of interpretation is adopted, individuals have fair warning of how their contract will be interpreted. If they really want grade A wheat, as normally understood, they can know that they should not put "grade B" in the contract. In this way, the rule will exert a pressure on individuals to express themselves in their contracts in a way that leaves no room for doubt about which obligations they intended to accept for themselves and which ones they expected the other party to fulfill.

As for damages, defenders of the traditional view argue that the law uses the reliance measure for breach of contract only when it is impossible to estimate expectancy-based damages or when there is no practical difference between the reliance and expectancy-based measures. Suppose I own a computer company and plan to put my wares on display at a big computer convention. I contract with you for equipment I need to set up the display. I go to the expense of transporting my computers to the convention site, but you breach the contract by failing to provide the other equipment on time. I may well have lost a number of sales as a result of being unable to put my wares on display, but there is no way to estimate how many sales I would have made had I been able to go through with the display. In such a case, the law will likely award reliance damages, and you will have to reimburse me for the costs I incurred in transporting my computers. Reliance damages thus become a fall-back when expectancy-based damages cannot be estimated. Expectancy retains its privileged position in awards for breach of contract. So the traditionalists argue.

ASSESSING TRADITIONALISM

Is the traditionalist view of private law a sound one? To the extent that it draws a distinction between public and private law on the basis of the alleged apolitical character of the latter, the traditionalist view seems dubious. The critics are persuasive in arguing that private law is political in several important ways. But traditionalism is on stronger ground in distinguishing contract from tort.

The key to the traditionalist position is that contractual obligations are self-imposed in a way that tort obligations are not. To sustain this position, it is not necessary, as some critics think, for the law always to decide contract cases on the basis of the subjective intentions and understandings of the parties. It is enough that the law provides practical means through which individuals can effectively express their intentions to accept certain legal obligations. In other words, the law must establish workable rules for individuals to follow when they intend to legally bind themselves to do something. It is then up to individuals to make proper use of those rules.

The critics of the traditional view may be right in suggesting that the particular contract rules the legal system comes up with will reflect certain views about good public policy and social justice. To that extent, the rules are political. But if the law establishes workable rules through which individuals can accept legal obligations they would not have but for their acceptance of them, then it does not refute the traditionalist to point out that sometimes individuals will not use the rules properly and end up having obligations imposed on them that they did not impose on themselves. Contractual obligations will still be largely self-imposed.

Nineteenth-century traditionalists saw contract law and its rules enabling individuals to undertake self-imposed legal obligations as a central part of the legal system. But as the importance of common law in general shrank over the course of the twentieth century, so did the importance of self-imposed legal obligations. In large and important areas of law, many of the obligations associated with making agreements are now imposed by society. In labor law, for example, owners and union representatives have a duty to bargain in good faith with one another. This is a duty imposed by society, and it overrides any contrary desires of the parties.

In light of such historical developments, it is impossible for contemporary traditionalists to share their nineteenth-century forerunners' conviction about the centrality of self-imposed obligations. However, critics of traditionalism go too far when they reject the very idea of a self-imposed legal obligation and attempt to collapse contract into tort.

SUBJECTIVE AND OBJECTIVE APPROACHES IN TORT LAW

We have seen that the law of torts imposes duties and that individuals can be held liable for violating those duties. Thus, the tort law concerning negligence imposes on individuals the duty to act with due care toward others and makes them liable if they cause harm as a result of violating that duty. And the law concerning battery imposes on individuals a duty to avoid physical contact with another without her consent and makes them liable if they cause harm as a result of violating that duty. But to what degree should the law look at the world from the perspective of the individuals on whom it is imposing its duties? This question has been examined and debated by legal thinkers under the rubric "subjective and objective" approaches to the law.

The subjective-objective debate appears in one form or another throughout the law, not only in tort law. Indeed, we have already come across an instance of it in our examination of different approaches to interpreting the terms of a contract. The subjective approach advocates interpretation in terms of what the parties to the contract intended and expected. The objective approach advocates interpretation in terms of the generally accepted meanings of terms.

In tort law, the subjective approach argues that the law should look at the world from the perspective of the particular individual involved in a legal case and should fine-tune its legal duties to fit the individual and his situation. The objective approach argues that the law should look at the world from a more objective perspective than that held by the particular individual in a case and should impose legal duties based on that more objective perspective. Let us consider a case that illustrates the differences between these approaches.

A Case of Self-Defense

Suppose Jones is sleeping in his home when intruders seek to enter it. He goes for his gun and yells that he will shoot if they do not go away. The intruders respond by throwing rocks at the home. An off-duty police officer in the area hears the commotion and proceeds to Jones's home, weapon in hand. Jones mistakenly believes the officer to be one of the intruders, sees him approaching with his gun, and shoots him.

Why did officer not announce presence? (handwritten margin note)

Has Jones violated a legal duty to act with due care? Jones would argue in court that he has violated no duty because he believed his life to be in danger and acted in self-defense. But a crucial question arises. Should a claim of self-defense be evaluated in terms of what the individual believed in the situation he was in; or should it be evaluated in terms of what a reasonable person would have believed in the individual's situation; or, finally, should it be evaluated in terms of the actual facts of the situation?

A subjective approach would argue that an individual's honest beliefs about the danger to his life and the necessity of using deadly force to preserve it are what count. In other words, the law should look at the situation from the individual's perspective. If Jones honestly believed that the officer was one of the intruders and bent on killing him and if he honestly believed that shooting was necessary to save his own life, then his claim of self-defense should be allowed. Assuming Jones had such beliefs, he violated no legal duty in shooting the officer. The duty should be tailored to fit the individual, and the law should not impose on any individual a duty to act in a way that, from the individual's point of view, will risk his own life.

A more objective approach would argue that Jones's honest beliefs about the danger and the necessity of shooting should not be the test for allowing his claim of self-defense. The law should adopt a more objective perspective in examining Jones's claim. In one version of this approach, the law should examine what a reasonable person would have believed in the same situation as the defendant. If the reasonable person would have believed that his life was in danger and shooting was necessary to save it, then the self-defense claim should be allowed. But if a reasonable person would not have believed such things, then the claim should not be allowed, regardless of Jones's own beliefs.

An even more objective approach would argue that the law should look at the situation in a completely objective manner and simply ask whether Jones's life was in fact in danger and whether his shooting was in fact necessary to save it. If the answer to both is affirmative, the claim of self-defense should be allowed. If the answer to either is negative, then the claim should not be allowed.

The Actual Person or the Reasonable Person?

Our focus here will be on the subjective approach and the reasonable-person version of the objective approach. Defenders of the subjective approach claim that it is more fair to individuals than the reasonable-person approach. Its fairness stems from the fact that it better reflects the actual blameworthiness or culpability of the individual. If Jones honestly believed that his life was in danger from the officer and could be saved only by shooting, then it seems he cannot be justifiably blamed for the shooting. He was doing what anyone who believed his life in danger would do: he acted to preserve it. His perspective thus determines the extent to which he is to blame and so should determine how the law imposes its duties and liabilities on him.

Defenders of the reasonable-person approach criticize this argument on several grounds. First, they claim that individuals can be legitimately blamed for failing to take reasonable steps to check whether their subjective beliefs are reasonable. Holding unreasonable beliefs does not absolve one of blame if one could have easily checked those beliefs and found them to be unreasonable but one neglected to do so.

For example, suppose a person believes that he is about to be attacked in his home by small but apparently menacing creatures. He gets his gun and begins firing away to stop them. In fact, it is Halloween, the "creatures" are children in costumes, and the person could have easily determined this if he had stopped to think for a moment and had observed more carefully what the "creatures" were doing. Defenders of a reasonable-person approach argue that this kind of example shows that simply having the honest belief that one is acting to save one's own life should not be enough to absolve one of legal liability.

In addition, critics claim that the subjective approach encourages individuals to wallow in their own subjective perspective without bothering to check to see how reasonable that perspective is. In contrast, by taking the perspective of the reasonable person and defining our legal duties in relation to that perspective, the law provides incentive to individuals to take steps to check the reasonableness of their beliefs.

The objectivists also contend that the subjective approach is excessively vulnerable to abuse because of the difficulties of confirming the claims individuals make about their subjective beliefs. It is too easy for an individual who is being sued for violating some legal duty to make up a story about his "honest" beliefs in order to escape liability.

The objectivists also attempt to turn the subjectivists' fairness argument on its head. They say it is unfair to others to make the legal duties and liabilities of a person dependent on his own subjective perspective: other people have no way of reliably knowing what that perspective is, and thus they cannot plan their activities to take account of it.

Finally, it is argued that a reasonable-person approach provides more certainty and uniformity in the imposition of legal duties. The duties imposed will not vary from person to person, depending on their subjective beliefs, but will be uniform across persons.

Subjectivists can respond that the reasonable-person approach will (in some cases) impose liability on persons even though they are without any personal fault. Suppose that, unlike Jones, a reasonable person would not have believed that the officer was in fact an intruder. But suppose Jones had been victimized by several assaults in the past, so he was more prone than the reasonable person to jump to the conclusion that he was under attack. From the reasonable person's perspective, Jones may have jumped the gun, but it hardly seems a matter of personal fault that he did so. Subjectivists can argue that a reasonable-person approach imposes excessive uniformity on persons. It fails to do justice to the fact that persons have very different experiences and very different perspectives arising from those experiences. The imposition of a generic reasonable-person standard on everyone rides roughshod over those differences.

Subcategorizing

This last point suggests a modification of the subjectivist position. The subjectivist's main goal of making the law more responsive than the reasonable-person approach to differences among individuals can be achieved without requiring the law to adopt the particular perspective of each individual. Having a different legal standard for every person is not needed. Instead, subjectivists can claim that the generic category of "reasonable person" is too broad and should be replaced with a series of more specific subcategories. For example, the experiences of persons who have been victimized by previous violent crimes might make their perspective on the world sufficiently different from that of the rest of us to subcategorize them. This would mean that in the earlier hypothetical case, Jones should be judged not by what some generic reasonable person would have believed in the circumstances but by what a person previously victimized by violent crime would have reasonably believed in the circumstances. The category "reasonable person" is simply too broad to take account of the differences in experience and perspective to which the law should be responsive. More specific categories are needed.

Defenders of a subjective approach might cite the example of sexual harassment to bolster their claim of the need for subcategorization in tort law. In some cases, sexual harassment can amount to the tort of battery; in others it can amount to the tort of intentional infliction of emotional distress.[5] To count as battery, the harassment must involve touching with an "unlawful" intent. To count as intentional infliction of emotional distress, the harassment must be "outrageous."

It is sensible to suppose that the sexually harassing conduct that reasonable women would regard as battery or intentional infliction of emotional distress is not necessarily identical to conduct that reasonable men would so regard. Women have different life experiences on account of their gender and might reasonably perceive certain unwelcome actions of a sexual nature as more serious than an average man would.

For example, a reasonable woman might perceive her employer's comments about her body as so demeaning as to be outrageous, whereas a reasonable man might think the remarks offensive or tasteless but not outrageous. Or a reasonable woman might perceive her employer's affectionate pat on her shoulder as battery, while a reasonable man might think the conduct out of place but not amounting to unlawful touching. And if the law uses the genderless standard of the reasonable person, the perspective of the reasonable women may be unjustifiably neglected or diluted.

Subjectivists who take the route of subcategorization could argue that moving to more specific categories would not encourage people to wallow in their own subjective perspective and avoid taking steps to determine whether their beliefs are reasonable. The law would still require people to do what is reasonable. It would merely recognize that what is reasonable for certain persons having certain life experiences is not necessarily reasonable for others having different life experiences.

Objectivists would reply that subcategorizing puts one on a slippery slope. Once one starts subcategorizing, there is no logical stopping point short of having the law adopt the perspective of each individual. That would take us back, of course, to the situation in which a different legal standard is used for every person, and people would be encouraged to wallow in their own subjective perspectives.

Subjectivists could respond by denying that subcategorizing puts one on such a slippery slope. The law already does subcategorize, for example, by having different standards for children than adults. Yet no one argues that this subcategorization logically leads to having a different legal standard for every person.

Objectivists will reply that everyone can agree that children should be treated differently than adults. And there are perhaps a few adult subcategories that everyone can accept, for example, those based on physical conditions such as blindness. But jettisoning the reasonable-person standard and replacing it with extensive subcategorization would open up a host of irresolvable controversies over what subcategories to use. While some would advocate subcategories based on gender, race, or economic class, others would reject such subcategories as inconsistent with the principle that all persons should be treated equally under the law. Extensive subcategorizing would entangle the law in a thicket of controversies that could not be settled except by the greater political might of one side or another.

At a minimum, it seems that advocates of subcategorization bear the burden of providing some account of which subcategories to use and why. Such an account might refute the claim that extensive subcategorizing would entangle the law in a thicket of intractable controversies. On the other hand, efforts to develop such an account might reveal all the more clearly the desirability of using a reasonable-person standard in determining tort liability.

THE DUTY TO AID

The Common-Law Approach

The law of torts covers the question of a person's legal duty to come to the aid of someone in need. The traditional common-law rule is that, in general, there is no duty to take action to aid another. There are exceptions, but historically judges have limited them to a fairly narrow range and have tried to draw clear lines around that range.

If a statute imposes a duty to render assistance, then the statute takes precedence over the common-law rule and aid must be rendered. If a person has a special legal relationship to the individual in need of assistance (for example, if one person is a lifeguard and the other a swimmer at the pool she has agreed to guard), then there is a legal duty to render assistance. If a person acted in a way that helped to bring about the dangerous situation in which someone now finds himself threatened, then there may be a legal duty to aid the threatened individual. But, in general, the position of judges in private-law cases has been to hold a very restrictive view of when there is a legal duty to render assistance.

The 1897 case of *Buch v. Amory* attempts to justify this restrictive approach by appealing to the difference between law and morality. The case involved an 8-year-old boy who trespassed onto the property of a textile mill. The boy did not understand English and did not leave the property when told to do so by the overseer. Instead, he went to his brother, who was an employee, and had his sibling show him how to operate the machinery. The 8-year-old's hand was crushed in the machinery as a result.

The boy brought a lawsuit against the company owning the mill for negligence. It was argued that the company had a legal duty to ensure that the boy was taken safely from the property, that it failed to meet this duty, and that, as a result, the boy suffered harm for which he now was demanding compensation.

The court threw out the case, contending that the company had no legal duty of care toward the boy, much less a duty to assist him in any way. The court stressed that its decision had to be based on legal duties, not moral obligations. It conceded that we have a moral obligation to come to the aid of those in need, whether we have a special legal relationship with them or not. We all stand under the same moral obligation that the good Samaritan discharged in the Biblical story when he assisted the injured stranger.

But law is different from morality and imposes much less stringent requirements to come to the aid of those in need. If a person causes harm through her actions, then she may be held liable for negligence if she acted carelessly. But, in general, the law does not hold a person liable for failing to prevent harm from occurring to someone else. "The duty to do no wrong is a legal duty. The duty to protect against wrong is, generally speaking and excepting certain intimate relations in the nature of a trust, a moral obligation only."[6]

The court's reasoning here is not wholly satisfying because it does not address the question of why, when it comes to helping others, the law should not be as stringent as morality or at least much more stringent than the traditional common-law rule. The court does not seem to be making an argument simply based on precedent; it is not just saying that, since prior legal cases refrained from imposing as stringent a view, we must do so as well. Such an argument would not have been very persuasive, since judges have always exercised the power to shape and modify the common law. Even if the court was not prepared to make huge changes in the common law regarding the duty to aid, it still could have nudged the law in the direction of morality. Instead, it refused to do so and implied that courts should not even begin making the legal duty to aid others more expansive than it already was. But why not?

The Ames Rule

Legal theorist James Barr Ames argued that the common-law rule should be altered to expand the scope of a person's duty to aid others. The revised rule he suggests would impose a legal duty to aid on someone who could save another from death or grave bodily harm with little or no inconvenience to himself. It would not matter whether any special legal relationship existed between the two. If I could save you from grave physical harm with little inconvenience to myself, then I would have a duty to do so under the Ames rule, even if we were total strangers.

Ames gives an argument for his proposed rule based on the idea that the purpose of law is to promote the general good of society as a whole.[7] His claim is that his rule would do a better job of achieving that purpose than the rule relied on by the court in *Buch*. For example, if I can save you from drowning simply by throwing you a life preserver located at my feet, then saving you would represent a net gain for society. The harm I save you from easily outweighs the slight inconvenience of bending over to get the preserver and toss it to you. Ames reasons that his rule would help motivate me to save you in such a situation, while the traditional common-law rule would not do so. Granted that my moral beliefs give me some motivation, I might need additional motivation actually to go ahead and save you. Ames thinks that his rule would give me, and others in a similar situation, such additional motivation. On the other hand, the traditional rule would give no such motivation. In that way, Ames claims that his rule would better promote social utility than the traditional one.

Even if the Ames rule would in fact provide increased motivation to help others in dire need, his argument for the rule would be questioned by many philosophers. First, it seems that an argument based on the general good of society would actually favor a duty to aid much larger in scope than even the Ames rule. If it would be a moderate inconvenience to me to save you from death, then there is still a net gain in social utility if I proceed to save you.

Indeed, there could be a net gain even if I would seriously injure myself by saving your life. Suppose I can save you from death but it would mean a year's stay in the hospital for me. That would still seem to involve net gain, since death is a more serious loss than a year in the hospital.

Some philosophers believe that arguments based on the idea that our highest obligation is to promote the general good of society place unreasonably severe duties on individuals to assist others. They would reject any such argument for expanding the traditional common-law duty to aid. But other types of argument can be given.

Many philosophers believe that the law should protect individual rights. The philosopher Joel Feinberg makes a rights-based argument for an expanded legal duty to aid similar in scope to the duty advocated by Ames. Feinberg is writing principally of criminal liability, as opposed to tort liability. But his position can be easily adapted to provide a rights-based argument for an expanded private-law duty to aid.

Feinberg and the Right to Assistance

Feinberg claims that in some situations an individual has a moral right to be assisted by a stranger, and in those cases the law should make assistance a legal duty. For example, suppose a child is drowning in a swimming pool, and all a stranger need do to save the child is reach out her hand and take the child from the water. The stranger can do this easily, and there is no one else in the vicinity who could save the child. Feinberg says the stranger not only has a moral duty to rescue the child, but that the child has a moral right to be rescued by the stranger. That the child has this right is reflected in how we would react were the stranger to knowingly fail to rescue the child. We would judge that the parents of the child could justifiably feel moral outrage at the stranger's inaction. Indeed, we would feel moral outrage ourselves, and such outrage is a sure sign that the child's rights have been violated by the stranger. Assuming, then, that the law's job is to protect individual rights, it should impose a duty on the stranger to rescue the child in this kind of case.

But what about the problem of drawing a line between the cases in which a duty to aid should be imposed and those in which it should not be? This problem is emphasized by the British statesman Lord Macaulay. He imagines a hypothetical case in which a man is about to cross a river that in fact is dangerously swollen and cannot be safely negotiated. Suppose another man knows of the danger, is by the river at the spot the first man is about to enter, and simply needs to call out a warning to prevent the first man from endangering his life. If there is a legal duty in this case, what about the case in which a man would have to walk fifty yards in the hot sun to give the warning? One hundred yards? A mile? Ten miles? One hundred miles?

Macaulay's point is that drawing a line to distinguish any of these hypothetical cases would be completely arbitrary; yet, it would be absurd to suggest that there should be a legal duty to travel ten miles to warn someone of a dangerous river, even if no one else could issue the warning. Thus, Macaulay concludes that we cannot start down this slippery slope and that we must hold that there should be no legal duty in any of these cases, including the first in which it was quite easy for the warning to be issued.

The law often deals with line-drawing problems by using the concept of reasonableness. It is a vague concept, difficult to define in a general way except in relation to equally vague terms such as justifiable, plausible, and the like. But precise definitions are often not needed for people to apply a concept to particular cases. And the law takes advantage of the fact that people can often come to a consensus about what is reasonable and what is not, when they deliberate about and discuss particular cases and facts.

The concept of reasonableness provides the law with a possible way of getting around Macaulay's problem. Suppose we understand Ames's expression "little or no inconvenience" as "no unreasonable cost, risk, or inconvenience." Someone will ask, "Who is to determine what counts as unreasonable?" And the answer will be what it usually is in our legal system: the jury, within some outer limits imposed by judges. If a jury is convinced that it was not an unreasonable inconvenience for a person to walk fifty yards to warn someone of a dangerous river, then the Ames rule will impose liability on that person. A defendant in such a case will have the opportunity to persuade the jury that certain facts made it unreasonable in his case, say, that he had a heart condition and walking fifty yards at a quick enough pace to warn the person about to enter the river might have precipitated a heart attack.

Epstein and Bright Lines

Some legal theorists are critical of the extent to which the law relies on vague concepts such as reasonableness. Richard Epstein, for example, argues that the duties imposed by law should be clearly defined: there should be "bright lines" that specify what one must do and what one need not do. Otherwise individuals do not have fair warning of what their legal duties are and cannot confidently plan their activities to avoid being held liable for their actions. And when individuals cannot confidently plan their activities for lack of fair warning, their right to liberty is being unfairly undermined by the law.

For Epstein, a basic test of any law that imposes a duty is that the law must be clear enough so that individuals can know in advance precisely what course of conduct will make them liable and what course will not. Epstein criticizes the Ames rule for flunking this test. And it flunks the test under the proposed interpretation that relies on the concept of reasonableness.

One might respond to Epstein by pointing out that the law, especially the private law, relies extensively on the concept of reasonableness. But Epstein could reply that the fact that the law is filled with bad things is no reason to add some more bad things to it. Even if we cannot eliminate the concept of reasonableness from the law, he might argue that we should minimize reliance on such vague ideas. To the extent that adopting the Ames rule would be moving in the opposite direction, it should not be adopted.

Epstein's argument against vagueness in the duties imposed by law places a high value on fair warning and on the individual's liberty to plan activities with the certain knowledge of how the law will regard those activities. But one might ask about the well-being and the rights of the persons who find themselves in life-threatening situations.

Epstein's response would be to deny that any individual has a moral right to assistance from someone who has not voluntarily agreed to provide that assistance. People do not have a right to get something for nothing from strangers. We have seen that Feinberg rejects this position, and it seems that we are faced here with fundamentally incompatible ways of understanding the rights-based approach to morality and law.

Even if one agrees with Epstein that individuals do not have a moral right to assistance, another argument against his view is possible: the added uncertainty that the Ames rule would introduce into the law is more than offset by the benefits the rule would bring to those who are saved from serious harm or death as a result of the rule. This argument brings us back to the approach Ames advocated: the law should promote the general good of society. Whether that approach can be modified to meet the objection that it places unreasonably heavy burdens on individuals to sacrifice for the good of others is an issue that philosophers are still debating. The controversy over the legal duty to aid thus leads to a difficult and continuing issue of moral philosophy.

SUMMARY

In this chapter, we have examined an area of law that does not receive as much attention from the public or philosophers as does constitutional or criminal law. Yet, private law raises issues of public policy and philosophy that are complex and important. The laws governing torts, contracts, and property establish the ground rules for crucial aspects of our lives: how the costs of the harms incurred in daily life are to be distributed; when the government will enforce the deals people make; what the government will defend when someone invokes his or her property rights. How the existing legal rules should be understood, and what rules we should have for these areas of social life, are questions that provide fertile ground for philosophical analysis and argument.

NOTES

1. The idea of harm as a setback to one's interests is rigorously explicated in Joel Feinberg, *Harm to Others* (New York: Oxford University Press, 1984), chap. 1.

2. Harms that the law does not prohibit at all are "private" in another sense: government does not act on behalf of society to prosecute those who commit such harms, nor does it provide a neutral forum in which private individuals can bring a lawsuit to gain compensation for the harm suffered.

3. The facilitative function of private law is examined in more detail in Chapter 6.

4. *Hotchkiss v. National Bank of New York,* 200 F. 287, 193 (S.D.N.Y. 1911).

5. Although many legal cases involving charges of sexual harassment are brought under Title VII of the federal Civil Rights Act of 1964, which forbids discrimination based on sex, it is also possible to bring such charges under a state tort claim. The Supreme Court has ruled that sexual harassment is a form of sex discrimination

prohibited by Title VII and that one form of illegal sexual harassment involves unwelcome sexual advances or actions of a sexual nature that create a "hostile environment." The Court has also ruled that a reasonable-person standard should determine what counts as a hostile environment. See *Harris v. Forklift Systems* 114 S. Ct. 367 (1994). Advocates of subcategorization would reject the reasonable-person standard for the reasons given later.

6. *Buch v. Amory Manufacturing Co.*, 69 N.H. 257, 44 A. 809 (1897), excerpted in *Cases and Materials on Torts,* 4th ed., R. A. Epstein, C. O. Gregory, and H. Kalven, Jr., eds. (Boston: Little, Brown, 1984), p. 373.

7. Philosophers call arguments based on the idea that our highest obligation is to promote the general good of society "utilitarian arguments." The philosophical theory behind such arguments is "utilitarianism," which will be explored in more detail in the next chapter. Utilitarianism seems to be the moral foundation of Ames's view of the law.

DISCUSSION QUESTIONS

1. In 1998, Jeremy Strohmeyer sexually assaulted and murdered a 7-year-old girl in the men's room of a Nevada casino. Strohmeyer had gone to the casino with his friend David Cash, a student at the University of California at Berkeley. Cash admitted that he had seen Strohmeyer drag the girl, Sherrice Iverson, into

the men's room and that Strohmeyer had confessed to murdering her after he came out. Cash did nothing to help the girl when Strohmeyer first grabbed her, nor did he notify the police of the murder.

Strohmeyer pled guilty to murder and was sentenced to life in prison. Many people called for the criminal prosecution of Cash for his failure to take any action to help the girl or notify the police after the murder. However, Nevada authorities determined that Cash had not committed any crime in the incident. Indeed, they implied that Cash's failure to help the girl had not even amounted to a tort for which he could be held liable. Cash remained a student at the University of California but was ostracized by many of the other students and was the target of public protests denouncing him.

Should there be a legal rule holding Cash responsible for his inaction? Should such inaction be a crime or only a tort? Is social ostracism and public denunciation sufficient "punishment" for Cash's behavior?

2. A basic moral principle to which most of us subscribe is that an individual can be legitimately held responsible only for what is within his or her control. Is that principle compatible with an objective approach to imposing tort liability? Consider your answer in light of the self-defense example.

ADDITIONAL READING

Ames, James Barr. "Law and Morals." *Harvard Law Review* 22 (1908), 97–113.

Atiyah, Patrick. *The Rise and Fall of Freedom of Contract.* Oxford University Press, 1979.

Cohen, Morris. "The Basis of Contract." *Harvard Law Review* 46 (1933), 553–592.

_____. "Property and Sovereignty." *Cornell Law Quarterly* 13 (1927), 8–30.

Coleman, Jules. "Contracts and Torts." *Law and Philosophy* 12 (1993), 71–93.

Cook, Walter Wheeler. "Privileges of Labor Unions in the Struggle for Life." *Yale Law Journal* 27 (1918), 779–801.

Epstein, Richard. "A Theory of Strict Liability." *Journal of Legal Studies* 2 (1973), 151–204.

Feinberg, Joel. "The Moral and Legal Responsibility of the Bad Samaritan." *Freedom and Fulfillment.* Princeton University Press, 1992.

Fletcher, George. "Fairness and Utility in Tort Theory." *Harvard Law Review* 85 (1972), 537–573.

Fried, Charles. *Contract as Promise.* Harvard University Press, 1981.

Fuller, Lon, and William Perdue. "The Reliance Interest in Contract Damages." *Yale Law Journal* 46 (1936–37), 52–96 and 373–420.

Gilmore, Grant. *The Death of Contract.* Ohio State University Press, 1974.

Hale, Robert. "Coercion and Distribution in a Supposedly Non-Coercive State." *Political Science Quarterly* 38 (1923), 470–494.

Holmes, Oliver Wendell, Jr. *The Common Law.* Little, Brown, 1963.

_____. "Privilege, Malice, and Intent." *Harvard Law Review* 8 (1894), 1–14.

Horwitz, Morton. *The Transformation of American Law, 1870–1960.* Oxford University Press, 1992.

Kronman, Anthony. "Contract Law and Distributive Justice." *Yale Law Journal* 89 (1980), 472–511.

Wells, Deborah, and Beverly Kracher. "Justice, Sexual Harassment, and the Reasonable Victim Standard." *Journal of Business Ethics* 12 (1993), 423–432.

White, G. Edward. *Tort Law in America.* Oxford University Press, 1980.

5

Criminal Law

TORTS AND CRIMES

In the previous chapter, we saw that the law of torts provides that compensation be given to those who are harmed by the illegal actions of others. If I punch you in the nose, then you can sue me for battery. If I carelessly do damage to your property or person, then you can sue me for negligence. Why, then, is it necessary to have a system of criminal law at all? Why is having a law of torts not enough?

Legal thinkers have taken two main approaches in providing a justification or rationale for the criminal law. One approach is utilitarian and is based on the idea that having a system of criminal law is necessary to promote the general good of society. The other is called retributivist. It is based on the idea that having a system of criminal law is necessary to ensure that wrongdoers receive what they deserve. Let us examine in more detail these two approaches.

A UTILITARIAN APPROACH

Bentham's Principle of Utility

A utilitarian approach to law rests on the idea that the law ought to promote the good of society as a whole. It stems from the general ethical theory, utilitarianism, which claims that the ultimate principle of morality is the principle of utility. One popular formulation of the principle of utility is this: one ought always to act so as to promote the greatest happiness for the greatest number. Utilitarians interpret the principle as applying to political institutions just as much as to private individuals. Governments and individuals alike stand under the basic moral obligation to do what promotes the greatest happiness for the greatest number.[1]

Utilitarians disagree with one another over how *happiness* is to be defined. In this chapter, we will focus on the definition offered by the father of modern utilitarianism, the eighteenth-century philosopher and social critic Jeremy Bentham.[2] Bentham understood happiness as the net balance of pleasure over pain. The more pleasure one experienced, and the less pain, the happier one was.

Bentham derived his conception of happiness from two ideas about good and bad. Pleasure is the only thing that is intrinsically good, that is, good in and of itself. Pain is the only thing that is intrinsically bad. Happiness can thus be understood as the net balance of what is intrinsically good over what is intrinsically bad. This point leads to another formulation of the principle of utility: one ought always to act so as to promote the greatest good for the greatest number.

Bentham contended that all of the morally relevant characteristics of pleasures and pains were quantitative in nature. His utilitarian morality would not recognize claims that some kinds of pleasure were qualitatively superior to others. The only differences that counted were ones that could, in principle, be measured: duration, intensity, and the like. Similarly, who experienced the pleasures did not matter: the pleasures of an aristocrat were no more important than those of a commoner. All that counted was how many individuals had the experience of pleasure and other quantitative aspects of the pleasure. The same went for pains: their quantitative aspects alone counted. The "felicific calculus" was Bentham's name for the set of rules for adding up the relevant dimensions of pleasure and pain in order to determine what course of action satisfied the principle of utility.

While the law of torts requires that wrongdoers compensate their victims for the harm done, the criminal law provides for the punishment of a wrongdoer. Since punishment involves some form of pain, utilitarians demand that there be some gain possible that more than makes up for the pain inflicted on the wrongdoer. For the utilitarian, the question of whether the existence of a system of criminal law can be justified thus comes down to the question of whether the practice of inflicting pain on criminals produces gains for society that more than make up for the pain.

For a utilitarian, if punishment caused pain to the wrongdoer but did nothing else, it could not be justified. It would simply be making matters worse by adding the pain of the wrongdoer to the pain of the victim. However, utilitarians have cited a number of factors as helping to provide a justification for criminal punishment. These factors are the "utilitarian aims" of punishment. In the eyes of a typical utilitarian, they more than make up for the pain inflicted on the criminal.

The Utilitarian Aims of Punishment

First and foremost is the aim of general deterrence. Punishing wrongdoers helps to deter other, potential wrongdoers. If pain to potential victims can be averted by using criminal punishment to deter potential wrongdoers, then criminal punishment can be justified from a utilitarian perspective. It will promote the greatest good for the greatest number if the pain prevented through deterrence is greater than the pain inflicted on the criminal wrong-doers. Punishment can provide such general deterrence, according to many utilitarians, because the chances of being caught and punished will create an incentive for at least some potential wrongdoers to obey the law.

A second utilitarian aim of punishment is called "special deterrence," which refers to the deterrence of the wrongdoer herself. If punishing her for her crimes helps deter her from future crimes, then the greatest good for the great-est number might be promoted. The fact of punishment, combined with the prospects of having to undergo it again, can create an incentive for a past wrongdoer to toe the line in the future.

A third utilitarian aim is referred to as "incapacitation," which is sometimes confused with special deterrence. Like special deterrence, it concerns someone who is being punished for a crime already committed. But unlike special deter-rence, it does not have to do with using punishment to create an incentive for him to obey the law in the future. Rather, it has to do with using punishment to limit his opportunity to commit further crimes. Imprisonment is the most common form of incapacitation. By isolating the wrongdoer from society and carefully regulating his conduct around the clock, imprisonment decreases his opportunities for additional crime. Of course, incapacitation typically ceases as soon as he is released from prison. But if special deterrence works, the punish-ment will continue to have its effect even after release.

A fourth utilitarian aim of punishment is rehabilitation, also often confused with special deterrence. The aim of rehabilitation is to change the moral char-acter of a wrongdoer so that it is not necessary to threaten her with punish-ment in order for her to obey the law. She will obey the law in the future as a matter of moral conscience, not because she fears being caught and punished once again. Thus, if rehabilitation works for a certain person, there is no need for special deterrence.

All of these utilitarian aims for punishment have one crucial feature in common. They involve inflicting pain now on the wrongdoer in order to pre-vent greater pain from being inflicted on society in the future.

A utilitarian justification for criminal punishment does not require that all four aims be successfully accomplished. Many people, for example, reject the idea that criminal punishment can rehabilitate wrongdoers. Even if they are correct, this does not defeat a utilitarian rationale for criminal punish-ment. For it still may be true that criminal punishment could be justified from a utilitarian viewpoint on the basis of general and special deterrence and incapacitation.

Criticisms of the Utilitarian Approach

The utilitarian justification for criminal punishment has been subjected to many criticisms. One of the most persistent is the claim that utilitarianism entails the morally unacceptable notion that innocent persons should some-times be deliberately punished by the authorities.

For example, suppose that a community is being terrorized by a criminal who has committed a number of murders. The police cannot find the perpetrator. However, there is an innocent person who could be easily framed. The community will then think that the perpetrator has been caught and its anxiety will be relieved. And the actual perpetrator may well be smart enough to cease his crime spree at that point, lest he push his luck too far and be caught. The innocent person who is framed no doubt suffers great pain. But the good to the community would seem to outweigh that pain, if, as utilitarianism insists, only the quantitative features of pleasure and pain can be properly taken into account.

The critics of utilitarianism argue that this kind of example shows that the theory is defective: any theory that approves of the deliberate punishment of an innocent person on the ground that the greater good of society will be served must be defective. The punishment of the innocent is inherently unjust and cannot be justified by claiming that it will maximize social happiness.

Notice that we are not dealing here with a case in which the police mistakenly think that the person is guilty. In the example, they know that he is innocent, but they can fabricate evidence to make him look guilty. Any system of criminal punishment will sometimes mistakenly prosecute and convict innocent persons. The point of the critics is that any acceptable system must refuse to prosecute and convict persons known by the authorities to be innocent. They argue that a utilitarian system flunks this test.

Utilitarians respond by arguing that the practice of framing innocent persons would not in fact serve the greater good of society. This is because the practice would cause a great deal of anxiety and fear among people generally: no one could be sure that he or she was immune to being framed. Thus, utilitarians claim that the practice of refusing to prosecute and convict those known by the authorities to be innocent actually promotes the greatest happiness for the greatest number, which is precisely why the practice is justified.

Critics reply that if the practice of framing innocents were kept secret from the public, then it would not cause general anxiety and fear. In that case, the practice could promote the greatest happiness for the greatest number, and so it would have to be approved by utilitarian thinking.

Utilitarians counter that the secret power to frame innocents would likely be abused by the authorities. The authorities would employ such power to promote their own interests at the expense of society. They would frame political and economic competitors in order to get more political power and economic wealth for themselves. When the authorities can ride roughshod over the rule of law in this way, the result is very bad for society. The principle of utility, properly applied, leads again to the conclusion that the authorities should not have the power to frame innocents, whether that power is kept secret or not.

Critics respond that the utilitarian keeps missing the point: one cannot entirely exclude the possibility of situations in which framing innocents would serve the greater good of society. The situations may be very rare, but they are not impossible. And in those situations, utilitarians are committed to approving the punishment of innocents.

The critics elaborate on this point by claiming that a central flaw in the utilitarian theory is that it focuses exclusively on the quantitative dimensions of pleasure and pain: how much, how many, and so on. The guilt or innocence of a person is not some quantitative feature of a person or her pains and pleasures. You cannot simply add up pleasures and pains on some kind of tote board, without taking into account whether the persons involved are innocent. The pain of an innocent person who has been punished for a crime she did not commit cannot be morally equated with the pain of a guilty person who has been punished for a crime she did commit, even if the quantitative aspects of the pain are exactly the same.

In addition, the critics argue that the utilitarian approach fails to treat individuals with the respect they are owed. It regards each individual merely as a means for promoting the overall happiness of society. That is why it can accept the punishment of innocents, for innocent individuals are not different from any other on the utilitarian approach: they exist only to be used for producing the greatest happiness for the greatest number.

Yet, the critics claim, such a view of individuals is morally unacceptable. Each individual has an inherent dignity that makes it wrong to regard her merely as a resource for maximizing the total good of society. Instead, dignity requires that each individual be treated in accordance with what she deserves. Accordingly, the idea of individual desert is at the center of the main alternative to utilitarianism, the retributivist approach.

A RETRIBUTIVIST APPROACH

Justice and Desert

Justice is served when those who are guilty of crimes are punished for their crimes. It is violated when the innocent are punished. According to retributivists, the reason is that the innocent do not deserve punishment, but the guilty do. The guilty deserve punishment because their actions have caused (or have risked causing) wrongful harm to someone.[3] Moreover, the harm the guilty inflict is not inconsequential but rather sufficiently serious for society to be concerned about. As long as these persons have no valid excuse or justification for what they have done, they deserve to be punished for their conduct. And the purpose of society's criminal justice system, according to the retributivist, is to give the guilty what they deserve.

Some critics of the retributive approach hold that advocating the punishment of criminals "because they deserve it" is actually advocating a thinly disguised form of revenge. Proponents of retributive punishment, the critics claim, are really basing their view on the idea that society should take vengeance on lawbreakers by paying them back with harm for the harm they have inflicted on society.

It may be true that a system of criminal law based on the retributivist approach would satisfy to some degree the desire for vengeance that persons naturally feel when they, or those with whom they identify, are victimized by the wrongful acts of others. We saw in Chapter 1 that one of the advantages of the rule of law was that it provided an orderly and restrained way of satisfying the desire for vengeance. But it is quite another thing to say that a retributivist system of criminal law is based on the notion that society should seek revenge against lawbreakers.

Retributivists would argue that there is a crucial distinction between the desire for vengeance and the desire to see justice done. Retributivism rests on the latter desire, not the former. The desire for vengeance seeks to harm someone, without necessarily stopping to ask whether the harm is really deserved. Like the Furies of ancient Greek mythology, the desire is blind to crucial moral concepts and considerations. It does not necessarily ask whether the individual against whom revenge is sought had an excuse or justification for the harm he inflicted. It does not necessarily distinguish between accidental and intentional harm. Vengeance per se only knows that harm was done and only wants to repay the one who did it by harming him in return.

In stark contrast, say the proponents of retributivism, their view of punishment rests on the desire for justice. As such, it necessarily incorporates moral concepts and considerations. It does not ignore whether an individual has an excuse or justification for the harm he did. It is not blind to the difference between accidental and intentional harm. To the contrary, such considerations are crucial to determining whether a person really deserves punishment.

Yet, one still might press the question: Why is punishment the appropriate way to treat persons who violate the criminal law? Exactly why do lawbreakers deserve punishment? Different versions of retributivism explain the appropriateness of punishment in different ways, each giving its own account of the crucial link between criminal punishment and criminal desert.

Why Punishment Is Deserved

According to one version of retributivism, punishment is an emphatic way of blaming and condemning the criminal. The criminal deserves blame and condemnation because of the wrongful harm he has inflicted (or risked inflicting). And emphatic blame is merited because the criminal law prohibits those kinds of harm that society rightly regards as most serious. Punishment is a relatively harsh form of blame and, as such, is appropriate for those who are guilty of relatively serious harms.

Another form of retributivism focuses on the educational and communicative aspects punishment. It holds that punishment is an emphatic way of communicating to the criminal that he has inflicted (or risked inflicting) wrongful harm on someone. Punishment teaches the criminal a harsh lesson. The harshness is appropriate on account of the serious harm the criminal has done (or risked). The main purpose of the punishment is not so much to blame the criminal (though the criminal does deserve blame) as to make him appreciate the wrongness of what he has done.

A third version of retributivism focuses on the unfair advantage that the criminal gains by violating rules that others follow. The criminal takes advantage of the law-abiding members of society by refusing to abide by the restrictions that others accept. The willingness of the law-abiding members of society to restrain themselves and obey the rules of the criminal law makes a relatively peaceful and orderly society possible. The criminal, however, refuses to similarly restrain himself: he takes the advantages of living in a peaceful and orderly society plus the advantages that come from breaking the rules that make such a society possible. He is, in effect, "double-dipping." This behavior is fundamentally unfair to those who restrain themselves and follow the rules.

On this third version of retributivism, the purpose of criminal punishment is to cancel out the unfair advantage that the criminal takes. In committing a crime, the criminal raises himself above the rest of society; he tells others, "You must play by the rules, but I am above the rules." In punishing the criminal, society brings him back down, nullifying the unfair advantage he took.

In the past, some retributivist thinkers argued that all criminals deserved punishment, regardless of the justice or injustice of their society and its laws. Few, if any, retributivist philosophers would accept such a view today. It is generally accepted that a precondition for the applicability of a pure retributivist analysis is that society and its system of criminal law be relatively fair and just. The question of exactly when and why disobedience to the criminal law is justified is a complex one. The main point to keep in mind here, though, is straightforward: nothing inherent to retributivism requires it to claim that anyone in any society who breaks the criminal law is always and necessarily deserving of punishment. The most convincing versions of retributivism hold, instead, that where society and its system of criminal law are relatively fair and just, those who commit crimes are generally deserving of punishment.

Criticisms of Retributivism

Morally Indifferent Conduct Retributivist justifications for the criminal law hinge on the claim that criminals engage in conduct deserving of punishment. The idea is that we should have rules of criminal law because certain conduct merits punishment, not that the conduct merits punishment because it has violated the rules of criminal law. After all, the point is to show that we should have a system of criminal law in the first place. It would be circular reasoning to say that criminals deserve punishment because they broke the rules and then to argue that we should have the rules because those who break them deserve punishment. The retributivist argument presupposes that the reason why conduct that is punishable under the criminal law deserves punishment is independent of the existence of the criminal law. Such conduct "naturally" merits punishment, which is why society should set up a system of criminal law to dish out the punishment.

The retributivist argument works best for the kinds of actions we immediately think of when we consider what the criminal law prohibits: murder, rape, theft, kidnapping, child molestation. It seems convincing, at least at first glance, that such actions naturally deserve punishment. But some conduct prohibited by the criminal law cannot be plausibly described as "naturally" meriting punishment. Public intoxication, the possession of a controlled substance, or even the possession of a concealed firearm do not seem to naturally call for punishment.[4] If the law prohibits them, then we might agree that those who do engage in these activities anyway deserve punishment. But in and of themselves the activities do not seem to call for punishment. They seem "morally indifferent."

The retributivist might respond by arguing that the criminalization of morally indifferent conduct can be seen as a kind of safeguard against conduct that is naturally blameworthy. People who are drunk in public tend to do things like harm property and start fights. People who carry concealed weapons may well use them to commit crimes. But the problem with this line of response is that it seems to be relapsing into a utilitarian approach, focusing on the prevention of harm to society.

The retributivist must explain why a person who is drunk in public deserves punishment for that, and the fact that public drunkenness is correlated with reprehensible conduct seems besides the point. After all, many people who are drunk in public do not do reprehensible things, so why do they deserve punishment just because others who are drunk in public do engage in reprehensible conduct? The retributivist must explain how public drunkenness as such naturally deserves punishment.

The Idea of Natural Desert In any event, the idea that any conduct—even murder or theft—naturally deserves criminal punishment can begin to look dubious on closer inspection. Criminal punishment refers to an organized and official response of society. It entails more than society generally thinking badly of someone or even criticizing and shunning the person. It involves the establishment by society of formal rules and of official institutions for enforcing those rules. Can one cogently argue that society should have such a system of rules and enforcement because certain conduct naturally merits the punishment that the system inflicts?

It is unclear that the argument can be made successfully. Retributivist justifications for the criminal law tend to conflate blame, punishment, and criminal punishment. These concepts must be clearly distinguished: one cannot simply assume that those who deserve blame thereby deserve punishment or that those who deserve punishment thereby deserve criminal punishment.

There is little doubt that murder, theft, and so forth naturally call for blame and condemnation. But blame and condemnation need not take the form of punishment. Someone can be blamed for his conduct even if he is not punished for it. To blame someone is to judge him (or his conduct) deficient in some morally significant respect. To punish someone is to intentionally deprive him of some good (other than the good of not being judged deficient), typically on the basis of the judgment that he is morally deficient. And to criminally punish someone is to punish him through the official organs of society established to enforce formal rules of law. Retributivist arguments must cogently show that the conduct prohibited by the criminal law naturally merits the kind of punishment that the criminal law inflicts.

As we have seen, a standard retributivist move is to claim that the conduct prohibited by the criminal law is especially harmful to others and to society as a whole, and so it deserves the especially harsh punishments of the criminal law. But it is doubtful that the forms of punishment provided by criminal law are necessarily harsher than more informal forms.

The criminal law provides for fines, imprisonment, and execution. In many cases, fines and even short terms of imprisonment may actually be less harsh than the social stigma and ostracism that comes from being a "criminal." The stigma and ostracism are not an official part of the criminal punishment. They are the kinds of penalty that societies without formal systems of criminal law rely on, and they can be very powerful. So even if we agree that certain conduct deserves harsh punishment, it does not follow that the punishment must take the form that the criminal law provides.

One could, of course, argue that in a large society like ours, stigma and ostracism would be relatively ineffective in deterring or incapacitating wrongdoers. Only fines, imprisonment, and execution will effectively deter potential wrongdoers or incapacitate those who have shown themselves prepared to do wrong. Such an argument is very persuasive, but it rests on utilitarian considerations, and what we are looking for is a retributivist justification of the criminal law.

Moral Blameworthiness and the Rule of Law Another difficulty with the retributivist justification of criminal law stems from one of the basic moral concepts it employs. The retributivist argument rests on the idea that the criminal is blameworthy for what she has done. This blameworthiness is not merely legal; it is moral. Remember that the argument is trying to justify the existence of the criminal justice system and that it would be circular reasoning to claim that there should be such a system because criminals do things that are legally blameworthy. The moral blameworthiness of the criminal's conduct is taken to justify the existence of a system that inflicts criminal punishment.

Yet, the criminal law neglects to take into account all factors that are relevant to moral blameworthiness, and it seems perfectly justified in neglecting to do so. One of the more obvious ways in which the criminal law screens out factors relevant to moral blame is that it does not allow accused criminals to invoke their motives as a defense. A person who steals in order to feed her hungry children cannot defend herself against criminal charges by claiming that her motive was a good one. Even if she is morally blameless on account of her motive, she is legally guilty. Surely her motive is a mitigating factor to be considered when it comes to sentencing. But the law declares it irrelevant to the question of guilt.

Excluding considerations such as motive seems justified because it makes the question of a person's guilt or innocence more clear-cut and less subject to relatively subjective assessments. Indeed, the rule of law requires that criminal guilt and innocence be determined by rules that clearly demarcate conduct that is prohibited from conduct that is allowed. Introducing all factors relevant to a person's moral blameworthiness—her motive, her childhood upbringing, her personal problems, and so on—would make such clear demarcations impossible.

Moreover, another and deeper conflict arises between the rule of law and the retributive argument for criminal punishment. If moral blameworthiness is the justification for having a system of criminal punishment, then it is unclear why we should refrain from punishing persons who are sufficiently blameworthy, even if we know that they have not violated any existing criminal law. Inflicting such punishment would, of course, be a gross violation of the principles of the rule of law.

Those principles require that all conduct subject to criminal punishment be defined clearly and in advance by society's official institutions. If you do something that is morally reprehensible but not a violation of the criminal law, the rule of law demands that you not be criminally punished. If you do something morally blameworthy, though not as reprehensible, and yet it is a violation of the criminal law, then the rule of law permits you to be criminally punished. These consequences of the rule of law seem to contradict the rationale for criminal punishment offered by retributivists.

Ironically, retributivists run into the same problem that they place at the feet of utilitarians: the punishment of those who have violated no criminal law. If utilitarianism seems to imply that such punishment is justified when the total social good can be advanced, retributivism seems to imply that it is justified when the individual is morally blameworthy to a sufficient degree. Both implications go contrary to the rule of law, and together they raise serious questions about the adequacy of either theory.

THE THERAPEUTIC MODEL

Rehabilitation, Not Punishment

Some thinkers have argued that we should reject the very idea that criminals ought to be punished. This line of thought can be traced back as far as Plato, who argued that it is unjust ever to knowingly inflict harm on anyone. His reasoning was that harming any person makes him a worse person, and a worse person is even more likely to commit unjust acts. Justice cannot allow us to make a bad person more unjust. Instead, it demands that we make bad people better and thus requires that we treat them in a way incompatible with harming them. If we understand punishment as the knowing infliction of harm in return for some offense or transgression, then Plato's position entails that punishment should be rejected in favor of some kind of rehabilitative approach.

Modern critics of punishment follow this line of thinking, although with a twist. Plato thought of bad people as suffering from a moral disease of the soul. In his view, curing that moral disease required philosophical enlightenment. Modern critics of punishment think of criminals and other "bad apples" as suffering from psychological disorders. In their view, curing such disorders requires psychiatric or psychological therapy. Thus, they contend that the punishment model should be replaced by a therapeutic model. The job of government should not be to punish lawbreakers but rather to help ensure that they are cured.

Defenders of the therapeutic model make both utilitarian and retributivist arguments. On the utilitarian side, they attack the practice of punishment as one that fails to promote the total good of society. Punishment actually adds to social misery, in their view, by reinforcing the criminal tendencies of the person punished. In response to the harm society inflicts on the criminal, the criminal's hatred of society grows. Moreover, while being punished, a first-time convict is exposed to other criminals, more hardened in their criminality than she is. She learns their criminal ways and methods, and her antisocial values are reinforced. In addition, the social stigma attached to criminality means that those punished as criminals will have a very difficult time getting back into society and becoming productive members of it.

What about the deterrent effects of punishment? Defenders of the therapeutic model claim that such effects are minimal. In their view, the main problem with utilitarian arguments based on deterrence is that they fail to recognize that criminality is the product of a psychological disorder. Threats of punishment can deter persons who control their conduct rationally, but we are dealing here with people whose mental disorders mean that they do not act rationally. Criminals do not respond to incentives in the same way rational persons do.

Proponents of the therapeutic model sometimes also invoke the retributivist idea of desert, although in a reverse kind of way. For they claim that the criminal does not really deserve punishment, and so if we are committed to giving people what they deserve, we cannot consistently advocate punishment. The criminal is not to blame because he is not responsible for the psychological disorder that is the cause of his criminal behavior. One proponent of the therapeutic model puts it this way: "It is our basic tenet that the criminal is a product of a vicious, emotionally unhealthy environment in the creation of which he had no hand and over which he had no control."[5] How would a therapeutic system work? The psychiatrist Karl Menninger was one of the leading proponents of such a system, describing it this way:

> [T]he convicted offender would be detained indefinitely, pending a decision as to whether and how and when to reintroduce him successfully into society. All the skill and knowledge of modern behavioral science would be used to examine his personality assets, liabilities and potentialities, the environment from which he came, its effects upon him, and his effects upon it. Having arrived at some diagnostic grasp of the offender's personality, those in charge can decide whether there is a chance that he can be redirected into a mutually satisfactory adaptation to the world. If so, the most suitable techniques in education, industrial training, group administration, and psychotherapy should be selectively applied.[6]

Criticisms of the Therapeutic Model

Critics of the therapeutic model have attacked it on a number of different grounds. First, some argue that it is impractical because we do not really have the understanding of human psychology that would be needed for it to work. Menninger's system is run by psychiatric and psychological experts who are given virtually complete power over the offender. At the very least, such experts should be expected to know which therapies work to change the behavior and character of persons who act in antisocial ways and which do not. Yet, it is very dubious to claim that anyone really has such knowledge.

But even if the experts did have such knowledge, problems persist with the therapeutic model. The model would seriously damage the rule of law in that it would give virtually uncontrolled discretion to psychological experts over the liberty and lives of offenders. Having expert knowledge does not necessarily mean that one has the moral integrity to use it wisely and properly. To eliminate the abuse of such uncontrolled discretion is one of the principal aims of the rule of law, and the therapeutic system would be very vulnerable to such abuse.

Moreover, the rationale behind the therapeutic approach implies that persons diagnosed as having a so-called "criminal personality" should be held for treatment even before they actually commit any crimes. Such preventative detention and treatment would be good for society and good for the individual, if the therapeutic approach is sound. The approach claims that crime is a symptom of some underlying mental disorder and that society's response should be to treat the disorder. In that case, it would seem to make more sense to treat the disorder before it causes social and individual harm.

The problem with such preventative detention is that it seriously violates the rule of law. Persons are deprived of their liberty by the official organs of society, even though they have not done anything that society has defined as a crime.

Defenders of the therapeutic approach may argue that the rule of law is applicable when government seeks to punish but is unnecessary where society has adopted a system of therapeutic rehabilitation to replace a system of punishment. However, such a view seems to fly in the face of what history and experience teach us.

For example, the Soviet Union treated many of those who violated its criminal laws as mental cases in need of therapy. The result was not some benign system that worked for everyone's benefit but rather grotesque abuses in which persons were subjected to degrading and inhumane treatment at the hands of those who were trying to implant in them the "socially correct" way of thinking.

Although a therapeutic system in Western countries would likely not be as bad as the Soviet system, it would still be subject to serious abuse. Moreover, it is difficult to see how any therapeutic system could avoid some kind of punishment to control those who would not voluntarily submit to therapy. Those individuals would have to be locked up and carefully monitored to prevent them from escaping. Although this may be done in the name of "curing" the persons, the involuntary deprivation of their liberty seems tantamount to punishment.

Advocates of the rule of law have long realized that it is important to restrain government's power to deprive persons of their liberty, not only when government intends to harm people but also when it intends to do good for them. For the efforts of government to do good cannot be entirely trusted. It seems naive to think that, if only we had a system of therapeutic treatment run by experts, then we could dispense with the rule of law in dealing with those accused of crimes or of having a criminal personality.

AMOUNT OF PUNISHMENT

A Utilitarian Approach

Assuming that it is legitimate for government to punish criminals, what standards should dictate the amount of punishment? Again, the utilitarian and retributive approaches yield different answers. Let us begin with utilitarianism.

The purpose of criminal punishment, in the utilitarian view, is to reduce the amount of pain in society as a whole over the long run by inflicting pain on the lawbreaker. In order to simplify matters, let us focus on the potential deterrent effects of punishment. As we have seen, there are ways other than deterrence in which punishment might reduce pain in society as a whole and thereby promote the greatest happiness for the greatest number. But deterrence is the effect that utilitarians tend to emphasize as contributing most to maximizing social happiness.

Suppose that a certain punishment is currently being employed for a given crime. Also suppose the same deterrent effect can be achieved by using a punishment that is less severe than the one currently employed. In the utilitarian view, this would mean that the current punishment is too severe: it inflicts an unnecessarily large amount of pain on the criminal. Recall that for the utilitarian, the pain of the criminal counts too in performing the calculations of the felicific calculus: that pain must be entered as a negative amount in calculating the greatest good for the greatest number. If the same overall deterrent effect can be achieved with a lesser penalty, then maximizing overall happiness requires that the lesser penalty be used.

On the other hand, if increasing the severity of a punishment can increase its deterrent effect, then the severity should be increased as long as the added deterrent effect is greater than the increased severity of the penalty. Thus, if increasing a penalty by twenty units of pain would deter additional crimes that would have caused thirty units of pain, then the penalty should be increased by that amount. Indeed, the penalty should be increased up to the point where the added severity is exactly matched by the additional deterrent value.

It is often said that punishment should be proportional to the seriousness of a crime: the more serious a crime, the more severe should be the punishment meted out for it. For the utilitarian, this proportionality principle must be understood in terms of the aim of maximizing social happiness. As a rule, more serious crimes inflict more pain on their victims and thus do more damage to the happiness of society. For the utilitarian, inflicting severe pain on those who commit such crimes could well be justified by the fact that such severe pain is still outweighed by the prevention through deterrence of even more severe pain to society.

On the other hand, inflicting severe punishments for minor crimes could detract from total social happiness by producing a net increase in pain. The deterrent effect of punishment can almost always be increased by increasing the punishment, but a greater deterrent effect does not always mean greater happiness in society. For the crime of bouncing a $20 check, life in prison will have a greater deterrent effect than three months in jail. But a utilitarian would argue that the pain inflicted on check bouncers by a life sentence is greater than the pain one prevents by using such a harsh punishment for such a relatively minor crime.

Criticisms of the Utilitarian Approach

Critics will respond that utilitarianism is again going astray. It is possible that, in at least some situations, imposing a severe punishment for a relatively minor crime such as bouncing a $20 check would have a deterrent effect on enough potential check bouncers that the total pain prevented by the punishment outweighs the pain inflicted by it. The utilitarian theory entails the judgment that, in such situations, the severe punishment should be imposed. But critics contend that such a judgment is unacceptable: no matter how big the deterrent effect might be, it is unjust to punish a minor crime like bouncing a $20 check with a severe penalty like life imprisonment.

In the eyes of its critics, the basic problems with utilitarianism remain the same, whether it is applied to the question of whether we should have criminal punishment or the question of what the proper amount of punishment is. Utilitarianism, they say, sometimes fails to give people what justice requires and violates human dignity. Critics are thus led to formulate an alternative, retributivist approach to the question of how much punishment may be legitimately inflicted on a criminal.

A Retributivist Approach

The retributivist approach begins with the idea that the severity of a punishment must be proportional to the seriousness of the crime. But this proportionality principle is not interpreted in terms of the goal of maximizing total social happiness. Instead, it is interpreted in terms of the degree of punishment the criminal's conduct deserves.

One common version of retributivism focuses on how morally blameworthy the criminal's conduct naturally is. In its most persuasive form, this version looks to the amount of harm the criminal causes (or risks causing) and the degree to which he is culpable (that is, morally to blame) for the harm.[7] The greater the harm, or the greater the culpability, the greater the blameworthiness.

For example, killing someone generally causes more harm than stealing from him, and intentional killing is generally more culpable than negligent killing. Thus, first-degree murder is more blameworthy and so deserves more punishment than both vehicular homicide (a form of negligent killing) and grand larceny. More generally, the punishment a criminal receives should be calibrated to reflect how morally blameworthy the kind of conduct he has engaged in is.

Notice that this approach differs from one that demands that the same harm be inflicted on the criminal as he inflicted on his victim: "an eye for an eye and a tooth for a tooth." Such a demand is called the *lex talionis* (law of retaliation), and it is sometimes thought to be an essential part of the retributivist approach to punishment. But it is more accurately thought of as belonging to the mind-set that existed before the establishment of the rule of law, when uncontrolled vengeance reigned. *Lex talionis* is the principle of the Furies, not a principle that could be accepted by a society ruled by law. For example, unlike vengeance, the rule of law distinguishes between accidental and intentional harm. And a retributivist approach that focuses on the natural blameworthiness of the criminal's conduct insists that such distinctions be taken into account when determining how much punishment a criminal deserves.[8]

Criticisms of Retributivism

This version of retributivism runs into the same difficulties encountered by the retributivist rationale for having a criminal justice system. Some crimes, like public drunkenness or carrying a concealed weapon, do not seem naturally blameworthy in and of themselves. Yet, those who commit those crimes seem clearly to deserve punishment.

More importantly, there is a conflict between the rule of law and the idea that the punishment of the criminal should reflect the moral blameworthiness of his conduct. The law does not take into full account all factors relevant to moral blameworthiness, and it seems that it could not do so while abiding by the principles of the rule of law.

The rule of law requires not only that crimes be defined in relatively clear and objective fashion but that the punishments for each crime be specified in the same way. The power of government to declare punishments must be controlled and regulated by relatively clear and objective rules, or else government will be free to impose arbitrary and capricious punishments. Yet, it seems that it is impossible to specify punishments using such rules while at the same time taking into full account all factors relevant to the moral blameworthiness of the criminal's conduct.

The rule of law is consistent with some degree of discretion on the part of the judge (or jury) in sentencing criminals. But it demands that such discretion be cabined, that is, that it operate within limits. The requirement to operate within legally defined limits means that a judge's decision making will be significantly different from what it would be were the judge to assess the natural blameworthiness of the defendant's conduct and impose a punishment based wholly on that assessment.

For example, some judges might think that the moral blameworthiness of the "white-collar" crime of illegally polluting the environment is insufficient to justify a prison sentence. These judges might think that from the perspective of moral blameworthiness, only a fine should be imposed. But if the law requires a prison sentence, such judges must set their moral beliefs aside and impose the sentence, though they may give the lightest prison sentence authorized under the law. Similarly, if other judges think the law too lenient on white-collar environmental crime, they are nonetheless barred by the rule of law from imposing a longer prison sentence than the maximum authorized by law.

Retributivists might argue that if white-collar environmental crime does not really deserve imprisonment (or, alternatively, if it deserves longer imprisonment), then the law should be changed to reflect the true moral blameworthiness of such conduct. But here we run head-on into another problem: in our pluralist society, people have conflicting views about moral blameworthiness. Some think that corporate pollution is extremely blameworthy—sometimes akin to murder—and would impose very severe prison sentences. Others think illegal pollution is only mildly blameworthy and should only be fined. And still others think that polluting the environment should not be a crime at all and that it should be handled by tort law exclusively.

One of the main purposes of the rule of law in a pluralist society is to establish ground rules that everyone can understand: the lines of the criminal law are to be drawn, and the penalties for crossing them are to be specified, so that anyone can know where the lines are and what penalties one is subject to for crossing them. Persons who cross those lines generally seem to deserve the specified punishments, whatever their "true" moral blameworthiness. If the idea of criminal desert is to be based on that of moral blameworthiness, we seem to need a version of retributivism that calibrates punishment to the blameworthiness of breaking the rules rather than to the natural blameworthiness of the criminal's conduct.

Davis's Version of Retributivism

In recent years the philosopher Michael Davis has developed such a version of retributivism. Like other retributivist approaches, Davis's approach holds that criminals are morally blameworthy for their conduct. But unlike other retributivists, he does not view criminal blameworthiness as a function of how naturally blameworthy the criminal's conduct is. Murder is surely naturally blameworthy, apart from society's rules that forbid it. Davis does not question that point. Instead, his idea is that criminal blameworthiness depends on something other than the natural blameworthiness of criminal conduct. That is why one can be criminally blameworthy for morally indifferent conduct such as public drunkenness or carrying a concealed weapon, according to Davis. But what is the something else?

In Davis's approach, conduct is morally blameworthy when it violates a system of rules that meets the following three conditions: (1) each person benefits from the rules, but only when others are generally willing to abide by them; (2) following the rules often requires a person to exercise self-restraint; and (3) persons are willing to exercise that self-restraint but only because they expect others to do so as well.[9] Davis argues that persons who violate rules that meet these three conditions are taking unfair advantage of those who play by the rules. The rule breakers are getting the benefits that come from the existence of the rules, but they are shirking their responsibility to do their part in upholding the rules. They are cheaters.

In Davis's analysis, criminals are essentially cheaters, which is why their conduct is morally blameworthy. Criminal conduct violates rules that meet the three conditions, and so takes unfair advantage of those who play by the rules of the criminal law. The moral blameworthiness of criminal conduct often extends beyond the mere fact that it amounts to cheating. Murder is blameworthy because it breaks the rules, but not only because it breaks the rules. Yet, criminal blameworthiness, as opposed to a more inclusive concept of moral blameworthiness, depends on the criminal's violation of the rules and not on any additional grounds for blame.

For Davis, then, punishment can be seen as the price that society attaches to infractions of its official rules. And the degree of punishment society imposes for each crime should be a function of criminal blameworthiness. Society's most severe punishment should be reserved for those crimes that take the greatest unfair advantage of those who play by the rules. And for each lesser crime, the punishment should be calibrated to reflect the degree of unfair advantage it represents relative to the other crimes.[10]

Davis's approach is not meant to answer the question "What conduct should be criminalized?" It leaves that question open, except to say that society needs to keeps some minimal level of order by means of its criminal laws. Instead, the aim of the theory is to explain the sense in which criminal conduct deserves punishment.

We have seen that other retributivist approaches run into trouble by using an inclusive concept of moral blameworthiness to explain why criminal conduct deserves punishment. Davis's theory avoids those problems by narrowing its focus to just one aspect of overall moral blameworthiness, namely, the unfairness in breaking rules from which one benefits because others have exercised the self-restraint needed to follow the rules. But if other versions of retributivism operate with an excessively broad concept of moral blameworthiness, is Davis's excessively narrow? Is it really possible to separate the question of what conduct should be criminalized from the question of why criminal conduct deserves punishment?

Criticisms of Davis

Do Homosexuals Deserve Punishment? Suppose that in a certain society homosexual conduct is criminal. Do those engaged in such an activity deserve punishment? For a retributivist who operates with a broad concept of blameworthiness, the answer will hinge on whether there is anything naturally blameworthy about homosexual conduct.[11] If the answer is no, then the conclusion will be that homosexual conduct does not morally deserve punishment and so should be decriminalized wherever it is against the rules. That seems like a sensible approach to the issue.

The approach that Davis's theory dictates, on the other hand, is more problematic. For his theory, the key question is: Are those engaged in homosexual conduct taking unfair advantage of the law-abiding members of society by failing to exercise the necessary self-restraint? That certainly seems like a relevant question, but how would Davis's theory go about answering it?

The theory requires us to set aside questions about whether homosexual conduct is naturally blameworthy and focus on the question of whether practicing homosexuals are taking unfair advantage of the law-abiding members of society. And to answer that question, we must ask whether the system of criminal law meets the three conditions that Davis sets out.

It would not be very difficult for a system of law to meet Davis's conditions, at least as he understands them. Davis argues that, even if there are unjust laws, those who violate them are generally taking unfair advantage of others. Thus, he writes:

> In most societies, I would, I think, have no trouble showing almost any criminal how his crime took unfair advantage. I need only show him that, though he may be a victim of injustice, his crime did nothing to make society more just overall and then ask him to consider how much worse his life would be if all police were fired, the courts closed, the prisons emptied, the law book burned, and everyone allowed the same license he took. Hobbes is a text for explaining law to criminals.[12]

The application of these remarks to the criminalization of homosexual conduct seems straightforward. Those who engage in such conduct when it is against the rules are taking unfair advantage of those who play by the rules, even if the rules are unjust. Such criminals would be much worse off without any criminal justice system: the Hobbesian state of nature is, after all, worse than living in a society that prohibits the kind of sexual activity in which one desires to engage. And being in constant fear for one's life does tend to dampen one's sex drive anyway. Moreover, homosexual conduct itself, as opposed to political demonstrations or organized campaigns to repeal antisodomy laws, is not likely to do much to advance the cause of winning equal treatment under the law for homosexuals. Thus, Davis's theory leads to the conclusion that those who engage in homosexual conduct when it is against the rules morally deserve punishment.

However, the way in which Davis's theory handles the question of homosexual conduct is unsound. A judgment about whether those who engage in such conduct are taking unfair advantage of those who play by the rules cannot be reasonably made without asking whether homosexual conduct is naturally blameworthy. If it is not blameworthy, then it is difficult to see how those who engage in it are taking unfair advantage of the rest of society, most of whom are quite happy to indulge their heterosexual appetites.

It simply does not make sense to separate the question of whether a certain form of conduct is naturally blameworthy from the question of whether those who engage in it are deserving of punishment. Yet, Davis's point in developing his theory was to render irrelevant to the issue of criminal desert any questions regarding the natural blameworthiness of the conduct that the criminal law prohibits.

Criminal Law and Private Law A related problem with Davis's theory concerns the distinction between criminal law and private law. Violations of the rules of criminal law call for punishment of the offender, while violations of private-law rules call for compensation of the victim. Yet, in both cases we are dealing with systems of rules that meet Davis's three conditions and so with conduct that takes unfair advantage of those who play by the rules. Why does breach of contract or defamation not deserve punishment, given Davis's theory?

Other retributivists might argue that such private wrongs are not sufficiently blameworthy in and of themselves to merit the harsh sanction of the criminal law. But that argument is not available within Davis's theory, which sets aside considerations of how naturally blameworthy the conduct prohibited by the criminal law is. The theory thus seems to collapse an important distinction between criminal behavior and the behavior that violates private-law rules.

Davis's theory may represent an advance in certain respects over other forms of retributivism: the unfairness generally involved when criminals flout the rules by which others play should be a central element of any view that holds that criminals deserve punishment. But once that view is accepted, it is difficult to develop an account of criminal desert that leaves entirely to the side questions about the natural blameworthiness of conduct that society declares criminal.

MENS REA VERSUS STRICT LIABILITY

The Guilty Mind

As we have seen, systems of law in Western civilization have traditionally operated on the idea that criminal liability should not be imposed on a person simply for acting in a way that causes (or risks causing) harm to another. There is no crime unless the person also has a "guilty mind." The following example illustrates this idea that a guilty mind is a necessary element of any crime.

Suppose you park your car in the lot at the mall. A professional car thief with a special key that fits all car locks is in the area, and he steals your car. I then park my car in the spot where yours had been. It is the same model, make, and year as yours, and your key fits the lock and ignition. I go off to do my shopping. You return to what you reasonably think is your car, get in, and drive off. Viewed from an external perspective, you acted in the same way that the thief who stole your car acted: you entered and drove off in a car that you did not own without permission of the owner. But your action is not a crime, while the action of the person who took your car is a crime. The difference lies not in the external action but inside the mind of each of you. Lawyers describe this by saying that the person who took your car had a guilty mind (in Latin, *mens rea*), while you did not.

Crimes are thus defined in way that combines two elements: the guilty act (*actus reus*) and the guilty mind. In our legal system, four kinds of mental states are used in defining the *mens rea* element of crimes: intention, knowledge, negligence, and recklessness. These mental states not only help distinguish what *is* a crime (the person knowingly taking your car) from what is *not* a crime (your unknowingly taking my car); they also help distinguish various kinds of crime from one another.

For example, different degrees of homicide are distinguished on the basis of whether the death was caused intentionally or not. First-degree homicide typically (though not always) requires that the death be caused intentionally. It would be a lesser degree of homicide if the intention were to cause serious bodily harm but not death. And it would be still a lesser degree if there were no intention to harm but death was the result of negligence, that is, a failure to exercise reasonable care.

Although the general principle in our legal system is that no crime has been committed without a guilty mind, there are exceptions. The exceptions fall into two broad categories: when the law imposes objective liability on a person and when it imposes strict liability on a person. These forms of liability involve holding an individual responsible for a harm she causes (or risks) regardless of whether she has a guilty mind.

Objective and Strict Liability

The law imposes objective liability on a person when it holds her liable for harm caused by her negligent or reckless action even when she was unaware of its negligent or reckless nature. For example, manslaughter is the negligent killing of another person, and such negligence is typically measured by an objective standard, not by the subjective perceptions of the accused person. It does not matter if the accused failed to realize that she was not exercising reasonable care. From her own subjective point of view, her conduct may have appeared reasonable, but if from some more objective viewpoint the conduct was unreasonable, then she may be judged negligent.

The law imposes strict liability on a person when it holds her responsible for harm caused by her action, even when she did not intend the harm or realize that her action would (likely) bring it about and even when the action showed reasonable care from an objective point of view. Strict liability goes a step beyond objective liability. If a person acts with reasonable care to avoid causing a certain harm but the harm happens anyway, then the criminal law cannot hold him responsible under the idea of objective liability. But in certain cases it will hold him responsible under the idea of strict liability.

Some examples of crimes that impose strict liability are statutory rape, bigamy, and interstate shipment of adulterated or tainted milk. Thus, a man is liable for rape in some jurisdictions for having sexual intercourse with a willing underage female even if he did not know she was underage and reasonably believed she was old enough, and he is liable for marrying two women even if he reasonably believed that his first wife was dead. Similarly, the owner of a company that ships milk interstate is liable if the milk is tainted despite the fact that she took reasonable precautions to ensure its quality.

The crime of felony-murder is often cited as another example of strict liability. If a person dies during the commission of certain felonies (such as armed robbery), then the perpetrator can be given the same punishment as if he had intentionally murdered the person. The perpetrator need not have intended the death or even have been aware that his actions risked causing the death of another. In that regard, it is like bigamy and statutory rape. But whether felony-murder counts as strict, as opposed to objective, liability depends on whether committing one of the specified felonies automatically means that one is failing to exercise reasonable care with respect to the lives of others.

The felony-murder rule can be interpreted as an instance of objective liability if one judges that any perpetrator of the felonies in question is failing to show reasonable care for the lives of others simply by virtue of the fact of committing those felonies. On the other hand, the felony-murder rule will be interpreted as an instance of strict liability if one judges that a person does not automatically put others at an unreasonable risk for their lives simply by committing one of the felonies in question.

Strict Liability: Against

However one interprets the felony-murder rule, many legal thinkers have argued that the law should never impose strict liability and should always require that a person have a guilty mind before criminal punishment is imposed on her. One argument for such a view is that strict liability is fundamentally unfair and a violation of important rule-of-law principles, because individuals do not have a fair chance of avoiding strict-liability offenses.

Suppose I own a company that ships milk interstate. In order to prevent any tainted milk from being shipped, I take reasonable precautions such as testing randomly selected batches of milk. Suppose that I am extracautious and go beyond the reasonable precautions, doing additional tests. Nonetheless, a shipment of adulterated milk gets through the precautions. I am guilty of a crime and subject to punishment, despite the fact that I have done everything that could be done, short of shutting down my business, to avoid committing it. That seems an unfair way for a government to treat its citizens.

In addition, one of the main purposes of the rule of law is to ensure that citizens can know in advance what actions will make them liable to punishment by the government and can adjust their behavior to avoid such actions. That is why the rule of law does not permit secret or retroactive laws or laws that require people to do what is impossible (for example, jumping over the moon).

In the view of critics, strict-liability laws are very much like laws requiring the impossible. Of course, I could avoid shipping adulterated milk by shutting down my business, so strictly speaking, one might say that I can avoid the crime. But I can avoid the crime of failing to jump over the moon by emigrating to another country or even by killing myself (unless the law is applied to dead people as well). The point of the critics of strict liability is that it is unreasonable to put people in a situation in which they can be sure of avoiding a crime only by emigrating or suicide, and it is also unreasonable to put them in a situation in which they can be sure to avoid a crime only by shutting down a perfectly legal business or by never having heterosexual intercourse (to avoid statutory rape laws) or by never getting divorced and remarried (to avoid bigamy laws). The rule of law, it is argued, does not permit a legal system to put people in such situations.

Strict Liability: For

Defenders of strict liability can reply that the rule of law is always a matter of degree and that a few, selected strict-liability offenses can be justified on utilitarian grounds. Imposing strict liability in some cases can promote the total social good by encouraging people to take all possible precautions in order to avoid certain harms. Someone who ships milk under a law that imposes strict liability for shipping tainted milk is likely to go to greater lengths to ensure that the milk is not tainted than someone who is under a law that requires *mens rea* or a law that imposes objective liability. If the extra harms prevented by a strict-liability rule (that is, harms above and beyond those prevented by a *mens rea* rule or objective liability) outweigh the costs of taking extra precautions (that is, costs above and beyond the minimal precautions a reasonable person would take), then we should have strict liability, from a utilitarian point of view.

Still, it might seem that we should not punish a person who takes reasonable precautions and more and yet still is unlucky enough to have tainted milk in his shipments. Yet, the defenders of strict liability can invoke another utilitarian consideration. It is much less costly to investigate and prosecute crimes that impose strict liability than crimes that involve an element of *mens rea* or objective liability. Society saves a great deal of time, money, and energy by making the shipment of tainted milk a strict-liability offense.

These utilitarian considerations may still seem insufficient to outweigh a basic unfairness in punishing persons who have taken reasonable precautions and more and yet are still unlucky enough to find they have caused some legally prohibited harm. Defenders of strict liability can respond to this claim of unfairness by pointing out that no one forces a person to engage in an activity covered by strict liability.

Moreover, it is not a secret that strict liability applies to those activities. If I want to make money in the business of shipping milk, I must assume the risk that, despite the precautions I take, I may end up being liable for shipping tainted milk. On the other hand, if I do not want to take that risk, I am free to sell the business to someone who is willing to that the risk. If large gains in social utility can be made by imposing strict liability for shipping tainted milk, there is nothing unfair or illegitimate about making those who enter the business of shipping milk assume the risk that they may be liable for shipping tainted milk regardless of the precautions they take. So the defenders of strict liability argue.

There is no guarantee, of course, that imposing strict liability for shipping tainted milk maximizes social utility, and the same goes for the other criminal offenses for which our law currently imposes strict liability. Whether social utility is maximized by strict liability needs to be argued separately for each of the crimes for which it is proposed. The main point of a philosophical defense of strict liability is that, in principle, the imposition of such liability for selected crimes could be justified.

But it is precisely this point that critics of strict liability deny. They claim that, in principle, imposing strict liability can never be justified. The problem is not that our law makes the wrong offenses into strict-liability crimes. The problem is that the criminal law should never impose strict liability for any crime.

Yet, it is unclear that such a sweeping case against strict liability can be made persuasively. For at least some activities, such as the shipment of milk, it does not seem unreasonable for the criminal law to confront individuals with the choice of either forgoing the activity or accepting the risk that they may be found liable regardless of personal fault. As long as fair warning is given and the penalties for violation are not unduly harsh, individuals are not necessarily put in an unfair situation when the law tells them that if they want the advantages that come from a certain activity, then they must be willing to run the risk of strict liability. Of course, before imposing strict liability for a certain activity, a legislature should have, on balance, evidence or reason to think that doing so would promote the general good. But if it has such evidence or reason, and the other conditions are met, then it is difficult to see why strict liability is necessarily an unfair form of criminal liability.

LIMITS OF CRIMINAL LAW

The Public-Private Distinction

The punishment of criminals represents in its starkest form the power of government over the inhabitants of its territory. Through the practice of punishment, the government takes away the liberty, property, and even the lives of individuals. For that reason, legal theorists typically argue that it is crucially important for government to follow the rule of law in exercising this awesome power. Criminal laws must be duly enacted, clear in meaning, applied prospectively, and meet the other formal requirements of the rule of law; government must give those accused of crimes a fair chance to establish their innocence and must satisfy the other rule-of-law principles.

But some theorists go further and argue that it is not enough for government to observe the principles of legality. They contend that certain areas of life are beyond the legitimate scope of the criminal law. Society may not use the criminal law to interfere with or regulate what persons do in these areas. It does not matter if the laws are duly enacted, clear in meaning, and so on. Certain kinds of activity simply should not be subject to the rules of criminal law.

It is here that we find another use of a distinction we have come across before: the public-private distinction. Some theorists use the distinction to draw the line between the area in which society may legitimately use the criminal law to regulate and control conduct and the area in which the criminal law may not be legitimately used. The private realm is where the criminal law may not legitimately interfere with the choices of individuals. The public realm is where it may so interfere. But what is the difference between the private and public realms?

J. S. Mill and the Harm Principle

The Principle One possible way to demarcate the private realm is provided by the philosopher John Stuart Mill in his book *On Liberty.* This work is regarded as a classic text of liberal political philosophy. *Liberal* here does not mean a commitment to such government programs as social security, unemployment insurance, and welfare. Rather, it means a commitment to the idea that each individual should have an extensive sphere of liberty into which government and society may not legitimately intrude. Liberal political philosophy describes this sphere as a zone of "privacy," and Mill's aim is to demarcate the boundaries of the sphere. In examining those boundaries, Mill is interested not only in the criminal law but in all of the ways in which society may interfere with the liberty of the individual. In addition to criminal punishment, these include such informal modes of regulation as ostracizing or stigmatizing individuals for their conduct.

In *On Liberty,* Mill formulates a principle to demarcate the activities with which society may legitimately interfere from those which it must leave the individual at liberty to carry out. The principle states that the only legitimate reason for society to restrict the liberty of one of its members is to prevent him from directly harming the interests of another. This has come to be called the "harm principle."

The harm principle implies that society may not legitimately use the criminal law to restrict activities that do not directly harm others. Mill describes such activities as "self-regarding," and they belong to the private domain beyond the legitimate jurisdiction of the criminal law and the other means used by society to restrict individual liberty. In contrast are activities that do directly harm the interests of others. Mill calls them "other-regarding" activities, and they belong to the public domain. Other-regarding activities are potentially legitimate targets for legal and social regulation.

Mill contends that the harm principle can be justified on the basis of the principle of utility, although he gives a somewhat different interpretation of utility than did Bentham. Mill believes that not only the quantity of pleasure but also its quality counts when determining the greatest happiness for the greatest number. Some pleasures, he believes, are qualitatively superior to others, and that superiority should be reflected in our judgments about what best promotes the total social good. In particular, Mill contends that the pleasures connected to our higher human intellectual and emotional capacities are the highest forms of pleasure, qualitatively superior to purely physical pleasures, for example.

Against Paternalism and Moralism For Mill, then, the greatest happiness for the greatest number is most effectively advanced by promoting the greatest intellectual and emotional development of the greatest number. And here is where the harm principle comes in. Mill believes that a society that adopts the principle will more effectively promote the greatest intellectual and emotional development of the greatest number than a society that does not adopt it. In order to see why he believes this, we must examine how societies that do not accept the harm principle operate.

All societies accept the idea that harm to others is one legitimate reason to restrict an individual's liberty. But many societies accept the notion that there are additional legitimate reasons. Thus, some adopt paternalism, the practice of restricting an individual's liberty for his or her own good. Paternalism can seek to protect or promote any aspect of a person's well-being: economic, physical, psychological, and so on. Even if an individual's conduct poses no risk of harm to others, a paternalist society may still seek to regulate or restrict it in order to protect or promote the individual's own well-being.

Arguments for paternalism are often made on utilitarian grounds. If the ultimate aim is to maximize social utility, it would seem to be a mistake for society to allow individuals to harm themselves or to neglect promoting their own good. For such harm or neglect detracts from total social utility. It would seem to be better, from a utilitarian perspective, for society to restrict people's liberties to ensure that they do not harm themselves or neglect their own good. We will examine Mill's responses to these points shortly.

Some societies adopt moralism, another practice that Mill regards as a violation of his harm principle. Moralism is the practice of punishing individuals for their immoral conduct, regardless of whether the conduct harms or victimizes any other, specific person. Much immoral conduct clearly does harm (or risk harm to) specific persons, and any society would regard such conduct as subject to restriction based on that reason. But even when immoral conduct does not victimize (or risk victimizing) others, a moralist society would declare that it ought to be punished in some way.

Moralism is often defended on the ground that it is morally fitting that immorality as such be punished. Immoral conduct is the sort of conduct that calls for punishment, just as morally upstanding conduct calls for reward of some sort.

In Mill's view, societies that accept either paternalism or moralism will fail to promote in the most effective way the greatest development of the higher faculties of the greatest number. The utilitarian argument for paternalism fails, according to Mill, for several reasons. First, individuals are in a better position to know what is good for them than society or government is. Each individual knows herself, her own needs, her own desires and aspirations, far better than society or government ever could. When society or government intervenes, even if the intervention is completely well intentioned, the actual result will likely be to make the individual worse off rather than better off.

In addition, even in a case in which society does know better than the individual what is good for her, paternalism fails to promote utilitarian aims in the most effective way. That is because paternalism undercuts the process by which individuals develop their higher, mental faculties. Essential to that process is thinking for oneself and using one's powers of thought and deliberation to decide where one's good lies and how to pursue it. Individuals will undoubtedly make mistakes in this process. But it is better to let individuals make those mistakes and learn from them than for society to compel people to act against their judgment. The development of one's higher powers depends on using them, even if one uses them incorrectly.

A society that adopts paternalism will thus block the greatest development of the higher powers of the greatest number. And moralism is no better than paternalism. In fact, for Mill it is worse, since it calls for inflicting punishment on persons without even pretending that there must be compensating benefits brought about by the punishment. For moralists, punishment is regarded as good for its own sake, an idea that is an anathema to utilitarians such as Mill.

In contrast to paternalist and moralist societies, Mill argues, a society that adopts the harm principle will best promote the greatest happiness for the greatest number. The development of the higher faculties will be encouraged because individuals will be free to make mistakes regarding their own good and to learn from those mistakes (assuming no harm to anyone else is involved). A Millian society will not treat its citizens like children who must be guarded to avoid harming themselves. Rather, it will treat them as independent persons capable of thinking for themselves and developing their powers through such a process. Nor will a Millian society inflict punishment on individuals for immoral actions that harm no one else. Rather, it will restrict punishment to those immoral actions that do (or risk doing) harm to others.

Criticisms of Mill   Mill's views about the legitimate basis for the restriction of individual liberties have been subjected to numerous criticisms. Some critics point out that Mill never sufficiently clarifies key concepts in his harm principle, like the concept of harm itself. At one point in *On Liberty,* Mill distinguishes harm from offense: it is one thing to harm a person; it is another to offend him. The distinction is important because Mill argues at that point that the fact that someone else is offended by your action is not a valid reason for society to restrict your liberty to do it. When you eat pork, certain people whose religion says that pork is unclean and should not be eaten may be offended. Mill's claim is that such offense is not a valid reason for society to deny you the liberty of eating pork.

Yet, at another place in *On Liberty,* Mill regards offense as a valid reason to restrict liberty. Thus, in discussing public nudity, he says that the offense it causes to other people is a valid reason for society to prohibit it. Given the harm principle, the implication is that in this case offense is a kind of harm. Mill thus seems unable to make up his mind as to exactly what counts as harm, which appears to reflect his failure to develop any clear account of the concept of harm.

Even if we can agree on what counts as harm, there are problems with the harm principle, in the view of some critics. They contend that Mill's utilitarian argument against paternalism is not convincing. Mill may be correct in saying that individuals generally know more about themselves than society or government could know, and he is likely correct in suggesting that individuals develop their higher faculties (in part) by learning from their mistakes. But Mill is too quick in drawing the conclusion that paternalism is never justified. In some aspects of contemporary life, for example, people as a rule do not know enough to effectively pursue their own good. For those aspects of life, utilitarianism will lead to the affirmation of paternalism, not its repudiation, the critics say.

Consider the medications used in the treatment of illness. As a rule, individuals do not have the training or knowledge to say which medications will help them and which may harm them. Taking the wrong medications (or wrong dosages) could cause dangerous and irreversible side effects, results that everyone would agree count as harm. In light of such potential harm, society is perfectly justified in requiring that individuals get the approval of those who do have the appropriate training and knowledge before they are permitted to purchase potentially harmful medications.

Yet, such a requirement is paternalistic: it is imposed for the good of individuals who might otherwise do harm to themselves by taking the wrong medication or dosage. Society's restrictions on the purchase of medications do not mean that it is treating adult individuals as if they were children. Rather, such restrictions mean only that society recognizes that most individuals cannot be reasonably expected to master the specialized body of knowledge needed to properly administer medication. Given that recognition, the most sensible way to promote maximum social utility is through restrictions on the purchase of medications. That is the view of many defenders of paternalism and critics of Mill, at any rate.

Other critics of Mill begin with the fact that some actions do not harm specific victims but do weaken or undermine the institutions that benefit society. When I evade my legal obligation to pay income taxes, my crime has no specific victim. You cannot point to any particular individual and say, "There is the victim of Altman's evasion of income taxes." That is because everyone is, in a sense, a victim. Income tax evasion weakens the institutions that we all rely on to perform essential services of government: maintaining domestic tranquillity, protecting us from foreign enemies, and so on.

Mill would clearly intend to cover such "diffuse" harms by his harm principle. He certainly would agree that society is justified in punishing tax evaders and the like. But by including such harm under his principle, Mill opens himself up for another attack. For it can be argued that moralism is justifiable on the basis of the idea that it is legitimate to restrict an individual's liberty to engage in immoral conduct that has no specific victim but that weakens institutions important to the health of society. If this argument is correct, it means that Mill's condemnation of moralism could be misguided, since his own principle might endorse rather than reject moralism. Let us turn to a more detailed examination of the issues raised by moralism.

The Devlin-Hart Debate

Devlin: Society's Right of Self-Defense A harm-based argument for moralism was developed by Patrick Devlin. According to his argument, every society has its own moral code, and the preservation of that moral code is essential to the well-being of the society. For society is held together most fundamentally by shared ideas about right and wrong, good and bad. These shared ideas are what constitute society's moral code, which provides individuals in society with structure and direction in their lives. When the code is violated, it is thereby weakened. And when society's moral code is weakened, society itself may be weakened. There may be no specific victims of immoral behavior, but that is not because there is no harm done to society. Rather, the harm done is diffuse but no less real than the harm done by actions that have specific victims.

For example, every society's moral code deals with matters such as marriage and family. The code answers the question of how family life should be organized. In some societies, the code demands monogamy as the basis of family life; in others, it encourages polygamy. Whatever moral code a particular society has, the entire society will be based on what the code says about marriage and family. The relations, expectations, plans, and aspirations of the members of society will presuppose the answer the code gives to the question of how family life should be organized. The economic, political, and social institutions of the society will be organized around that answer. And for Devlin, the implication is that conduct violating the code is a potential threat to society.

Devlin proceeds to argue that society has the right to protect the moral code on which it is built. Such protection is a matter of self-defense for society. For a society to neglect to protect its moral code would be tantamount to it acquiescing in harm that could lead to its internal disintegration. But since the very existence of society is potentially at stake, society has the right to use its most potent domestic weapon, the criminal law, to preserve its moral code.

In addition, Devlin argues that there are no areas of life that one can automatically say are off-limits to the criminal law: the liberal idea of a zone of privacy forever beyond the legitimate regulation of the law is misguided. Mill's liberal followers in the twentieth century argued, for example, that sexual relations between consenting adults should be off-limits to the criminal law. Such relations are none of the law's business, they argued, because consenting, adult sexual partners do not harm anyone else by their sexual conduct, no matter how unconventional the conduct may be. But Devlin responds that such conduct can cause harm if it violates society's moral code. There may be no specific victim, such as one finds in cases of murder or rape. But there may be the kind of diffuse harm that weakens the moral foundations of society.

Hart versus Devlin Devlin's argument has been criticized by H. L. A. Hart, who contends that it rests on a faulty conception of the relation between society and its moral code. Although any society needs some moral code, it does not necessarily need to preserve the exact moral code it has at a given time. Societies can remain perfectly healthy and vibrant even as their moral codes change. And a moral code changes only when people act in ways that go contrary to it.

Devlin can consider such action a threat to society because he fails to see that a moral code may change without posing any threat of social disintegration. Surely, some changes in a society's moral code might bring harm to the society and even threaten its existence. For example, if society no longer condemned the indiscriminate use of violence, then it would likely be well on its way to disintegration. But that does not mean that any change in a society's existing moral code represents a threat.

Society may have a right to defend itself using the criminal law—although even that right would seem to depend on the kind of society it is. But even granting the general right of a society to defend itself, Hart argues that it does not follow that society has the right to use its criminal laws to enforce each and every part of its moral code.

Hart is especially concerned to protect from legal interference the private sexual practices of consenting adults. Society's moral code may condemn homosexuality, for example, even when practiced in private by consenting adults. Devlin thinks that such conduct is the law's business and that society may legitimately criminalize it. But Hart argues that Devlin has no empirical evidence that such conduct poses any threat to society. Indeed, Hart suggests that the evidence is all on the other side: historically, societies have been threatened by internal disintegration when persons were at liberty to victimize others with impunity, but not when they were at liberty to engage in private, consensual sexual practices regarded as "deviant."

Devlin's reply is that any violation of a society's moral code has the potential to harm the society. It is true that with some violations the potential may not be realized and harm will be avoided. But there is no way to draw a hard-and-fast line and say that violating these parts of society's moral code is permissible because it can never cause harm, but that violating these other parts is not permissible because it can do so. Immoral conduct in any area, if sufficiently widespread, can do serious harm to society, and immoral conduct in one area can spread into another. Accordingly, no area of life that is of concern to society's moral code can be marked off as beyond the legitimate limits of its criminal law.

But for Devlin this does not mean that society should straightaway criminalize all conduct that violates its moral code. He proposes that society refrain from criminalizing immoral conduct that has no specific victims unless the conduct is judged by society to be so abhorrent that it cannot be tolerated. He also suggests that society be sensitive to the value of privacy when deciding to criminalize immoral conduct of that kind. If such conduct cannot be reliably detected without giving the police expansive powers to intrude into the homes and bedrooms of citizens, then that is a consideration against criminalizing the conduct. But again, it is society's right to balance the considerations, pro and con, and arrive at a judgment. No one can sensibly say that this is an area of life that is none of the law's business, regardless of how strongly society's moral code condemns the conduct and regardless of the harm to society's practices that may be done by not criminalizing the conduct.

Devlin does not wish to claim that a society's moral code can never change for the better. He recognizes that history renders such a claim false. But Devlin does claim that such changes bring with them a danger to society. The danger is that any such change will involve a period of time when the old moral code (or some part of it) has been rejected but the new one has not yet been accepted by a sufficiently large portion of the population to be effective in regulating people's conduct. This interim period is one in which society is vulnerable to those few who disregard morality entirely and are concerned only with pursuing their own self-interest. The interim period unleashes these amoralists from the constraints of social morality.

For Devlin, the criminal law has an important role to play in ensuring that society is not seriously harmed by such individuals. Its role is not to make moral change within society impossible. Rather, its role is to help regulate the process of change by making it more deliberate and by deterring the amoralists from taking advantage of the change. The law can do this only if it is slow to change, moving behind the curve of moral change.

Thus, Devlin argues that changes in society's morality should not be immediately reflected in law, since such changes may turn out to be passing fads. In addition, even if the new morality is not a passing fad, retaining criminal sanctions based on the older morality will help ensure that those who violate the law are motivated by sincere moral beliefs and not simply by amoral desires. Those motivated by amoral desires are less likely to run the risk of criminal punishment for their conduct than those motivated by sincere moral beliefs.

Assessing Devlin's View: The Role of Rights Devlin's arguments presuppose that any conduct posing a potential danger to society is within the realm of what can be rightfully criminalized. For him, the degree of the danger is a factor to be weighed in the balance with others such as the administrative costs of criminalization and the harm to values such as privacy. The answer to the question of whether certain conduct should be criminalized depends on how the various factors balance out. One can never say in advance of such balancing that the result must come out against the criminalization of certain kinds of potentially dangerous conduct. And society's judgment as to where the balance falls is final, not in the sense that society cannot be wrong in its judgment, but in the sense that society has the right to act on its judgment regardless of whether it is wrong. Since immoral conduct is always a potential danger, in Devlin's eyes, he concludes that society always has the right to use the criminal law against conduct it regards as immoral.

Although Devlin says that individuals have rights, too, he makes those rights wholly subordinate to society's judgments about what conduct should be criminalized. In his analysis, individual rights play no role in limiting society's right to act on its judgments or in limiting how society may balance the various factors on which its judgments are to be based. For him, individual rights are just another factor to be weighed by society along with whatever other variables it deems relevant in whatever way it sees fit.

Devlin insists that one cannot justifiably say that certain conduct can never be criminalized by society no matter what. One must take account of the circumstances and the potential consequences of allowing any sort of conduct, whether the conduct be public or private.

Devlin's insistence on this point is sensible and would not be opposed by Hart. But Devlin's approach contains a fundamental weakness, and Hart's criticisms do not get to the heart of it. The basic weakness is not that Devlin fails to provide empirical evidence that homosexuality is a sufficiently serious danger to society or that he exaggerates the extent to which one part of social morality is connected to another. Devlin is, in fact, quite prepared to say that, given the way that the pros and cons balance out, there is insufficient reason to criminalize homosexuality.

The basic weakness is that Devlin is operating with a seriously inadequate conception of individual rights: such rights should be not seen as just another factor to be weighed in the balance by society in whatever way it sees fit. Devlin assumes that an individual right must either be absolute, so that society cannot interfere with it no matter what, or else it must be just another factor to be balanced in whatever way society sees fit. He chooses the latter view. But individual rights can be something more than just another factor to be weighed by society however it deems fit and something less that an absolute guarantee that must be respected in every conceivable situation.

For example, individual rights might require society to accept certain significant risks that it may prefer not to accept. And individual rights might require society to produce fairly persuasive evidence that a certain conduct poses a significant risk before it can go ahead with criminalization. In both scenarios, society would not have the right to act on any judgment it might happen to make about an activity it deems a risk. The risk would have to rise above a certain level, and society would have to produce evidence to show that it was so.

Hart is correct to demand that Devlin produce evidence that decriminalizing homosexual conduct would pose a significant risk. But he fails to articulate the moral basis of the demand: that individuals have a right to practice in private the consensual sexual activities of their choosing.

This right is rooted in a more abstract right of individuals to make decisions central to their lives and human identity, as long as the decisions do not victimize others. Hart stresses how a person's sexual impulses are such an important and insistent part of his or her life and how private sexual practices, if consensual, do not victimize anyone. But he needs to take the next step and say that this is a reason for accepting the existence of an individual right protecting those practices. And such a right requires a society to do more before it interferes with those practices than simply say, "On balance, we sincerely think it best for these practices to be criminalized."

Consider the less controversial case of freedom of religion. When it was first proposed in Western society during the sixteenth and seventeenth centuries, many believed that it posed a mortal danger to society. This was because the societies of the time were organized around a single religious faith, and opponents of freedom of religion claimed that it would cause society to unravel by weakening the religious bonds that held it together. Proponents of religious liberty made strong counterarguments that it was the policy of intolerance that led to social turmoil and that a policy of religious toleration would actually promote civil peace.

The logic of Devlin's position forces him to say that if society agreed with the opponents of religious liberty, then it could rightfully proceed with a policy of intolerance even if there was no good evidence to support the idea that society would unravel without intolerance. Indeed, even if the risk to society was very small from recognizing religious liberty and even if the probable outcome of such recognition was the civil peace predicted by the advocates of toleration, Devlin would have to say that society has an unrestricted right to enforce religious intolerance.

What is missing from such an analysis is any recognition of the possibility that the right of religious liberty places a burden on society to show that the danger is more than minimal. If, like religious worship, an activity is central to a person's life and fails to victimize anyone, then society must meet a substantial burden before it may rightfully criminalize the conduct. At a minimum, it must show with persuasive evidence or argument that the danger of diffuse harm to society is both real and more than minimal.

But is the situation the same with conduct contemporary society regards as immoral? Consider again the case of homosexual conduct. Persons with homosexual desires reasonably regard sexual relations with partners of the same sex as having central importance to their lives, just as religious persons reasonably regard their forms of worship to be central to their lives. In addition, homosexual activity between consenting adults, like many forms of religious worship, harms no unwilling victims. Accordingly, one can argue that, just as there is a right to engage in a specific form of religious worship, there is a right to engage in homosexual activity.

Some persons might claim that the risk of tolerating homosexual conduct is that too many people will turn away from heterosexuality and the population of society will plummet dangerously. But if there is a right to engage in private, consensual sexual relations, then the claim would need to be backed up with evidence. Society could not rightfully criminalize homosexual conduct just because most people in it sincerely believe that such conduct poses a danger of causing serious diffuse harm. There must be solid evidence or arguments showing that such a danger exists and that it is not simply a minuscule one. If there is no such evidence and society criminalizes homosexual conduct anyway, it has acted beyond the limits of its rightful powers and has violated the rights of its citizens.

SUMMARY

In this chapter, we have examined a number of philosophical problems related to the criminal law: Why should there be a system of criminal law? Would a system of criminal therapy be better than a system of criminal punishment? How much punishment should be imposed on criminals? Does strict liability have a legitimate place in criminal law? And what are the moral limits of the criminal law? Philosophers have used a variety of approaches in grappling with these questions. They have developed and applied utilitarian, retributivist, and rights-based theories in order to come up with defensible answers. Each type of theory has its strengths and weaknesses in dealing with the problems of the criminal law. Each comes in different forms and versions, and perhaps no single theory is adequate to the problems raised.

NOTES

1. Early utilitarians tended to treat each society as a self-contained unit. Contemporary ones often take account of the effects of actions and government policies on the happiness of persons in other societies.

2. There are many different versions of utilitarianism, differing not only over the definition of happiness but also over such questions as whether the principle of utility is to be applied directly to each action or rather to the social rules under which specific actions are to be judged. Criticisms of one version do not necessarily apply to other versions.

3. The issue of whether the harm must be inflicted on another, identifiable individual—the victim—is a separate question examined later in this chapter. Retributivism as such does not address the issue.

4. See Michael Davis, *To Make the Punishment Fit the Crime* (Boulder, CO: Westview, 1992), chap. 1.

5. Benjamin Karpman, "Criminal Psychodynamics: A Platform," in J. G. Murphy, ed., *Punishment and Rehabilitation* (Belmont, CA: Wadsworth, 1973), p. 131.

6. Karl Menninger, "Therapy, Not Punishment," in J. G. Murphy, ed., *Punishment and Rehabilitation,* p. 136.

7. The most prominent proponent of this form of retributivism has been Andrew Von Hirsch. See his *Doing Justice* (New York: Hill & Wang, 1976).

8. Some retributivists reinterpret the *lex talionis* so that it takes account of such

distinctions as that between accidental and intentional harm. They also reinterpret "an eye for an eye" to mean that punishment should reflect the seriousness of the crime but not necessarily amount to the same kind of harm the criminal inflicted. This reinterpretation is needed to avoid the implication that rapists should be raped and torturers tortured, implications that are morally unacceptable. It is also needed to avoid the absurd implication that those guilty of attempted (but unsuccessful) murder should be punished by having an unsuccessful murder attempt made on their lives.

9. Davis enumerates four separate conditions, but I think the three formulated here capture everything essential in his four.

10. Davis uses an economic model to fill out his notion that criminal punishment is the price society makes someone pay for taking unfair advantage of the law-abiding members of society. The details of that model will not be of concern to us here.

11. I leave aside the question of whether the retributivists can explain why someone deserves punishment for doing something that is not naturally blameworthy but that is correlated with conduct that is naturally blameworthy. See the previous discussion of public drunkenness.

12. Davis, *To Make the Punishment Fit the Crime,* p. 221. Hobbes argues that without government and positive law, society could not exist, and there would be a war of every person against every person.

DISCUSSION QUESTIONS

1. In most states having capital punishment, the law allows juries to consider "victim-impact" evidence when deciding whether or not to inflict the death sentence. Such evidence is introduced by the prosecution and typically involves the character of the victim and the impact of the murder on the victim's immediate family. The evidence is heard during the punishment phase of the trial, after the defendant has been found guilty.

The Supreme Court initially ruled that the use victim-impact evidence in capital cases was unconstitutional, but soon overruled its own precedents and allowed such evidence. And the Court's approval of victim-impact evidence has proved to be controversial among legal thinkers and jurists.

Critics of victim-impact evidence argue that its use is at odds with the rule of law and fundamental principles of criminal law. Juries who hear such evidence are swayed by emotion, not by the kind of clear and objective standards that the rule of law demands. Moreover, our system of law defines crimes and the punishments that go with them on the basis of the harm done to the direct victims. In a murder, the victim—legally speaking—is the person who is killed, not her family, friends, lovers, classmates, or anyone else. And it should be irrelevant to the law whether the victim has a morally good character or not: to make the victim's character legally relevant would make a mockery of the important principle of equal justice for all under the law.

Advocates of victim-impact evidence argue that it is relevant to determining how much harm a murderer has done and that it is legitimate for the law to consider such harm in determining whether to impose the death sentence on a murderer. After all, we sensibly punish murder more harshly than attempted murder, and the only difference is the amount of harm actually caused by the crime.

Should victim-impact evidence be allowed in the punishment phase of capital cases?

2. Is there any validity to the therapeutic model? Would society be better off if it adopted such a model for certain crimes, such as those connected to the use of drugs?

ADDITIONAL READING

Beccaria, Cesare. *On Crimes and Punishments.* Bobbs-Merrill, 1963.

Bentham, Jeremy. *The Theory of Legislation.* Routledge and Kegan Paul, 1931.

Davis, Michael. *To Make the Punishment Fit the Crime.* Westview, 1992.

Devlin, Patrick. *The Enforcement of Morals.* Oxford University Press, 1965.

Dolinko, David. "Some Thoughts About Retributivism." *Ethics* 101 (1991), 537–559.

Ezorsky, Gertrude, ed. *Philosophical Perspectives on Punishment.* State University of New York, 1972.

Feinberg, Joel. *Harm to Others.* Oxford University Press, 1984.

_____. "The Expressive Function of Punishment." *Doing and Deserving.* Princeton University Press, 1970.

Fletcher, George. *Rethinking Criminal Law.* Little, Brown, 1978.

Friedrich, Carl, ed. *Responsibility.* Liberal Arts Press, 1960.

Hampton, Jean. "The Moral Education Theory of Punishment." *Philosophy and Public Affairs* 13 (1984), 208–238.

Hart, H. L. A. *Law, Liberty, and Morality.* Stanford University Press, 1963.

_____. *Punishment and Responsibility.* Oxford University Press, 1973.

Hershenov, David B. "Restitution and Revenge." *Journal of Philosophy* XCVI:2 (February 1999), 79–94.

Kadish, Sanford. *Blame and Punishment.* Collier-MacMillan, 1987.

Kant, Immanuel. *Metaphysical Elements of Justice.* J. Ladd, trans. Bobbs-Merrill, 1965.

Katz, Leo. *Bad Acts and Guilty Minds.* University of Chicago Press, 1987.

Menninger, Karl. *The Crime of Punishment.* Viking Press, 1968.

Mill, John Stuart. *On Liberty.* Hackett, 1979.

Morris, Herbert. "Persons and Punishment." *Monist* 52 (1968), 475–501.

Murphy, Jeffrie, ed. *Punishment and Rehabilitation,* 2d ed. Wadsworth, 1985.

_____. *Retribution Reconsidered.* Kluwer, 1992.

Paul, Ellen, Fred Miller, and Jeffrey Paul, eds. *Crime, Culpability, and Remedy.* Blackwell, 1990.

Pincoffs, Edmund. *The Rationale of Legal Punishment.* Humanities Press, 1966.

Primoratz, Igor. *Justifying Legal Punishment.* Humanities Press, 1989.

Rawls, John. "Two Concepts of Rules." *Philosophical Review* 64 (1955), 3–32.

"Special Topic: Criminal Law Theory, Retributivism, and Beyond." *UCLA Law Review* 39:6 (August 1992).

Ten, C. L. *Crime, Guilt, and Punishment.* Oxford University Press, 1987.

Von Hirsch, Andrew. *Doing Justice.* Northeastern University Press, 1986.

Wasserstrom, Richard. "Strict Liability in the Criminal Law." *Philosophical Issues in the Law.* K. Kipnis, ed. Prentice-Hall, 1977.

6

Law and Economics

THE ECONOMIC ANALYSIS OF LAW

Positive law is made and maintained by the decisions and actions of human beings. In light of that fact, it is reasonable to think that fields of study focusing on human behavior and institutions can contribute to the understanding of the law. Accordingly, it is unsurprising to find that such fields as sociology, psychology, and anthropology have made important contributions to the study of law. Psychologists, for example, have studied how verdicts in criminal cases are affected by whether the prosecution or the defense goes last in giving its closing statement to the jury. And anthropologists have described and contrasted the distinct ways in which different cultures handle disputes that break out among their members. But in recent years, some thinkers have proposed that the principles of economics provide the best way to describe, explain, and evaluate the rules of any system of positive law. These thinkers have established the "law and economics movement."

The law and economics movement is part of a trend that uses economic ideas, such as the concept of efficiency, to account for decisions and practices seemingly far removed from the impersonal transactions of the marketplace. For example, economic analyses have been given of dating, courtship, and marriage. The underlying idea here is that the principles of economics do not apply merely to some narrowly restricted range of human behavior; they apply to human activities and practices across the board, including the law.

We should be careful to distinguish among three separate theses belonging to the law and economics approach: the descriptive, the explanatory, and the evaluative. The descriptive thesis holds that economic concepts and principles provide illuminating descriptions of legal rules. The explanatory thesis holds that economic concepts and principles help provide the best explanation for why society has the legal rules it has. And the evaluative thesis holds that economic concepts and principles provide sound criteria for evaluating legal rules and determining which ones society ought to have.

The descriptive and explanatory theses are made more specific by proponents of law and economics by focusing on particular areas of law and their economic efficiency. Accordingly, two of the principal claims of law and economics are (1) the rules of common law are economically efficient, and (2) the rules of common law are what they are because they are economically efficient.

These two claims about the efficiency of the common law are specifications of the descriptive and explanatory theses, respectively. It is clear that the explanatory claim presupposes the truth of the descriptive one: efficiency cannot explain the rules of common law unless we suppose that the common law can be accurately described as efficient in the first place.

What about the reverse relationship: Does the descriptive thesis presuppose the truth of the explanatory thesis? The answer is no, because the common law could be economically efficient even though its efficiency is not what explains it. In such a case, it would still be important to know that the common law was efficient. Showing that it was so would contribute to our understanding of the common law, even if we would need to look beyond efficiency for an explanation of why it contains the particular legal rules it does.

The evaluative thesis of law and economics is made more specific by the claim that economic efficiency provides a criterion for evaluating the law: other things being equal, inefficient legal rules should be replaced by efficient ones, and efficient ones should be maintained. These evaluative claims about efficiency stand or fall, regardless of whether the law as a whole (or some area of it) is explained by its economic efficiency or is even efficient in the first place. The idea that the law should be efficient must be defended or criticized apart from the other claims of the law and economics movement about what the law is and why it is.

ECONOMIC RATIONALITY

In this section, we will focus on the economic concept of rationality. It is one of two concepts at the center of how the economic approach describes, explains, and evaluates human actions and institutions. The other concept is that of efficiency, which we will examine in the next main section.

Rational Action

From the economic perspective, human action is essentially rational, and the rationality of an action is a function of its costs and benefits to the agent. Costs and benefits refer to the entire range of considerations that make something better or worse for an individual. Monetary considerations are included, but costs and benefits are not restricted to financial gains and losses. Suppose I receive an award for my work. Suppose that no money goes along with the award and that having it will not indirectly increase my income in any way (unlike, say, an Olympic gold medal). Still, the award would count as a benefit as long as it made me better off in some way, for example, by increasing my prestige among my colleagues or just by making me feel good.

According to the economic approach, each individual is the ultimate judge of what makes her better or worse off. In other words, each person's preferences determine what counts as a cost or benefit for her.[1] Moreover, the economic approach assumes that all costs and benefits can be mathematically represented in terms of some common unit of measurement. In practice, monetary units (for example, dollars) are used. Thus, gaining prestige among my colleagues is not itself monetary compensation, but its value to me can be represented in terms of dollars.

Rational decisions reflect the net benefits of the decision. In other words, they reflect the gains minus the losses. For economic analysts, the crucial gains and losses are the marginal ones. Marginal costs and benefits are the ones added to (or subtracted from) what one already has. By focusing on marginal costs and benefits, one can determine when one has maximized one's net benefits.

An Example: The Rational Athlete

Consider an athlete whose training involves sit-ups in order to increase the strength of her abdominal muscles. Suppose that we ignore all of her other aims in life and focus only on her task of strengthening her abdominal muscles. If she has done fifteen sit-ups at a certain training session, doing an extra, sixteenth sit-up will bring an added benefit. But the extra benefit will be less than the extra benefit of doing the tenth sit-up after having already done nine of them. The marginal benefit of the sixteenth sit-up is still positive, but it is not as high as the marginal benefit of the tenth.

In general, the marginal benefits of a beneficial activity decrease as the activity continues. Similarly, the marginal benefits of a good thing decrease as one obtains more of the thing: the added benefit of a loaf of bread is less to you if you already have ten loaves than if you only have one.[2]

Benefits are maximized when one engages in a beneficial activity until the point at which its net marginal benefits drop to zero. After that point, further activity decreases one's overall benefits, while up to that point, further activity increases the benefits. Of course, even beneficial activities have costs that must be accounted for in determining their net marginal benefits, in particular, the opportunity cost of forgoing some other activity. Suppose that by doing sit-ups our athlete is forgoing another exercise, say, leg lifts, which provides the next best way of increasing the strength of her abdominal muscles. The cost of doing sit-ups is determined by how much benefit she forgoes by not doing the leg lifts. How many sit-ups would she do, assuming she is rational?

Suppose that the marginal benefit of the thirtieth sit-up is greater than that of the first leg lift, but the marginal benefit of the thirty-first sit-up is less than that of the first leg lift. She would maximize her net benefits by doing thirty sit-ups and then switching to leg lifts. How many leg lifts would she do? Assuming she is rational, she would perform each additional leg lift until the marginal benefits decrease so as to become equal to the marginal costs. Past that point, she would be detracting from her net benefits instead of maximizing them.

According to economic analysis, then, rational action maximizes one's net benefits, and maximizing one's net benefits entails acting to the point at which marginal benefits minus marginal costs becomes zero.

Rationality and Uncertainty

In most situations in life, it is not certain what the gains and losses will be from any given choice or action. Rational choice under such conditions of uncertainty is handled using the idea of expected benefits (or losses). The expected benefit of a choice is simply the benefit multiplied by the probability of its occurrence. If there is a 10 percent chance (0.10) of my receiving $10, then my expected benefit is $1.

Economic analysts will concede that not all human conduct is rational in exactly the way they describe. But they will insist that their idea of rational action provides a very good approximation of much human conduct, applicable across the spectrum of human activities. Moreover, economic analysts will contend that their approach provides the most systematic and comprehensive approach to describing and explaining human conduct. It might be possible to come up with counterexamples, in which persons do not maximize their net (expected) benefits. But there is no alternative theory that does a better job than the economic approach. It may not be perfect, because humans are not always perfectly rational, but the economic approach is by far the best game in town.[3] Or so the economic analysts of law argue.

ECONOMIC EFFICIENCY

The economic concept of efficiency concerns the costs and benefits of an action, rule, or institution to society as a whole rather than to a specific individual. The concept rests on the idea that society is simply the sum of the individuals who make it up. Accordingly, the costs and benefits to society as a whole is a function of the costs and benefits to each affected individual. But how are the costs and benefits to different individuals to be compared and weighed against one another?

Utilitarianism and Beyond

Economic thinkers developed their answer to this question by considering the problems with a utilitarian approach and formulating several alternatives to it. Let us examine the utilitarian approach and the problems it encounters.

In its classic formulation, the utilitarian approach holds that the total good to society of some act or rule is determined by the net balance of pleasure over pain produced by the act or rule. The net balance is calculated by summing up the pleasure produced for each individual (taking into account its intensity, duration, and so on) and subtracting the pain produced for each individual (also taking account of its intensity, duration, and so on). If we used this approach to define efficiency, we would say that an efficient act or rule is one that maximizes the net balance of pleasure over pain, summing up the pleasures and pain over all affected individuals.

The critical problem that economic thinkers see in this approach to defining efficiency is that it assumes one can compare the pleasures and pains of different persons and say how much more one person's pleasure (or pain) is than another's. The simple fact seems to be that there is no way to make such "interpersonal utility comparisons."

Jack may be able to say reliably that his pleasure in eating fried chicken outweighs his pain in having indigestion. Or that his pleasure in playing basketball is greater than his pleasure in playing cards. But how can anyone determine how much more (or less) Jack's pleasure in playing basketball is than Jill's pleasure in playing cards? It seems that there is no way to compare the subjective experiences of different individuals because that would demand the impossible task of getting inside their heads. Yet, if we want to know whether it is efficient for Jack and Jill to play basketball or to play cards, a utilitarian approach to efficiency demands that we make such comparisons between the pleasures of Jack and those of Jill.

Pareto's Concepts of Efficiency

Vilfredo Pareto, an economist, developed two concepts of efficiency that circumvented the problem of interpersonal utility comparisons. The two concepts are called "Pareto optimality" and "Pareto superiority." Both concepts enable one to measure the efficiency of different ways of allocating society's resources, and both can be applied without getting inside the minds of the affected persons and comparing their subjective experiences. Let us examine their meanings.

Suppose that all of society's resources are in a box, waiting to be allocated to its members. Suppose that X represents one specific allocation of those resources. X is Pareto-optimal if and only if there is no way to change that allocation to make at least one person better off without making anyone worse off. Conversely, X would fail to be Pareto-optimal if and only if there were some way to change the allocation so as to make at least one person better off without making anyone else worse off.

Pareto superiority involves a comparison between any two ways of allocating the same set of resources. Let X represent one way of allocating the resources and Y another. X is Pareto-superior to Y if and only if at least one person is better off with X than with Y and no one is worse off with X than with Y. And if some persons are better off with X than with Y but others are worse off with X than Y, then we cannot say that either X or Y is Pareto-superior. X and Y are noncomparable.

Both Pareto optimality and Pareto superiority dispense with interpersonal utility comparisons in the determination of efficiency. For they only require us to determine for each affected individual whether he or she would be better off, worse off, or the same under various, possible allocations. And according to the economic analysts who use these Pareto criteria, it is not necessary to get inside anyone's head in order to determine whether someone is made better off or not by some change in the allocation of resources. That is because a person's behavior will show whether he is made better off or not. If a person would voluntarily pay (that is, give up some valuable resource of his) in order to move from what he has with allocation X to what he would have with Y, then that person is better off with Y than with X. And if the person would pay to avoid moving from what he has with X to what he would have with Y, then he is worse off with Y than with X.

For example, suppose that Jack and Jill are the only two people involved, that X consists of Jack having a cow and Jill having a horse, and that Y consists of Jill having a cow and Jack having a horse. Suppose further that X is the current allocation and that Jack and Jill can get together and strike a bargain without incurring costs such as hiring lawyers and paying postage and other "transaction costs" (that is, the costs of negotiating and making an agreement).

If Jack is willing to give Jill his cow in order to gain her horse, then he would be better off under Y. If Jill is willing to trade her horse to get Jack's cow, she too would be better off under Y. Accordingly, they will voluntarily exchange their possessions and move from X to Y. That move will be a Pareto-superior move, because it will produce an allocation that is Pareto-superior to the allocation from which they started. Whether it is Pareto-optimal will depend on whether they are willing to undertake any other exchange. If not, Y will also be Pareto-optimal.

The concepts of Pareto optimality and Pareto superiority are thus understood by economists in terms of economic exchange: each voluntary exchange produces an outcome that is Pareto-superior to the starting point (assuming that no one is affected other than the parties to the exchange), and the point at which no further voluntary exchange takes place (assuming no transaction costs) represents a Pareto-optimal distribution.

The Pareto criteria thus circumvent the problem of interpersonal utility comparisons by making the economic behavior of a person the measure of his or her well-being. Yet, certain difficulties make the criteria almost worthless in evaluating legal rules and systems.

The Limitations of Pareto's Efficiency Concepts

The first problem stems from the fact that economic exchanges typically have effects on third parties that can make them worse off. While a voluntary exchange makes the parties to the exchange better off—at least according to economic theory, it may make persons who are not parties to the exchange worse off. If I buy my groceries from Jill's store rather than Jack's, I might be making Jack worse off by increasing the profits of his competitor who could then use the extra profits to offer better services and take away more of Jack's business.

The Pareto criteria give us no way of comparing and evaluating the outcomes of such exchanges. As soon as even one person is made worse off by some transaction, the Pareto criteria are silent on whether the transaction produces an improvement or not. The starting point and outcome are noncomparable. Since most transactions have these third-party effects, the Pareto criteria are usually inapplicable.

Second, virtually any change in existing legal rules or social policies will produce some winners and some losers. It does not matter whether the change is a radical one (such as replacing a command economy with a market one) or a more modest one (such as lowering tax rates). In almost every case, a change in the status quo will make at least one person worse off. This means that the Pareto criteria are practically useless for judging proposed changes in legal rules and policies, for the criteria will again be silent on the question of which is better, society before the change or after.

Kaldor, Hicks, and Posner

The severe limitations of the Pareto criteria have led some economic analysts of law to develop and employ yet another standard of efficiency: the Kaldor-Hicks criterion. According to this standard, the move from one allocation, X, to another, Y, is an improvement in efficiency if and only if those who benefit from the move gain enough extra benefits so that they could fully compensate those who lose out from the move. Fully compensating a loser means giving her enough benefits so that she is as well off as she was before the move from X to Y. The Pareto demand that efficiency improvements help at least some and harm no one is replaced by the requirement that overall improvements outweigh overall harm. To that extent, the Kaldor-Hicks standard is similar to the principle of utility, which allows trade-offs between the gains of some and the losses of others.

In addition, a leading economic analyst of law, Richard Posner, has proposed a way of interpreting Kaldor-Hicks that enables the criterion to avoid the problem of interpersonal utility comparisons. He calls his version of Kaldor-Hicks "wealth maximization," and it appears to give us the best of both worlds. We can use it to weigh the gains of some against the losses of others but without doing any interpersonal utility comparisons.

According to Posner's wealth maximization criterion, the efficient allocation of society's resources is the allocation that puts each resource in the control of the person who values it the most. And efficient legal rules are ones that serve to bring about such an allocation. But the degree to which a person values a resource is not defined in terms of the pleasure or happiness or satisfaction she would receive from possessing it. Such a definition would throw us back into the intractable problem of getting inside the heads of others. Instead, the value that a person places on possessing something is determined by her economic behavior: how much she is willing and able to pay to obtain it, if she does not already have it, or how much she asks for in order to give it up, if she does already possess it.[4]

Posner's wealth maximization standard is the most useful of the efficiency criteria that have been developed by economic analysts of law. Accordingly, when we discuss efficiency, the idea should henceforth be understood in terms of wealth maximization.

Scarcity and Efficiency

On the economic view, efficiency is important for virtually every human society because humans generally live under conditions of scarcity. Scarcity means that the resources we need to satisfy our preferences are too few for everyone to get all that they would prefer to have.

The implication of scarcity is that some potential, preference-satisfying uses for a given resource must be denied when that resource is put to a different use. The efficient use of a resource by society means that the resource is allocated to the use(s) that has the highest value, as measured by how much people are willing to pay.

Does the law help society deal with scarcity by promoting efficiency? According to many economic analysts, the rules of common law do so: they are efficient in that they generally ensure that resources wind up in the hands of those who put them to their highest-valued use. In the next section, we will examine the descriptive claim that the common law is efficient. Later, we will turn to the claim that its efficiency is what explains why the common law has its particular rules.

THE EFFICIENCY OF THE COMMON LAW

As we saw in Chapter 4, the common law consists of the judge-made system of legal rules that govern property, contracts, and torts. Although much of it was originally inherited from England, the common law underwent modification and development at the hands of American judges. Economic analysts of law often claim that the rules of common law, on the whole, lead to an economically efficient allocation of resources.

Contract Law

Promoting Efficient Exchange In order to promote efficiency, a system of legal rules must ensure that resources end up in the hands of those who place the most value on them. If you value my wheat more than I do and I value your corn more than you do, it is inefficient if I keep the wheat and you keep the corn. That is because the two resources, wheat and corn, are not in the hands of the people who value them the most. Economic analysts argue that market transactions are vital in promoting efficiency because the transactions help ensure that resources end up in the hands of those who value them the most.

Accordingly, an efficient system of law must have rules that enable persons voluntarily to exchange the resources they possess. In the common-law system, according to economic analysis, the rules of contract law help to ensure that resources get transferred to those who value them the most. The rules are especially important in those situations where the parties to a contract do not simultaneously exchange their respective goods.

For example, suppose that my wheat is ready for harvesting and delivery now but that your corn will not be ready until next month. We might enter a contract in which I deliver the wheat to you before you deliver the corn to me. When I deliver the wheat, though, I am in a vulnerable situation. Now that you have my wheat, you might be tempted to hold onto your corn. The rules of contract law aim to deter such inefficient behavior on your part and thus give me sufficient assurance to send you my wheat. Only in that way will the economically efficient transaction occur. Accordingly, the rules of contract law provide that you must pay damages to me in case you breach our contract.

Suppose, however, that someone else who values your corn even more than I do gets in contact with you after I have delivered my wheat to you but before you have delivered your corn to me. She makes you a better offer for the corn than I made. Thus, it would be more economically efficient for that person to get the corn than for me to do so: she values it more. Does the law allow that to happen? Yes, because contract law only requires you to pay me the cash value of the corn to me. If you get a better offer for the corn from someone else, then you can pay me that cash amount and still have some left over for yourself. Everyone ends up better off, and economic efficiency is promoted.

Certain kinds of contracts are legally unenforceable, for example, those made as a result of duress. If you coerce me into signing a contract with you at gunpoint, the law will refuse to enforce the contract. Economic analysts point out that the rule regarding duress is economically efficient. If I do not willingly enter into a contract with you for something I possess, economic analysis will conclude that you do not really value the item more than I do. If you did, then you would voluntarily pay me for it. For the economic analyst, a person's willingness to pay is the most reliable evidence of the value of something to that person.

According to economic analysis, it is not efficient for society's legal system to enforce every promise or agreement, even when we ignore the ones made under duress. Enforcement uses society's resources, and if it costs more to enforce a contract or promise than the net gain that accrues as a result of meeting its terms, society will have lost more than it gains. Economic analysis claims that contract law contains a doctrine that helps society avoid the inefficient enforcement of such promises and contracts, the doctrine of consideration.

The Doctrine of Consideration *Consideration* is defined by the law as something of value that is given or promised in exchange for something of value. If I offer to sell you my car and you promise to pay me $500, then your $500 and my car both count as consideration: in consideration of your money, I will give you my car, and in consideration of my car, you will give me your money. Consideration is the essence of the deal we make.

The doctrine of consideration says that in order for a promise or agreement to be legally binding, each party must give consideration for what the other gives (or promises). This means that "gratuitous" promises are not legally binding. Thus, suppose I promise to give you $10 so you can buy a new compact disc, and I ask for nothing (and you offer nothing) in return. The promise is without consideration and so is gratuitous. It is not legally binding and so, in general, I may change my mind the next day without incurring legal liability.

Does the doctrine of consideration promote efficiency? Economic analysts say yes. They claim that it excludes from legal enforcement relatively trivial "social" promises whose enforcement would be economically inefficient. After all, it uses up society's resources when you take me to court in a dispute over my promise to give you $10 to buy a compact disc or when Joe takes Jane to court in order to settle a dispute about whether she promised to go out on a date with him. The valuable time of judges, lawyers, and court employees could be more efficiently spent if such informal social promises were denied legal enforcement, which is what the doctrine of consideration does.

Economic analysts also argue that the doctrine excludes from enforcement those agreements that are so vague that the courts would, in effect, be required to define the terms. In order for there to be consideration, there must be a definite something—a sum of money or a specific item or a specific promise of such—that is given in the exchange. Where nothing definite is given or promised, the courts have no specific bargain to enforce. That means that the courts would have to set the terms of the bargain in order to enforce it. But that is largely inefficient because the parties themselves are in a much better position than the courts to say what contract terms make them better off. The parties know better what value they place on things and what it is worth to them to obtain the item that the other party is offering. As a general rule, efficiency demands that the parties to a contract set the terms themselves and that courts restrict themselves to enforcing the terms that the parties have set. Accordingly, the doctrine of consideration helps promote efficiency by telling potential contract partners, "You need to settle on the specific terms of the contract yourselves, and, if you fail to do so, we are not going to formulate the terms for you."

Contract law generally requires that there be consideration for a promise to be legally enforceable. But it also keeps courts out of the business of evaluating whether the consideration given for a particular promise is adequate. The law is concerned with the existence of consideration but not with its adequacy. In other words, the courts will not inquire into whether each of the parties to a contract is getting his or her money's worth.

Economic analysts argue that the law's refusal to consider adequacy is efficient. This is due to the fundamental economic principle that individuals are in the best position to say what something is worth to them. The principle helps explain why it is efficient for courts to insist on definite consideration before they will enforce a contract, but it also helps explain why it is efficient for them to avoid questions about the adequacy of consideration. If you are the one in the best position to say what something offered as part of a contract is worth to you, then the courts should not second-guess whether you are getting your money's worth.

Negligence and the Hand Formula

The common law not only sets the rules for the enforceable bargains people make. One of its important functions is to enable those injured by another's negligence to gain compensation. The tort law sets the rules covering negligent behavior, including the criteria that determine what behavior counts as negligent.

Negligence is ordinarily explained as the failure to exercise reasonable care in one's activities. But what level of care is reasonable? Economic analysts claim that the idea of efficiency can help answer that question. Reasonable care, they say, is economically efficient care.

Suppose that unusually cold weather causes the underground water pipe that I installed to burst, causing damage to your property. Was I negligent in not putting the pipe deeper in the ground, where it would not have frozen and burst? The economic analyst will answer this question by comparing the cost of putting the pipe deeper to the expected cost of the burst pipe. The expected cost of the burst pipe is obtained by multiplying the probability that the pipe would burst by the harm done. Suppose that the probability of such a burst was 0.01 and that $1,000 worth of harm was caused. That means that the expected cost of the harm was $10. Suppose that it would have cost me an extra $20 to have put the pipe deep enough to avoid the bursting. Then it would *not* have been "cost-justified" to have placed the pipe that deep: it would have cost more than its expected benefit of saving $10. Taking precautions that are not cost-justified is not economically efficient.

Suppose, however, that it would have only cost me $8 to have placed the pipe deep enough to avoid the bursting. Then it *would* have been cost-justified to place the pipe that deep, and for that reason it would have been economically efficient to do so. Thus, I was acting in an inefficient way by not placing the pipe that deep, and according to the economic interpretation of negligence, I was being negligent.

The economic interpretation of negligence was first proposed by the famous judge Learned Hand. Judge Hand ruled that a defendant was negligent if the cost of precautions that could have prevented the harm she caused was less than the expected harm. Thus, the so-called "Hand formula" for negligence is that a defendant is negligent if and only if B is less than PL—where B = the cost of preventative measures, P = the probability of harm, and L = the harm caused.

Hand's formula is, however, not exactly correct, from an efficiency standpoint, because it is based on total costs rather than marginal ones. True economic efficiency does not merely require that the total cost of preventative measures be less than the total expected cost of the harm avoided. It requires that each additional dollar spent on prevention save at least one additional dollar in expected costs. Suppose that by an additional $6 spent on my water pipe I could have reduced expected accident costs from $10 to $3. That represents a net saving to society of $1 and so is efficient, at least compared to my spending no additional money on the pipes. But also suppose that the seventh extra dollar I spend would only bring down the expected accident costs by another $0.50. Then it would be inefficient for me to spend seven extra dollars. I should only spend $6 (at most), since the marginal benefit of that seventh dollar is less than a dollar.

On the economic view, then, the common-law doctrine of negligence promotes efficiency by encouraging persons to take cost-justified measures to prevent harm to others. It holds them liable for carelessness if but only if they failed to invest resources in prevention up to the point where additional investment would cost as much or more than the expected marginal savings.

Property

In addition to negligence and contracts, an important part of the common law covers the ownership and use of property. Economic analysts claim that these common-law rules are efficient as well.

Consider the rule that a property owner owes no duty of care to a trespasser. If I own land that has hidden pits and crevices on it, the common law does not require me to post signs that would warn trespassers of the danger. Suppose you come onto my land without my consent and fall into a pit, injuring yourself. Under the common law, I am not liable for the harm, since you are a trespasser, regardless of whether I was negligent in failing to fill in the pit or take other precautionary measures.

The economic understanding for the rule is that it promotes efficiency because the trespasser can generally avoid the cost of injury more cheaply than the landowner can: he need only refrain from trespassing, which will usually cost less than my filling the pit, putting a fence around it, or taking some similar precautionary measure. Requiring the trespasser to shoulder the costs of the injury creates an incentive for potential trespassers to refrain from that kind of illegal action. And since the potential trespasser can take measures to avoid the costs of trespassing injuries more cheaply than can landowners, efficiency is thereby promoted, according to economic analysts.

The trespassing example can be generalized to cases in which both parties are engaged in perfectly legitimate activities. In many types of disputes, the uses to which two people put their respective pieces of property end up causing harm to one of the properties. It is efficient for the harm to be avoided, but this can be accomplished only if one of the parties alters his use of his property. Economic analysis says that in such cases of "incompatible" property use, the common law typically assigns rights to the parties based on which one can take steps that avoid the harm more cheaply. The cheaper "cost avoider" is given the burden of altering his use of his property, while the other party is given the legal right to continue using his property as he has been.[5]

Suppose a railroad emits sparks and that, once in a while, the sparks will cause a fire that burns down the crops on a farm adjacent to the railroad. The railroad could prevent the sparks by slowing its speed by 15 mph. But that slowdown will cost the railroad $100 in revenues. The farmer could prevent the fires by not planting on land within thirty feet of the tracks. But not planting on that land will cost the farmer $50 in revenues. The common law will, according to economic analysis, give the railroad the right to emit sparks and put the burden of avoiding fires on the farmer, the cheaper cost avoider. The farmer will have no choice but to refrain from planting crops within thirty feet of the tracks.

THE COASE THEOREM

One of the more surprising ideas of the law and economics movement concerns cases of incompatible property uses, like the railroad and farmer example. The idea is that in these cases, the property owners would invariably arrive at the efficient outcome, regardless of how the law assigned rights, as long as there are no transaction costs and the owners cooperatively negotiate a solution to their dispute. For example, even if the law denied to the railroad the right to emit sparks and assigned to the farmer the right to grow crops next to the tracks, the efficient outcome would still occur. How is that possible if it is inefficient for the farmer to have the right to grow crops adjacent to the tracks and thus prevent the railroad from emitting sparks?

The answer stems from the fact that the railroad could and would buy the farmer's right from him. It is worth $100 for the railroad to be able to emit sparks, since that is its marginal benefit from traveling at a speed that would emit sparks. It is worth $50 for the farmer to grow crops within thirty feet of the tracks, since that is the marginal benefit of planting on that land. If the farmer is given the right, then the railroad could offer him something between $50 and $100 to refrain from growing crops on land within thirty feet of the tracks. The farmer has incentive to take such an offer, because he would be able to get more than the $50 he gets from planting on that land by making the deal. And the railroad has incentive, because it would then be able to earn an extra $100 in revenues from running at a higher speed. If there were no transaction costs and neither party stubbornly held out for a better deal (for example, the farmer did not hold out for a price of $99.99 and the railroad did not hold out for a price of $50.01), then both parties would arrive at a mutually acceptable price that allowed the railroad to run its trains at spark-emitting speed.

More generally, a theorem of the economic analysis of law is that an efficient allocation of resources will occur through market transactions, even if the initial allocation made by the law is inefficient, as long as transaction costs are zero and the parties negotiate cooperatively. This is called the Coase theorem, after the man who discovered it.

It may seem that the theorem has a paradoxical consequence for the main explanatory thesis of the law and economics movement. That thesis, which we will explore in detail shortly, holds that the efficiency of common-law rules is what explains why we have them. The Coase theorem seems to render such an explanation silly. For the theorem entails that efficiency will result no matter what the common-law rules are. If the goal is efficiency, it does not seem to matter whether the legal rules themselves assign rights and resources in an efficient way.

However, three crucial points must be kept in mind before concluding that it does not matter if common-law rules are efficient. First, market correction of inefficient allocations is possible only if legal rules allow the market transactions that make the corrections. So to the extent that we are assuming that society eventually produces efficient allocations, legal rules must promote such efficiency by allowing for the market correction of legally generated inefficiencies. This is why economic analysts regard rules governing economic exchange as vitally important in promoting efficiency.

Second, in the real world there are transaction costs. The costs involved in negotiating and entering an agreement include the costs of identifying and contacting the other parties, the cost of the time spent negotiating, the cost of lawyers, the cost of drawing up the documents, and so on. In some cases, transactions costs are so high that the law cannot rely on the market to correct inefficient allocations. The law needs to get the allocation right, the first time.

Third, in some situations, incentives for hold-out behavior decrease the chances for a Coasian bargain that corrects for legal mistakes. If the railroad had to negotiate with many farmers instead of just one, some of them might try to take advantage of the situation. They might wait until the railroad had deals with most of the others farmers and then hold out for the highest possible price. In such a situation, the few hold-outs would have great bargaining leverage against the railroad, since the railroad would not be able to run its trains consistently at the higher speed unless it had an agreement with every farmer. But if enough farmers adopt a hold-out strategy, such behavior could scuttle any deal with the railroad and result in the railroad running its trains at the lower speed. That would be an inefficient outcome. In contrast, an efficient legal rule would respond to the hold-out problem by simply assigning to the railroad at the outset the right to run trains at the spark-emitting speed.

AN EFFICIENCY EXPLANATION OF COMMON LAW

We have seen that there are many rules of common law that economic analysts describe as promoting efficiency. Let us assume for the moment that the descriptions are right and that the rules of common law largely promote efficiency. Is there reason to conclude that their efficiency is what explains the existence of the common-law rules?

Economic analysts of the law answer in the affirmative. They contend that the common law is (largely) efficient, but they also claim that its efficiency explains why it contains the rules it does. The latter claim, however, needs to be supported by additional argument, over and above whatever arguments may establish the efficiency of the common law. Even if we grant that the common law is efficient, it does not automatically follow that its efficiency is what explains it.

Posner's Argument

Richard Posner presents one argument for the efficiency-based explanation of common law. It rests on two key premises (aside from his descriptive thesis that common law is largely efficient). First, a social consensus holds that efficiency is a good thing for society. Second, the common law is an ineffective way to redistribute the resources of society in order to assist some politically active interest group. In Posner's view, the truth of the first premise inclines the judges who fashion the rules of common law to make them efficient. And the truth of the second premise means that no significant countervailing force will incline judges to assist some particular interest group at the expense of economic efficiency. The upshot is that judges will fashion the common law so as to make it (largely) efficient.

Let us grant for the moment that there is a social consensus in favor of efficiency. Why does Posner argue that the common law cannot be effectively used for redistributive purposes? He claims that any efforts to use the common law to benefit a certain interest group at the expense of efficiency will be canceled out by the economic behavior of the parties involved. For example, suppose that a judge wants to help tenants at the expense of landlords by fashioning common-law rules that make it more difficult for landlords to evict tenants who do not pay their rent. Posner says that landlords will simply cancel out the intended effect of the new rules by raising their rents to cover the extra losses. Or suppose that a judge wants to help farmers at the expense of railroads by formulating common-law rules that make railroads liable for damage to crops caused by sparks. The railroads will simply raise the rates they charge to cover the additional expense, and farmers will end up paying more to get their crops to market.

Posner is not arguing that all redistributive efforts always fail due to the economic behavior of the affected parties. He is arguing that redistributive efforts that rely on the common law will fail. But he concedes that efforts relying on legislation, say the tax code, may succeed. Funding food stamps by taxing the rich at a higher rate than the poor may indeed succeed in redistributing resources from the well-off to the poor. The difference with common-law rules, for Posner, is that they are unable to work like the progressive income tax scheme. And with redistribution out of the common-law picture, the inclination of judges to promote the agreed-on value of efficiency will operate largely unhindered.

Criticisms of Posner

The basic problem with Posner's argument for an efficiency explanation of the common law is that it does not take adequate account of the possibility that noneconomic reasons exist for the common law and that it just so happens that the rules that stem from those noneconomic reasons are also largely efficient. For example, many legal thinkers explain the rules of common law in terms of moral, rather than economic, principles and concepts. They contend that the rules are to be explained in terms of society's judgments about justice and fairness, not its judgments about the most efficient use of resources. Assuming that Posner and other economic analysts are right that the common law is efficient, its efficiency might only be a side effect, not the true basis, of the law.

Posner responds to the claim that social morality, not economics, explains the rules of common law by arguing that principles of morality and fairness typically promote efficiency. Honesty and industriousness, for example, are not only regarded as moral virtues in our society; they are also economic virtues because they help efficiency.

But even if Posner is right about the efficiency of society's moral rules, he is missing the point. The question is whether social morality or economic efficiency (or both, or something else entirely!) explains the common law. Pointing out that social morality is generally efficient, even if true, does not answer the question, much less establish that the correct answer is "economic efficiency."

Social Morality versus Efficiency

Any explanation of legal rules in terms of social morality has one major advantage over a competing explanation in terms of economic efficiency. As we have emphasized at several points, positive law is made and maintained by the human beings who make up a society. And human beings generally think and make judgments much more readily and more often in terms of their social morality than in terms of economic efficiency. Indeed, very few people ever think or make judgments in terms of economic efficiency in its Kaldor-Hicks sense. The upshot is that explaining any area of law in terms of social morality need not go beyond what persons ordinarily and often do, while explaining the law in terms of efficiency does not permit such a simple and direct route.[6]

If economists made the law, then it might be reasonable to expect that it could be explained in terms of its efficiency. After all, economists often, if not always, think and make judgments in terms of that concept. But economists do not make the law, and an efficiency explanation relies on a concept that is not in the conscious thinking of those persons who do make it. The idea of efficiency is, for the most part, "external" to the deliberations and decisions of legislators and judges. Unless there is some strong reason to think that such an "external" concept better explains the law than the "internal" concepts of society's morality, it would seem that the social-morality approach is more plausible.

What would count as a strong enough reason? In scientific inquiry, hypotheses that are contrary to common sense often end up confirmed as true. Common sense says combustion is a process in which some substance is driven out of the burning material. Scientific inquiry says that combustion is a process in which oxygen combines with the burning material. Could it be the same with legal rules, that common sense says social morality, not efficiency, explains the common law, but scientific inquiry says common sense is wrong? Undoubtedly, the proponents of law and economics would like to think of their enterprise as "scientific," but there are reasons to doubt that it has achieved that status.

THE SCIENTIFIC STATUS
OF LAW AND ECONOMICS

Scientific Method

Scientific hypotheses are put to the test of experimental confirmation. The experiments are based on predictions logically derived from the hypothesis and statements describing the experimental conditions. The predictions anticipate events (or conditions) that are not likely to occur (or exist) unless the hypothesis is true. And the predicted events must be publicly observable: whether they actually occur must not be subject to reasonable disagreement. If the events do indeed occur as predicted, then the hypothesis is confirmed. Before the hypothesis is accepted by the scientific community, though, the experimental result must be replicated by independent investigators. The requirement of replication serves as an additional check against the influence of personal biases. The point of scientific experimentation is to confront any hypothesis with the facts making up the world in such a way that the scientific enterprise becomes self-correcting and consensus-generating. False hypotheses are eventually revealed as such, and the scientific community comes to general agreement on hypotheses that are (approximately) true.[7]

Is Law and Economics Scientific?

How well does law and economics measure up to the standards of scientific inquiry? Is there anything in the law and economics approach that is analogous to experimental confirmation? Earlier it was suggested that there is no commonsensical reason to expect that the rules of common law will turn out to be economically efficient. Suppose we treat that as the "prediction" of law and economics: it will turn out, contrary to commonsensical expectations, that the rules of common law are generally efficient. The "experimental" test will then be whether it can be shown that the various rules are efficient. To the extent this can be shown, it counts as experimental confirmation of the hypothesis that efficiency is what explains the common-law rules.

However, there are two serious problems with this way of trying to make law and economics "scientific." First, the "experimental test" looks more like a test of the ingenuity of the proponents of law and economics than a test of the truth of their hypothesis that efficiency is what explains the common law. Undoubtedly, Posner and his colleagues have displayed great ingenuity in arguing that various common-law rules are actually efficient. But these arguments are hardly equivalent to experimental confirmation in science. There is nothing analogous to a publicly observable event, whose occurrence or nonoccurrence is beyond reasonable disagreement. Instead, there are arguments containing a great deal of conjecture, assumption, and interpretation. At best, the arguments show that it is a plausible hypothesis that common-law rules are efficient. But they do not confront that hypothesis with facts in the world in anything like the way that scientific experimentation does.

Consider the economic analysis of the common-law rule that says a property owner has no duty to warn a trespasser of hidden dangers on her property. That analysis claims that the rule is efficient, because it costs less for a person to refrain from trespassing than for an owner to warn anyone on the land of the dangers. Perhaps that analysis is accurate. But perhaps the rule is actually inefficient, because in many cases it might be cheaper for an owner to put up a warning sign than for a trespasser to determine the exact borders and nature of the owner's property. What law and economics gives us is no more than a plausible hypothesis.

A second problem with the attempt to make law and economics scientific concerns the "prediction" that, contrary to common sense, common-law rules will turn out to be efficient. This "prediction" fails the requirement that it be unlikely to turn out true unless the hypothesis is true that the common law is explained by its efficiency. It could well turn out that the common law is generally efficient, even if its efficiency is not what explains it. This is because efficiency may well be a by-product of what does provide the best explanation of the common law.

Suppose that common-law rules substantially reflect social morality and that the rules also are largely efficient. Posner assumes that this supposition could be true only if social morality is explained by its efficiency. If he were right and the supposition were true, efficiency would be the underlying explanation of the common law. Common sense would not be so much wrong as superficial in its social-morality explanation. For there would be something underlying social morality, efficiency, that provides the deeper explanation of the common law.

Yet, it is entirely possible that the common law is efficient because it substantially reflects social morality. Contrary to what Posner assumes, social morality may be more fundamental than efficiency and may explain both the content of common law and why it is efficient.

Recall that what is efficient depends on the preferences of individuals in society. Social morality could play a large role in determining individual preferences. Obviously not all preferences conform to social morality—or else no one would ever do anything regarded as wrong by the lights of social morality. But it is also true, if less obvious, that many of our preferences do conform to social morality.

For most people, there are costs to having preferences that go against that morality—a guilty conscience, disapproval of one's friend and acquaintances, criminal sanctions in some cases—and these costs could play a substantial role in forming and shaping our preferences. And for most people, having preferences that conform to social morality offers benefits: there is a better chance of getting what one prefers. Again, such benefits could decisively shape our preferences.

Suppose it turns out, then, that the free market established by the rules of contract law is efficient. This outcome might simply reflect the fact that social morality encourages preferences that can be better satisfied through such a market (for example, preferences for consumer goods) and discourages ones that are more difficult to satisfy through the market (for example, preferences for democratic processes in the workplace). Social morality would provide the best explanation of both the common law and its efficiency.

This possibility does not show that Posner and his cohorts are wrong when they claim that economic efficiency is what explains the common law. Yet, at this stage in our understanding of the law, the idea that its efficiency is what explains the common law remains a suggestive but unconfirmed hypothesis.

THE EVALUATION OF LAW:
SHOULD LAW MAXIMIZE WEALTH?

We now turn to the evaluative aspect of the law and economics movement: its claims about what the law should be. Like the explanatory claims, the evaluative ones revolve around the idea of economic efficiency. According to the economic analysts, the idea enables us to compare the effects of adopting different legal rules and, by such comparison, to evaluate the rules.

The Biggest Pie?

A standard claim of the law and economics movement is that efficient legal rules create the "biggest economic pie." Various interest groups may fight one another over how the slices of the pie are to be distributed, but it is in everyone's interests to have legal rules that create the biggest pie. After all, the more there is to fight over, the better off everyone seems to be. For that reason, economic analysts say that efficiency is a "neutral" value that all can endorse, whatever their differences about the just or fair distribution of resources. And for that reason, economic analysts claim that efficient legal rules are, insofar as they are efficient, good legal rules.

The claim that efficient legal rules create the biggest pie seems to be conflating the idea of efficiency as wealth maximization with a very different idea of efficiency. That different idea can be called "productive efficiency," which can be explained in terms of a simple example.

Imagine a society whose sole product is widgets. The society faces a choice between mutually exclusive legal rules A and B. Suppose that the choice of rule A will lead to a higher output of widgets per work hour. We can then say that A has greater productive efficiency than B.

Legal rules can promote productive efficiency in a number of distinct ways. For example, they may create incentives for society's laborers to work harder or faster in a given period of time. Or they may create incentives for persons to come up with technological innovations that increase the output of a given period of labor time. Or they may create incentives for persons to invest in available technology that increases the output of labor.

The idea of productive efficiency is logically distinct from that of wealth maximization. For a society to have the highest possible output per work hour is one thing; for it to allocate goods and services into the hands of those who value them the most, as measured by their willingness and ability to pay, is quite different. When economic analysts of law refer to the size of the pie, sometimes they are referring to productive efficiency and sometimes to wealth maximization, and it is not always clear which one.

Moreover, it would seem misleading to refer to wealth maximization as the creation of the biggest pie possible. For the concept of wealth maximization is about who gets what slice; it is not about the overall size of the pie. Strictly speaking, it would be more accurate to claim that wealth maximization ensures that each person gets the particular slice of pie for which he or she is willing and able to pay the most.

However, Posner would argue that there is an empirical connection between wealth maximization and productive efficiency. The connection stems from the fact that the slices of the pie are economic goods that can be used to make other goods (used to "grow" the pie). The degree to which I value some good will depend, at least in part, on how productively I can use it. The more I can make with it, the more value it is to me. And when I obtain the good through market transactions, I have every incentive to use it as productively as I can, for such use maximizes its value to me.

Other Virtues of Wealth Maximization?

In Posner's view, the wealth maximization standard has many other virtues in addition to promoting productive efficiency. Among the most important is that it provides a stronger support for individual rights than utilitarianism. Consider slavery. Slaves do not have any legal right to their own labor: they must work for the master and cannot decide to withhold their labor or to work for someone else who is offering a better deal. Our belief that no one should be a slave rests on the idea that everyone has a moral right to their own labor. But what is the basis of such a right? Utilitarianism bases the "moral right" on the claim that slavery fails to maximize the net balance of pleasure over pain.[8] But Posner regards that as a weak basis: there could be circumstances in which the pleasure of the slave owners and their families outweighs the pain of the slaves. He suggests that maximizing wealth, as opposed to utility, provides a stronger basis for the right to one's own labor.

The value of a slave's labor is much greater to the slave than to the owner. After all, everything the slave produces goes to the owner, with nothing to the slave. This reality creates a powerful incentive for the slave to work very unproductively. In contrast, as a free person with a right to his own labor, the individual has a strong incentive to work as productively as possible. This means that a person's labor is of greatest value to himself, and so maximizing wealth requires that the right to such labor be given to the individual and not to anyone else.

This conclusion of Posner's may seem a bit bizarre in light of the fact that he insists that the value of something to a person is a function of how much they are willing and able to pay for it. If a slave has nothing to pay for his freedom, does it not have zero value to him, given Posner's criterion for measuring value?

Posner's answer is that the slave can borrow the amount of money that represents the value of his freedom to him. That amount would be more than the owner would be willing to pay to keep him a slave, and so wealth maximization requires that the right to a person's labor be assigned to the person himself rather than to someone else. The fact that a slave who is forced to borrow to buy his freedom would have a large debt is irrelevant in Posner's view. For wealth maximization tells us that we should assign to every person the right to freedom from the beginning. The borrowing scenario is simply a hypothetical device that helps us determine who values the slave's freedom more—the owner or the slave himself—and thus enables us to determine whether there is moral right to freedom or a right to own slaves.

Wealth Maximization and the Poor

Markets and the Work Ethic Some critics of Posner charge that the wealth maximization standard is biased against the poor in society. They point out that a person's willingness and ability to pay for something is a function of his or her wealth. The wealthy are in a position to shell out more money for something than the indigent (or to borrow more, if they do not have enough cash on hand), and so they will end up getting much more of society's goods and services if Posner's wealth maximization standard is used. The fact that an indigent person may desire some good much more than a wealthy person or may derive much more pleasure from it is irrelevant according to Posner's standard.

Yet for Posner, one of the strengths of wealth maximization is that it does not allocate goods based simply on the intensity of a person's desire for it or the amount of pleasure she would receive from it. Such utilitarian bases for allocation flout an important moral intuition: people are not entitled to goods simply by virtue of wanting them or getting pleasure from them. Posner believes that people should have to work for what they get, and wealth maximization reinforces this work ethic. Wealth maximization supports a market society (recall the efficiency of market transactions), and in such a society the wealth of persons is generally a reflection of their productive labor. At least that is Posner's view of the matter.

The claim that wealth maximization is biased against the poor is one aspect of a broader criticism of the evaluative side of the economic approach to law. According to that criticism, reliance on notions of economic efficiency for evaluating the law is biased in favor of a right-wing political agenda. Efficiency-based recommendations, it is charged, invariably favor the sorts of solutions to social problems that political conservatives advocate.

Efficiency and the Welfare State Posner's claim about how the market rewards the work ethic is dubious: many thinkers, including conservatives, have pointed out how success in the market is often more a matter of luck than of any work ethic. But even if we reject Posner's claim, the general charge that the economic analysis of law exhibits a political bias is mistaken in a number of key respects. First, it is simply not true that efficiency-based recommendations invariably favor conservative solutions over liberal ones. Consider, for example, the question of whether government should operate a welfare program to prevent the poorest from starving or suffering similar serious deprivation. Liberals have, of course, been strong advocates of such welfare policies. Conservatives tend to be skeptical or downright hostile toward them.

Yet, Posner quite plausibly points out that a welfare system could well be justified on the basis of economic efficiency. Private charity is likely to prove insufficient, and starving persons will not generally die quietly in the street. They will commit crimes in order to feed themselves and their children. It may well be more efficient economically to establish welfare programs to ensure that such persons are fed than to leave them no choice but to feed themselves through criminal activity. That is because crime creates very heavy social costs: people spend a great deal to avoid being crime victims (buying alarm systems, not going out at night, and so on), and society spends a great deal investigating and prosecuting crimes and in imprisoning offenders. Running a welfare system may not be cheap, but it may well be cheaper for society than paying the increased costs of crime that would ensue were there no welfare system.

Another efficiency reason for some kind of a welfare program is rooted in the altruistic desires of many citizens. These citizens have a preference that their fellow citizens not suffer from drastic deprivation. If enough people who are well-off have such a preference, then a welfare program might be called for on efficiency grounds.

It may be asked why efficiency cannot be served by having altruistic citizens donate to private charity. What is the need for the liberal, government-imposed solution? Posner points out that there is an efficiency-based justification for reliance on government in this context. Although a well-off person may really want to see all the poor fed, the donations to private charity of others may make her contribution unnecessary. And her contribution, by itself, will not determine whether there are enough total contributions so that all the poor can be fed. Thus, a rational incentive exists for the well-off person to hold back from giving to private charity—in the hopes that others will give and make her contribution unnecessary—so that she can be a "free rider." As a free rider, she would get what she wants—all the poor fed—but not have to pay for it. But since each well-off person would have a rational incentive to refrain from donating so she could be a free rider, the result is likely to be a lower level of actual charitable contributions than would be efficient. And as Posner points out, government action solves this free-rider problem by financing a welfare program out of taxes that the well-off person has no choice but to pay.

There are many social problems in which a free-rider analysis can lead to liberal solutions. Environmental problems are rife with free-rider considerations, and many proponents of law and economics argue that strict environmental laws of the sort typically favored by political liberals are needed to promote efficiency. This is not to say that there is unanimity among the proponents of law and economics on environmental issues or any other politically controversial topic. But that very point takes us to the nub of the problem with the claim that law and economics has an inherent conservative bias: many proponents of law and economics use its ideas to advocate liberal solutions to policy issues.

POLITICAL DISAGREEMENT
IN LAW AND ECONOMICS

What Kind of Market?

The views that economic analysts of law have on current issues span the political spectrum from liberal to conservative. There is general agreement among them that Kaldor-Hicks efficiency is a politically neutral value that society should take account of in developing its law. And the free market is uniformly endorsed as the main engine of the economic system. But there are serious disagreements as well that lead to very different conclusions about what kinds of legal policies society should adopt.

Roughly, we can distinguish between a conservative and a liberal side to the law and economics movement. The two sides disagree over the extent to which the market should be left to operate free of legal interference and regulation. The liberal side advocates greater legal regulation and interference than does the conservative. The disagreement is rooted in conflicting conceptions of the efficiency and morality of unregulated market outcomes.

Conservatives versus Liberals

Those on the conservative side of the law and economics movement tend to think that the market almost always produces efficient outcomes and so is only rarely in need of legal correction in order to achieve efficiency. They do not reject the existence of transaction costs and other factors that interfere to some extent with the efficiency of market operations. But they judge that such interferences are usually minimal and that legal efforts to alter market outcomes usually create more inefficiency than they correct.

In contrast, the liberal side sees a greater need for legal correction of the market. It holds that transaction costs, free-rider problems, and other factors that interfere with market efficiency are more extensive than the conservative side admits. And it believes that legal regulation or circumvention of the market can effectively counteract such costs and problems and yield efficient outcomes for society.

In addition, those on the liberal side tend to subscribe to theories of justice that claim the priority of justice over efficiency and that require substantial redistribution from the outcomes produced by the market, even when the market is operating efficiently. For example, their theories of justice generally hold that government must provide significant assistance to the indigent and significantly reduce the disparities in wealth and income that result from the operation of market forces.

In contrast, those on the conservative side either deny that justice is a value that can take priority over efficiency or else hold a theory of justice according to which market outcomes are essentially just. Thus, the conservatives argue that, when transaction costs do interfere with the efficiency of market exchange, the law should generally "mimic the market." In other words, the law should produce the same outcome the market would have produced had transaction costs not interfered.

Conservatives who deny that justice takes priority over efficiency tend to be skeptical of all value judgments other than those about efficiency and to adopt a "deflationary" attitude toward such judgments. They regard judgments about justice and other moral values as no more than expressions of personal preference. Such subjective moral preferences can be incorporated along with all the other preferences people have in order to decide what is most efficient, that is, what maximizes the satisfaction of preferences. But these law and economics conservatives doubt that justice and other moral values can provide legitimate constraints on the pursuit of efficiency.

Notice that this deflationary attitude toward values other than efficiency sharply distinguishes these law and economics conservatives from many of the political groups in society that are regarded as conservative.

For example, consider fundamentalist religious groups that favor state-sponsored prayer in school, oppose homosexual rights, reject abortion, and otherwise argue that moral values must be enforced by the government. Such groups do not conceive of the moral values they advocate as personal preferences to be cranked into the efficiency equation along with the differing personal preferences of their political opponents. Rather, they think of their moral values as the true ones and as disqualifying from consideration any preferences that conflict with those values. Such persons might consistently adopt the other elements of conservative law and economics: the efficiency of markets and so on. But they would have to judge that, where market transactions would violate their moral values, the market must yield.

Some law and economics conservatives reject the deflationary account of justice and morality. They believe that justice is the primary value to which social institutions must conform. But they wind up with the same conclusion that the deflationary conservatives endorse: the free market should be largely left alone to operate without legal interference or regulation. This is because they hold to a theory of justice that says that market outcomes are largely just. Liberals, in turn, will counter with a view that questions the justice of market outcomes.

IS EFFICIENCY A NEUTRAL VALUE?

Though the liberal and conservative wings of the law and economics movement disagree on key economic and philosophical points, they do agree that Kaldor-Hicks efficiency is a politically neutral value that society should promote through its laws. They claim that it is politically neutral in the sense that it is a value that all in society should be able to agree on. All should be able to agree on efficiency because it is in the equal interests of all in society to maximize efficiency: everyone is better off if the economic pie is as large as possible.

In that respect, advocating efficiency is very different from advocating a pro-life or pro-choice position on abortion or advocating in favor of or against homosexual rights. The values relating to abortion and sexuality are controversial and cannot be agreed on by all in society. In contrast, Kaldor-Hicks efficiency is said to be a value all can agree to, even if there are other and more controversial values that each group in society also wishes to pursue. But are the law and economics advocates correct in their view of Kaldor-Hicks efficiency?

The main argument of these economic analysts hinges on a distinction between the total value of society's economic pie, on the one hand, and how the pie is sliced up and distributed among the different groups in society, on the other. Making the pie as valuable (that is, as big) as possible is one goal; dividing it up in a certain way is another. Everyone in society can agree on the first goal, even as they disagree over what the second one should be and work out their disagreements in the political arena.

The distinction between maximizing the value of the economic pie and distributing the slices of the pie in a certain way is unobjectionable as a matter of logic. However, it cannot be relied on to claim that it is in everyone's equal interest for society to maximize efficiency. That is because one cannot assume that, once Kaldor-Hicks efficiency is achieved, all interest groups have a real shot at winning the political game of distribution. Such an assumption glosses over the fact that certain groups in society have a decided advantage when it comes to dividing up the extra pie. In particular, those groups that are already economically well-off are likely to have a great advantage in the political game that determines how the fruits of increased efficiency are to be distributed. The argument that Kaldor-Hicks efficiency is a politically neutral value is thus blind to the fact that economic wealth confers political power and that society is structured so that certain groups are much more likely than others to gain the extra benefits of increased efficiency.

The argument is also blind to the fact that the burdens of maximizing the total value of the pie are likely to fall disproportionately on the shoulders of certain groups in society. For example, efficiency might be maximized by having certain groups of workers do more in less time with the same technology. Just as society is structured so that the extra benefits of increased efficiency are likely to be enjoyed by certain groups, it is structured so that the burdens of producing those extra benefits fall on certain groups. And it is unlikely that those who get the extra benefits will be those who bear the extra burdens.

Another argument for the neutrality of efficiency is tied to the deflationary view of moral values held by some in the conservative wing of law and economics: all such values are personal preferences to be cranked into the efficiency equation to determine which legal rules ensure the maximum level of preference satisfaction in society as a whole. No values are given special status or privilege in the efficiency equation: preferences in favor of homosexuality are treated on a par with those against it; preferences against abortion are treated on a par with those in favor of allowing women the choice of abortion. Since all values are treated equally, the efficiency equation is neutral.

This argument poses a big problem, however. To adopt the deflationary view of morality and justice is already to be biased against the views of those who think that justice and morality impose constraints on the pursuit of efficiency. The deflationary view is itself just one among many in society. When society adopts and acts on that view to the exclusion of others, it lacks neutrality just as much as when it adopts and acts on a particular conception of justice or morality. For society has then elevated one view, and its preferred value of efficiency, over all other views and values. Whether or not the pursuit of efficiency is justified, it is not politically neutral.

THE VALUE OF EFFICIENCY

Dworkin's Critique of Efficiency

If Kaldor-Hicks efficiency is not a neutral value, can it be regarded as an important social value at all? Ronald Dworkin expresses great skepticism about the value of Kaldor-Hicks efficiency, at least when interpreted according to the wealth-maximizing idea that the value of something to a person is determined by how much he or she is willing and able to pay for it. Dworkin argues that (1) there is nothing intrinsically good about Kaldor-Hicks efficiency, and (2) any interesting claims about its instrumental value are dubious.

Advocates of the evaluative side of law and economics agree that there is nothing intrinsically good about ensuring that things end up in the hands of those who value them the most. Instead, they rest their case on the instrumental value of efficiency, not its intrinsic value. The pursuit of Kaldor-Hicks efficiency by our legal and political institutions will, they believe, bring important benefits to society: a higher average standard of living, better protection for individual rights, and greater reward for virtues such as industriousness and diligence. According to law and economics advocates, these benefits of efficiency are why it should be used as a standard to evaluate legal rules.

Dworkin counters this view by distinguishing two claims. First is the claim that sometimes the pursuit of efficiency in the law is the best way to bring about some important social benefit. Second is the claim that the single-minded pursuit of efficiency in some area of law (or law as a whole) is always the best way to bring about some important social benefit.

Dworkin regards the first claim as trivial: no sensible person would doubt that in some cases doing the efficient thing will benefit society. If that is all the advocates of law and economics mean when they say that Kaldor-Hicks efficiency should be an evaluative standard for the law, then their view is not false but trivial and uninteresting.

Dworkin regards the second claim as interesting but unproven and implausible. It is much more sensible to believe that the best way to protect individual rights, for example, is not by pursuing efficiency but by directly granting people their rights. Sometimes it is best to approach a goal indirectly. Baseball players often say that trying to hit a home run is a bad way to go about actually hitting one: instead you should simply keep your eye on the ball and try to make contact. Dworkin concedes that a similar indirect strategy may sometimes mean that promoting efficiency is the best way bring about some intrinsic social good. But it strains belief to hold that the only goal that the law should ever aim at directly is Kaldor-Hicks efficiency.

Taking Efficiency Seriously

Defenders of the evaluative side of law and economics can agree with Dworkin that it is trivial to hold that pursuing efficiency sometimes brings social benefits and implausible to hold that efficiency is the only goal that the law should ever aim to promote. But they can argue that there a great deal of room between the trivial and the implausible for an evaluative standard of efficiency. Kaldor-Hicks efficiency, they can contend, is an important evaluative standard for the law to use: it is not the only standard that judges or lawmakers should focus on, nor is it so insignificant a standard that it should be largely ignored. Efficiency is not all-important, but it should be taken seriously.

This counter to Dworkin requires giving up the deflationary view of values other than efficiency. If efficiency is not all-important, then there must be other important values that are irreducible to efficiency. But the counter also raises a crucial question. How important is Kaldor-Hicks efficiency? How seriously should it be taken? At this point, I think there is no alternative but for the law and economics movement to shift gears. It must go beyond its formal economic principles and make explicit the tacit interpretation of human history and society that underlies it.

The importance that the movement places on efficiency stems from a certain understanding of history, especially the history of the twentieth century. According to that understanding, some societies almost entirely ignored efficiency, and the results were catastrophic for them; while others took efficiency seriously, with largely beneficial results. In the first category, for example, are the old Soviet Union and Eastern bloc, and, until recently, China. The results of refusing to take efficiency seriously were economic stagnation, political repression, and a culture of sloth and indolence. In the second category are the United States and other Western industrialized nations (at least during certain periods).

The results of taking efficiency seriously have been economic growth, political liberty, and a culture that values hard work and innovative thinking. This is, of course, a very oversimplified account of history and even a caricature of it. But it brings into bold relief the essential understanding of history that leads the advocates of law and economics to insist that efficiency be taken seriously.

Dworkin might respond by pointing out that interpretations of twentieth-century history do little to settle disputes over how important efficiency is as an instrumental value. For example, some thinkers interpret history as suggesting that the welfare state does not take efficiency seriously enough: though not nearly as bad, the welfare state is similar to communist regimes in creating economic stagnation and a culture of sloth. Others reject that interpretation and argue that the welfare state does take efficiency seriously enough. This disagreement over how to interpret the history of the welfare state may be one of the sources of the divisions between the conservative and liberal wings of the law and economics movement. The two wings clearly differ in the importance they accord to Kaldor-Hicks efficiency as a normative standard for law, and it is doubtful that any move to history can resolve those divisions. Rather, the move will simply lead to conflicting historical interpretations.

So it does seem true that looking to history to provide a definitive resolution to the question of how seriously efficiency should be taken is bound to fail. Yet, looking to history can still lead us to conclude that taking efficiency seriously is important. Advocating Kaldor-Hicks as an evaluative standard for law need not be seen in terms of Dworkin's stark dichotomy: either it is trivial or implausible. It can be seen as occupying a middle ground. When that middle ground is specified more clearly, it will turn out to be contestable. It will rely on judgments about history and society that are open to question and challenge. Law and economics advocates may be reluctant to make their stand on such contestable terrain. Yet, if they wish to vindicate their evaluative standard from Dworkin's dichotomy of triviality or implausibility, the advocates of law and economics have no choice.

NOTES

1. Accordingly, economists sometimes talk of costs and benefits in terms of preference satisfaction.

2. Philosophers and economists refer to this phenomenon as "decreasing marginal utility." In this context, the term *utility* is equivalent to benefits.

3. One way in which real people fall short of perfect rationality is that all of us sometimes act on the basis of false beliefs and misinformation. This fact raises complications that any full account of the concept of rationality must address. The complications are side-stepped in the simpler account examined in this chapter.

4. There is usually a difference between a person's asking price—how much she would ask to part with something she already has—and her offering price—how much she would be willing to pay for that same thing if she did not already have it. Posner suggests that both prices must be used in determining something's value to a person, under his wealth maximization standard. In practice, though, he seems to rely mostly on the offering price.

5. The kind of legal right involved here is one that implies a duty on the part of others not to interfere with the activity protected by the right.

6. The hypothesis that social morality explains the common law does not by itself entail that each and every aspect of social morality is reflected in the common law's rules and doctrines. One could expect, for example, that practical considerations would demand rules that in some way depart from social morality. Thus, morality says that even gratuitous promises should be kept, but practical considerations may dictate that such promises not be legally enforceable. Such considerations may well reflect efficiency-related concerns about how society's resources are used, but they would serve to qualify and modify at the edges legal rules and doctrines whose fundamental source is social morality.

7. Some recent philosophies of science have suggested that there are no "brute facts" with which to confront scientific hypotheses. These skeptical philosophies assert that everything—every occurrence, every situation—is a matter of interpretation, and there are no objective limits that can be placed on interpretation. Virtually all advocates of law and economics quite correctly reject these skeptical philosophies of science. It may well be true that there are no brute facts in the sense of facts that any person is logically compelled to accept, regardless of what else she believes. But there certainly are facts that no reasonable person can deny. It is simply not reasonable to deny that litmus paper turns red when placed in vinegar, that the weight of a given amount of mercury prior to combustion is less than the combined weight of the ash and remaining mercury after combustion, and that Halley's comet has a period of seventy-six years. And facts of this kind give science the leverage it needs to confront its hypotheses with the world.

Moreover, there is a crucial difference between systems of thinking that are self-entrenching and those that are self-correcting. The former do not in the least attempt to confront their ideas with the facts: quite the contrary, they attempt to shut out any facts inconsistent with their ideas. Stalinism (Soviet communism) is a good example of such a system of thought. It suppressed "inconvenient" facts that showed its ideas were mistaken. Any reasonable person can easily see the difference between the Stalinist suppression of facts and science's systematic testing of its hypotheses.

8. Following Bentham, many utilitarians are averse to any talk about moral, human, or natural rights. Mill is less hostile, but his account of rights still makes them derivative from social utility.

DISCUSSION QUESTIONS

1. As we saw in Chapter 4, the general common-law rule is that an individual has no legal duty to aid another person unless there is some kind of special legal relationship between the two. The counter-rule proposed by Ames is that a person should have a duty to aid anyone in grave danger as long as the person can do so with little or no inconvenience to himself. Which rule is more efficient economically? Why? Should considerations of economic efficiency determine which rule we should have?

2. Suppose that you get a thrill from killing people and I am willing to let you kill me for $100,000. The money will go to my needy family, for which I cannot provide due to serious disability. Could such a transaction be economically efficient? Under the law, your action would count as murder even if I had voluntarily agreed to it. Is there an argument based on economic efficiency for the way the law is?

ADDITIONAL READING

Baker, C. Edwin. "The Ideology of the Economic Analysis of Law." *Philosophy and Public Affairs* 5 (1975), 3–48.

Becker, Gary. *Essays in the Economics of Crime and Punishment.* Columbia University Press, 1974.

Calabresi, Guido. *The Costs of Accidents: A Legal and Economic Analysis.* Yale University Press, 1970.

Coleman, Jules. *Markets, Morals, and the Law.* Cambridge University Press, 1988.

———. "Efficiency, Auction, and Exchange: Philosophic Aspects of the Economic Approach to Law." *California Law Review* 68 (1980), 221–249.

Dworkin, Ronald. "Is Wealth a Value?" *A Matter of Principle.* Harvard University Press, 1985, pp. 237–266.

Goodman, John. "An Economic Theory of the Evolution of Common Law." *Journal of Legal Studies* 7 (1978), 393–406.

Hardin, Russell. "The Morality of Law and Economics." *Law and Philosophy* 11 (1992), 331–384.

Kelman, Steven. "Cost-Benefit Analysis: An Ethical Critique." *Regulation* (Jan.–Feb. 1981), 33–40.

Kuperberg, Mark, and Charles Beitz, eds. *Law, Economics, and Philosophy.* Rowman and Allanheld, 1983. [Contains important articles by Coase, Posner, Calabresi, Melamed, Coleman, and Fletcher.]

Pennock, J. Roland, and J. W. Chapman, eds. *Ethics, Economics, and the Law.* New York University Press, 1982.

Polinsky, A. Mitchell. *An Introduction to Law and Economics.* Little, Brown, 1983.

Posner, Richard A. *Economic Analysis of Law,* 5th ed. Little, Brown, 1998.

———. "The Value of Wealth: A Comment on Dworkin and Kronman." *Journal of Legal Studies* 9 (1980), 243–252.

"Symposium: Efficiency as a Legal Concern." *Hofstra Law Review* 8: 3 (Spring 1980).

"Symposium: The Future of Law and Economics." *Hofstra Law Review* 20:4 (Summer 1992).

Tribe, Laurence. "Policy Science: Analysis or Ideology." *Philosophy and Public Affairs* 2 (1972), 66–110.

7

※

Feminism and the Law

FEMINISM VERSUS THE
TRADITIONAL VIEW OF WOMEN

Woman's Place

In virtually all societies throughout history, men have occupied positions of power, prestige, and wealth in far greater numbers than have women. Monarchs and presidents, tribal chiefs and military commanders, high priests and influential thinkers, captains of industry and leaders of finance: the overwhelming percentage of such persons have been male. Everyone can name a few women who are exceptions to the rule. But it cannot be reasonably denied that such women are indeed exceptions and relatively rare ones at that.

In addition, in virtually all societies women have been the primary ones to raise children and attend to domestic chores, while men have maintained ultimate power over the family. Again, there are some exceptions, but the overwhelming percentage of heads of families have been men, while the vast proportion of caregivers for the young have been women.

To most people, the foregoing arrangements have seemed perfectly natural and unobjectionable. For thousands of years, it has been almost universally accepted that the social role of women is dictated by certain unalterable biological and psychological facts about them. Only women can bear children or breast-feed infants; women are more nurturing and caring of the young than men; and women are naturally more emotional and less rational than men, as manifested in the stronger emotional ties they have to their children. According to the traditional view, such ideas about the biology and psychology of being a woman represent empirically obvious facts that fit together perfectly and add up to the conclusion that women are naturally suited for the role of wife, child rearer, and homemaker and unsuited for such roles as head of household, political leader, or captain of industry.

Moreover, from the traditional perspective, women have not been shortchanged by accepting the roles of wife, child rearer, and homemaker: it is in those roles that they can find meaning and fulfillment in their lives. Indeed, women have chosen their place in society of their own accord, prompted by their natural desires for motherhood and child rearing. And they have found that their natural place in society brings with it its own kind of power and influence, different from that which men have, but no less important to society. Accordingly, all of society benefits when women stick to their natural roles within it and men to theirs. That has been the traditional view, at any rate.

The Feminist Rebellion

Feminism is at its core a rebellion against the traditional view of women and their role in society. In the feminist view, societies have systematically and unjustifiably consigned women to a social status inferior to that of men. Societies have deprived women of valuable opportunities they routinely give to men. They have blocked women's access to the positions of power and influence routinely occupied by men. And societies have generally devalued women: women's experiences, social roles, interests, ideas, and words are all treated as less important and less deserving of attention and respect than those of men.

Moreover, the subordinate social status assigned to women is not dictated by any biological or psychological facts about them, nor is the role freely chosen by them. Rather, it has been imposed by society and enforced by a range of informal and formal sanctions. It is true that only women can bear or breastfeed children. But feminists argue that these biological facts do not by themselves entail that women must bear most of the burden for taking care of and raising children. Nor do they imply that men must be the ultimate decision makers in the household. Authority in the family can be shared equally by men and women, and men can contribute equally to child rearing. But men generally refuse to accept such arrangements, defending their male privilege against the efforts of women for fair and equal treatment.[1]

Nor are there any psychological facts about women that justify the lower value placed on their experiences, ideas, and words. Many people believe that women are too emotional or psychologically unstable to be given the most responsible roles in society. But for feminists such beliefs about the psychology of women are bogus rationalizations of the subordinate status of women in society. The beliefs are part of the ideology of male dominance: they help make that dominance appear right, natural, and necessary, but the beliefs are nonetheless unjustifiable. Thus, feminists vigorously reject the view expressed in the following statement by the conservative religious and political figure Pat Robertson: in marriage women "have accepted the headship of a man, your husband. . . . The husband is the head of the wife, and that's the way it is, period."[2]

In the view of feminists, then, society has been dominated by men, in the interests of men, and against the interests of women. The term *patriarchy* is often used by feminists to refer to such a society. Patriarchy involves the systematic subordination of half of society—women—by the other half—men.

Some persons insist that patriarchy is inevitable: the superior strength and rationality of men, they argue, means that men will invariably control society and dominate women. Such a view is suggested in Pat Robertson's claim that the dominance of the husband over the wife is "the way it is, period."

Feminism rejects every argument that purports to establish the inevitability of patriarchy. It claims that patriarchy can and should be eradicated, and it is committed to that goal. Patriarchy should be eradicated because it unjustifiably subordinates the lives and interests of half of society to the other half. It can be eradicated because women can fight back against their subordination and seize from men the power to control their own destinies. Contemporary feminist philosopher Patricia Smith sums up the feminist position this way: "Feminists think that patriarchy (the subjugation of women) is not good, not ordained by nature, and not inevitable."[3]

It is important to recognize that not all persons who sincerely claim to be concerned with the interests of women are feminists. The key question is how one interprets those interests. Someone who interprets women's interests in terms of the traditional view of women is not a feminist. Such a person may be sincerely concerned to protect the interests of women, but from a feminist perspective she has fundamentally misunderstood what those interests are.

TYPES OF FEMINISM

Two Central Issues

There are many different types and versions of feminism. These differences reflect disagreements among feminists on key questions about society and politics. For our purposes, two central issues divide contemporary feminism.

The first concerns the existence of patriarchy in societies such as Canada, the United States, and other Western nations. Some types of feminism hold that patriarchy in such societies is not a thing of the past: it continues to exist in the present. Patriarchy is "alive and well," as Patricia Smith puts it.[4]

Yet, other types of feminism hold that patriarchy has been largely eliminated from Western societies: only its scattered remnants are left, and women have moved close to achieving equal standing with men. One proponent of this view, Christina Sommers, calls her position "equity feminism," and she says, "The equity agenda may not be fully achieved, but by any reasonable measure, equity feminism has turned out to be a great American success story."[5]

The second issue dividing contemporary feminists concerns the legitimate scope of government's power to use the law to advance or protect the interests of women. The issue can be subdivided into two distinct questions. The first concerns whether it is legitimate for the law to ban pornography and to place other substantial restrictions on how persons express and enjoy themselves, when those restrictions affect what John Stuart Mill and other thinkers regard as the individual's private sphere of liberty.[6] Some types of feminism assert that it is legitimate for the law to impose such restrictions as part of an effort to promote the interests of women, while other types deny the legitimacy of any such use of the law.

The second question concerns whether it is legitimate for government to treat women according to different rules than it treats men. All types of feminism affirm the principle that the interests of women must be given equal weight with those of men. But feminists disagree over the implications of the principle for whether it is legitimate for government to treat women by different rules than it does men.

For example, some feminists argue that a genuine commitment to equality requires that courts give women a preference over men when marital assets are divided up in a divorce case. These feminists claim that the preference is needed to help balance out the disadvantages women suffer from marriage and from social norms generally. But other feminists argue that the only legitimate way for government to treat men and women is to apply the same rules to both, with no one being given any special benefit or burden on the basis of gender. This debate among feminists will be explored in detail later in the chapter.

Liberals, Radicals, Progressives, and Conservatives

We are now in position to describe several distinct types of feminism, depending on their answers to the questions about patriarchy and the legitimate scope of government's power to advance the cause of women. All types reject the traditional conception of women and their role in society, and all four affirm the equal standing and dignity of women with men. That is what makes them feminist views. But beyond that, they disagree over important questions of social and legal philosophy.

Liberal feminism combines the following three ideas: (1) patriarchy has been largely eliminated from Western societies, (2) there is a private sphere of individual liberty with which government and law may not legitimately interfere, and (3) government must treat men and women by the same rules.

Radical feminism repudiates each of the three ideas of liberal feminism, and in that sense is at the opposite end of the feminist spectrum. It holds (1) patriarchy still exists in Western societies, (2) government may legitimately interfere with the so-called private sphere of individual liberty, and (3) in order to help eliminate patriarchy, government may treat women according to different rules.

Progressive feminism stands between the liberal and radical versions. It agrees with radical feminism that patriarchy continues to exist, but it does not accept the radical view of the legitimate scope of government power. One version of progressive feminism accepts the liberal idea that there is a private sphere of individual liberty with which government and law may not interfere. Another version accepts the liberal idea that women must be treated by the same rules as men. And a third accepts liberal claims both about individual liberty and about treatment by the same rules.

Conservative feminism also stands between liberal and radical feminism, though in a quite different location than does progressive feminism. It agrees with the liberal view that patriarchy has been largely eliminated from Western societies, but it rejects the liberal view of the limits of the legitimate scope of government action. One version of conservative feminism accepts the radical view that government and law may legitimately interfere with the so-called private sphere of individual liberty. So conservative and radical feminists could agree, for example, on the banning of pornography.

Another version of conservative feminism accepts the radical view that it is sometimes legitimate for government to treat women by different rules than it treats men. So conservative and radical feminists could agree, for example, that courts should give a preference to mothers in child custody hearings. Yet a third version of conservative feminism would accept the radical view both on the private sphere and on differential treatment.

In the remainder of this chapter, we will focus mainly on liberal and radical feminism, not because they are the only consistent types but rather because they incorporate the essential claims out of which both progressive and conservative feminism are constructed.

THE QUESTION OF PATRIARCHY

Virtually all feminists agree that some existing societies are patriarchal: some Middle Eastern, African, and Asian societies, for example, are said to pervasively subordinate the lives and interests of women to those of men. And all feminists agree that women in societies such as the United States are treated in unfair and disadvantageous ways. But a deep split exists among feminists over how that treatment is to be understood. Liberal feminists understand the treatment as discrimination, while radicals understand it as oppression.[7] This crucial distinction between discrimination and oppression divides feminists on the key question of whether contemporary Western societies are patriarchal.

Discrimination and Oppression

The idea of discrimination has many possible meanings. In the context of discussions about the treatment of women in society, discrimination is best interpreted as a form of unfair treatment that (1) deprives someone of an important good (a right, opportunity, commodity, and so on) to which she is entitled or imposes on her some substantial burden (a cost, obligation, and so on) that she should not be made to bear and (2) grants to others that same kind of good or declines to impose on them that same kind of burden.

Accordingly, discrimination involves a contrast in the treatment of distinct persons or groups. If everyone is being treated unfairly, then that is surely wrong, but it would be misleading to describe the treatment as a form of discrimination. Thus, it is wrong for everyone to be forced to pay excessive taxes, but no discrimination is involved. In contrast, if certain persons are forced to pay excessive taxes while others are not, we can say that discrimination is leveled against the former group.

The idea of oppression builds on but goes beyond that of discrimination in a crucial way: it links the discriminatory treatment of persons to the overall structure of society. To claim that certain persons are victims of oppression is to claim that the discriminatory treatment they receive is built into the very structure of society. Society's practices, laws, norms, customs, and institutions work together to treat these persons, but not others, in certain unfair and disadvantageous ways.

The existence of patriarchy entails the oppression of women, not merely discrimination against them. Patriarchy means that the very structures of society—its system of laws, customs, norms, and expectations—operate in unison to the unfair disadvantage of women and to the unfair advantage of men.

The existence of some laws or practices that discriminate against women would not by itself establish (or presuppose) that women are oppressed or that patriarchy reigns in society. For such laws or practices could, in theory, be exceptions to the way society generally treats women. In contrast, if patriarchy exists in a given society, it means that such laws and practices are not the exception but the rule: they are part of a whole system of social practices, customs, norms, rules, and expectations that work against the interests of women and in favor of the interests of men.

Is Patriarchy a Thing of the Past?

Feminist thinkers are deeply split over whether the unfair and disadvantageous treatment women receive in the United States and similar societies should be seen as a matter of discrimination or a matter of oppression. Those who see it as discrimination but not as oppression believe that in the past our society was a patriarchy and did systematically oppress women but that the unfair treatment of women is no longer built into the very structure of society in the way it once was. In the past, men could vote, but women could not; men would routinely serve on juries, while women mostly did not; husbands were in legal control of all marital assets; and men generally enjoyed legal privileges and rights that women were denied.

But liberals will argue that the situation is dramatically different today. They will not deny the existence of some sex discrimination, but they will argue that discrimination against women has been largely eliminated from the laws and official policies of society. Moreover, our laws enable women who are the victims of discrimination to get legal redress for the harms inflicted on them. Liberal feminists thus argue that our society is dramatically different from the days when its laws and policies operated in unison to put women at an unfair disadvantage.

Radical feminism claims that we must not look simply at the formal legal rules and policies of society in order to determine whether it is still systematically oppressing women: we must look at all of its informal norms, rules, and practices as well. For example, the mother, not the father, is still expected to do the lion's share of the work involved in raising children and keeping the household in order (that is, doing the cooking, cleaning, shopping, errands, and so on). Even in families in which both parents are employed outside the home, women are expected to keep the household running and in fact put in far more time in taking care of domestic affairs than men.

According to radical feminism, patriarchy disadvantages women in far more ways than by unfairly distributing the burden of raising a family. For example, powerful institutions in society generally take the word of a man more seriously than they do that of a woman, other things being equal.

In the view of radical feminists, the oppression of women starts long before they have become adults. Society's norms and expectations are geared toward discouraging girls from aspiring to positions of power and influence occupied by men. Girls are systematically encouraged to have lower expectations for themselves than do boys. For example, they are dissuaded from pursuing their interests in science and mathematics, while boys are encouraged to pursue science projects and take the most difficult math courses. The self-confidence of girls is undercut, while that of boys is bolstered.

For the radical feminist, then, from childhood to adulthood, society's expectations and norms disadvantage women relative to men. It is misguided to think that equality between the sexes exists just because laws and other official policies are the same for men and women. For those laws and policies are operating in the context of a society whose practices and expectations do not treat men and women equally.

In the remainder of the chapter, we will examine in more detail the ways in which radical and liberal feminists disagree over the nature of contemporary society and the way the law should promote women's equality. At the end of the chapter, we will take up the question of which view of society—the liberal or the radical—is more accurate.

THE QUESTION OF PRIVACY: A RADICAL VIEW

Feminists disagree over the liberal idea that there is a sphere of private conduct in which individuals should be at liberty to act without interference by government or law. This disagreement implicates some of the most important social and legal issues of our time. It is at the center of the controversies over abortion and equal rights for homosexuals. And it provides one of the main targets that radical feminists attack in their criticisms of liberal feminism.

The Problems with Privacy

On the surface, the liberal idea of privacy may seem like good one: it marks off a zone in which one should be free from the surveillance and regulation of public authorities. And that kind of freedom seems like something we should all celebrate. But radical feminists argue that appearances are deceiving. They attack the liberal idea of privacy from two directions.

First, they claim that law and official government policy are, from the very beginning, inextricably entangled in the so-called private domain. The domain of marriage and the family, for example, is regarded by liberals as belonging to the very heart of the zone of privacy into which government should not intrude. But marriage and the family are extensively regulated, controlled, and even constituted by law and official policies. Radicals point out that the law is what determines which relationships count as marriages and which do not; the law is what determines when a marriage has begun and when it has ended; the law is what determines which groups of persons count as a family and which do not.[8] Thus, radical feminists argue that conceptually it makes no sense to argue that there is a "private" sphere of marriage and family life from which government should be barred.

Radical feminists also mount a second line of attack on the liberal idea of privacy. They argue that, in practice, the idea has helped reinforce and perpetuate the patriarchal power men have over women. Their key claims are that women are oppressed within the "private" sphere of the family and that the liberal idea of privacy is an obstacle to eliminating that oppression. It is an obstacle because it helps perpetuate the idea that family matters are "nobody else's business." Let us explore these radical claims in more detail.

Fighting "Private" Oppression

For radical feminists, effectively fighting against patriarchy means that we must make what takes place within the "private" domain of the family a matter of public and political concern. This is a central part of the meaning of the feminist slogan "The personal is political."[9]

Consider the matter of wife battering, often cited by radical feminists to support their view. It has always been a crime for one person to physically assault another, certain exceptions aside, such as one boxer punching another in the middle of a match. Radical feminists claim that a husband's battering of his wife was historically an exception as well. Thus, some feminists cite a ruling of a North Carolina court from 1868 that it was legally permissible for a husband to strike his wife because "every household has and must have a government of its own . . . and we will not interfere or attempt to control it."[10] Even if wife battering once was a formal exception to the rule against assault, it no longer is. Yet, radical feminists argue that to a disturbing degree it remains an informal exception. Police and judges are extremely hesitant to get involved in cases of wife battering. Radical feminists argue that a principal reason for this hesitation is the continuing belief that the family is a private domain into which the law should not as a rule intrude: family disagreements are a private matter that should be settled within the family.

This belief was expressed by O. J. Simpson when police came to his home to investigate reports that he was beating his wife. He told them, "This is a family matter. Why are you making a big deal out of it?"[11] Radical feminists argue that such thinking is widespread and responsible for an epidemic of wife abuse. Again, the interests of women suffer as a result of the idea of a zone of privacy, and the fight against patriarchy means a fight to eliminate the oppression of women in the so-called private sphere.

Feminist thinker Rhonda Copelon puts the radical view succinctly: "Marital privacy has operated historically to justify state nonintervention in the family and thus to reinforce patriarchal power."[12] And Catharine MacKinnon levels a similar criticism of the idea of privacy: "The legal concept of privacy can and has shielded the place of battery, marital rape, and women's exploited labor."[13]

Women's Labor

MacKinnon's reference to "exploited labor" refers to a recurrent theme among radical feminists. They point out that women do the vast majority of the unpaid work involved in raising children and caring for the household. This is true even when the woman also has a paying job outside the home.

The zone-of-privacy idea seems to imply that we should view these family work arrangements simply as the result of the personal and purely voluntary choices of the women and men involved. But radical feminists argue that such a view is deeply mistaken. Those "personal" and "voluntary" choices reflect and reinforce an important truth about society as a whole and the distribution of power within it: society is patriarchal, and so men are in position to advance their interests at the expense of women.

In the view of radical feminists, it is not some inexplicable coincidence that, in almost all families, the woman bears a disproportionate share of the burden of the unpaid work of the family. It is the very predictable result of the way girls and boys are socialized and of the way women and men are treated in society.

Children are raised to expect that it is the girls who will have the job of raising children and that the job will be done without financial compensation. As they play with their dolls and play house, girls are in training for the future role society expects of them. These expectations are reinforced by the way society treats adult women and men. Women who do not stay home to raise their kids are typically viewed with disapproval, while men who stay home to raise their kids are typically viewed as inadequate.

According to this radical feminist analysis, men benefit at the expense of women from these social expectations and norms. The mother tends to become economically dependent on the father, to the extent he sticks around. This gives the father much more say in the way the family operates: the fact that he is bringing home the paycheck (or the larger of the two paychecks) gives him leverage over the mother and the ability to enforce his wishes over hers. If the mother tries to insist on an equal voice, he can explicitly or tacitly threaten to leave, leaving her and the children destitute. In the meantime, the father gets someone to raise his kids, do his laundry, cook his meals, clean his home—all for free and all the while developing his workplace skills and increasing his value in the labor market.

ABORTION RIGHTS:
BEYOND PRIVACY TO EQUALITY

Abortion and the Indigent

The radical criticisms of the liberal idea of privacy lead naturally to the conclusion that the legal right to abortion should not be based on any general right of privacy. Accordingly, many radical feminists repudiate the privacy-based reasoning of the Supreme Court in the famous case of *Roe v. Wade,* which held that women have a constitutional right to an abortion. The Court argued that the right of abortion was based on a general right of privacy that protected certain intimate and personal decisions from government interference. Those decisions included the decision of a couple to use contraceptives and that of a woman to terminate her pregnancy.

Yet, many radical feminists contend that a privacy-based argument in favor of abortion rights is seriously, even fatally, flawed. They argue that the defects of such reasoning go beyond the conceptual and practical problems with the liberal idea of privacy, discussed in the previous section. Their contention is that the privacy-based argument has harmed those women who are most in need of effective control over when and whether to bear children, namely, women who are unable to afford an abortion.

The radicals contend that when the right to an abortion is based on the idea of privacy, it follows that government has no responsibility to pay for the abortions of indigent women. If a woman's decision to obtain an abortion is a truly private matter, beyond the legitimate concern of government, then a woman cannot demand that government subsidize her decision: whether she can afford an abortion is a strictly private matter with which government should not be concerned. Indeed, radical feminists claim that the Supreme Court has drawn precisely this conclusion, in a ruling that government has no constitutional obligation to pay for an indigent woman's decision to have an abortion.[14]

Radical feminists insist that all women, indigent or not, be able to control when and whether they bear children. Without that control, women can fall too easily into the traps and snares of patriarchy: they become mothers in circumstances where they do not desire to raise children, and yet society exerts great pressure on them—not on the fathers—to be the principal caregiver. This serves to replicate the patterns and relations of patriarchy.

Women who can afford an abortion may be better off than they were before the Supreme Court recognized a constitutional right to an abortion. Yet, on the radical analysis, women who cannot afford an abortion are left without any effective right to an abortion: all they have is a formal right that exists on paper but not in their real lives. The result is a setback for the political cause of true equality for all women.

Equality: Eradicating Women's Oppression

If a privacy-based argument for abortion rights is flawed both philosophically and politically, what kind of argument would be better? Radical feminists contend that an argument based on the idea of equality is superior, and they develop such an argument in a way that ties the abortion issue to their claims about patriarchy.

The argument operates from the premise that patriarchy is alive and well and oppresses women. The eradication of that oppression and the establishment of true equality between men and women require the elimination of laws that reflect and reinforce patriarchy. Laws that criminalize abortion fit into that category because they deprive women of control over when and whether they will bear children. For the reasons cited earlier, mothers—as the principal caregivers for children and caretakers of the household—have much less opportunity for professional and personal development and for economic independence than do fathers. Accordingly, in order to eradicate women's oppression and establish the equality of men and women, society must eliminate laws that deprive women of control of when and whether they will bear children.

Many people will object to this argument by claiming that women can be required to carry their pregnancies to term without being oppressed as long as they have the option of putting their babies up for adoption. But radical feminists will counter this objection with two points.

The first point concerns the medical dangers and disabilities associated with carrying a pregnancy to term. Those dangers and disabilities put women at a relative disadvantage to men, quite aside from the question of who is to care for the child after its birth. Some critics of radical feminism might reply that those disadvantages can be largely, though not entirely, canceled out—if society provides all pregnant women with good health care. Yet, few if any radical feminists will accept such health care as an even remotely adequate substitute for the right to terminate a pregnancy.

This brings us to the second and more fundamental point: the option of putting one's baby up for adoption is largely illusory, in the eyes of radical feminists, because social expectations and norms regarding the role of women effectively coerce many women into keeping the baby and raising it themselves. The option is one that can be taken only in the face of intense psychological and social pressure that reflects and reinforces the traditional view of women.

Moreover, such pressure is exercised after years of socialization in which girls are taught that their most important role in life is to be a mother. In these circumstances, the large majority of women will end up keeping their child if the pregnancy is brought to term, which will then continue the cycle of patriarchal oppression in which the mother becomes the principal caregiver, while the father has the opportunity for economic independence and career advancement.

From a radical feminist perspective, linking abortion to equality helps focus attention on the fact that patriarchy is reinforced and supported when women cannot control whether and when they bear children. Laws against abortion are to be rejected, in the radical view, mainly because they are part and parcel of the system of women's oppression, not because they represent the invasion of some private domain by the government.

Moreover, the equality-based argument for abortion rights can be used to support the idea that society must guarantee all women an effective right to an abortion, not simply a formal right. Real equality between men and women requires that all women have an effective right to abortion, which would make it incumbent on government to subsidize the decisions of indigent women to terminate their pregnancy.

Radical feminists also contend that focusing on equality rather than privacy helps expose a crucial but usually unstated premise of the pro-life movement. That movement paints the abortion issue in terms of a conflict between the right to life of the fetus and the right to choose of the woman. It claims that the right to life must, as a rule, take precedence. However, many radical feminists argue that the traditional view of women underlies this claim about the overriding importance of the fetus's life. Pro-lifers are so ready to discount the importance of a woman's choice to terminate her pregnancy and to elevate the importance of the fetus because they believe that women should be mothers and child rearers.[15] Thus, Copelon describes the pro-life position this way: the goal is "not simply to save fetuses but to return woman to her 'proper place'—to assure that motherhood remains her primary preoccupation."[16]

For radical feminists, then, the central conflict of the abortion debate is not between differing views of the fetus but between differing views of women. The issue of abortion is seen as a major battleground on which the struggle between the traditional and the feminist conceptions of women is being fought out. And should the pro-life side win, it would give aid, comfort, and support to those who hold the traditional view and strengthen the grip that patriarchy has over women in our society.

ABORTION RIGHTS: A LIBERAL VIEW

Defending the Right of Privacy

Liberal feminists have generally supported a privacy-based argument for abortion rights. The idea of privacy was central in the legal briefs filed with the Supreme Court by feminist lawyers in *Roe v. Wade*. For example, Harriet Pilpel's brief claimed that "the right to an abortion must be viewed as a corollary of the right to control fertility which was recognized in *Griswold*. [It] is an aspect of the right to privacy and liberty."[17]

More recently, Kathleen Sullivan has defended a privacy-based argument according to which a "bedrock" principle in our legal system is that "we, unlike

China, . . . do not allow reproduction to be regulated by the state."[18] Any such regulation would constitute a legally intolerable invasion of privacy.

In the view of these feminist thinkers, a right to privacy is firmly rooted in our nation's legal traditions. They contend that the idea that the law protects a general right of privacy makes sense of and helps justify a wide range of legal precedents and doctrines. The idea of a private domain of individual choice is thus seen as an essential part of our scheme of government and law.

Moreover, feminist supporters of the idea of privacy claim that it is a gross misuse of the idea to employ it for the protection of rapists and wife batterers. The point of the right to privacy is not to let the strong abuse the weak by having government turn its back. Rather, the point is to prohibit government from using its power to dictate to individuals how they must conduct their intimate affairs even when they are not abusing any other person. To that extent, liberal feminists claim that legal recognition of the right to privacy enables women to have more control over their own lives.

Liberal feminists also reject the radical claim that a privacy-based argument for abortion rights undercuts the idea that government should pay for the abortions of the indigent. The purpose of the right of privacy is to help empower individuals by prohibiting government from telling them how to conduct their intimate affairs. If government provides funding of abortions for poor women, it is not telling them they must get an abortion. That would be an invasion of privacy.

In contrast, government funding for abortions simply provides an indigent woman with the resources she needs to carry out a decision to terminate her pregnancy, and the decision is itself left up to the woman. This is not an invasion of privacy any more than it is an invasion of the privacy of the elderly for the Medicare program to provide them with health insurance. In both cases, the government is providing resources so that individuals can effectively exercise control over their lives. The purpose of the right of privacy is in no way undercut; to the contrary, it is reinforced by expanding a woman's feasible options.[19]

Liberal Equality

Nonetheless, some liberal feminists believe that a privacy-based argument for abortion rights should be supplemented by an equality-based argument. For example, before her appointment to the Supreme Court, Ruth Bader Ginsburg wrote about abortion: "Nor is the overriding issue state versus private control of a woman's body for a span of nine months. Also in the balance is a woman's autonomous charge of her full life's course. . . her ability to stand in relation to man...as an independent, self-sustaining, equal citizen."[20]

For Ginsburg and many other liberal feminists, an equality-based argument for abortion rights is also needed. But it will be very different from the equality-based argument offered by radical feminists. The central contention of the latter argument is that antiabortion laws reflect and reinforce society's patriarchal oppression of women. The central contention of the liberal argument is that antiabortion laws discriminate against women. Let us examine the liberal version of the equality argument in more detail.

According to liberal feminists, antiabortion laws place serious burdens and disadvantages on women from which men escape altogether. By requiring women to carry their pregnancies to term whether they want to do so or not, such laws impose significant medical risks on women and disrupt their lives in ways that men do not experience. These burdens and disruptions are neither trivial nor necessarily temporary. They can disrupt a women's career, undermine her economic independence, drive her into poverty, and, in some cases, lead to lasting physical disability or death.

Pregnancy is the result of the sexual activity of a man and a woman. When the law prohibits women from terminating their pregnancies, it is treating their sexual activity in an unfair and disadvantageous way relative to the way it treats the sexual activity of men. The law is guilty of discrimination based on sex, the liberal argument holds, since it singles out women for disadvantageous treatment. Accordingly, the law is a violation of the constitutional requirement that all persons receive the equal protection of the laws.

Note that this argument does not depend on the radical feminist claim that society as a whole systematically oppresses women. The liberal argument from equality is that antiabortion laws are discriminatory against women, not that they are part of a patriarchal system that oppresses women.

The liberal argument thus focuses on the disadvantages imposed on women by the antiabortion laws in and of themselves, quite apart from how other laws or social rules may or may not disadvantage women. There is no general indictment of society as one that systematically and pervasively deprives women of opportunities, rights, and goods that it routinely grants to men. Rather, the argument focuses narrowly on the direct impact that antiabortion laws have on the interests and lives of women.

This liberal argument from equality can be quite easily combined with the liberal argument from privacy. The key idea joining the two is this: discriminatory treatment is especially objectionable when it concerns matters, such as sexual conduct and reproduction, that belong to the intimate, private realm.

The law demarcates a private realm in large part because the activities belonging to it have a special importance to individuals and the way they give meaning and direction to their lives. Discriminatory treatment of women is objectionable even when it concerns opportunities and rights that are not crucially important, for example, the right to administer the estate of a deceased relative.[21] But discriminatory treatment is all the more objectionable when it concerns matters of critical importance to individuals, such as the decision to a bear a child.

ABORTION RIGHTS: THE
LIBERAL OR RADICAL APPROACH?

We have seen that at least two approaches are possible in developing a feminist argument for a constitutional right to an abortion. A liberal approach combines the idea that antiabortion laws invade a zone of individual privacy that should be free of government interference with the idea that such laws discriminate against women and so violate their equal rights. A radical approach rests on the idea that antiabortion laws are part and parcel of the society-wide oppression of women and so violate their equal rights.[22]

As we have examined the right of privacy in some detail in Chapter 3, our focus here will be on the competing liberal and radical versions of the equality-based argument. Which of the two is better?

Let us begin by distinguishing two separate issues raised by the question. The first asks, Which version of the equality argument makes the better legal argument that the Constitution should be interpreted as protecting the right to abortion? The second asks, Which version makes the better moral argument that women should have a basic, legally protected right to abortion?

Sometimes the best legal argument for recognizing a certain right will be different from the best moral argument for recognizing that same right. We saw in Chapter 2 that both legal positivism and the strongest form of natural law theory—Dworkin's interpretive version—agree that legal argument is different in important ways from moral argument. Let us, then, first consider the abortion issue from the perspective of legal argument.

The Legal Argument

From the perspective of the law, the radical approach has one fatal disadvantage from which the liberal approach does not suffer: the radical argument has implications that no court would, or should, accept. At the center of the radical analysis of abortion is the view that women are so oppressed by society that they are routinely coerced by the force of social expectations and norms into bearing and raising children. Such a view may or may not be accurate, but it could not be consistently enforced by any court in our legal system. That is because the view calls into question the legality of much of what every court takes for granted.

For example, the radical view would bring into question the validity of marriage: can women really voluntarily choose to get married, if patriarchy routinely coerces them as the radical feminist analysis suggests? Would not the agreement to get married typically be one made under coercion, and would not marriage itself be a kind of slavery? Moreover, if the view is correct that patriarchy routinely coerces women into bearing children, it would bring into question the voluntary nature of most, if not all, heterosexual intercourse: would there be any clear difference between rape and intercourse that was "voluntarily" chosen by the women?

Some radical feminist thinkers have not hesitated to suggest that the marriage contract is made under coercion, that marriage is a form of slavery, and that there is no clear difference between rape and "voluntary" intercourse. While these feminists are admirably consistent in their view of American society as an oppressive patriarchy, judges do not share that view and cannot consistently enforce it. Most judges will perceive the radical view as a gross exaggeration of the sex-based discrimination whose existence they are prepared to concede. And they will point out that, while discrimination is a wrong that our law clearly condemns, there is no legally recognized wrong of oppression.

Moreover, even if the radical view is not an exaggeration, the norms of our legal system simply do not permit courts to engage in the wholesale repudiation of laws whose validity is recognized by almost all of society. Judges who are convinced of the accuracy of radical analysis should acknowledge that courts should refrain from enforcing it.

The liberal analysis has no such shortcomings when presented as part of a legal argument. Courts are quite prepared to accept the contention that society sometimes discriminates against women, even if they are not prepared to accept the radical notion that it pervasively oppresses women. And the liberal charge that antiabortion laws are guilty of discrimination against women does not imply that marriage laws or rape laws are of suspect validity. Courts can accept the liberal version of the equality argument without committing themselves to the wholesale repudiation of laws whose validity is acknowledged by virtually all of society.

When viewed from a legal perspective, then, the liberal argument is superior to the radical one. Judges can accept the liberal argument as consistent with the norms of our legal system, while they cannot and should not accept the radical argument when presented as a legal one.[23]

The Moral Argument

How does the radical argument fare when presented as a moral one in favor of a basic, legal right to an abortion? The answer to that question turns in large measure on the issue of whether women continue to be oppressed by patriarchy in our society. We will take up that complex issue again later in this chapter.

For the sake of argument let us assume for the moment that radical feminists are right in claiming that patriarchy still exists. Let us also assume that the recognition of a basic, legal right to abortion is important for the elimination of patriarchy. The radical feminists would still need to make the additional moral argument that the importance of eradicating patriarchy overrides any competing considerations that may stem from the moral standing of the fetus. Without that argument, they would not be able to legitimately conclude that society should recognize a basic, legal right to abortion.

Pro-life advocates claim that the life of the fetus has an intrinsic moral value that must be protected by the state. Radical feminists typically refuse to take this claim at face value. They see the claim as deceptive and ideological: the claim purports to assert the moral importance of fetal life, but what is really behind the assertion is the idea that women should play the traditional role of bearing and raising children. The claim is a pro-patriarchy claim and not, as it seems at first, a pro-fetus one.

This response to the pro-life position is, however, inadequate. It sidesteps the question "Does the fetus have the moral significance ascribed to it by the pro-life position?" The question cannot be legitimately sidestepped; it must be confronted directly. The pro-life claim cannot simply be dismissed by invoking either the pro-patriarchal effects or pro-patriarchal motivations that purportedly lie behind the claim.

Catharine MacKinnon attempts to avoid questions about the value of the fetus by saying abortion is not a moral issue but a political one. However, her reasoning rests on a false dichotomy: an issue must be either moral or political and cannot be both. In fact, some moral issues are also political ones, and the abortion issue is one of those. It is a moral issue because it involves questions about the moral obligations we have. It is a political issue because it involves questions of how women can gain standing in society equal to that of men. MacKinnon's effort to sidestep moral questions thus fails.[24]

Liberal feminists are also sometimes guilty of failing to address pro-life claims about the value of the fetus. They sometimes contend that the fundamental question is the procedural one, "Who is to decide, the woman or the state?" and that the substantive question "What is the moral value of the fetus?" can thus be avoided. But this view is wrong, and liberal feminists cannot in fact avoid the substantive question.

Liberal feminists are committed to prohibiting the state from interfering with a woman's decision to terminate her pregnancy, and such a commitment presupposes that the fetus does not have the moral value that pro-life advocates ascribe to it. That is because pro-life advocates claim the life of the fetus is so important and so deserving of protection that it overrides the woman's choice to terminate her pregnancy. The attempt to make the abortion issue a completely procedural one simply begs the question.

THE DIFFERENCE DEBATE

Men and women are different from each other in some obvious ways and perhaps some not-so-obvious ones as well. Are any of these differences good reasons for society to have different rules for women than for men? This question is one aspect of what is called the "difference debate" in feminism.

Some feminists assert that the rules for women should be the same as the rules for men.[25] They do not deny that there are certain differences between the sexes, but they believe that the fair treatment of both men and women requires that the rules be the same for both.

Other feminists assert that, in some important respects, the rules for women should be different from the rules for men. They claim that there are certain differences between the sexes that make it unfair to women when society applies exactly the same rules to them as to men. They believe that fair treatment of women requires some difference in treatment.

What is the relation of the difference debate to the disagreements among feminists over whether the unfair treatment of women is a matter of oppression or discrimination? Conceptually, there is no necessary connection. The radicals' claim that women are oppressed by society entails neither that society should apply the same rules to both men and women nor that it should apply different rules; the same is true of the liberals' claim that the unfair treatment of women is discrimination, not oppression. Nonetheless, there is some connection between the difference debate and the dispute over oppression.

Radical feminists typically argue that the overriding goal of society should be the elimination of patriarchy and that the goal cannot be effectively pursued if the same rules are always applied to men and women. The same-rules strategy will only perpetuate the inequality of women because women's oppression stems largely from society's informal expectations and norms rather than from its formal rules and policies. Special rules for women are sometimes justified in order to counteract the disadvantages placed on them by society's informal expectations and norms. For example, society puts women at an economic disadvantage, and so it is unfair if judges make child custody decisions based mainly on a parent's economic status. Women should be given allowance in such hearings in order to compensate for the economic disadvantages society imposes on them. That is the view of many radical feminists, at any rate.

In contrast, liberal feminists argue that the past oppression of women has been eliminated for the most part and that this happy outcome is mainly the result of the successful demand that there be the same official rules for women as for men. As for society's informal practices and expectations, liberals argue that they will change as more women begin to occupy positions that society's rules once reserved for men. Treating women by different rules and giving them special allowances send the unfortunate message that women are really inferior to men and need special help or protection. Such a message would reinforce the traditional conception of women and their role in society, thus subverting the feminist aim of achieving equality. If women are to achieve full equality in every sphere of society, then they must not demand special treatment or protection; instead, they must insist on being treated according to the same rules that men are.

Pregnancy Benefits

Let us turn to an example in order to explore further the different ways in which liberal and radical feminists approach the issue of whether society should have the same rules for both men and women. Suppose that Jack and Jill work in the same job for the same organization. Jill becomes pregnant and as a result is unable to work from June 1 to June 30. Jack gets into a car accident, as a result of which he is unable to work during the exact same period of time. Consider the following four possibilities:

1. The organization has no disability program: anyone who is unable to work due to a disability of any kind will not get paid for the period of time in which he or she does not work. Neither Jack nor Jill receive any disability benefits from the company.

2. The organization has a disability program that covers those who are unable to work because of accident or illness but does not cover those unable to work because of pregnancy. A person who is injured in a car accident will still get his or her wages while recovering and unable to work. A woman who is pregnant and unable to work because of the

pregnancy will not get paid until she returns to work. Jack will receive disability benefits from the company, but Jill will not.

3. The organization has a disability program that covers those who are unable to work due to pregnancy but does not cover those unable to work due to accident or illness. Jill will receive benefits from the company, but Jack will not.

4. The organization has a disability program that covers those who are unable to work because of accident, illness, or pregnancy. The benefits received by the employees with disabilities are the same, regardless of the source of the disability. Both Jack and Jill will receive benefits.

During the 1970s, the constitutionality of a program like number 2—covering accidents and illness but not pregnancy—was challenged on the grounds that it constituted sex discrimination. The Supreme Court rejected the challenge.[26] On the Court's reasoning, such a program does not draw a distinction between men and women, treating the latter less favorably. Rather, it draws a distinction between nonpregnant persons and pregnant persons, treating the latter less favorably. Since unconstitutional sex discrimination can occur only where the distinction drawn is between men and women, there is no such discrimination in a case like this. So said the High Court.

Most feminists have rejected the Supreme Court's reasoning. They contend that program 2 places women at an unfair and unconstitutional disadvantage relative to men, since it excludes from coverage a disabling condition from which only women can suffer and there is no comparable "men only" condition that is likewise excluded from coverage. But serious disagreement persists among feminists over program 3—giving Jill benefits for her pregnancy but none to Jack for his accident. Liberal feminists reject it; radical feminists support it. Let us examine this disagreement.

Special Treatment or Equal Treatment?

Liberal feminists reject programs such as number 3 because they claim that it gives unjustifiable special treatment to women, and liberals insist on the same treatment for both men and women. If women are covered for their disabilities, then men should be covered as well: the same rules should apply to both sexes.

Radical feminists typically support programs like number 3, or at least regard the programs as justifiable. They deny that such programs amount to "special treatment" in any objectionable sense. Rather, they see the programs as treating women differently but justifiably so in light of the oppression from which women suffer.[27]

Radical feminists believe that society strongly discourages women from establishing their economic independence from men. Society's informal expectations and practices tell women that they should be housewives, that it is the role of the husband and not the wife to be the principal breadwinner, that a mother who has a career is suspect as a mother, and that being a mother is the most important role for a woman. Such messages discouraging economic independence play an important role in women's oppression: they help perpetuate the patriarchal system in which women are dependent on and subordinate to men.

Almost any policy or program that helps women establish their independence from men would be supported by radical feminists as a blow to patriarchal oppression. A company disability policy that covered pregnancy would help women in that way: they would not have to quit their job and would not be financially penalized for having a baby. They could be both mothers and economically independent workers.

For many radical feminists, it is misguided to object to a program such as number 3 on the grounds that it amounts to "special treatment." Adopting the exact same policy for men and women would ignore the fact that society does not discourage men in the way that it discourages women from being economically independent. Society does not tell men that they should be househusbands, that the wife should be the principal breadwinner, that a father with a career is suspect as a father, and so on. Women are entitled to differential treatment from policies and laws because that is the only way that the oppressive treatment they get from society in general can be counteracted and eventually eradicated. And if equality demands that everyone be treated *fairly,* then equal treatment actually requires that women be treated differently from men.

Liberal feminists argue against differential treatment, even when the rules appear to treat women more favorably. They claim that such treatment, in addition to being unfair to men, can easily backfire against women. After all, differential treatment is at the heart of the traditional view of women and their role in society: women should be treated differently by society's laws and policies because their natural role in society is different from that of men. Liberal feminists typically argue that any claim to differential treatment for women plays into the hands of traditionalists who will take such claims as evidence of their beliefs about the natural role of women.

Radical feminists will respond by charging that the liberals have greatly underestimated the extent to which society's informal expectations and practices unfairly disadvantage women. Such disadvantages cannot be effectively counteracted by treating men and women as if they were similarly situated in society. And women are not treated fairly if those disadvantages are ignored. Thus, imagine a public school in which certain students had the textbooks for their classes but others were denied the books. It would hardly be fair treatment if teachers used exactly the same standards to grade both groups of students. Those denied textbooks are in a different situation than the others, and they are unfairly treated if that difference is ignored and exactly the same rules are applied to them as to the students with the textbooks.

Persons who are differently situated should not always be treated in exactly the same way, and radical feminists argue that women are differently situated than men in crucial respects that the liberal view ignores. In particular, society systematically places women in a disadvantageous situation relative to men. The disadvantages are more easily overlooked than the disadvantage suffered by the schoolchildren who are denied textbooks in the example. That is because those disadvantages imposed on women seem so natural from the perspective of people within a patriarchal system. After all, such a system teaches everyone from the time they are born that women ought to be mothers and housewives and men ought to be breadwinners and head of the family.

Liberals can concede that women are differently situated than men in contemporary society, though they will contend that radical feminists have greatly exaggerated the disadvantages women suffer as a result of the difference. And liberals will contend that the best way to move toward a society in which women are not at any disadvantage relative to men is by insisting on a policy of applying the same rules in the same way to both men and women.

Such a "same treatment" policy anticipates the kind of society toward which we should be working, a society in which no one suffers from unfair disadvantage on account of sex. In the view of liberals, the goal of a society that treats men and women fairly must be prefigured in the policies we use to achieve it. And, for liberals, that means that the policies must not hand out special advantages on the basis of sex to either men or women.

Women's Values?

Some feminists claim that the socially relevant differences between women and men go well beyond the obvious fact that only women can become pregnant. For example, they contend that men and women have fundamentally different values and ways of thinking about moral questions. Women place greater emphasis on establishing and maintaining human relationships and on caring for others. They think that it is more important to act in a way that shows care and concern for others than to obey abstract rules and regulations. In contrast, men emphasize individual rights, following rules, and the freedom to act as one wishes without having to rely on or care for others.[28]

Many feminists argue that women's values are as valid as the values of men, if not more so. These feminists contend that the law needs to be reconstructed to better reflect the values of women. After all, it is men who have created and shaped our system of law. In doing so, they have followed the values they deem especially important. In law, as in the rest of society, women's values have been shortchanged. For example, abstract rights of individuals have taken precedence over relationships and caring. Some feminists argue that the balance needs to be dramatically shifted, giving more importance to what women value and less to what men do.

Yet, not all feminists have accepted claims about essential moral and psychological differences between men and women. Some of the critics agree that there are differences but not ones reflecting the "essential nature" of men and women. Rather, the differences are said to be a result of the oppression of women by men. Catharine MacKinnon puts the point succinctly: "Women value care because men have valued us according to the care we give them," and men are in charge.[29]

Other feminists question whether the differences are real at all, or at least whether they constitute any sharp distinction between men and women.[30] For these feminists, it is crucially important that men have created and shaped our legal system, but its importance is not because men have fundamentally different values than women. Rather, it is because men have used their power to create law to their advantage and to the disadvantage of women.

This debate among feminists cannot be settled at this stage of our scientific knowledge about the sexes. There is insufficient evidence to affirm or deny that the moral thinking of women is fundamentally different from that of men. Further study and argument will be needed to determine reliably whether such differences exist and, if so, what their source is.

In the meantime, it is still possible to argue that the law overemphasizes certain values, such as abstract rights, to the exclusion of others, such as caring. In the end, the decisive question is not whether caring is a woman's value and abstract rights a man's value. Caring and rights are clearly both important to a humane and just society. Rather, the decisive question is an ethical one: how should the law reflect and balance the different values that all reasonable persons would endorse?

PORNOGRAPHY: FREE SPEECH AND WOMEN'S RIGHTS

One of the most important disagreements among contemporary feminists concerns the issue of pornography. Some feminists argue that the freedom of speech guaranteed by the First Amendment to the Constitution should be interpreted as protecting pornography. Others argue that pornography does not fundamentally present a free speech issue at all. Rather, they contend that it is an issue that concerns the equal standing of women in society. And such feminists argue that there should be laws that restrict the manufacture, distribution, and display of pornography.

Liberal feminists support First Amendment protection for pornography, while radical feminists support its legal suppression. In order to clarify feminist approaches to the issue of pornography, let us first examine the arguments behind these two conflicting feminist views.

A Linchpin of Patriarchy

For radical feminists, pornography is a linchpin of patriarchy. In a system that subordinates women to men, one of the key aspects of that subordination concerns sexuality. Men define and control the sexuality of women, and their definition stipulates that women exist for the sexual pleasure of men. Since women are mere "instruments" for men's pleasure, they may be treated in whatever way a man chooses; they may even be raped, bound, beaten, or murdered for the sexual excitement it may give a man.

In the eyes of radical feminists, pornography plays a central role in defining women as mere instruments of men's sexual pleasure. Catharine MacKinnon, a prominent proponent of this view, explains it this way: "Pornography sexualizes rape, battery, sexual harassment, and child sexual abuse. . . . Through this process pornography constructs what a woman is as what men want from sex."[31] And to get what they want from sex, men need women who are subordinate and servile, who have no value in themselves but who exist merely for the sake of male pleasure. This is the kind of woman men find in pornography.

As MacKinnon sees it, "Pornography is integral to attitudes and behaviors of violence and discrimination that define the treatment and status of half the population."[32] That half, of course, consists of women. "Women are oppressed socially," she asserts, and pornography is central to that oppression.[33]

For MacKinnon and other radical feminists, then, pornography contributes to society's devaluing of women and their interests, and it provokes serious harm, including violence, against women. The existence of a multibillion-dollar pornography industry refutes the idea that in our society women count as much as men do, and as long as there is such an industry, women will not have equal standing with men. The eradication of patriarchy calls for the eradication of the pornography industry, and the legal suppression of that industry and its product is the means we need to adopt in order to accomplish that goal. That is the radical view of the matter.

To support their contentions about the oppressive effects of pornography on women, radical feminists point to a number of scientific studies showing that exposure to pornographic materials alters the attitudes and behavior of men toward women. In particular, the studies show that exposure to violent pornography tends to make men more tolerant of, and oblivious to, the sexual abuse of women. And it tends to increase their sexual aggressiveness against women. Moreover, radical feminists point to anecdotal evidence from women who tell of how pornography led the men in their lives to abuse them.[34]

Protecting Pornography

Liberal feminists oppose the legal suppression of pornography, arguing that such a policy will do more harm than good to society in general and to women in particular. Adopting arguments used by philosophers and jurists, they point both to the advantages of free expression—even when it is pornographic expression—and to the dangers of its suppression.

Liberal feminists typically argue that a wide range of free expression is crucial to a healthy democracy, since government by the people requires that the people be free to express their ideas, attitudes, and opinions. It is also essential to social and political progress: if people are not free to express ideas and attitudes that others find offensive, false, or outrageous, new and better ways of organizing society and its political practices will be stifled. This includes the progress all feminists are working to achieve in eradicating the abusive and discriminatory treatment of women.

Nadine Strossen, a prominent proponent of the liberal feminist view, emphasizes that "feminists, like all who seek social change and equality, are especially dependent on free expression."[35] She insists that strong legal protections for freedom of speech have been essential to the struggles of all groups that have fought against discrimination in our society. The civil rights struggle of African-Americans during the 1950s and 1960s would have been much more difficult had the speech of those involved been subject to legal suppression. And women have themselves benefited enormously from the fact that no court and no government official can silence feminist authors and speakers because they are seen by some as wrongheaded or even dangerous to society.

Reinforcing these advantages of free expression are the dangers of its suppression. For liberals, government's authority to restrict expression must be severely circumscribed on account of the abuses to which it is subject. Government will be tempted to silence views that challenge its legitimacy, competence, or integrity. It will be prone to suppress opinions and attitudes simply because they are unpopular. For these reasons, restrictions on expression must be drawn as narrowly as possible and must meet a heavy burden of proof: those who propose restrictions must show that they are necessary to meet some very important social goal.

Liberal feminists typically contend that the evidence is woefully insufficient to support radical claims that the legal suppression of pornography is necessary for advancing the cause of women. For example, Strossen claims that it is simply a "speculative possibility" that pornography causes harm to women in the way radicals like MacKinnon contend it does.[36]

At the same time, many people would be only too happy to suppress feminist ideas, and Strossen argues that it would be risky and foolish to play into the hands of such people by chipping away at protections for free speech. The legal suppression of pornography would only increase the chances of these people getting what they want. It would set a risky legal precedent that could easily backfire against women and lead to restrictions on feminist speech. In fact, Strossen argues that this has actually happened in Canada where legal restrictions on pornography that were supported by some feminists have been used by the authorities to suppress sexually explicit, pro-feminist material.[37]

Strossen and other liberal feminists contend that the best remedy for pornography and other "bad" speech that denigrates women is not legal suppression but more speech by the advocates of women's equality.[38] The free marketplace of ideas must be vigorously protected, even when some persons purvey ideas about women's inferiority by using pornographic images. The way to counter pornography degrading to women is for feminists to criticize its message, not for government to censor it.

Silencing Women

In reply to liberal arguments about free speech, radicals claim that the liberals are ignoring a crucial fact: feminists and women generally may not be censored by government officials, but their speech is devalued and dismissed by society at large. Protecting speech from government interference has value for those whose speech society listens to, takes seriously, and regards as authoritative. Its value is much more dubious for those whose speech society ignores, ridicules, or dismisses. For such people, the fundamental "speech problem" is not government censorship; rather, it is society's denigration, devaluation, and dismissal of them and what they say.

In a patriarchal society such as ours, radical feminists contend, the speech of women is devalued, denigrated, and dismissed. The inevitable effect is the silencing of women. Women are inhibited from voicing their views and ideas by a society that treats those views and ideas as unworthy of serious attention because they are those of women. And in our particular society, pornography plays a major role in creating and perpetuating such an attitude toward women and their speech.

Legal restrictions on pornography, radicals argue, are essential in working toward a society in which what women say is given the same respect, attention, and authority as what men say. To say that pornography should be countered by more speech in the free marketplace of ideas, rather than by legal restrictions, is to ignore the role pornography plays in silencing women.

As radicals see it, pornography itself is deeply subversive of the marketplace of ideas because of the way it treats half of the potential contributors to that marketplace. Accordingly, they argue that restrictions on pornography would actually create a fuller and more robust interchange of ideas and views by helping eliminate the factors that currently inhibit women from giving voice to their views and ideas.

As for liberal claims that restricting pornography is simply too risky, radicals reply that restrictions can be formulated that do not unduly threaten forms of expression that should remain legally protected. They assert that pornography is clearly distinguishable from those forms of expression and that laws can be developed that define with sufficient precision what does and does not count as pornography. Indeed, MacKinnon and her ally, Andrea Dworkin, have been the principal architects of such legislation. One of the laws they helped draft was challenged as unconstitutional in the case of *American Booksellers Assn. v. Hudnut.*

Later in the chapter, we will look at the *Hudnut* case in some detail. However, before turning to that case, it will be helpful to examine more carefully the connection between the question of whether women are still oppressed by patriarchy and the issue of pornography.

The Harm of Pornography

We have seen that radical feminists contend that pornography not only causes harm to women but also causes enough harm to justify legal restrictions on it. Liberals need not deny that pornography does cause some harm, for example, by provoking some men to rape or otherwise abuse women, but they deny that whatever harm is caused is sufficient to justify legal restrictions. Part of the explanation for this disagreement may be in differing standards of proof each side brings to the issue: the liberal side may demand more conclusive proof of harm than the radical side. But even if this is so, it would not explain why liberals demand more proof.

A deeper explanation of the disagreement about harm to women may lie in the very different ways in which liberal and radical feminists view society as a whole. Recall that radical feminists contend that women are still oppressed by patriarchy, while liberals reject such a claim. This difference can help explain why liberals and radicals take the positions they do on pornography. Let us see how.

Suppose that radical feminists are right and that women are oppressed by society. Further suppose that pornography causes some of the abusive and unfair treatment from which women suffer. In that case the harm caused by pornography to women includes the harm of helping perpetuate a system of oppression. Each act provoked by pornography that treats a woman abusively or unfairly will not count simply as an isolated injustice to a particular woman. Rather, in addition to being that, each such act will reinforce the social system of injustice that puts all women down. The harm it causes women will therefore be greater than the harm of a truly isolated act of injustice.

Now suppose that liberal feminists are right and that women are not oppressed but they sometimes suffer from discriminatory treatment. Further suppose that pornography causes some of that discriminatory treatment. Each act provoked by pornography that treats a woman unfairly or abusively will be a more or less isolated act of injustice against that woman. It will not include the further harm of reinforcing a social system of oppression.

It turns out then that the harm of pornography, assuming it exists, is much greater on the radical's understanding of contemporary society than it is on the liberal's understanding. And the greater the harm caused by a certain form of expression, the stronger the justification for its restriction. Thus, it should not be surprising to find that radical feminists see pornography as very harmful to women and support its suppression, while liberal feminists see it as less harmful and oppose its suppression.

Now let us turn to an actual legal case in which these feminist arguments about pornography are implicated. The case will enable us to further explore feminist views on pornography in relation to a specific law defining and prohibiting pornographic materials.

PORNOGRAPHY ON TRIAL: *AMERICAN BOOKSELLERS ASSN. V. HUDNUT*

The Ordinance

This case from the 1980s involved an ordinance enacted by the city of Indianapolis. The legislation had as its explicit purpose to outlaw the manufacture, distribution, display, and consumption of pornographic materials within the city. To this end, the law provided that women who were harmed by pornography could sue those involved in its manufacture, distribution, or display. One provision of the law made "trafficking" (that is, producing, distributing, or displaying) in pornography unlawful and authorized any woman to bring a legal complaint in order to stop it.

Traditionally, legal efforts to restrict pornography rested on the idea that obscenity was one of a limited number of categories of expression that were unprotected by the First Amendment. The Supreme Court found it difficult to define obscenity, but in the landmark case of *Miller v. California* (1973), the

Court formulated a three-part test for obscenity. In order for material to be deemed obscene, all of the following conditions must be met:

1. The average person, applying contemporary community standards, must find that the material, taken as a whole, appeals to the prurient interest (that is, to an abnormally lustful interest in sex).
2. The material must depict in a patently offensive way sexual acts specifically enumerated in a relevant state or federal law.
3. The material, taken as a whole, must lack serious literary, artistic, political, or scientific value.

MacKinnon and other feminists supporting the Indianapolis ordinance reject the obscenity approach. They believe that the fundamental problem with pornographic materials is not that they portray sex in an offensive way. Rather, the problem is that they degrade and debase women. Because of this degradation and debasement, pornography denies women the equality to which they are legally entitled under the Fourteenth Amendment to the Constitution. For MacKinnon and other feminists, pornography is basically a civil rights issue: for government to tolerate pornographic materials is for government to acquiesce in a practice that discriminates against women and denies them real equality.

The Indianapolis ordinance defines pornography in a way that accords with this civil rights approach: it is the graphic sexually explicit subordination of women, whether in pictures or words, that also includes one or more of the following:

1. Women are presented as sexual objects who enjoy pain or humiliation; or
2. Women are presented as sexual objects who experience sexual pleasure in being raped; or
3. Women are presented as sexual objects tied up or cut up or mutilated or bruised or physically hurt, or as dismembered or truncated or fragmented or severed in body parts; or
4. Women are presented as being penetrated by objects or animals; or
5. Women are presented in scenarios of degradation, injury, abusement, torture, shown as filthy or inferior, bleeding or bruised, or hurt in a context that makes these conditions sexual; and
6. Women are presented as sexual objects for domination, conquest, violation, exploitation, possession, or use, or through postures of servility and submission or display.[39]

This definition of pornography is designed to apply not merely to "hardcore" materials that contain graphic scenes of sexual intercourse, fellatio, and so on. It is also meant to apply to "soft-core" materials, including magazines like *Playboy* and *Penthouse* that are readily available at many newsstands. These magazines contain pictures that debase and devalue women by showing them in servile and submissive positions and on sexual display: the women are depicted as there for the sexual taking. According to the ordinance, such pictures amount to the subordination of women and thus count as pornographic.

The obscenity approach allows *Playboy* and similar magazines to circulate unimpeded: the articles that surround their pictures mean that, when taken as a whole, they have serious literary or political value. Accordingly, the magazines pass the *Miller* test and do not count as obscene. In contrast, the Indianapolis ordinance does not allow a magazine to insulate its sexually explicit pictures from legal restriction by surrounding them with legitimate material. If the pictures subordinate women, they count as pornography even if the surrounding material is not pornographic.

The Indianapolis ordinance was challenged as an unconstitutional infringement on freedom of speech. Some feminists joined in the opposition to the ordinance, while others defended it. MacKinnon was one of its prime defenders, resting her argument on the claim that pornography causes serious harm to women: it incites men to rape and sexually brutalize women; it makes men insensitive to violence against women; it causes men to devalue and disrespect women. Moreover, she contended that the women who participate in its manufacture are often beaten and brutalized to ensure that they do what the pornographer wants them to do.

The Ruling: Easterbrook's Opinion

Both the Federal District Court and the Circuit Court of Appeals declared Indianapolis's antipornography ordinance unconstitutional.[40] Writing for the Circuit Court, Judge Frank Easterbrook conceded that there was evidence showing that pornography contributed to the unfair and abusive treatment of women. He wrote, "Depictions of subordination tend to perpetuate subordination. The subordinate status of women in turn leads to affront and lower pay at work, insult and injury at home, battery and rape on the streets."[41]

Why, then, did Easterbrook strike down an ordinance prohibiting materials that produce such harmful consequences? The answer he gives makes three main points. First, the consequences of pornography fail to show that it is not a form of speech; rather, they show that it is a powerful form of speech. Second, when government acts to restrict speech, its restrictions must be "viewpoint-neutral"; that is, they must not be biased for or against any particular point of view in society. Third, the Indianapolis ordinance is not viewpoint-neutral. Let us examine each point in turn.

Easterbrook agrees with MacKinnon that pornography can alter for the worse the attitudes and actions of men toward women. But he argues that, in altering attitudes and actions, pornography is no different from political speeches, religious art, television programs, and countless other parts of popular culture. It may be "bad speech," but it is clearly speech. Thus any government restrictions that affect it must be viewpoint-neutral.

This brings us to the heart of Easterbrook's argument: the principle of viewpoint neutrality. The principle is so important, in his view, because any other principle "leaves government in control of all the institutions of culture, and the great censor and director of which thoughts are good for us."[42] The viewpoint-neutrality principle guarantees that "[t]he state may not ordain preferred viewpoints" in the regulation of speech.[43] And it may not single out certain viewpoints, declare them to be mistaken, and silence those who give voice to them. Easterbrook holds that this restriction on the power of government is central to our political system and demanded by the Free Speech Clause of the First Amendment.

The final step in Easterbrook's argument centers on the question of whether the Indianapolis ordinance violates the principle of viewpoint neutrality. His answer is that it does. Referring to the ordinance, he claims, "This is thought-control. It established an 'approved' view of women, of how they may react to sexual encounters, of how the sexes may relate to each other."[44] If women are depicted in subordinated or servile positions, then the use of sexually explicit images or language is forbidden by the ordinance. But if women are depicted as the equals of men, then sexually explicit images and language are permissible. This violates the principle of viewpoint neutrality. Easterbrook concludes that the ordinance is unconstitutional.

MacKinnon's Criticisms

In the years since *Hudnut* was decided, MacKinnon has criticized Easterbrook's reasoning and elucidated her own arguments in favor of the Indianapolis ordinance. In criticizing Easterbrook, MacKinnon makes several key points.

First, she claims that Easterbrook is inconsistent in his reliance on the principle of viewpoint neutrality. He struck down the Indianapolis ordinance because he says it was not viewpoint-neutral. But MacKinnon points out that laws against obscenity and child pornography are not viewpoint-neutral either. Antiobscenity laws are biased against the view that graphic and explicit depictions of sexuality are good. Child pornography laws are biased against the view that sex between adults and children is natural and healthy. Yet, Easterbrook was not prepared to strike down either antiobscenity or child pornography laws, despite their viewpoint bias. This shows that he is inconsistent in his reliance on viewpoint neutrality, using it to strike down laws that restrict viewpoints with which he agrees and to uphold laws restricting viewpoints he rejects.

MacKinnon's second main charge against Easterbrook concerns the harm that pornography does to women. Although Easterbrook concedes the existence of the harm as an empirical matter, his argument does not allow it to play a role in determining the constitutionality of the Indianapolis ordinance. According to MacKinnon, his analysis of the First Amendment implies that "no amount of harm of discrimination can outweigh the speech interests of bigots, so long as they say something while doing it."[45]

As MacKinnon sees it, Easterbrook is saying the harm done to women by pornography is legally irrelevant because pornography is speech. His view is reflected in his statement that the harms caused by pornography simply show its power as speech. But MacKinnon points out that the same could be said of libel or treason or other forms of speech that have the power to do great harm and are legally prohibited on account of that power. Instead of treating pornography like these other forms of harmful speech, Easterbrook gives it special and unwarranted legal protection. He declares, in effect, that the harm done to women by pornography does not count in favor of its legal restriction but against it! Once again, the legal system has devalued women and their interests.

This brings us to MacKinnon's third main charge against Easterbrook. His approach incorporates a very general and fundamental defect in our legal doctrine: "the constitutional doctrine of free speech has developed without taking equality seriously."[46]

The Fourteenth Amendment guarantees the equal protection of the law to all persons. MacKinnon argues that this guarantee of equality must be taken seriously when it comes to interpreting and applying the First Amendment. And taking equality seriously in that context means giving weight to the harms done to disadvantaged and subordinated groups by certain forms of speech. MacKinnon writes:

> When equality is recognized as a constitutional value and mandated, the idea that some people are inferior to others on the basis of group membership is authoritatively rejected as the basis for public policy. This does not mean that ideas to the contrary cannot be debated or expressed. It should mean, however, that social inferiority cannot be imposed through any means, including expressive ones.[47]

The Psychology of Pornography

In conjunction with her criticisms of Easterbrook and his approach to the First Amendment, MacKinnon has developed an account of the nature of pornography. The account is intended to show how pornography imposes social inferiority on women and how it is essentially different from simply expressing or debating ideas about the role of women.

In MacKinnon's view, opponents of antipornography legislation have consistently failed to understand the insidious way pornography helps to form the psyches of men. Once that is understood, anyone committed to women's equality will appreciate pornography's extremely harmful character and also see why the free-speech arguments against the Indianapolis ordinance are so misguided.

In MacKinnon's analysis, pornography forges a connection in the minds of men between the pleasure of sexual excitement and release, on the one hand, and the degradation of women, on the other. This connection is created by psychological conditioning: when two things are repeatedly presented together, the mind will associate the two. And if one of the things is perceived as good, then the other will come to be seen as good as well. Pornography conditions men to perceive the degradation of women as good because it leads men to associate their sexual pleasure with the degradation of women. It can achieve this conditioning because it causes sexual arousal in men at the same time it degrades women.

According to MacKinnon's analysis, only pornography has this power to condition men, through sexually arousing them, to perceive the degradation of women as good. And it is this unique feature of pornography that makes the free-speech arguments so misguided, in her view. The idea that women should be subordinated to men can be articulated, discussed, and debated with no violation of women's civil rights. A philosophical or religious essay defending patriarchy, for example, would not run afoul of MacKinnon's ordinance.

Pornography is different, MacKinnon argues, because it has a very different relation to the idea of women's subordination. It does not present the idea as an idea, making it then possible to discuss and debate it. Rather, pornography psychologically shapes the minds of men so that they perceive women as inferior, and it uses the intense pleasure of sex to accomplish this effect. For MacKinnon, then, pornography is not a legitimate part of the marketplace of ideas.

MacKinnon is sometimes portrayed as someone with a prudish revulsion toward sexual pleasure. That portrayal is based on a serious misunderstanding. What revolts her is not sexual pleasure as such but rather sexual pleasure derived from the degradation and humiliation of women. Unlike the person who sees something intrinsically wrong in the pleasures of sex, MacKinnon condemns those pleasures insofar as they are tied to the treatment of women as inferior beings. The misunderstanding of her view arises because, like all radical feminists, she sees such treatment as pervasive in our society.

Evidence of Harm?

Feminist arguments about pornography, such as MacKinnon's, bring into focus the issue of pornography's harm to women. Is there good evidence for it? If so, how great is the harm, and is it enough to justify the legal suppression of pornography? It is difficult to see how the legality of the Indianapolis ordinance can be responsibly decided without tackling these questions. The better the evidence and the greater the harm to women, the stronger will be the case for upholding the legality of the ordinance.

MacKinnon seems to grasp this point much better than Easterbrook does. His concession that pornography helps perpetuate the subordination of women seems to admit that radical feminists are right in claiming that pornography helps cause serious and pervasive harm to women. But once that concession is made, Easterbrook does not have much choice if he wants to strike down the Indianapolis ordinance except to declare the harm caused by pornography legally irrelevant to whether it can be restricted.

If the harm were relevant, it would be necessary to give the harm great weight: what could be a more compelling consideration than pervasive and serious harm to half the population? But having acknowledged pornography's harm to women, to then declare the harm legally irrelevant certainly requires a better justification than Easterbrook provides. Saying, as Easterbrook does, that the harm only shows how powerful pornography is as speech completely misses the point: the greater the harm caused by pornography or libel or treason or whatever form of expression, the stronger the case for restricting it.

Liberal feminists opposed to the Indianapolis ordinance are in a better position than Easterbrook. Their counter to MacKinnon is not the implausible claim that the harm of pornography does not count. Rather, their counter is the claim that the harm does not count enough to justify restrictions. Liberal feminists would argue that, contrary to MacKinnon's claims, no good evidence shows that pornography causes substantial numbers of men to seriously abuse women. And even if there are isolated acts of abuse caused by pornography, that cannot be regarded as a basis for restricting pornography unless one is prepared to censor virtually every other form of expression as well. Movies about bank robbery might be shown to persuade some people to try it themselves. But no reasonable person would argue that such a showing would be sufficient to restrict movies about bank robberies.

MacKinnon has two options in responding to this liberal feminist line of argument. The first is to argue that, leaving aside the question of whether women are pervasively oppressed by society at large, liberal feminists have greatly underestimated the harm that pornography causes to women through the acts of men. In MacKinnon's view, the evidence unambiguously demonstrates that pornography's harm adds up to the "carnage" of women.[48] The second option is for MacKinnon to engage liberals on the issue of whether women are oppressed by society.

The first option uncouples the argument for restricting pornography from the controversial claim about the systematic oppression of women. But problems arise with the argument. Even if one agrees that the scientific evidence shows that pornography tends to cause some men to abuse and discriminate against women, the evidence does not show how much that happens. MacKinnon thinks the "body count" is high, but the fact is that scientific studies simply do not even begin to tell us what the body count is. This is an especially important point for those liberals who see the Constitution's commitment to free speech as placing a substantial burden of proof on those who would restrict expression.

MacKinnon might respond by pointing out that there are no scientific studies showing that obscenity or child pornography does great harm, and yet the law allows its restrictions. But liberals who oppose restrictions on pornography can reply that the law is wrong to allow restrictions on obscenity—those too should be struck down. And liberals can argue that there is an essential difference between child pornography and adult pornography: children lack the autonomy that adults have, with the result that they are much more vulnerable to exploitation and abuse. And it would be absurd to demand a scientific study to prove the point.

MacKinnon could reply that women also lack autonomy in a patriarchal society that oppresses them: just as the inequality of power between adults and children renders children subject to abuse and exploitation by pornographers and their customers, the inequality of power between men and women renders women subject to abuse and exploitation by pornographers and their customers.[49] But notice that this reply reintroduces the claim that society systematically oppresses women. That claim may be correct. But it is not a claim that can be unambiguously established by scientific studies, as we will see in the next section.

Moreover, the claim that society systematically oppresses women is no more acceptable for courts to adopt as a basis of decision in the context of pornography than in the context of abortion. For the fact is that the claim would have revolutionary implications for the law that extend far beyond the question of whether the Indianapolis ordinance is constitutional. If women are oppressed in the way MacKinnon and other radical feminists suggest, then the validity of a whole range of currently unquestioned laws and legal contracts would be called into question.

As was pointed out earlier in this chapter, marriage laws would be of dubious validity, since the society's oppression of women presumably forces them into marriage when it may not be what they really want. And rape laws would need to be greatly expanded in scope, since society's oppression would presumably force many women into heterosexual relations they do not really want.

Perhaps it is true that gender equality demands very different rules than society now has for marriage, rape, and anything else concerning the relations between men and women. But the norms of our legal system do not permit judges to strike down an array of laws whose validity is accepted by almost all of society. Feminists who support restrictions on pornography such as those contained in the Indianapolis ordinance must make their legal argument without the help of the contention that society is a patriarchy that systematically oppresses women. The argument may not be impossible to make persuasively in that case, but it becomes more difficult to do so.

PATRIARCHY REVISITED: THE ROLE OF REASON

Beyond Statistics

We have seen that several important disputes among feminists turn on the question of whether women are oppressed by patriarchy. Radical feminists assert the existence of such oppression, but liberals deny it. Who is right? Answering that question is well beyond the scope of this chapter. But some points can be made that may help to clarify how one should go about arriving at an answer.

Many people would reject out of hand the claim that women in contemporary society are oppressed by patriarchy. The mainstream view is that liberal feminists are right in saying that patriarchy has been largely eliminated. In contrast, the radical claim that patriarchy is still around is well outside the mainstream. But it would be a mistake to dismiss a view simply because it lies outside of the mainstream opinions of society.

One of the most notable features of past societies is that their mainstream was blind or indifferent to the injustices they perpetrated. It is a well-known historical fact, for example, that well into the nineteenth century, those in favor of abolishing slavery were viewed by mainstream opinion as far-out and dangerous radicals. Similarly, throughout that century most people—including women—saw no serious injustice in the denial of a woman's right to vote, and those in favor of women's suffrage were viewed as dangerous and irrational.

In light of this kind of historical evidence, it is reasonable to believe that our current mainstream is blind to serious social injustices. Feminists who say that patriarchy still exists lay claim to being the abolitionists and the women suffragists of our time: they claim to see the current injustices that the rest of society cannot or will not see.

The problem, though, is that many groups today say they are the true heirs of the moral prophets of the past, including groups whose views are antithetical to the radical feminist position. For example, radical pro-life groups that advocate violence in order to stop abortions claim to be the abolitionists of the present day, trying to make a morally blind society see the light. So even if we are blind to some current injustice, how can we determine who the real moral prophets are?

The only reliable way to assess any view, including that of radical feminism, is to rationally analyze the arguments and the evidence for it. Radical feminists sometimes cite an array of statistics as confirmation of women's oppression. For example, the statistic that women earn on average only 59 percent of what men do is commonly cited, as are statistics allegedly showing half of all women are victims of rape or attempted rape and that over three million women a year are battered by their live-in partners.[50]

The accuracy of such statistics has been challenged by liberal feminists. For example, it is claimed that the statistic comparing women's earning with men's is outdated, that women's earning power relative to men has gained steadily over the past decade, and that the gender gap in earnings for younger workers is only about 10 percent at present.[51] Likewise, it is claimed that statistics on rape and other forms of abuse against women have been exaggerated. Some critics of radical feminism have even argued that statistics actually show that men are worse off in society than women.[52]

As everyone knows, statistics are easily manipulated, especially for political purposes. If the issue is the validity of some statistical study, there is no substitute for a detailed examination of that particular study. But some general points can still be made.

First, aggregate empirical data about women in society are relevant and even essential in deciding whether claims of women's continuing oppression are accurate. Despite their manipulability, statistical data are not dispensable: they are important in forming an overall picture of the lives of women.

Second, statistical data by themselves cannot settle the question of whether women are systematically oppressed by patriarchy. The question of patriarchy implicates subtle and contestable judgments, not only about the effects but also about the meaning of society's practices, rules, and expectations. Do those practices and expectations consistently demean and degrade women, conveying the message that men are superior and women inferior? Do they restrict and stunt the growth of women's potentialities? Do they provide men with decidedly better prospects for a good life?

These are not questions of simple empirical fact, like the question of how many births occurred in the country last year. They are questions that are interpretive and moral as well. And where one interpretation stands against another, one moral judgment against its contrary, the practice of reasoned argument and counterargument is the only reliable way to determine which view is better.

Is Reason "Male"?

Some radical feminists will respond by rejecting the practice of reasoned argument and counterargument.[53] They would contend that such a practice is as much a part of patriarchy as the other norms, laws, and institutions that make up our male-dominated society. In the eyes of these radical feminists, it is a "male" assumption to presume that human reason, through the use of argument and counterargument, will lead us to reliable moral, political, and empirical conclusions. These feminists reject such an assumption, often invoking intuition as a superior source of insight into the world. In their view, relying on "human" reason (that is, male reason) and its practice of argument and counterargument in order to assess the validity of radical feminism is like relying on cigarette company studies to determine the validity of the surgeon general's warning that smoking is unhealthy: in both cases there is a built-in bias against what one is evaluating.

Yet radical feminists are contradicting themselves when they reject the practice of argument and counterargument by claiming that the practice is male-biased. For in that very claim lies an argument as to why they should not have to formulate arguments and counterarguments in defense of their views. There is thus a fatal contradiction in the radical feminist rejection of reasoned argument. Such feminists purport to reject the practice of reasoned argument, but they in fact engage in it themselves.

In spite of this contradiction, radical feminists still might be right in their claims regarding the pervasive oppression of women by society. And it may even be true that much of the argument and counterargument that takes place in society is infected by a male bias. But the existence of such a bias would simply mean that it should be eliminated, not that the very practice of reasoned argument and counterargument should somehow be dispensed with. Accordingly, radical feminists cannot consistently or legitimately refuse to argue for their own claims or against the claims of their opponents. Of course, the same goes for the opponents of radical feminism.

SUMMARY

Two decades ago, the systematic study of law had barely begun to take account of the ideas of feminism. Today, it is not possible to think about law adequately without taking account of feminism's concepts and claims. In this chapter, we have examined only a few of the many areas of law to which feminist thought has contributed. We have seen that it challenges and criticizes traditional views and widely accepted assumptions. In that respect, feminist thinking about the law has begun to take its place as a vital part of the process of reasoned reflection and argument that has helped to shape the Western tradition in legal philosophy.

NOTES

1. Many feminists, though not all, use the distinction between sex and gender to challenge the traditional view of women. *Sex* refers to the possession of reproductive organs of a certain kind, while *gender* refers to certain social roles and cultural expectations that society associates with reproductive organs of a certain kind. For example, to talk about a person's capacity to give birth is to talk about her sex, while to talk about society's expectation that she be a housewife is to talk about her gender. Feminists often argue that one's sex does not logically determine what social role one should play. More exactly, the possession of female reproductive organs does not entail that one's primary role should be housewife and homemaker, and the possession of male reproductive organs does not entail that one should be a head of the household or primary breadwinner.

Other feminists have tried to collapse the distinction between sex and gender by arguing that all concepts and categories are socially constructed. This argument confuses a concept with what the concept refers to in the world. People had reproductive organs before anyone developed the concept of reproductive organ. The concept may be socially constructed, but the organs themselves are not.

2. Quoted in Albert R. Hunt, "O. J. and the Brutal Truth about Marital Violence," *Wall Street Journal,* June 23, 1994, p. A15.

3. Patricia Smith, *Feminist Jurisprudence* (New York: Oxford University Press, 1993), p. 3.

4. Smith, *Feminist Jurisprudence,* p. 143.

5. Christina Hoff Sommers, *Who Stole Feminism?* (New York: Simon & Schuster, 1994), p. 22.

6. See the discussion of Mill and the harm principle in Chapter 5.

7. For convenience, the term *discrimination against women* will be used instead of the more accurate but longer *discrimination against women as women*. It is possible for women to be discriminated against but not as women. For example, a woman might be discriminated against as a Jew or as an Arab. In this chapter, discrimination against women as women is the relevant form of discrimination. Similar considerations apply to the term *oppression.*

8. Recall H. L. A. Hart's idea of power-conferring legal rules, discussed in Chapter 2: rules covering marriage empower individuals to get married. Also, compare this line of radical feminist argument with the legal realist attack on the public-private distinction, examined in Chapter 4.

9. The first line of radical feminist attack on the liberal idea of privacy might be summarized as "The political is personal"; that is, the rules enacted in the political sphere help constitute the personal sphere of society.

10. Cited in Joan Hoff, *Law, Gender, and Injustice,* p. 277. Hoff omits an important qualification made by the court in this case following its assertion that it will not attempt to interfere with the family: "unless in cases where permanent or malicious injury is inflicted or threatened, or the condition of the party intolerable" (*State v. Rhodes,* 61 N.C. 445, 448 [1868]). Hoff and many other feminists also cite this case to support their contention that a legal rule of the time permitted a husband to strike his wife with a stick no larger than the width of a thumb. However, *State v. Rhodes* explicitly rejects the so-called rule of thumb, even though it was supported by "some of the old authorities" (at 450).

11. Simpson is quoted as having made that statement in 1989. See "Review of Records Shows Simpson Abused Wife," *Washington Post,* June 16, 1994, p. A3.

12. Rhonda Copelon, "Beyond the Liberal Idea of Privacy: Toward a Positive Right of Autonomy," in *Judging the Constitution,* Michael McCann and Gerald Houseman, eds. (Boston: Scott, Foresman, 1989), p. 298.

13. Catharine MacKinnon, *Feminism Unmodified* (Cambridge, MA: Harvard University Press, 1987), p. 101.

14. *Harris v. McRae,* 448 U.S. 297 (1980).

15. Many feminists also argue that if men had to be the child bearers, child rearers, and homemakers, then pro-lifers would not

value the life of the fetus so highly and the freedom of the woman so minimally. This claim is captured in a cartoon cited by Susan Moller Okin. The cartoon shows several male justices in their robes, looking down in great surprise at their bellies, which are swollen by pregnancy. One of the justices is saying, "Perhaps we'd better reconsider that decision." See Okin, *Justice, Gender and the Family* (New York: Basic Books, 1989), p. 102.

16. Copelon, "Beyond the Liberal Idea of Privacy," p. 287.

17. Cited in David J. Garrow, *Liberty and Sexuality* (New York: Macmillan, 1994), p. 502.

18. Kathleen Sullivan, "Review of *Liberty and Sexuality* by David J. Garrow," *New Republic* (May 23, 1994), p. 44.

19. Liberals can make a privacy argument against the Supreme Court's decision to uphold a law denying government funds to indigent women for abortions. The law at issue in the case of *Harris v. McRae* provided government funds for childbirth even as it denied funds for abortion. A privacy argument can be made that this funding pattern was an illegitimate attempt by government to manipulate the private, reproductive choices of women.

20. Ruth Bader Ginsburg, "Some Thoughts on Autonomy and Equality in Relation to *Roe v. Wade*," 63 *North Carolina Law Review* 375, 383. (Ginsburg cites the work of Kenneth Karst in this passage.)

21. The Supreme Court struck down a state law giving automatic preference to men over women in the choice of estate administrator: *Reed v. Reed*, 404 U.S. 71 (1971).

22. Some "pro-life" conservative feminists do not believe that there is any inconsistency in promoting equality for women while also denying that women should have any legal right to an abortion. See Pamela Erens, "Anti-Abortion, Pro-Feminism?" *Mother Jones* (May 1989), p. 31.

23. The plurality opinion in the Supreme Court's most recent major consideration of the right to an abortion employed mainly a privacy-based argument. However, there was also language suggesting that the equal standing of women in society is at stake in the abortion issue: "The destiny of the woman must be shaped to a large extent on her own conception of her spiritual imperatives and her place in society." See *Planned Parenthood v. Casey*, 60 L.W. 4795, 4800 (1992).

24. See "Not a Moral Issue," in *Feminism Unmodified* (Cambridge, MA: Harvard University Press, 1987).

25. The phrase *rules for women* should be understood as shorthand for *rules for women as women,* and the phrase *rules for men* should be understood in a similar way.

26. *Geduldig v. Aiello*, 417 U.S. 484 (1974).

27. One need not be a radical feminist in order to support a program like number 3. A conservative feminist might do so as well, as could someone who has a traditional view of the role of women. For example, traditionalists and conservative feminists might argue that childbearing is sufficiently important for society that it is legitimate to single it out for financial support. However, radical feminists would make a very different argument in favor of the program.

28. The idea that men and women are essentially different in their mode of moral thinking was suggested by Carol Gilligan in her influential *In a Different Voice* (Cambridge, MA: Harvard University Press, 1982).

29. MacKinnon, *Feminism Unmodified,* p. 39.

30. Some feminists go so far as to suggest that neither women nor men have any essential nature—psychological, biological, or otherwise—and that the distinction between men and women is completely artificial or, as they put it, "socially constructed." This is not a plausible view. See note 1.

31. MacKinnon, *Feminism Unmodified,* p. 171.

32. *Ibid.,* p. 175.

33. *Ibid.,* p. 207.

34. Anecdotal evidence is generally a weak basis on which to rest general claims about cause and effect. It involves none of the careful controls that are necessary to sound scientific reasoning. Some radical feminists will reject scientific reasoning as male-biased. But would those feminists be

prepared to reject the scientific studies that show cigarette smoking causes cancer or that bacteria and viruses cause disease? Would they accept anecdotal evidence that demons and spirits cause illnesses like tuberculosis? These questions suggest that it is very difficult to reject scientific reasoning in a logically consistent way. Some of the problems with anecdotal evidence about pornography are described in *Attorney General's Commission on Pornography: Final Report* (Washington, DC: U.S. Department of Justice, 1986), pp. 312–315.

35. Nadine Strossen, "A Feminist Critique of 'The' Feminist Critique of Pornography," 79 *Virginia Law Review* (1993), 1099, 1169, and 1185.

36. Strossen, "Feminist Critique," 1185.

37. Strossen claims that, ironically, the Canadian authorities seized as pornographic books authored by Andrea Dworkin, a close collaborator of MacKinnon's. See "Feminist Critique," 1146–1147.

38. Justice Brandeis argued that in the face of evil speech, "the remedy to be applied is more speech, not enforced silence." *Whitney v. California,* 274 U.S. 357, 377 (1927) (J. Brandeis, concurring).

39. Quoted in *American Booksellers Assn. v. Hudnut,* 598 F. Supp. 1316, 1319 (1984).

40. The Supreme Court did not agree to hear the case, leaving the decision of the Circuit Court of Appeals to stand.

41. *American Booksellers Assn. v. Hudnut,* 771 F.2d 323, 328 (1985).

42. *Hudnut* at 329.

43. *Hudnut* at 325.

44. *Hudnut* at 327.

45. Catharine MacKinnon, *Only Words* (Cambridge, MA: Harvard University Press, 1993), p. 93.

46. *Ibid.,* p. 71.

47. *Ibid.,* p. 106.

48. *Ibid.,* p. 37. Thus MacKinnon might argue that the harm of bank robberies falls more or less randomly on the population as a whole, while the harm of pornography falls squarely on the shoulders of women.

49. *Ibid.,* p. 91.

50. Statistics regarding income differentials between men and women can be found in Okin, *Justice, Gender and the Family.* The figure on rape is cited by MacKinnon, *Only Words,* p. 7. The statistic on domestic violence is derived from a study by the Commonwealth Fund and is cited in many sources, including Don Colburn, "Domestic Violence," *Washington Post,* Health Section, June 29, 1994, p. 9. The validity of these statistics, and others cited by feminists to prove the oppression of women, is challenged in Sommers, *Who Stole Feminism?*

51. See Sommers, *Who Stole Feminism?,* pp. 238–241.

52. For example, the life expectancy of men is significantly lower than that of women, and more men die as a result of crimes of violence than women. See Warren Farrell, *The Myth of Male Power* (New York: Simon & Schuster, 1993).

53. Not all radical feminists reject the practice of argument and counterargument. Some—like Catharine MacKinnon—accept the practice and engage in it with great vigor and skill.

DISCUSSION QUESTIONS

1. Is society still a patriarchy? What kinds of evidence and considerations are relevant to the question?

2. Is the kind of antipornography law supported by Catherine MacKinnon and Andrea Dworkin best understood as a civil rights law for woman or as a form of censorship? In what respects is it like the civil rights laws that protect persons from racial discrimination? In what respects is it like government censorship of

unpopular ideas? Does it make a difference that the antipornography law does not provide for any criminal prosecution but only for lawsuits brought by private parties?

ADDITIONAL READING

Bassham, Gregory. "Feminist Legal Theory: A Liberal Response." *Notre Dame Journal of Law and Ethics* 6 (1992), 293–319.

Cornell, Drucilla. *The Imaginary Domain: Abortion, Pornography, and Sexual Harassment.* Routledge, 1995.

Dworkin, Andrea. *Intercourse.* Free Press, 1987.

Dwyer, Susan, ed. *The Problem of Pornography.* Wadsworth, 1995.

Frug, Mary Jo. *Postmodern Legal Feminism.* Routledge, 1992.

Frye, Marilyn. *The Politics of Reality: Essays in Feminist Theory.* Crossing Press, 1983.

Gavison, Ruth. "Feminism and the Public-Private Distinction." *Stanford Law Review* 45 (1992), 1–42.

Goldstein, Leslie. *Feminist Jurisprudence: The Difference Debate.* Rowman and Littlefield, 1992.

Hoff, Joan. *Law, Gender, and Injustice: A Legal History of U.S. Women.* New York University Press, 1991.

Lederer, Laura. *Take Back the Night: Women on Pornography.* William Morrow, 1980.

MacKinnon, Catherine. *Feminism Unmodified.* Harvard University Press, 1987.

———. *Only Words.* Harvard University Press, 1993.

Markowitz, Sally. "Abortion and Feminism." *Social Theory and Practice* 16 (1990), 1–17.

Minow, Martha. *Making All the Difference.* Cornell University Press, 1990.

Nedelsky, Jennifer. "Reconceiving Autonomy: Sources, Thoughts, and Possibilities." *Yale Journal of Law and Feminism* 1 (1989), 7–36.

Nussbaum, Martha C. *Sex and Social Justice.* Oxford University Press, 1999.

Okin, Susan Moller. *Justice, Gender and the Family.* Basic Books, 1989.

Rhode, Deborah. *Justice and Gender.* Harvard University Press, 1989.

Scheppele, Kim. "The Reasonable Woman." *The Responsive Community* 1 (1991), 36–47.

Schulhofer, Stephen. "The Gender Question in Criminal Law." Paul, Ellen, Fred Miller, and Jeffrey Paul, eds. *Crime, Culpability, and Remedy.* Blackwell, 1990.

Smith, Patricia, ed. *Feminist Jurisprudence.* Oxford University Press, 1993.

Strossen, Nadine. *Defending Pornography.* Scribner, 1995.

"Symposium: Feminism and Political Theory." *Ethics* 99:2 (January 1989).

Winston, Kenneth, and Mary Jo Bane, eds. *Gender and Public Policy.* Westview, 1993.

8

▨

Race and American Law

RACE, CITIZENSHIP, AND IDENTITY

Human beings are agents capable of initiating and controlling their own activities. We do not simply react to external stimuli, as does a rat running through a maze. We act. And when we act, what we do is based to a large extent on our conceptions of who we are and how we are connected to—or separated from—other human beings. Those young Americans who signed up to serve in the armed forces during World War II thought of themselves as Americans, with a duty to their fellow citizens, to previous generations of Americans, and to generations still to come. The law may have made it a legal obligation to serve in the military. But for many of those who served, it was not primarily the law but their sense of who they were—their sense of identity—that obligated them to serve.

In the modern world, a sense of national identity has decisively shaped the course of history. After all, it was not only Americans who were motivated by their sense of themselves as a nation. The Germans, Japanese, and many others besides were also driven by a sense of national identity.

But if national identity has been so influential in modern history, racial identity has not been far behind. Indeed, the two forms of identity have been deeply intertwined. For example, the Nazis conceived of the national German identity in racial terms: supposedly, true Germans belonged to a master race, the Aryan race, while Jews and Gypsies belonged to inferior races. And until very recently, even people who were born and raised in Germany could not become citizens unless they had German ancestors.

In the United States, too, national identity has been linked to race. For much of our history, the United States has been a "white nation." Whites have had legal privileges and rights denied to others and have enjoyed a social status above that of other racial groups. Nonwhites were truly second-class citizens, when they were permitted to be citizens at all. From 1791 until 1870 federal law prohibited anyone born in another country from becoming a citizen unless they were white.[1] And in its infamous *Dred Scott* decision of 1857, the Supreme Court declared that even emancipated blacks could not be full citizens and had no constitutional rights that whites were bound to respect.[2]

The amendments to the Constitution adopted in the wake of the Civil War embodied the principle that American citizenship was open to both whites and blacks and that all citizens should be treated as equals under the law. In addition, Congress amended federal law, allowing blacks to become naturalized citizens and guaranteeing all black citizens the same civil rights as whites. Yet, naturalized citizenship was still denied to Asians and all other races, who were discriminated against in many ways by both law and social attitudes.

Moreover, when it came to black Americans, the reality of American life fell far short of the new principles enshrined in the Constitution and other federal laws. Even when the law did not discriminate against blacks on the basis of race, social attitudes most definitely did. Blacks were widely regarded as innately inferior to whites in moral character and intelligence. Prior to the Civil War, many states prohibited blacks from testifying in court against any white person. After the Civil War, federal law overturned such prohibitions, thereby giving blacks the same right to testify as whites had. But social attitudes meant that white judges and juries were unlikely to find the testimony of blacks as credible as that of whites. Moreover, whites continued to find many ways to use the legal and political system to ensure that blacks would be only second-class citizens.

JIM CROW AND THE ONE-DROP RULE

The most blatant violation of the Constitution's promise of equal citizenship for blacks came in the form of the "Jim Crow" system that developed in the South at the end of the nineteenth and beginning of the twentieth century. During that period, southern whites acted to ensure that the Civil War Amendments would be a dead letter in that part of the country. For example, the Fifteenth Amendment had outlawed the denial or abridgement of the right to vote on account of race, color, or previous condition of servitude. But southern states found many ways to deny blacks their right to vote and to exclude them from the political process.

As the first decade of the twentieth century drew to a close, rigid racial segregation and the exclusion of blacks from positions of power and privilege had become entrenched facts of life in the South. This was the Jim Crow system of racial oppression. Blacks were victimized by systematic racial prejudice in the North as well, but it did not match the level of oppression that they faced in the Jim Crow South.

The force of the law was a key factor upholding the South's system of racial separation and exclusion, but it was not the only factor. Law worked hand in hand with social attitudes and with the very real threat of violence to ensure that blacks would be systematically deprived of the opportunities and benefits that whites took for granted.

Under the Jim Crow system, blacks were treated as a subordinate caste, fit only for the most menial of occupations, prohibited from using the same public facilities as whites, barred from marrying whites, and required to act in a subservient manner in every interaction with whites. Blacks who did not follow the rules were severely condemned, physically beaten, legally prosecuted, and in some cases lynched by white mobs.

With such serious consequences attached to racial identity, it was important to be clear exactly who was black and who was white. Racial identity may seem an obvious matter. But the fact is that race is understood in the United States in a very different way from how it is understood virtually anywhere else in the world. In the United States, anyone with a black ancestor is generally considered black. This is known as the "one-drop rule," referring to the idea that a single drop of "black blood" makes one black.

In other countries, individuals who have a mixed racial ancestry have a different racial identity and social status from those whose ancestors all belong to the same racial group. This is true even in countries that have had systems of racial division and oppression. For example, in South Africa's system of racial apartheid, a clear distinction was drawn between blacks and coloureds. Coloureds included those who had some Asian or black ancestry, and only those with all black ancestors were counted as blacks.

The one-drop rule was at the center of the Jim Crow system, aggressively enforced by prevailing social attitudes. Moreover, the legal system helped to support the idea that a person was black even if she had only one black ancestor going back several generations. It is true that state laws did not always provide that anyone with any black ancestor was to be counted as black. For example, in some states the relevant statutes provided that persons had to be at least 1/32 black in order to be counted as a black. In other states, the required fraction of "black blood" was 1/8. But in all states, a relatively small fraction of black ancestry would make one black. And in many instances, legal disputes over race were decided by juries who were informally guided by the one-drop rule in their deliberations.

One of the most infamous cases in the history of the Supreme Court involved a man most of whose ancestors were white but who was judged by law and social custom to be black. The Court heard the case in the last decade of the nineteenth century, just as southern whites were establishing the Jim Crow system. And the consequences of the Court's decision would reverberate through the twentieth century.

SEPARATE BUT EQUAL: THE *PLESSY* CASE

In 1890 the state of Louisiana enacted the Separate Car Act, requiring separate but equal accommodations for whites and blacks in all passenger railways, with the exception of streetcars. The Act authorized train conductors to determine the race of passengers, assign them to the appropriate cars, and refuse admittance to anyone seeking to use a car other than the one assigned. The Act also made the conductors and railroad companies immune to any lawsuit for damages stemming from their refusal to admit a person to a car on account of race.

Apparently intending to challenge the constitutionality of the Act, in 1892 Homer Plessy tried to board a "whites-only" passenger car and was ejected by the conductor, who had evidently been told that Plessy was black. Plessy was, in fact, only 1/8 black, that is, he had one black great-grandparent, and he appeared to be white. As provided by the Act, Plessy was arrested and charged with a crime. Plessy then challenged the legality of the charge, arguing that the Act violated the Fourteenth Amendment's requirements of equal protection and due process.

Plessy argued that the Act's enforced separation of the races stamped blacks as inferior to whites, unfit to share the same accommodations with them. Such separation therefore violated the Equal Protection Clause of the Fourteenth Amendment, which prohibits states from denying anyone "the equal protection of the laws."

Plessy contended further that the Separate Car Act violated the Due Process Clause of the Fourteenth Amendment, prohibiting states from denying anyone "due process of law." The Act violated that clause because it gave the train conductor the power to arbitrarily determine a passenger's race. Louisiana had no statutory definition of *white* or *colored* at the time on which conductors could base their determination. Moreover, conductors and their companies were immunized by the Act from any lawsuit stemming from an incorrect identification. In Homer Plessy's view, such immunity meant that conductors had uncontrolled discretion in assigning passengers to cars.

In *Plessy v. Ferguson,* the Supreme Court rejected Homer Plessy's challenge to the constitutionality of Louisiana's Separate Car Act.[3] In doing so, the Court made the "separate-but-equal" doctrine part of our constitutional law. That doctrine had been originally developed in state and federal courts as a common-law rule regulating common carriers such as streetcars and railroads. According to the doctrine, the enforced separation of the races in common carriers was legal as long as it was reasonable, and it was reasonable as long as the separate accommodations were equal.

The Supreme Court itself had endorsed the separate-but-equal doctrine in 1878 in a case involving common-law and statutory considerations. In his concurring opinion in *Hall v. DeCuir,* Justice Clifford explained why he thought it reasonable for common carriers to enforce separate accommodations:

> It is not an unreasonable regulation to seat passengers so as to preserve order and decorum, and to prevent contacts and collisions arising from natural or well-known customary repugnancies which are likely to breed

disturbances, where white and colored persons are huddled together without their consent.[4]

In *Plessy,* the Supreme Court held that the Equal Protection Clause incorporated the separate-but-equal doctrine and that Louisiana's Separate Car Act, by providing for separate but equal accommodations for whites and blacks, was consistent with the Clause. The Court measured the Act's constitutionality on the basis of a reasonableness standard and judged that it passed the test. Reasonableness, the Court said, is to be determined "with reference to the established usages, customs, and traditions of the people, and with a view to the promotion of their comfort and the preservation of the public peace and good order." And looking to those factors, the Court maintained that "we cannot say that a law which authorizes or even requires the separation of the two races in public conveyances is unreasonable."[5]

In addition, the Court rejected Plessy's claim that the Separate Car Act stamped blacks as racially inferior to whites. The Court claimed that if blacks interpreted the Act in that way, "it was not by reason of anything found in the act, but solely because the colored race chooses to put that construction on it."[6]

Moreover, the Court rejected Plessy's due process argument. It said that Louisiana had conceded the unconstitutionality of the provision of its Act that had given conductors immunity from liability for misidentifying a person's race. This concession entailed that anyone claiming to have been misidentified could bring a lawsuit in which a court would give him or her a fair hearing to determine racial identity and award damages if appropriate. In the Court's view, the possibility of such a suit meant that the Act, expunged of the immunity provision, did not violate due process.

The Court concluded its analysis of the case by commenting on the limits of law in dealing with problems of racial inequality. The law can and does give the two races equal political and civil rights, but it cannot eliminate social prejudices. "If one race be inferior to the other socially, the Constitution of the United States cannot put them on the same plane."[7]

The sole dissent in *Plessy* was registered by Justice Harlan. He argued that "our Constitution is colorblind" and so does not permit any public authority to take account of the race of American citizens.[8] Harlan rejected the reasonableness standard and instead embraced a categorical prohibition of racial classifications by the state. Determining the reasonableness of legislation was a job for legislators, not for courts: it called for policy judgments based on the weighing of various factors. Courts should not make policy judgments but judgments of principle. And the principle that states may not classify their citizens by race was at the heart of the Equal Protection Clause.

Referring to the Separate Car Act, Harlan contended that it "puts the brand of servitude and degradation" on blacks, for the obvious purpose of the law was to prevent blacks from traveling in cars reserved for whites, not to prevent whites from traveling in cars for blacks. He added that whites and blacks had a common interest in opposing race hatred but that laws mandating racial segregation were certain to arouse such hatred. Indeed, Harlan predicted that laws such as the Separate Car Act would "stimulate aggressions, more or less brutal and irritating, upon the admitted rights of colored citizens."9 His prediction turned out to be exactly right.

The majority decision in *Plessy* is now widely regarded as one of the worst in the Court's history. But the fact is that a strong argument can be made that it was legally correct. Justice Harlan's principle of colorblindness certainly captures a moral ideal of considerable cogency. But it is not easy to read that ideal into the body of American law that existed in the late nineteenth century. Many legal precedents had established that government could classify persons by race as long as the classifications were reasonable, and there was little legal support for the idea of a categorical ban on racial classifications.

Some nineteenth-century lawyers and politicians did, indeed, advocate a categorical ban. Prominent among them was Senator Thaddeus Stevens who, after the Civil War, proposed an amendment to the Constitution that would prohibit government from classifying citizens on the basis of race. But Stevens's proposal was defeated: it represented a view that was seen as too radical by most people. For example, Stevens's proposal would have invalidated the laws against racial intermarriage that existed in many states at the time, and only the most radical advocates of racial equality then favored the elimination of such laws.

The Equal Protection Clause was adopted as a more moderate alternative to Stevens's proposal. The vague language of the Clause would allow courts to invalidate some laws that classified by race, for example, laws that kept blacks from serving on juries. But it would also allow courts to uphold other such laws that seemed more reasonable to most white Americans in the period after the Civil War.

Subsequent to the ratification of the Fourteenth Amendment, radicals insisted that the Equal Protection Clause be construed to prohibit all official racial classifications. But such an interpretation was difficult to square with the rejection of Stevens's proposal and with the fact that the same Congress that voted for the Fourteenth Amendment also established racially segregated public schools in the District of Columbia. So despite the radicals' view, the courts generally interpreted the Equal Protection Clause in terms of a reasonableness standard.

Justice Harlan's dissent did provide a compelling account of why the Separate Car Act was so bad from the point of view of public policy and morality. Segregation laws did, indeed, stimulate racial hatred and aggression against blacks. And it was entirely reasonable to expect such consequences. But Harlan's dissent failed to come to grips with the legislative history behind the Fourteenth Amendment and the weight of judicial precedent in favor of a reasonableness standard.

A REASONABLE DISSENT FROM
PLESSY: LAW AND SCIENTIFIC RACISM

A more cogent dissent from the decision in *Plessy* would have used Justice Harlan's points about the intensification of race hatred and aggression to argue that the Act failed to meet the reasonableness standard. Instead of pronouncing a broad and categorical ban on all racial classification, the dissent would have been on more solid legal ground if it had been limited to arguing that the state lacked sufficiently good reason to require segregation on public transportation, especially in light of the potential dangers cited by Harlan.

Whether the Act in and of itself stamped blacks with the brand of racial inferiority, it could have been easily interpreted as doing so, not only by blacks, but by whites as well. And to the extent that it was so interpreted by whites, it would likely stimulate the racial prejudice and aggression against the rights of blacks about which Harlan had warned.

The Court majority in *Plessy* invoked the traditions and customs of the South in finding that the Separate Car Act was not unreasonable. But two points tell against the Court's finding in that regard. First, the Civil War Amendments surely entailed that traditional and customary racial practices in the South could not be taken as the measure of reasonableness: those Amendments were decisive repudiations of such practices.

Second, there was no evidence that society was being harmed by the absence of enforced racial segregation on public transportation. The Court in *Plessy* alluded to Justice Clifford's concurrence in *Hall* in which he cites the danger of interracial violence should public transportation be racially integrated. But there was no evidence of such violence: the Louisiana law was a response to a nonexistent problem.

Undoubtedly, many whites favored segregation for fear of a broader and more diffuse problem: they believed that integration would lead to "race mixing," and race mixing would weaken society. By "race-mixing," people meant interracial sexual intercourse (miscegenation). And the fear was that the children of such relations would be defective on account of the supposed fact that they were the hybrid offspring of two distinct racial types. Moreover, it was widely believed by whites that miscegenation between whites and blacks would pollute and degrade the white race. Such a belief was, of course, closely tied to the one-drop rule.

It was not only uneducated southern whites who held these racist beliefs about the effects of miscegenation. Some of the most prominent scientists of the day, including professors at universities such as Harvard and Yale, endorsed them as well. The late nineteenth century was the heyday of scientific racism: a set of ideas asserting the supremacy of the white race over all others and claiming that experimental evidence confirmed such supremacy.[10]

We now know that such experiments were seriously flawed. But at the time they were widely accepted. And if leading scientists of the day supported scientific racism, then how could the Supreme Court in *Plessy* have decided that laws enforcing a separation of the races were unreasonable?

The answer is that the Civil War Amendments are best construed as embodying the principle that government may not act on the basis of ideas of racial supremacy. Whatever conclusions scientists or anyone else may draw about race and racial hierarchy, it is prohibited for government to enact laws or to otherwise proceed on the premise that one race is superior and another inferior.

On this interpretation of the Civil War Amendments, it is not that the Constitution is "blind" to the race of American citizens, as Harlan would have it. Rather, it is that the Constitution is "deaf" to claims of racial superiority by some citizens over others. Just as the Religion Clauses of the First Amendment mean that government must not act based on sectarian religious beliefs, the Equal Protection Clause means that it may not act on claims of racial supremacy.

The framers of the Bill of Rights well understood the conflict and social disorder that could easily be unleashed if government acted on sectarian religious claims. Each religious faction would fight fiercely for control of the government so it could ensure that its vision of religious truth would prevail. Severe religious antagonism, hatred, and oppression would result.

When it comes to claims of racial supremacy, a similar logic prevails. Allowing government to act on claims of racial supremacy would be a prescription for severe racial conflict and oppression. Indeed, that is the great insight behind Justice Harlan's dissent in *Plessy,* an insight eclipsed by his remark that the Constitution is colorblind.

It is noteworthy that the Court's opinion in *Plessy* did not invoke scientific racism or any other claims about the racial supremacy of whites to support its finding that the Louisiana statute was not unreasonable. Indeed, such claims would have entirely undercut the equality part of the separate-but-equal doctrine. If claims of white supremacy were legally valid grounds for government action, it is not clear why separate facilities for blacks would have to be equal to those of whites. The absence of any explicit reference to claims of white supremacy testifies to the Court's implicit acceptance of the principle that government may not act on such claims. But once those claims are disqualified as a basis for Louisiana's statute, the state is left only with the unconvincing argument that the law is reasonable because it averts interracial violence on public transportation. In short, once racist ideas are disqualified from serving as a legitimate basis for a law, the Separate Car Act cannot meet the reasonableness test. And that is why the Act should have been declared unconstitutional.[11]

BEYOND SEPARATE
BUT EQUAL: THE *BROWN* CASE

The Small Steps to *Brown*

Legal change is rarely revolutionary. The process of revising and reinterpreting the law is more typically an incremental one in which small steps over time add up to substantial changes. Some steps are undoubtedly larger and more important than others, but smaller steps usually precede and pave the way for the larger ones.

It is with this incrementalist view of legal change in mind that we should approach one of the most celebrated judicial decisions in the nation's history: the Supreme Court's ruling in *Brown v. Board of Education,* handed down in 1954. The Court declared unconstitutional state laws that enforced racial segregation in public schools. In doing so, the Court held that the doctrine of separate but equal has no place in public schooling. The irony is that the legal path to *Brown* was paved with a series of decisions that rested squarely on *Plessy's* doctrine of separate but equal.

In the wake of *Plessy*, it was an open question as to how seriously courts would enforce the "equal" part of the doctrine of separate but equal. Prior to *Plessy*, black plaintiffs had won several common-law cases by persuading courts that the accommodations reserved for blacks were inferior to those reserved for whites. And strict judicial enforcement of the equality provision would have taken some of the sting out of racial separation. But as Jim Crow took hold in the South, such enforcement was not to be. Southern states routinely provided inferior facilities for blacks and sometimes provided none at all.

Beginning in the early 1930s, lawyers working for the National Association for the Advancement of Colored People (NAACP) developed and implemented a long-term legal strategy attacking Jim Crow. In its initial phases, the strategy was aimed at making the pay of black school teachers equal to that of white teachers and at ensuring that blacks would have access to state-run graduate and professional schools.

In the South, substantial pay disparities existed between black and white teachers who were equally qualified. Moreover, southern states operated all-white graduate and professional schools, without providing any such education for blacks, much less an equal education.

The NAACP sought to make the South take seriously the equality requirement of the separate-but-equal doctrine. While it may seem that such a strategy would only entrench the legal separation of the races, the reality was that it would be very costly for states to provide all-black schools and facilities that were truly equal to the existing all-white ones. The potential costs might convince southerners to admit blacks to their all-white institutions.

Moreover, the NAACP ultimately aimed to show that over the decades of Jim Crow, enforced racial separation had invariably led to unequal treatment of the races. Even if separate but equal was not a logical contradiction, it was a practical one: in the real world of American life, separate would never be equal.

In an important pre-*Brown* case, the Supreme Court heard a legal challenge against the University of Texas brought by a black mail carrier, Heman Sweatt. The university's law school had rejected Sweatt's application on grounds of race. The state told him that he could attend, instead, an all-black law school staffed by three part-time faculty members that it had just established in the basement of a Dallas office building. While arguing in court that the all-black school was equal to the one at the University of Texas, the state made plans to establish in Houston a permanent law school for blacks with greatly improved facilities and faculty. By the time the case reached the Supreme Court in 1950, the new school was ready and had even received accreditation.

The Court declined to declare that state-enforced racial segregation in education was inherently unconstitutional. It was not yet ready to take such an important and controversial step. But it did take the equality requirement of the separate-but-equal doctrine as seriously as possible. It held that the all-black school in Houston was not the equal of the University of Texas law school. Texas had acted unconstitutionally in denying Mr. Sweatt admission on account of his race. The Court ruled that equality in legal education meant not only equality of factors that could be objectively measured—number of faculty, size of library, and so on. It also meant equality in such factors as the reputation of the faculty and the position and influence of alumni. By such intangible criteria, the two schools were decidedly not equal.

The ruling in *Sweatt* was relatively narrow: it applied to law school education and perhaps to all graduate-level schooling. It did not apply to public schools. But *Sweatt's* emphasis on the intangible factors in education would foreshadow the Court's ruling when it finally did confront the question of whether state-enforced segregation in public schools violated the Constitution's principle of equality.

Brown: Constitutional Equality

The NAACP's legal attack on Jim Crow culminated in the Supreme Court's 1954 decision in *Brown v. Board of Education.* The Court ruled on the constitutionality of government-enforced racial segregation in public schools. The Court held that "in the field of public education the doctrine of 'separate but equal' has no place. Separate educational facilities are inherently unequal."[12]

Before reaching its conclusion, the Court considered the history behind the ratification of the Fourteenth Amendment. Despite an exhaustive review of that history, the Court said, there was no conclusive answer as to whether the Amendment was intended to prohibit state-enforced segregation in public schools. The framers and ratifiers disagreed among themselves on the extent, if any, to which government should be allowed to classify persons by race.

The Court proceeded to suggest that, even if there had been consensus among the framers and ratifiers, the case should not turn on their understandings: "We cannot turn the clock back to 1868."[13] The Court went on to explain that public education had become a central task of government in the century since the Fourteenth Amendment became part of the Constitution. Whatever the framers thought about public education, its centrality to life in the twentieth century meant that if states provided public education, then they had a duty to do so on an equal basis for all their citizens.

State-enforced racial segregation violated that duty, the Court held.[14] Prohibiting black children from attending schools with whites, solely on account of race, "generates a feeling of inferiority as to their status in the community that may affect their hearts and minds in a way unlikely ever to be undone."[15] The Court then cited several social science studies to support its finding of the harmful psychological effects on black schoolchildren of segregation. Thus, the intangible factors of self-esteem and self-respect provided the Court the grounds on which it declared Jim Crow education unconstitutional.

In an effort to mitigate southern antagonism to its ruling, the Court did not order an immediate end to segregated schooling, but rather instructed the parties to the case to submit legal briefs on how desegregation could best proceed. A year later, in *Brown II,* the Court ordered that desegregation proceed with "all deliberate speed," a flexible standard that could take account of local conditions, and the Court gave federal district courts the job of overseeing the process.[16]

Despite the Court's efforts to soften the blow to the South, southern states simply refused to desegregate. White politicians, school officials, and ordinary citizens engaged in a massive campaign of resistance, denouncing the Court's decision as an illegitimate and draconian violation of the rights reserved to the states under the Constitution. Their views were captured in a statement placed into the *Congressional Record* in 1956 and signed by almost every southern senator and representative at the time. The so-called "Southern Manifesto" decried the *Brown* decision as an exercise of "naked judicial power" and called for the use of "all lawful means" to resist and reverse the decision.[17] Segregationists did not, however, restrict themselves to lawful means in their opposition to the Court. In addition to legal challenges to desegregation orders, there were threats, violence, and the simple refusal to obey court decisions. The result was that a full ten years after *Brown,* there had been virtually no desegregation in the states of the old Confederacy.

White southerners were not the only ones who challenged the legitimacy of the Court's decision. Even some northern liberal legal scholars had their doubts. Indeed, it does not seem very difficult to poke holes in the Court's reasoning. The Court rested its ruling that segregation is "inherently unequal" on a handful of social science studies that concluded that segregation makes black schoolchildren feel inferior. Even if those studies were well-designed, the Court's reasoning displays a rather weak understanding of scientific inquiry.

A handful of studies cannot conclusively establish any conclusion, especially when the studies are of such complex psychological matters as racial identity and feelings of inferiority. The Court had deemed its review of the history of the Fourteenth Amendment as "inconclusive," and it should have made the same judgment about the scientific studies of the psychological effects of segregated schooling on black children.

But the critical weakness in the Court's reasoning in *Brown* is that it rests on a misconception about where the burden of proof should lie. The Court reasoned on the tacit premise that the opponents of segregation had the burden of showing that it did harm to black schoolchildren. Instead, the Court should have placed the burden on the supporters of segregation to show that they had good reason to treat black and white schoolchildren differently. And it should have refused to listen to any reason that invoked the natural superiority of one race over another. For as we saw in our analysis of *Plessy,* the Equal Protection Clause is best construed as excluding such reasons from governmental decision making. And without such reasons, it is difficult to see how the enforced racial separation of schoolchildren can be convincingly justified.

The South's support for school segregation rested squarely on the belief in white intellectual and moral supremacy. Southern whites continued to fear the "dilution of white blood" from miscegenation. They continued to think that blacks had inferior intellects and stronger criminal propensities, supposedly making a black presence in white schools a threat to the education and safety of white children.

If such fears and beliefs were deemed constitutionally impermissible reasons for any state policy or law, southern states would be left grasping at straws in their efforts to justify school segregation. In *Brown,* the Court would have been on firmer ground had it pushed the South to justify its practice of school segregation and found the proffered justifications wanting.

THE CIVIL RIGHTS REVOLUTION

Beyond Litigation

The Supreme Court followed the *Brown* decision with a series of rulings declaring unconstitutional segregation in parks, restrooms, swimming pools, and other state-run facilities. But southern states resisted those rulings, just as they resisted *Brown.* And if push came to shove, they often chose to shut down a public facility rather than agree to its racial integration.

Moreover, President Eisenhower was very reluctant to use the power of the federal government to force states to abide by the rulings of the Court. Although he did deploy federal troops in one notable instance, to implement the integration of Central High School in Little Rock, Arkansas, the president failed on the whole to use his powers to ensure that the Supreme Court's rulings were followed.

By the early 1960s, it had become clear that litigation was not enough to accomplish a civil rights revolution. Thanks to *Brown,* significant desegregation had taken place in the border states. But the deep South was another matter: the revolution that southern blacks hoped for, and southern whites feared, did not take place.

The missing ingredients for a genuine civil rights revolution in the United States were social agitation and electoral politics. Social agitation would come in the form of grass-roots protest marches, demonstrations, and boycotts aimed at segregated facilities, public and private. Working through their churches and civil rights organizations, blacks throughout the South would mobilize to demand their rights as American citizens.

The civil rights protestors also understood that ending racial injustice required more than the effective enforcement of the Supreme Court's rulings against segregation. Those rulings were limited to state-run facilities, on the theory that the Equal Protection Clause applied to the actions of state governments but not to the discriminatory actions of businesses or other private organizations. In addition, southern states continued their long-established practice of preventing blacks from registering and voting.

The pervasive discrimination against blacks meant that a thoroughgoing civil rights revolution would not only need to enforce *Brown* and its progeny. It would also need the enactment of new laws effectively guaranteeing the right to vote and prohibiting racial discrimination in such areas as employment and public accommodations. And that is where electoral politics became important: if such laws were to be enacted, the elected officials in the federal government had to do it. And so social agitation had to be combined with political dealmaking to complete the civil rights revolution.

Social Agitation: Martin Luther
King, Jr. versus George Wallace

The year 1963 was a crucial one for the civil rights movement. Nearly a decade had elapsed since the Supreme Court's decision in *Brown,* and Jim Crow still reigned throughout the deep South. In January of that year, George Wallace was sworn in as governor of Alabama. He declared in his inaugural speech, "Segregation now; segregation tomorrow; segregation forever." Moreover, as the year began, civil rights for blacks was not an issue on the radar screen of most white Americans. But that would soon change dramatically.

Civil rights protestors conducted a series of peaceful demonstrations that southern police authorities met with brutal force. Television cameras captured the police brutality and broadcast it to the nation. By mid-year, civil rights had become a nationwide issue and the protestors had gained the respect and support of many whites throughout the country.

The high point of the civil rights movement that year came at a mass rally, "The March for Jobs and Freedom," held in August in Washington, DC. Hundreds of thousands of blacks and whites from across the land assembled before the inspiring monument to Abraham Lincoln. And there they heard the cadences of Reverend Martin Luther King, Jr., as he captured the moral essence of the movement that he had helped to lead:

> Five score years ago, a great American, in whose symbolic shadow we stand today, signed the Emancipation Proclamation. This momentous decree came as a great beacon light of hope to millions of Negro slaves, who had been seared in the flames of withering injustice. . . . But one hundred years later, the Negro still is not free. . . .
>
> Let us not seek to satisfy our thirst for freedom by drinking from the cup of bitterness and hatred. We must ever conduct our struggle on the high plane of dignity and discipline. We must not allow our creative protest to degenerate into physical violence. . . .
>
> I have a dream that one day this nation will rise up and live out the true meaning of its creed—we hold these truths to be self-evident that all men are created equal.
>
> I have a dream that one day on the red hills of Georgia the sons of former slaves and the sons of former slave owners will be able to sit down together at the table of brotherhood. . . .
>
> I have a dream that my four little children will one day live in a nation where they will not be judged by the color of their skin but by the content of their character.[18]

Earlier in 1963, King had been jailed on a criminal charge stemming from his role in organizing a series of peaceful demonstrations against segregation. The demonstrations took place in Birmingham, Alabama, one of the most segregated cities in the South. Just before his arrival there, a new and more moderate city government had been elected in the place of the previous, hardline segregationist one. The old government officials, however, claimed that the elections were illegal, and the dispute was taken to court.

Meanwhile, King and other civil rights leaders proceeded with their plans for nonviolent rallies and marches. City ordinances required a parade permit for such demonstrations, but city officials made it clear that they would not issue one to the protestors under any circumstances. The city also went to state court and received a court order prohibiting King and his colleagues from conducting the demonstrations. King defied the order and the judge found him in contempt of court. He was jailed.

King's decision to defy the court order was criticized not only by hardline segregationists but also by political moderates who wanted to end segregation but who called for a less confrontational approach. These moderates included white clergymen, and they argued that all sides in the dispute over segregation must obey the laws and the orders of the courts. Just as George Wallace cannot justifiably thumb his nose at the Supreme Court, Martin Luther King cannot justifiably violate the orders of a duly constituted court of Alabama, unless and until those orders are dissolved by that court or a higher one. In short, the rule of law must be respected.

The moderates agreed with King that segregation must be eliminated. But they suggested that he and other civil rights leaders should show more patience in pursuing that goal. Birmingham's new city officials should be given a chance to address the city's racial problems. Negotiation, not confrontation, was the key to resolving those problems.

King ardently disagreed with the moderates' approach, and while in Birmingham jail, he wrote an open letter to a city newspaper responding to their views. He argued that it was unreasonable to ask blacks to show more patience: they had been victimized by centuries of brutal injustice, humiliation, and degradation. Moreover, the dichotomy between negotiation and confrontation was a false one. Confrontation was an essential tool in getting business leaders to the negotiation table. And nonviolent confrontation can generate "creative tensions" that lead to negotiated solutions.

King also sketched a theory of law to respond to the moderates' charge that, just like George Wallace, he was guilty of damaging the rule of law. King insisted that there was a crucial distinction between just and unjust laws. The latter kind violated a higher law, natural law. For that reason, unjust laws lack legal authority and do not impose on us any obligation to obey them. And the same goes for unjust court orders.

King contended that an individual is justified in violating an unjust law or court order as long as he does so openly, nonviolently, and with a willingness to accept the penalty and the purpose of eliminating the injustice. Someone who breaks an unjust law in that way is not showing any disrespect for the rule of law. Quite the opposite, such a person is showing the highest regard for the law.

The laws upholding segregation were unjust, King explained, for multiple reasons. Such laws degraded and demeaned blacks; they imposed on the black minority burdens that the white majority itself refused to bear; they were enacted by a process that was not really democratic due to the political exclusion of blacks; and even when appearing to be impartial, they were applied in a racially biased manner.

King's letter lays out the justification for his strategy of nonviolent civil disobedience. He provides a compelling account of the injustices of Jim Crow and is convincing in his claim that blacks had already waited far too long to receive equal treatment.

But his reliance on traditional natural law theory weakens his argument. As we saw in Chapter 2, there are serious problems with any such version of natural law theory. King would have done better to dispense with natural law theory and to have emphasized that the rule of law had long ago been undermined in the South by the system of white supremacy. Under Jim Crow, whites were effectively above the law in their relations with blacks: far too often, whites were not called to account by the law for the illegal harm they visited upon blacks. More generally, southern officials applied the law in a racially biased manner that effectively deprived blacks of many of their legal rights. In short, the South was a system of arbitrary white rule.

In such a situation, violating laws and court orders does not necessarily harm the prospects for building a true rule of law. King's key insight, obscured by the language of natural law theory, was that a strategy involving peaceful, open, and limited lawbreaking could help establish the rule of law in a situation where it had broken down. By focusing his campaign of civil disobedience on those laws and court orders that sustained segregation, King's strategy was aimed at the heart of the system that made a mockery of the rule of law. Only when all races received the equal protection of the law would the rule of law be a reality. That day would come only with the demise of Jim Crow. And King reasonably believed that his campaign of civil disobedience would have a better chance of destroying Jim Crow much sooner than any strategy that declined to disobey the dictates of the South's system of arbitrary racial government.

Contrary to the suggestions of the moderates, then, King's strategy could not be equated with George Wallace's defiance of the Supreme Court, even from the perspective of the rule of law. Wallace's defiance helped perpetuate the system of arbitrary rule by whites over blacks. King's strategy would help destroy that system and replace it with a true rule of law. But before the benefits of the rule of law could be enjoyed by southern blacks, aggressive action in the halls of the federal government would prove necessary.

THE CIVIL RIGHTS ACT OF 1964

When 1963 came to a close, the nation was still mourning the loss of its young leader, John F. Kennedy. Several months before his assassination, President Kennedy had introduced a civil rights bill into Congress. Civil rights laws had been enacted by Congress in 1957 and 1960, but the power of southern congressmen meant that these laws lacked the aggressive provisions that could challenge and destroy Jim Crow. President Kennedy's bill was stronger and included a ban on discrimination in public accommodations and in employment by businesses with federal contracts. But civil rights leaders wanted stronger enforcement provisions and a broader ban on employment discrimination. Working with their liberal allies in Congress, they persuaded President Kennedy to go along with a stronger bill, though he feared that it would not pass.

Indeed, prospects for the bill's passage looked rather bleak in the Fall of 1963. But then came the assassination, and the situation changed dramatically. The new president, Lyndon Johnson, made the passage of the bill his top priority. And he called on the nation to support the bill as a memorial to the slain president. The nation responded, and strong public support for the bill helped secure its enactment.

The Civil Rights Act of 1964 contained broad prohibitions on racial discrimination in public accommodations, employment, and programs receiving federal funds. But the law raised serious legal questions. Certain of its provisions, including the sections on public accommodations and employment, were arguably unconstitutional.

In the *Civil Rights Cases* of 1883, the Supreme Court struck down a federal civil rights law quite similar to the 1964 legislation. The law had prohibited discrimination in public accommodations and transportation. Congress claimed the authority to enact such a law on the basis of the Fourteenth Amendment. Section 5 of the Amendment authorized Congress to enforce "by appropriate legislation" the Equal Protection Clause and other provisions of the Amendment.

But the Court ruled that the Fourteenth Amendment had not given Congress the authority to prohibit "individual invasion of individual rights." Congress could bar states from legislating in ways that invaded the right of individuals to equal treatment. After all, the Amendment says that "no state" shall deny anyone the equal protection of the law. But the decision of a business owner to serve whites only or to segregate blacks from whites was not the action of any state. It was private action and, as such, was beyond the jurisdiction of Congress.

In *Civil Rights Cases,* the Court established a doctrine that has guided the interpretation of the Fourteenth Amendment ever since: the "state action" doctrine. The Amendment, said the Court, applied to the actions of states or agencies acting under state authority; it did not apply to the actions of private individuals or organizations. And the state action doctrine created a big problem for the proponents of the Civil Rights Act of 1964. For the Act to be upheld as constitutional, they had to find some way around the doctrine.

Perhaps surprisingly, the advocates of the Act found their answer in the provision of the Constitution that gives Congress the authority to regulate interstate commerce (the "Commerce Clause"). Beginning in the late 1930s, the Supreme Court had given that authority a very broad interpretation, so that just about all economic activity in the country could be deemed to be involved in interstate commerce.

The modern industrial economy into which America had developed in the early twentieth century meant a pervasive movement of goods, services, and people across state lines. If a motel had guests from another state, it was involved in interstate commerce. If a restaurant bought some of its food from an out-of-state supplier, it was involved in interstate commerce.

The development of the national economy thus gave the advocates of the Civil Rights Act of 1964 a constitutional argument that could not have been made in the nineteenth century. And in a series of rulings, the Supreme Court accepted the argument: the Civil Rights Act of 1964 was within Congress's authority under the Commerce Clause. The fact that the Act aimed to end discrimination, rather than, say, increase the Gross Domestic Product, was beside the point for the Court. Regardless of the aim, Congress was regulating interstate commerce, and that was sufficient to judge it constitutional.

Nonetheless, the Court's use of the Commerce Clause to uphold the Civil Rights Act of 1964 is problematic. To see why, let us look more closely at the Clause and why it is in the Constitution.

Recall that the Constitution does not grant Congress the power to enact whatever legislation it deems necessary for the national good. Rather, it enumerates the specific kinds of powers that Congress may exercise, and congressional authority under the rule of law is limited to those powers. The Commerce Clause specifies one such power, that of regulating interstate commerce.

In upholding the Civil Rights Act, the Court essentially said that, in acting under the Commerce Clause, Congress may act for noneconomic reasons, as long as the activity it regulates is connected to interstate commerce. But this is a very strained interpretation of the Clause.[19]

Consider the question of why it makes sense for the Constitution to have the Commerce Clause. The answer is clear. Having the Clause makes sense for economic reasons: it empowers Congress to look out for the nation's economic well-being. The point is not simply that the framers intended the Clause to empower Congress to act for economic reasons rather than ethical reasons. Rather, the point is that the only sensible rationale for having the Clause in the Constitution is an economic rationale.

In upholding the 1964 act on Commerce Clause grounds, the Court disregarded the economic rationale and chose to read the Clause in a literalist way. The Clause does not explicitly say that Congress needs economic reasons to regulate interstate commerce; it just says that Congress is authorized to regulate such commerce.

However, there is a serious problem with this literalist approach. It is not reasonable to consistently apply the approach to the Commerce Clause, and the Court itself has recognized that fact. For example, a literal understanding of the term *commerce* would have made it impossible for Congress to regulate many kinds of economic activities, such as the production of goods or the hiring of labor, that the Court has in fact included under the term. Production and hiring are, literally speaking, distinct from commerce. But the Court has sensibly chosen to construe *commerce* as referring to economic activity generally. In doing so, the Court left literalism behind and looked to the rationale for the Clause. And that same rationale is what makes problematic the argument that the Civil Rights Act was within Congress's authority under the Commerce Clause.

So is there any better way to argue for the constitutionality of the Civil Rights Act? Perhaps there is. Consider again the state action doctrine. The usual understanding of it is that it imposes a single requirement on the interpretation of the Fourteenth Amendment: the Amendment must be construed to apply only to the actions of a state and not to those of a private person or organization. In fact, though, the usual understanding conflates two separate requirements: (1) the Amendment applies only to states and not to private parties, and (2) the Amendment applies only to actions and not to omissions, that is, not to failures to act. By retaining (1) but giving up (2), we can develop an alternative argument for the constitutionality of the Civil Rights Act.

Philosophers draw a distinction between negative duties and affirmative ones. The former require one to refrain from taking a certain kind of action, while the latter require one to take a certain type of action. The Equal Protection Clause of the Fourteenth Amendment has been interpreted by the Court as imposing a strictly negative duty on states: they must refrain from acting to deny anyone the equal protection of the law. But even if we agree that the Amendment applies only against states and not private parties, there is no good reason to limit the meaning of the Clause to negative duties. If states fail to act to protect persons from conditions or practices that make them second-class citizens, then such omissions should be considered violations of equal protection.

Southern states clearly violated equal protection when they practiced racial segregation. But the second-class status of blacks and other racial minorities was not simply a function of what states did to them. It was also the result of exclusionary practices by companies making employment decisions and businesses serving whites only. Acts of private discrimination worked hand in hand with acts of state discrimination to subordinate blacks.

Prior to 1964, some states had in fact enacted laws to protect persons against racial discrimination in employment and public accommodations. But obviously not all of them did, and the existing state civil rights laws were insufficient to establish equal standing for blacks in American society. Without effective state action against private discrimination, blacks were left vulnerable to many of the practices and actions that made it impossible for them to have the status of equal citizens. States were thus in violation of their affirmative obligations under the Equal Protection Clause.

The remedy for this state inaction was not for courts to force states to enact effective civil rights legislation. Even if it had been feasible, such a course would have been a serious judicial invasion of the authority of states under the Constitution. Rather, the remedy was for Congress, acting under Section 5 of the Fourteenth Amendment, to enact civil rights legislation. In short, the Amendment can be construed as placing affirmative duties on states and authorizing Congress to act if states fail to act to meet those duties.

The Commerce Clause is about Congress's power to act for the purpose of promoting and protecting national economic interests. The Fourteenth Amendment is about Congress's power to act for the purpose of guaranteeing an equal status for all citizens, regardless of race. The effort to defend the constitutionality of the Civil Rights Act on the basis of the Commerce Clause proved to be a success. But it was a success in spite of its weakness. A better approach would have defended the Act squarely on the basis of the Fourteenth Amendment.

THE VOTING RIGHTS ACT:
RACE AND DEMOCRACY

The Civil Rights Act of 1964 was followed the next year by the Voting Rights Act. For decades southern states had illegally prevented blacks from registering and voting. This exclusion of blacks from the political process was a critical element in maintaining white supremacy. And only very aggressive intervention by the federal government in the electoral processes of southern states could overcome that exclusion.

The Fifteenth Amendment had prohibited any denial or abridgement of the right to vote on account of race. But within a few decades of its adoption, it was a dead letter in the South. Southern whites employed a variety of strategies to prevent blacks from exercising their right to vote.

Aside from brute force and threats of violence, one of the most effective strategies for disenfranchising blacks was the literacy test. A number of southern states enacted laws that required citizens to pass a test of their literacy and/or their knowledge of law and government in order to register to vote. On account of the poor education they received, if they received any at all, such tests effectively disqualified most southern blacks. Moreover, white election officials applied the tests in a discriminatory way, making the tests much more difficult for blacks than for whites.

Civil rights laws enacted by Congress in 1957, 1960, and 1964 all contained provisions protecting the right to vote. But they were ineffective. The reason was simple: they placed the onus on individual blacks to bring a lawsuit if they believed their rights had been violated. Even if black plaintiffs won these suits, this case-by-case approach could hardly make a dent in the South's systemic denial of the right to vote. The individual plaintiffs might win a court order directing that they be registered, but most of the black population would remain disenfranchised.

The Voting Rights Act rejected the case-by-case approach. It mandated sweeping changes in southern electoral systems and put the force of the federal government behind that mandate. Up to that time, state and local governments controlled registration and voting, with the federal government playing virtually no role. State and local control was generally understood to be an aspect of federalism, the constitutional doctrine that divided powers between the federal government and the states. By 1965, Congress and the president had come to the conclusion that federalism was not working to protect the right to vote. The Voting Rights Act thus authorized a substantial role for the federal government in what had previously been left up to states.

Section 2 of the Act reaffirmed the Fifteenth Amendment ban on the denial or abridgement of the right to vote on account of race or color. In later years, Section 2 was extended to protect certain linguistic minorities, such as speakers of Spanish and of indigenous Alaskan languages.

Section 4 abolished literacy tests for five years in southern jurisdictions. That section was subsequently amended to provide for a permanent ban on such tests everywhere in the country. Section 5 required certain jurisdictions, mainly in the South, to get approval in advance from the federal government for any changes they intended to make in their voting procedures or practices. Sections 6 through 8 provided for federal officials to register persons to vote and oversee the voting process. And Sections 11 and 12 provided for federal criminal penalties for anyone found guilty of interfering with another's right to vote.

The Voting Rights Act proved to be a great success. In its wake, the number of blacks registered to vote increased dramatically throughout the South. And the number of black elected officials also began to climb. In 1965, there were fewer than 100 such officials in all of the states of the deep South. By 1989, the number had climbed to over 3,000.

Nonetheless, the provisions of the Act gave rise to many legal cases and controversies. One such controversy revolved around the ban on literacy tests. Gaston County in North Carolina filed suit to be allowed to reinstate its literacy test, which had been suspended by Section 4. The county argued that it had not applied the test in a biased manner and should be allowed to resume its use. The federal government opposed resumption of the test on the ground that, even if administered fairly, the use of the test would be discriminatory. The test would disqualify a disproportionate number of blacks because blacks had received inferior public schooling to whites. For years, the county had operated a segregated school system in which educational opportunity for blacks was far worse than that for whites.

The county countered that it was now equalizing the educational opportunities for blacks and whites and so should be allowed to resume the test. But in *Gaston County v. U.S.,* the Court agreed with the federal government.[20] A test that was itself impartial and was impartially administered could still be discriminatory in operation. The critical fact was that the test would help to perpetuate the effects of the county's past racism. It was such racism that resulted in an inferior education for blacks. Using the test now would allow that racism to result in additional harm to blacks in the form of their exclusion from the electoral process.

The *Gaston* case shows clearly how a "facially neutral" practice, as lawyers call it, can be discriminatory in operation. The legacy of past racism can be perpetuated by practices that, on the surface, appear unbiased and even quite reasonable. It was not unreasonable to think that voters should be required to demonstrate basic literacy and a minimal understanding of law and government. After all, when a voter casts a ballot, she potentially affects not only her own life but the lives of all other citizens as well. It makes sense to expect that those who exercise this civic responsibility will be minimally informed, and a literacy test could help weed out those unable to meet that expectation. And over the years several states, under their constitutional authority to set voting qualifications, had decided to adopt such tests.

But even if we grant that literacy tests are quite reasonable in the abstract, the particular facts of American history made them discriminatory, at least in cases such as *Gaston*. The Court in *Gaston* made it clear that its ruling was based on the county's long-standing practice of racially segregating schools and underfunding blacks ones. The Court noted that the practice had only recently been discontinued and that it was unrealistic to think that its effects would vanish in just a few years. So the Court's decision was relatively narrow in scope, even as it recognized a wider point, namely, that reasonable and facially neutral tests can be discriminatory.

THE BLACK POWER MOVEMENT

In one of the great ironies of American history, the anger and frustration of blacks exploded into mass violence in the very years that the civil rights movement achieved its stunning victories with the Civil Rights Act of 1964 and the Voting Rights Act of 1965. There had been race riots before in the nation's history, but in most instances the rioters were white, who went on rampages against blacks. Starting in 1964, riots were predominantly by blacks and, perhaps surprisingly, they were not by southern blacks but rather by the inhabitants of urban ghettoes in northern cities and in California.

Out of the riots of the mid-1960s a new movement emerged that claimed to give voice to the grievances of the rioters and of blacks more generally. It was the Black Power movement, and it was far more militant than the one led by Martin Luther King. In their book *Black Power,* two of the leaders of the movement, Stokely Carmichael and Charles Hamilton, declared: "The advocates of Black Power reject the old slogans and meaningless rhetoric of previous years in the civil rights struggle. The language of yesterday is indeed irrelevant: progress, nonviolence, integration . . . these terms must be set aside or redefined."[21]

For the Black Power movement, the legislative victories of the civil rights movement did not amount to real progress. Blacks continued to suffer from poverty, unemployment, disease, premature death, and dilapidated housing at rates far higher than did whites. The new federal laws had not made a dent in such dramatic racial disparities. Moreover, the Black Power leaders accused northern liberals of hypocrisy: the segregation of blacks in the destitute urban ghettoes of the North was as racially oppressive as the conditions blacks faced in the South. Northern liberals could see the racism of southerners but not their own.

Black Power advocates argued that whites—northern and southern—would never willingly relinquish their racial dominance. Blacks could not depend on whites in their fight for racial equality, nor should blacks seek as their immediate goal integration into mainstream white society. That society was racist to the core, and integration would amount to nothing more than capitulation to a profoundly antiblack system. Thus, Carmichael and Hamilton wrote, "[W]e reject the goal of assimilation into middle-class America because the values of that class are anti-humanist and because that class as a social force perpetuates racism."[22]

The advocates of Black Power did not wholly repudiate the principle that people should be colorblind. But they argued that the nation was a long way from the day when such a principle could serve as a reasonable basis for action. Carmichael and Hamilton put the point this way: "[W]hile color blindness *may* be a sound goal ultimately, we must realize that race is an overwhelming fact of life in this historical period. There is no black man in this country who can live 'simply as a man.' His blackness is an ever-present fact of this racist society, whether he recognizes it or not."[23]

Moreover, many of the leaders of the Black Power movement argued that blacks should abandon the commitment to nonviolence, a hallmark of Martin Luther King's approach. They pointed out that whites had not hesitated to use violence to defend Jim Crow. Between 1880 and 1940, there were over 3,800 reported cases of lynchings, the vast majority of which were aimed at black men who in one way or another challenged the system of white supremacy. And as civil rights protestors of the 1960s increasingly refused to accept white hegemony, whites struck back with a ferocious violence. Civil rights workers were beaten and murdered. Black churches were bombed, including the infamous incident in Birmingham in 1964 that killed four black schoolgirls. Moreover, many advocates of Black Power thought of the police who patrolled the ghettoes of the North and West as an occupying army whose purpose was to keep blacks subordinate to whites.

The advocates of Black Power argued that, in order for blacks to defend themselves and gain the equality that is rightfully theirs, they must be ready and willing to resort to arms. Carmichael and Hamilton wrote: "From our viewpoint, rampaging white mobs and white night-riders must be made to understand that their days of free head-whipping are over. Black people should and must fight back. . . a 'nonviolent' approach to civil rights is an approach that black people cannot afford. . ."[24] And Huey Newton, one of the founders of the Black Panther Party, put it simply: "When the people move for liberation, they must have the basic tool of liberation: the gun."[25]

It is unlikely that a substantial percentage of American blacks ever fully supported the Black Power movement. The riots notwithstanding, most blacks understood that Martin Luther King was right in rejecting a strategy of violence. If the fight for racial justice came down to an armed confrontation between blacks and whites, there was no doubt that blacks would suffer a staggering loss. Moreover, despite the Black Power movement's contempt for middle-class American life, many blacks aspired to become part of that life.

Yet, Black Power did express a rage and frustration that was widespread among American blacks. And it helped to focus attention on what many blacks and whites reasonably saw as the fundamental issue: the reality of life faced by blacks across the nation. That reality could be boiled down to a simple proposition: a black baby born anywhere in America in the 1960s had life-prospects far worse than a white one. It is a reality that would stubbornly persist through the remaining decades of the twentieth century.

THE IDEA OF INSTITUTIONAL RACISM

In their efforts to understand and articulate the situation of blacks, the leaders of the Black Power movement formulated a new concept: institutional racism. Although the movement itself died out during the early 1970s, the idea of institutional racism took root and has become part of the way many thinkers and activists understand the problems of race in America.

Among the first to formulate a conception of institutional racism were Carmichael and Hamilton. They defined racism as "the predication of decisions and policies on considerations of race for the purpose of *subordinating* a racial group. . . ."[26] They went on to argue that racism "takes two closely related forms: individual whites acting against individual blacks, and acts by the total white community against the black community. We call these individual and institutional racism."[27]

Individual racism involves actions obviously intended to harm blacks. Institutional racism is more subtle, but its effects are much more far-reaching. "When white terrorists bomb a black church and kill five black children, that is an act of individual racism. . . . But when in that same city—Birmingham, Alabama—five hundred black babies die each year, because of the lack of proper food, shelter, medical facilities . . . that is a function of institutional racism."[28]

For Carmichael and Hamilton, institutional racism is the product of the normal functioning of our social institutions and of the harmful effects those institutions have on blacks. And they link institutional racism to the prejudices of whites: "Institutional racism relies on the active and pervasive operation of anti-black attitudes. . . ."[29] This link seems necessary given their general understanding of racism in terms of decisions and policies undertaken with "the purpose of subordinating a racial group."

But what if certain institutions or practices had the effect of harming blacks even if that was not the purpose of the people running the institutions? Would that still be institutional racism? A strict application of the Carmichael-Hamilton conception would seem to answer in the negative. Yet, much of what they say in condemning the impoverished and degrading conditions in which blacks lived suggests that institutional racism against blacks can exist apart from any prejudicial attitudes on the part of whites. And later theorists would explicitly formulate a conception of institutional racism that would detach the idea of racism from that of personal prejudice. According to that conception, social practices and institutions are racist when they systematically result in putting blacks as a group (or some other racially subordinate group) at a disadvantage relative to whites (or some other racially dominant group). No one involved in the institution need have a desire—overt or covert—to harm blacks. The racism is found strictly in the disparate consequences for different racial groups of the institution or practice.

Those who adopted the idea of institutional racism used it to indict America's institutions as racist. The proof, as they saw it, was in the dramatic and persistent racial disparities generated by those institutions when it came to income, wealth, health, housing, employment, life-expectancy, and the other variables that indicate a group's quality of life. Focusing on personal prejudice made it seem that racism was simply a matter of the invidious acts of a few isolated individuals, when in fact it was a matter of how society systematically operated to make the life-prospects of blacks far worse than those of whites.[30]

But others rejected the idea of institutional racism and the claim that America was a racist society. They held that racism was fundamentally a matter of personal prejudice: the desire to disadvantage persons on account of race. And they pointed to polling data and other evidence that personal prejudice had diminished markedly in the country during the late 1960s and 1970s.

The debate over institutional racism raises important questions about American society. Are we still a racist society? Is racial discrimination so pervasive and deep in our institutions and practices that it amounts to systemic racial oppression? How severely does racism disadvantage minorities? Answering these questions would require a detailed sociological and historical study, well beyond the scope of this chapter. But it is crucial to recognize that one cannot address those questions reasonably without an understanding of the nature of racial discrimination and how we can judge when and where it exists. And those matters were at the heart of a series of legal cases decided by the Supreme Court. Let us turn to those cases and see whether we can shed some light on the nature and scope of discrimination. We will see that there are important insights behind the idea of institutional racism, even though it is a mistake to think that disparate racial consequences can, by themselves, make an institution or practice racist.

RACIAL DISCRIMINATION:
INTENT VERSUS DISPARATE IMPACT

For many years, the Duke Power Company had deliberately limited black workers to the worst-paying and most onerous jobs. In 1965 the company terminated its practice of job segregation, but it adopted a policy requiring workers to have a high school diploma or pass a general intelligence test in order to get transfers to better-paying jobs within the company.

Black employees sued the company, alleging that its use of the tests was discriminatory. They pointed out that the tests did not measure the ability to do the particular jobs in question and that blacks were disproportionately disqualified from the higher-paying jobs. In *Griggs v. Duke Power*, the Court agreed with the black plaintiffs and ruled that the company's use of the tests was racially discriminatory, in violation of the Civil Rights Act.[31]

The relevant section of the Act declares, "It shall be an unlawful employment practice for an employer to limit, segregate, or classify his employees in any way which would deprive or tend to deprive any individual of employment opportunities . . . because of such individual's race. . . ."[32] The Court ruled that this prohibits not only intentional and overt discrimination but also "practices that are fair in form but discriminatory in operation."[33]

Employers could use tests that had a disproportionate racial impact, but the employers had the burden of establishing that the tests were "demonstrably a reasonable measure of job performance."[34] More generally, the Court held that employment practices having a negative impact disproportionately falling on racial minorities were legal only if the practices were necessary to serve some legitimate goal of the business. This has been called the "business necessity test."

The lower courts had found that Duke Power had not adopted the tests with the intention of disadvantaging blacks, but for the Supreme Court that finding did not settle the case: "good intent, or absence of discriminatory intent does not redeem employment procedures or testing mechanisms that operate as 'built-in headwinds' for minority groups and are unrelated to measuring job capability."[35] The company could not meet the business necessity test, and so the Court judged its practices discriminatory.

The Court's decision in *Griggs* formed the basis of the "disparate-impact" theory of racial discrimination. According to that theory, the idea of racial discrimination is not limited to intentional efforts to disadvantage persons on account of race. It covers actions and practices that have a disproportionate negative impact on a racial minority, regardless of intent.[36]

And going beyond the reasoning in *Gaston,* the disparate-impact theory does not require that the negative impact be a legacy of past intentional discrimination by the party currently charged with discrimination. Even if Duke Power had never intentionally discriminated in the past, it would still be guilty of discrimination for its testing policies, under the disparate-impact approach. What counts are the consequences for racial minorities of a given practice, not whether the party charged with discrimination is now acting, or has ever acted, with the intent to disadvantage minorities.

A number of legal thinkers endorsed the disparate-impact theory as the best account of racial discrimination against minorities. And the theory clearly reflects the influence of the idea of institutional racism in its focus on the consequences for racial minorities of an action or practice. But the Supreme Court itself soon backed away from any general endorsement of the theory.

In *Washington v. Davis,* the Court faced the question of whether the Equal Protection Clause prohibited a police department's use of written tests in making employment decisions when the tests had a disproportionate impact on blacks.[37] There was no charge that intentional discrimination motivated the use of the tests. Thus, the question was whether the disparate-impact theory was to be used in explaining the meaning of the Fourteenth Amendment.

The Court answered by rejecting the disparate-impact theory for purposes of constitutional law and embracing the much narrower "intent theory" of discrimination. According to the intent theory, only actions and practices that are undertaken with the intent of disadvantaging persons on account of their race can count as racial discrimination. Relying on that theory, the Court ruled that the police department tests were not discriminatory under the Equal Protection Clause, because the department had not used them with the intent to disadvantage racial minorities.[38]

Accordingly, current law operates with two differing accounts of racial discrimination, one for the Civil Rights Act of 1964 and the other for the Equal Protection Clause of the Constitution.[39] But which account is the better: disparate impact or intent?

Advocates of the intent theory of discrimination insist that actions and practices can be discriminatory only if prejudicial reasons lie behind them. Consider the following example developed by the philosopher J. L. A. Garcia in the course of his argument that actions are not made racist by their consequences.[40]

Suppose space aliens decide to attack earth, focusing the brunt of their attack on Africa. The aliens harbor no racial bigotry. They are attacking Africa for military reasons, not reasons of prejudice. The attack has a disparate impact on blacks as compared to whites. Yet, Garcia points out that it is not sensible to describe the attack as racist, since there is an absence of any racial bigotry on the part of the aliens.

Garcia's example casts serious doubt on the soundness of the disparate-impact approach. The alien attack may be immoral, but it is not racially discriminatory, despite the disparate racial impact. The example shows that what makes actions or practices discriminatory are the prejudicial reasons behind them, not their consequences.

Yet, we still need some way of accommodating certain insights of the advocates of the disparate-impact theory. For example, they cogently point out that actions not motivated by prejudice can be still be discriminatory if they carry forward or exacerbate the harmful effects of past prejudicial acts. We found just such a situation in the *Gaston* literacy test. And advocates of disparate impact are certainly right in thinking that the harmful effects of racial discrimination on the lives of minorities are what has made such discrimination such a great wrong in our society.

But these insights can be accommodated without giving up a central idea of the intent theory: what makes actions and practices discriminatory are the prejudicial reasons behind them. The key is to see that prejudicial reasons can include more than what intent theory, as conventionally understood, is prepared to recognize. When someone acts in a deliberate effort to harm minorities, we have a clear example of a person acting for a prejudicial reason. And that is the sort of case the conventional version of intent theory is designed to capture. But it is also prejudicial for someone to be indifferent to harm suffered by minorities when that same person would not be indifferent to a similar harm suffered by white individuals. And the conventional intent theory would not count such a case as an instance of discrimination.

Consider the case of the racial disparities caused by the much longer mandatory prison sentences handed out for crack cocaine violations than for powder cocaine offenses. Crack users tend to be black; powder users tend to be white. The result of the law is that blacks get far harsher sentences for drug offenses than do whites. Suppose that white lawmakers would have been less harsh with crack users had most of those users been white and that the lawmakers are indifferent to the long sentences received by crack users because most of the users are in fact black. In such a situation, it would be fair to attribute prejudice to those lawmakers, even on the assumption that they were not deliberately (or even unconsciously) trying to harm blacks. Their prejudice would rest in a racial double-standard that was more cold-hearted toward the suffering of blacks than that of whites.

In a similar way, the idea that racial indifference can be a form of prejudice helps explain cases such as *Gaston* and *Griggs,* where facially neutral practices are deemed discriminatory because of the way in which they perpetuate the legacy of past discrimination. In those cases, past discrimination consisted of deliberate acts of racial exclusion and subordination that resulted in inferior educational and employment opportunities for blacks. The requirements of a literacy or intelligence test, though reasonable in the abstract, would have carried forward the harmful effects of that past discrimination by disproportionately excluding blacks from the political process or from better-paying jobs. And an indifference to those consequences of the tests can be reasonably deemed a form of prejudice because one can sensibly think that whites would not have shown such indifference toward the continuing effects of past injustice had the victims been other whites instead of blacks. The whites in charge would likely have modified voting or job requirements that disproportionately disqualified their own racial group.

Thus, it is possible to accommodate the insights behind the disparate-impact theory within the framework of an approach that understands discrimination as rooted in prejudicial motivations. Such an accommodation would enable the law to recognize a subtle but important form of discrimination: an indifference to the harms suffered by minorities when there would have been a response had the same harms befallen whites. The conventional version of intent theory would let such discrimination pass by without legal condemnation. But a revised version would judge it for what it is: a form of racial discrimination that, no less than the intent to harm, can unfairly put minorities at a significant disadvantage.

CRITICAL RACE THEORY

Overview

Critical Race Theory (CRT) is an approach to understanding issues of race, law, and society that has emerged over the past decade or so. It echoes some of the ideas of the Black Power movement. Although Black Power was mainly a social activist movement and CRT is principally an intellectual one, important similarities—along with some crucial differences—can be found between them.

As the Black Power activists argued in their time, Critical Race theorists (CR theorists) hold that American society remains deeply racist and that such racism is fundamentally a matter of the racial inequalities that result from the normal functioning of American institutions. The aim of CR theorists is to uncover, analyze, and combat the racial subordination that they see throughout society. And, like their Black Power forerunners, they hold that this racism cannot be effectively combatted on the basis of colorblind policies and actions. Society is emphatically not colorblind, and CR theorists assert that is wrongheaded to think that colorblind policies can rectify the severe disadvantages from which persons suffer on account of their color.

On the other hand, in contrast to Black Power, CRT does not call for armed struggle.[41] Rather, it seeks to improve the conditions of minorities through the combined use of social activism, political mobilization, creative legal interpretation, and—for some CR theorists—disobedience to the rule of law.

CR theorists tend to agree with the Black Power movement that the civil rights laws of the 1960s were quite ineffective in improving the lives of minorities. And like Black Power advocates, they regard grass-roots action by minority organizations as central to the task of securing racial equality.

But unlike Black Power activists, the proponents of CRT see the law as a potentially effective tool for combatting racism and moving toward racial equality. They criticize judicial decisions and doctrines that undercut that potential and argue for doctrines and creative legal interpretations that will help promote the cause of racial equality.

For example, advocates of CRT argue that the free-speech principles of the Constitution should be interpreted to permit university regulations against racist speech and to allow civil lawsuits based on the harm caused by such speech. In recent years, courts have repeatedly invalidated on First Amendment grounds university hate-speech rules.

CR theorists do not argue that the legal regulation of racist speech would by itself make a large dent in the problem of racial subordination. But they argue that the hostility to such regulation reflects a more general phenomenon in America society, a phenomenon that plays a key role in perpetuating racial subordination: the tendency to discount or downplay the harmful effects of activities when the victims are mainly racial minorities. For CR theorists, the legal regulation of racist speech would be a significant move in the direction of taking seriously the harm suffered by minorities.

One of the distinctive aspects of CRT is its use of stories, both real and hypothetical. Conventional legal scholarship revolves around the logical analysis of legal doctrines, principles, and theories. And the work of CR theorists often involves such analyses. But CRT also includes narratives in which race is the major theme.

One of the most widely discussed CR narratives is Derrick Bell's hypothetical story set in the future about space aliens who promise the American people vast reserves of gold and very advanced technology so that the country will be able to solve the severe environmental and economic problems from which it is then suffering. The aliens' only condition is that America turn over to them the country's entire black population. Bell's story tells of the political and ethical debates that are triggered by the space aliens' proposal.[42]

Other CR narratives recount episodes in the lives of CR theorists themselves. For example, Patricia Williams tells of the time a clerk working at Benetton's in New York City refused to buzz her into the store during store hours, presumably because Williams is black.

The use of narratives has proved very controversial among legal scholars. Critics of CRT point out that stories cannot prove, or even provide convincing evidence for, CRT's claims about racism in American society. And the critics are right: such claims can be reliably established only on the basis of systematic scientific inquiry about society and careful logical and moral analyses that proceed in light of what scientific inquiry shows. The scientific inquiry would need to examine such matters as life-expectancy, infant mortality, health, income, wealth, and education. The logical and moral analyses would need to elucidate and clarify such concepts as those of racism and injustice and, with the help of such analyses, evaluate the facts disclosed by the scientific study of society.

Narratives are a useful and compact way of encapsulating various views about race in American society. CR theorists think that our currently popular story lines are much too optimistic. They reject the mainstream narratives that treat the enactment of the civil rights laws of the 1960s as the rightly celebrated climax of the long struggle for racial equality. They seek alternative narratives that suggest the continuation of pervasive racial subordination.

Perhaps the view encapsulated in the mainstream narratives is too optimistic. But the cogency of any view about race in America depends not on how captivating or aesthetically pleasing the corresponding story is but rather on the empirical evidence and moral analyses that can be marshaled to support it.

Nonetheless, it is possible to understand CR narratives in a way that is different and more defensible than their critics take them. The narratives can be construed as an effort to prod white Americans into examining more carefully what many take for granted about race, namely, that widespread racial injustice is a thing of the past. The examination requires systematic social, logical, and moral inquiry, but the prod to such inquiry can be stories about race in America.

Another very controversial aspect of CRT stems from the fact that some of its proponents are prepared to defend disobedience to the rule of law in the fight against racial subordination. They contend that the American system of law is heavily tilted against nonwhites, and that any simple endorsement of the rule of law will help perpetuate white domination. The pursuit of substantive justice for racial minorities, some CR theorists argue, justifies disregard for the rule of law. Let us examine those arguments more closely.

Racism and the Rule of Law

Some contemporary conservatives contend that racism is no longer a major problem in American society. Thus, Dinesh D'Souza declares the "end of racism" in a book in which he argues that whatever inequalities now exist between the races are not due to racism and do not amount to racial injustices inflicted on minorities by whites.[43] But for those who agree with CRT in rejecting such a view, the question arises as to whether the current fight against racism can justifiably take the form of deliberately violating the law.

Some CR thinkers answer that question in the affirmative. And the violations of the law that they seem prepared to countenance go beyond the kind of nonviolent public protest practiced by Martin Luther King. Consider the ideas of one prominent advocate of CRT, Richard Delgado.

Delgado has a rather broad understanding of when the fight for racial equality may ignore the requirements of the rule of law. He writes that "minorities should invoke and follow the law when it benefits them and break or ignore it otherwise—when it gets in the way, is unresponsive, or is adverse to their interests."[44] Delgado calls this way of thinking about the law "legal instrumentalism."

Legal instrumentalism clearly aims to deflate the importance often attached to the rule of law. Delgado sees that importance as an obstacle in the path of minorities who are seeking substantive justice for themselves:"The law-lover will subscribe to mythic, heroic views about the rule of law and insist that everything be addressed within that framework. We, by contrast, will take a more utilitarian view of law.... We'll ask, 'What can law do for us at this time and place?'"[45]

Delgado does not advocate violent methods, but unlike Martin Luther King, he does not oppose them as a matter of principle. For Delgado, the question of using or forgoing violence is strictly a pragmatic one: which tactic will help the cause of minorities and which will not? Whatever helps the cause is justifiable.

It is difficult to find a persuasive moral argument for Delgado's deflation of the rule of law. Delgado is not simply saying that racism is so pervasive and harmful that some departure from the rule of law is justified. He is saying that the rule of law does not apply to minorities who are fighting for racial equality. Thus, legal instrumentalism is not only incompatible with strict adherence to the rule of law; it is incompatible with qualified versions of the rule of law that would draw a limited exception for the kind of nonviolent public protests conducted during the civil rights movement.

So even if we concede that racism is sufficiently pervasive and harmful to permit some departure from the rule of law, we are a long way from justifying Delgado's sweeping legal instrumentalism. And even if we concede that his instrumentalism would be justified in conditions where minorities were enslaved or oppressed as under Jim Crow, we are a long way from justifying Delgado's approach under current conditions.

Moreover, Delgado glosses over the question of how one is to determine which laws advance minority interests and which do not. Within minority communities, there is significant disagreement over how best to promote racial equality. Adherence to the rule of law is a way of handling disagreement and deciding on which view, among a number of competing reasonable ones, society is to act. Perhaps Delgado would prefer for minorities to set up their own legal and political system and make decisions through such institutions as they establish. But the fact is that no such institutions exist, and in their absence, Delgado's legal instrumentalism seems to license each individual member of a minority group to decide for him- or herself whether and when following a certain law is good for the group. Even granting the existence of widespread racial injustice, it is difficult to see why such a position is morally defensible.

Another view of when minorities are justified in departing from the rule of law for reasons of racial equality comes from CR theorist Paul Butler. A former federal prosecutor, Butler argues that in cases of nonviolent, victimless crimes, such as drug possession, black jurors have a moral responsibility to vote to acquit black defendants, even when guilt has been proved beyond a reasonable doubt. He tells us that this kind of "jury nullification" for reasons of race already takes place in cities like the District of Columbia and that it is even discussed at training sessions for federal prosecutors.[46] Butler seeks to justify this practice of racial jury nullification.

Affirming the view of other CR theorists, Butler contends that "criminal law is racist because, like other American law... it is an instrument of white supremacy."[47] Due to racism, past and present, "the majority of African-Americans receive few meaningful educational and employment opportunities."[48] The "inevitable result" is that blacks commit proportionally more criminal offenses than whites and so are disproportionately incarcerated. Butler explains: "In other words, racism creates and sustains the criminal breeding ground, which produces the black criminal. Thus, when many African-Americans are locked up, it is because of a situation that white supremacy created."[49]

Butler proceeds to argue that the black community is better off when blacks who are guilty of nonviolent, victimless crimes are acquitted. He points to the sizeable percentage of young black men who are imprisoned, especially for offenses such as drug possession, and he contends that the incarceration of so many black youth does serious additional harm to a black community already severely disadvantaged in many other ways by racism. And Butler emphasizes that there are alternatives to incarceration, such as drug treatment programs, that would be far better for the black community than locking up those who are guilty of nonviolent, victimless crimes.

Butler concedes that his proposal is subversive of the rule of law. For jurors to ignore the law and facts of a case and to acquit a defendant they know to be guilty is a serious departure from the rule of law. But Butler argues that the application of drug-possession laws to blacks is an injustice and that "there is no moral obligation to follow an unjust law."[50] Moreover, Butler points to "the continuing failure of the rule of law to protect African-Americans," as evidenced by recent Supreme Court decisions striking down affirmative action policies helpful to blacks.

In certain ways, Butler's approach is more restrained than Delgado's legal instrumentalism. Butler's proposal operates within a specific institutional context, that of the jury, and is designed to apply to a limited number of criminal offenses. He clearly wants to draw a line at violent offenses, pointing out that violent black offenders harm the black community. Indeed, most violent crime committed by blacks is against other blacks.

But Butler's argument ignores the extent to which nonviolent crimes such as drug possession help promote the drug trade and the violence associated with it. And even if drug treatment programs are better than prison for the offender and the community, acquitting drug offenders does not increase the limited funds available for such programs. Such acquittals simply place the offenders, untreated, back on the streets. So it is far from clear that the black community would really benefit were Butler's proposal to be followed.

Even assuming that the community did benefit, it does not follow that the proposal should be endorsed. Butler's argument rests on the questionable moral premise that whatever promotes the well-being of the black community is

justified. Much should indeed be done—by blacks and whites—to help rectify the effects of racial injustice. But "much" is not "anything and everything."
Greater support for drug treatment programs would surely be justified. But in
a democratic society, individuals have a responsibility to abide by the law, and
only compelling reasons can absolve a person of that responsibility.

Butler suggests that blacks are in fact absolved of the responsibility because
of the political system's "failure to protect blacks from a tyrannical majority."
The result of that failure "is that the majority rule of whites over African-
Americans is, morally speaking, illegitimate." And Butler sums up his view of
contemporary American democracy: "blacks are unable to achieve substantial
progress through regular electoral politics."[51]

But Butler fails to make a convincing case for his dismissive attitude toward
the existing democratic process. He cites the inability of the congressional
Black Caucus to amend a recent federal crime bill in a way that would have
made it more difficult to impose the death sentence on blacks. But he makes
no mention of the Civil Rights Act of 1991, which reaffirmed the disparate-
impact approach of *Griggs* in the face of hostile Supreme Court rulings. And
he does not bring up the amendments to the Voting Rights Act that were
adopted in 1982: the amendments strengthened considerably the protections
that racial minorities have under the Act and were also adopted in response to
Supreme Court rulings viewed as hostile to the rights of minorities.

Of course, one cannot settle the question of whether the existing democratic process affords sufficient opportunity for racial progress by invoking a
few examples. Nor can one avoid the difficult question how much progress has
been made, or how oppressive are the current conditions of racial minorities.
But if the rule of law is to be disregarded and existing democratic processes are
to be circumvented, a fairly high burden of persuasion should be met.

In the context of the early 1960s, Martin Luther King and his fellow civil
rights activists could meet that burden. White officials in the South systematically violated the rule of law in their treatment of blacks. The political process
there was effectively closed to all but whites. Rates of poverty, illiteracy, and
unemployment for blacks were staggering. King's targeted program of civil disobedience was reasonably calculated to counteract racial oppression, while at
the same time showing respect for the rule of law and for the potential of the
national political process to produce meaningful progress on racial issues.

In the context of the early twenty-first century, it is far from apparent that
the proposals of CR thinkers to circumvent the rule of law and the processes of
electoral politics can be justified. It is true that the rule of law and electoral politics should not be regarded as sacred. In circumstances of dire and entrenched
injustice, it can be right to disregard them. But a strong presumption should be
made in favor of the rule of law and electoral politics. And proposals to disregard
them should be accepted only after a very convincing case is presented that there
is a dire and entrenched injustice, that such proposals will likely be effective in
ameliorating the injustice, and that alternatives which respect the rule of law and
electoral politics will likely be ineffective. It will not be an easy case to make. But
if CR thinkers are to vindicate their views, they must make it.

AFFIRMATIVE ACTION

A generation ago, the American legal scholar Alexander Bickel wrote that "discrimination on the basis of race is illegal, immoral, unconstitutional, inherently wrong, and destructive of democratic society."[52] Bickel was criticizing university admissions policies that took race into account and gave a preference to racial minorities in the admissions process. And he was articulating a principle of colorblindness that he thought captured the moral essence of the *Brown* decision. He explained: "If the Constitution prohibits the exclusion of blacks and other minorities on racial grounds, it cannot permit the exclusion of whites on similar grounds; for it must be the exclusion on racial grounds which offends the Constitution, and not the particular skin color of the person excluded."[53]

Bickel was positing a fundamental legal and moral right of individuals not to be treated on the basis of their race. But notwithstanding his criticisms, during the 1970s policies that took race into account proliferated in both the private and public sector. Companies adopted race-conscious recruiting and hiring policies; unions used such policies in admitting members to apprenticeship programs; the federal government used them to ensure that federal contractors would employ minority subcontractors; colleges and universities followed them in recruiting and admitting students and in hiring faculty.

Some of these "affirmative action" policies simply expanded the pool of applicants for a position to include more minorities, but many of them altered the criteria for hiring or admission in a deliberate effort to increase the chances of minority applicants. Some of the policies imposed fixed quotas, while others counted race as one factor among many.

But what all these affirmative action policies had in common was that they took race into account and sought greater inclusion in the mainstream institutions of our society for racial minorities who had been historically excluded from them.[54] Even policies that simply expanded the pool of applicants were not strictly colorblind, for they deliberately sought out racial minorities to bring into the pool.

However, the debate over affirmative action has centered on policies that adjust admissions or hiring criteria so as to increase the chances of minority applicants. In the remaining sections of this chapter, we will focus on those aspects of the debate that concern college and university admissions.

The Law and Politics of Affirmative Action

Alan Bakke was a white male from a blue-collar family who twice applied for admission to the medical school of the University of California at Davis. He was rejected both times, despite the fact that his MCAT scores and GPA were substantially higher than racial minorities who were admitted. The medical school had established a dual-track admissions program. Any applicant could apply to the regular track, where he or she would compete against all of the other applicants. But 16 places in the incoming class of 100 were reserved for certain minority groups. Applicants who belonged to those minority groups were asked on the application if they wished to be considered for the reserved places in this "special" admissions program. And as a white, Bakke was ineligible to apply through the program.

Bakke sued the university, claiming that he had been illegally denied admission. He claimed that the medical school's admission program violated the Civil Rights Act of 1964 and the Equal Protection Clause of the Constitution. Both of those legal provisions, Bakke contended, prohibited universities from using race-conscious admissions processes.

The Supreme Court struck down the Davis admissions policy and ordered that the school admit Bakke. But the Court was deeply divided on the legal basis for its ruling, and no single view commanded a majority of the justices.

One group of four justices argued that the plain meaning of the Civil Rights Act prohibited any university receiving federal funds from using race as a factor in the admissions process. The relevant section of the law reads: "No person in the United States shall, on ground of race, color, or national origin, be excluded from participation in . . . or be subject to discrimination under any program or activity receiving Federal financial assistance."[55] For this group of justices, any reliance on race in an admissions program is clearly inconsistent with the Act.

Another group of four justices distinguished race-conscious programs that assist minorities historically disadvantaged by prejudice from programs that stigmatize or demean persons on account of race. The old segregationist policies in the South would fall into the latter category and are violations of the Equal Protection Clause. The special admissions program at Davis, though, was completely different. It was not racially demeaning but rather sought to remedy the continuing effects of past prejudice by helping historically disadvantaged groups. And this group of justices argued that a program having that purpose was legally valid.

The remaining justice, Lewis Powell, argued that all government policies and programs that classified persons by race should be subject to "strict scrutiny." Applying strict scrutiny meant that a policy would be judged constitutional under the Equal Protection Clause only if it were shown to be necessary in order to serve some compelling societal interest. A compelling interest is an interest of the highest order of importance, and so strict scrutiny sets a very high hurdle for any policy to clear.

Powell argued that the Davis program failed to clear that hurdle. The program did help to ensure diversity on campus, and in the university context, diversity is a compelling interest. But Powell went on to argue that achieving diversity did not require a dual-track admissions program, reserving a specified number of places based on race. Such a "quota" system was not necessary because diversity could be achieved simply by making race one of the factors by which all candidates were judged. All applicants could then compete for all of the places in the incoming class, and diversity would be promoted. Accordingly, Powell ruled that the Davis program was unconstitutional, even though other race-conscious programs were not.

Ironically, although no other justice endorsed Powell's analysis, his position effectively became the law of the land: after *Bakke,* colleges reasonably concluded that they could take race into account to achieve diversity even if they could not establish racial quotas or racially separate admissions programs. But in the wake of *Bakke* it was unsettled whether strict scrutiny would apply to all racial classifications by government or only those that stigmatized persons by race. The question was eventually settled in a series of cases in which the Court made it clear that strict scrutiny would apply to all racial classifications.

Critics of affirmative action are generally satisfied with judicial rulings that apply strict scrutiny to such policies, for these rulings almost always invalidate the policies. But the critics have also worked to enact state and federal laws prohibiting any policies that involve racial preferences. And their greatest victory so far has been California's Proposition 209. Adopted by referendum in 1996, the proposition provides that "the state shall not discriminate against, or grant preferential treat to, any individual or group on the basis of race, sex, color, ethnicity, or national origin in the operation of public employment, public education, or public contracting."[56]

The critics have been less successful in other states and in Congress, but they continue to press their arguments. Following Bickel, they invoke a principle of colorblindness. But they also claim that a range of undesirable effects for blacks and other minorities flow from race-conscious admissions policies.

Such effects, the critics argue, include: the perpetuation of the racist notion that racial minorities are incapable of excelling in academics; the stigmatizing of minority students, who are looked on by their fellow students as "charity cases" who would not have been admitted had they not been given an unfair advantage; the corrosion of the self-confidence of minority students, who are admitted to schools whose academic standards they have not been adequately prepared to meet; the removal of an incentive for minority students to study hard in high school, since they know that they do not need to excel to be admitted to an excellent college; the reinforcement and perpetuation of the scientifically dubious and socially toxic concept of race, since individuals are given an incentive to think about themselves—and others—in terms of their "race."

If these effects are indeed a product of race-conscious admissions policies, then they would certainly count against the policies.[57] However, all policies have undesirable effects, and it is necessary to weigh against them the potential benefits in order to make a reasoned judgment about the desirability of the policy. For example, some minority students might have their confidence shaken at elite schools, but many more may not, and the economic and social advantages that accrue to the many as a result of attending such a school may outweigh the shaken confidence of the few.

In addition, beyond any cost-benefit analysis of affirmative action policies is the fundamental moral issue raised by Bickel: Regardless of the cost-benefit calculus, do individuals have a moral right that their race not be taken into consideration in admissions decisions?

If the answer is that there is no such right, then we still might look at the negative effects of affirmative action and, weighing them against the positive ones, decide that race-conscious policies should not be used. And if the answer is that such a right does exist, then we still must ask whether there are other rights that might override any right to be treated in a colorblind manner. But the question of our rights in regard to race remain at the center of the affirmative action debate.

Let us examine more closely this matter of individual rights. We will see that the question of whether race-conscious admissions violate such rights is a very complicated one. And we will also see that, even after addressing the matter of rights, the social effects of affirmative action policies remain a very important part of the debate.

Individual Rights

The Right of Nondiscrimination If there is a right to a colorblind admissions process, then it clearly cannot itself be a fundamental moral right. This is because truly fundamental moral rights must be sufficiently general and abstract that they can apply across the range of societies and eras. It does not make sense for a fundamental right to apply only to societies with formal institutions of higher education, and for that reason a right to a colorblind admissions process is simply too culturally and historically specific to count as fundamental. But such a right might be derivable from a more fundamental right.

Many people think that the more fundamental right is the right not to be treated on the basis of a characteristic over which one has no control. But it is not plausible to think that there is any such right. Blind people do not have their rights violated when the law prohibits them from driving a car. Short people do not have their rights violated when they fail to get a spot on the basketball team because they are not tall enough.

A more plausible candidate for a fundamental right is the right of individuals not to be treated on the basis of a characteristic of theirs that is irrelevant to the task at hand.[58] Let us call this the "right of nondiscrimination." Blindness is not irrelevant to driving, and so a law against blind people driving is not a violation of the right. But, the argument goes, race is irrelevant for purposes of university admissions, and so race-conscious admissions programs violate the right of nondiscrimination.

There are two possible lines of counterargument to this effort to establish that race-conscious admissions policies violate a moral right of nondiscrimination. First, one might question whether there really is such a right. Second, one might concede such a right but argue that the critics of race-conscious admissions policies misunderstand and misapply it. Let us look at how each response might play out, beginning with the question of whether there really is a right of nondiscrimination.

To treat a person on the basis of some irrelevant characteristic is, by definition, irrational: what makes a characteristic irrelevant is that it provides no rational basis for deciding how to act in the situation at hand. But one can argue that there is no general moral duty to act rationally toward others and no corresponding right to be treated rationally by others. Consider the following hypothetical example.

Suppose you are a salesperson, and you offer me a great deal on some item that I want. But I buy the item at another store, for a higher price, simply because I do not like the color of your shoelaces. I have acted irrationally and I have even harmed you insofar as you have lost out on a sales commission. But I did not violate any basic moral duty to you, and you did not have a moral right that I buy the item from you, even if you did offer it to me at the lowest price.

Of course, many instances of irrational conduct do violate rights. If I had killed you on account of your shoelaces, then I would have been guilty not only of irrationality but of violating your rights as well. But that just goes to show that irrationality per se does not constitute a rights violation: only certain kinds of irrational conduct toward others constitute such a violation.

A proponent of a moral right of nondiscrimination could reply to this counterargument in the following way. If I do no wrong in refusing to buy a product from you on account of the color of your shoelaces, then it should be the same if I refuse on account of the color of your skin. But it is clear that refusing on account of skin color is wrong. So refusing to buy on account of shoelace color is wrong as well, and the moral right to nondiscrimination explains why both refusals are wrong.

However, it is not clear that the skin color and shoelace examples call for the same moral judgment. In arguing that there is a difference, some might point out that you can change your shoelaces but not your skin color. Yet, that does not seem to get to the heart of the matter. You lost the sales when I noticed your shoelaces, and the fact that you can wear different laces tomorrow is beside the point. If you have a right to nondiscrimination, then I have violated it regardless of whether you can change your laces.

A better account of the moral difference between the two hypothetical cases would involve the historical and social facts about race discrimination. The history of our society has been one in which people have been defined in terms of race and systematically advantaged or disadvantaged on account of their race. Since racial identity does not provide any moral justification for such systematic advantage or disadvantage, our society has been guilty of serious racial injustice. And acts of racial discrimination, such as refusing to deal with individuals in certain ways, have been the driving force behind this racial injustice. Accordingly, if I refuse to deal with you on account of your skin color, I am helping to keep alive the legacy of our nation's history of racial injustice.

By contrast, in the shoelace example there is no systemic injustice that my actions help keep alive. My action is simply a highly idiosyncratic irrationality that makes no contribution to the subordination of any social group. Moreover, as opposed to racial subordination, systematic shoelace subordination could not occur in the real world. If an individual were placed at a serious disadvantage by others on account of the color of her shoelaces, she would simply change her laces. So systematic and serious disadvantage due to shoelace color could not get a foothold in society.

The situation is different with racial characteristics because, unlike the color of one's shoelaces, they are immutable. Thus, while immutability does not explain why racial discrimination is wrong, it does explain why racial discrimination can get a foothold in society and result in severe and systemic disadvantage.

So we have a reasonable argument for the conclusion that, while racial discrimination is wrong, shoelace discrimination is not. And the argument suggests that we should understand the right of nondiscrimination more narrowly than our original formulation. It should be instead understood as the right not to be treated on the basis of an irrelevant characteristic that has been used to create systemic and serious disadvantage for some social group. Race and shoelace color are both irrelevant characteristics, but, of the two, only race has been used to create such disadvantage.

It is true that this narrower right of nondiscrimination would appear not to be truly fundamental but rather derived from a more basic right of equality. After all, the moral equality of humans would seem to be the best explanation of why individuals have a right not to be treated on the basis of irrelevant characteristics that have generated severe, systemic disadvantage. But it does seem quite plausible that the narrower right to nondiscrimination is a genuine moral right even if it does not go all the way down to the foundations of morality. Accordingly, the critics of race-conscious admissions policies do make a reasonable claim when they assert the existence of a moral right of nondiscrimination. But are they properly applying that right when they invoke it to argue that such admissions policies are wrong?

The Relevance of Race Even granting the existence of a (narrow) right of nondiscrimination, it is possible to argue that race-conscious admissions policies do not violate it. One way to develop this line of argument is by trying to show that race can be a relevant factor in the admissions process. And so advocates of affirmative action argue that academic skills and capabilities, while of prime importance, are not the only factors relevant to admission. The advocates argue that race is relevant, too, because race is tied to the responsibility of a university to ensure diversity within its student body and to help ameliorate the effects of society's past racial injustice. Let us examine these arguments more closely.

Proponents of race-conscious admissions often claim that such a policy is needed to ensure diversity on campus. The quality of an education that a student receives is in part a function of the varied experiences and perspectives her fellow students bring with them: students receive a better education and are better prepared to meet their civic responsibilities when their fellow students have a variety of backgrounds and perspectives. And race-conscious admissions are needed to make sure that diversity within the student body is achieved. So argue the advocates of affirmative action.

But when their argument is couched simply in terms of "diversity," the advocates of race-conscious admissions are unpersuasive. A student body can be diverse in all kinds of ways other than racially: economically, politically, religiously, geographically, and so on. Diversity in those respects can be guaranteed without taking race into account.

Thus, defenders of affirmative action need to argue not simply that diversity is important, but that racial diversity is important. And the way to make that argument is to emphasize that in our society racial categories and identities have been, and continue to be, extremely prominent. Space-alien anthropologists who wanted to understand American society would have a large gap in their understanding if they failed to grasp the existence and significance of race. In our society, the experiences and perspectives of persons differ not only by economic class or geographical background: they also differ by race in important and systematic ways. Accordingly, race is relevant to the legitimate goal of ensuring the inclusion of the differing racial experiences and perspectives that are part of American society.

Before we turn to some counterarguments against the "racial diversity" argument, let us examine how affirmative action advocates appeal to past racial injustice in order to show how race is relevant to admissions decisions. The argument goes as follows.

Those who run institutions of higher education may reasonably regard their schools as having a social responsibility to help rectify the effects of society's past racial injustice.[59] Among those effects is the disparity in economic well-being and educational attainment between minority groups and whites. Even granting that racism in American society has greatly attenuated over the past generation, the racial disparities that persist are in large measure a product of past racism. There are, of course, many ways in which a school might try to meet any responsibility it may accept to decrease racial inequality in wealth, income, and education. But one way is to increase the number of minorities admitted to the school. Accordingly, race is a factor relevant to the legitimate goal of mitigating the inequalities that are the legacy of racial injustice.

Affirmative action critics will not be persuaded by these appeals to racial diversity and the mitigation of racial inequality. One of their principal counterarguments hinges on the point that an inevitable by-product of an admissions process that gives a preference to racial minorities is that innocent whites are unfairly harmed. Diversity and mitigating racial inequality may be fine as goals, but race-conscious admissions policies are a morally objectionable way of pursuing them.

Yet, we must ask: why are such policies morally objectionable? The original argument was that the policies violated the right of nondiscrimination by taking account of some irrelevant factor that has been used to create systemic disadvantage. But race cannot be irrelevant to the admissions process if racial diversity and racial equality are legitimate goals. So why is the right of nondiscrimination violated?

Critics of affirmative action might claim that the goals are in fact illegitimate for a university to pursue, but a more persuasive argument would be that, even assuming the goals to be legitimate, they are not compelling enough to justify the harm done to innocent whites, like Allen Bakke. Such whites have their rights violated insofar as they are harmed for reasons that may not be wholly irrelevant to the tasks of higher education but are insufficient to justify inflicting the harm on an innocent person.

However, advocates of affirmative action are dubious of such arguments based on innocence. They regard the arguments as a diversion from a crucial fact about American society: whiteness confers on people a substantial, lifelong advantage ("white skin privilege"). Whether or not Bakke himself was ever guilty of personally acting in a discriminatory manner, he and his ancestors benefited from white skin privilege. He may have had other strikes against him, especially if he came from an economically insecure working-class background. But his race was not one of them; rather, it was something that counted in his favor in the eyes of society. For the minorities who were admitted in his stead, their race was something that counted against them in the eyes of society. And the preference received by those minorities from the admissions program was relatively small compared to the lifelong racial preference that all whites, including Bakke, enjoy.

Affirmative action critics have a lower estimate of the social advantages that come simply from being white and a higher estimate of the harm done by race-conscious admissions to blue-collar whites. While the advocates of affirmative action suggest that white skin privilege defeats the claims of whites that their rights are violated by affirmative action policies, critics argue that the harm whites suffer from such policies is a direct violation of their rights.

But there is another sort of harm that is important to the debate. Critics contend that race-conscious admissions programs harm academic standards, while advocates dispute that contention. And this aspect of the debate moves us away from the issue of individual rights to a consideration of the broader social effects of race-conscious policies on our institutions and, ultimately, on our self-conceptions.

Social Effects: Academic Values and Racial Identities

Many affirmative action critics argue that, in practice, such programs substantially lower academic standards. Minorities admitted under such programs have much lower scores on objective tests of academic ability than the rest of the students. Even if racial diversity and the mitigation of past injustice are legitimate goals for a university to pursue, it is wrong to pursue them in ways that harm the core academic values of a university.

Notice that the argument has shifted at this point from individual rights to institutional values. The contention of the critics is that affirmative action harms the core values of higher education. If they are right, their point counts as a strong consideration against race-conscious admissions policies, even if such policies do not violate the individual's right of nondiscrimination.

Affirmative action advocates recognize the importance of academic values and reply that their policies do not do harm to academic standards. The advocates suggest that "objective" tests of academic ability are in fact racially biased and are unreliable predictors of success in school or in life. Accordingly, they reject the focus on standardized tests and argue for a broader way to assess the potential contributions an applicant can bring to a college and to society generally.

The effects on core academic values is one important aspect of the debate. But also central to the debate are the effects of affirmative action on the prominence of race in American society.

Advocates of affirmative action insist that race counts in contemporary society: we are not colorblind and should not base policy on the premise that we are. But the critics can agree that society is not currently colorblind and that race does count in American society. Their argument is that society's goal should be to make race count less in the lives of individuals and that the best strategy to accomplish that goal is to reject policies that make it count. The problem with race-conscious policies is that they make race count, and in doing so they entrench racial categories and racial identities. Affirmative action ties the individual all-the-more tightly to his or her racial identity.

Affirmative action advocates can reply that the primary task for society when it comes to race is to eliminate the systemic harm done to persons on account of their race. That harm is reflected in persistent racial inequalities across a range of social indicators reflecting the quality of life: income, wealth, health, education, and so on. To effectively undo that harm and mitigate those inequalities, we must take account of race. And as racial inequalities are reduced, the social salience of race will recede.[60] In contrast, permitting racial inequalities to persist will far more effectively entrench the social importance of race than affirmative action policies ever could. As long as race remains strongly correlated with quality-of-life indicators such as wealth and life-expectancy, racial categories and identities will invariably be of great importance to individuals.

It would not be difficult to continue the arguments and counterarguments over affirmative action. The issue raises deep and complicated questions of morality, psychology, society, history, and law. And the divisions that separate the antagonists in the affirmative action debate are perhaps too deep to be bridged by reasoned argument. But it may not be expecting too much to think that those on all sides of the debate can be convinced that simple slogans cannot settle the issue. And perhaps it is not expecting too much to think that those on all sides can be convinced that their opponents have arguments that may have some element of truth and must be taken seriously.

SUMMARY

Race has been at the center of American history. Racial identities have been critical to the way Americans think about themselves and treat others. Racial questions have confronted American society and law with their most urgent moral tests. For nearly two centuries, the nation failed those tests. Some think we are still failing. Perhaps they are right. But even if they are, it is implausible to deny that over the past half century the country has made substantial and virtually irreversible progress in matters of race.

Some CR thinkers argue that any racial progress that has been made in America is precarious and likely to be reversed. Such is one of the main points of Derrick Bell's space-alien story. Indeed, Bell once suggested that the racial situation in the year 2004 will not be much different from the Jim Crow era 100 years before.

The reversals anticipated by Bell and other CR thinkers have yet to take place, and there is no sign that they will. History certainly tells of episodes in which previous moral progress was dramatically reversed and undone. Certainly, the example of Nazi Germany must haunt anyone who thinks seriously about the possibility of such reversals.

But history also tells us that reversals are far less likely when moral progress has become rooted in the institutions and laws of a country. And in that respect we have good reason to reject pessimism about America's racial future. The legal accomplishments of the civil rights era may have fallen far short of bringing about racial justice. But they have created a system of laws and institutions that virtually exclude the possibility of a return to anything like the days of Jim Crow. And they have created a system that gives civil rights activists considerable leverage in their fight for greater racial equality. For a nation whose history has been steeped so in racial prejudice and oppression, those are no small accomplishments.

NOTES

1. Ian F. Haney Lopez, *White by Law* (New York University Press, 1995).

2. *Scott v. Sandford*, 19 How. 393 (1857).

3. *Plessy v. Ferguson*, 163 U.S. 537 (1896).

4. *Hall v. DeCuir*, 95 U.S. 485 (1878).

5. *Plessy* at 550–551.

6. *Plessy* at 551.

7. *Plessy* at 551.

8. *Plessy* at 559 (Harlan, J., dissenting).

9. *Plessy* at 560 (Harlan, J., dissenting).

10. Such experiments included the measurement of the brain sizes of individuals of different races. For an account and critique of those experiments, see Stephen Jay Gould, *The Mismeasure of Man*, rev. and expanded ed. (Norton, 1996).

11. Suppose, however, there was a problem with whites attacking blacks on integrated railroad cars. Could the state then have met the reasonableness test in requiring segregation? I do not think so. Under any realistic scenario, the attacks would have been inspired by racist beliefs. If the state were to adopt enforced segregation as a response, it would have effectively been permitting such beliefs to dictate public policy. Instead of enforced segregation, the state should be deterring racist attacks by vigorous enforcement of the laws against assault and battery.

12. *Brown v. Board of Education*, 347 U.S. 495 (1954).

13. *Brown* at 492.

14. It is important to keep in mind the distinction between *de jure* and *de facto* segregation. The former is segregation decreed by the law, while the latter is segregation that is not the result of any legal decree but rather of the decisions of private parties. The ruling in *Brown* applied only to the former kind of segregation.

15. *Brown* at 494.

16. *Brown v. Board of Education*, 349 U.S. 294 (1955).

17. 102 Congressional Record 4515–4516 (1956).

18. *Martin Luther King, Jr. Papers*, available on the web at: www.stanford.edu/group/King/Docs/march.html.

19. It should be noted that in a series of cases from the early 1900s, the Supreme Court upheld on grounds of the Commerce Clause laws enacted by Congress for essentially noneconomic reasons. Such laws included the Mann Act of 1910, which outlawed the transportation of women across state lines for immoral purposes such as prostitution. For reasons to be noted shortly, I find these precedents to be questionable. But even if the precedents are treated as settled law, the strongest argument for the constitutionality of the Civil Rights Act of 1964 is one based on the Fourteenth Amendment. That argument is given in the following text.

20. *Gaston County v. U.S.*, 395 U.S. 285 (1969).

21. Stokely Carmichael and Charles V. Hamilton, *Black Power* (Vintage, 1967), p. 50.

22. *Ibid.*, p. 41.

23. *Ibid.*, p. 54.

24. *Ibid.*, pp. 52–53.

25. Huey P. Newton, "In Defense of Self-Defense," rpt. in Peter Levy, ed., *Documentary History of the Modern Civil Rights Movement* (Greenwood Press, 1992), p. 186.

26. *Black Power*, p. 3.

27. *Ibid.*, p. 4.

28. *Ibid.* The actual number of children killed was four.

29. Ibid., p. 5.

30. Recall from Chapter 7 the claim of radical feminists that discrimination against women is systemic and so amounts to oppression and the counterclaim of liberal feminists that such discrimination consists of relatively isolated acts.

31. *Griggs v. Duke Power,* 91 S. Ct. 849 (1971).

32. *Griggs* at 851.

33. *Griggs* at 853.

34. *Griggs* at 856.

35. *Griggs* at 854.

36. An aggressive version of the disparate-impact approach would find discrimination whenever there is a negative impact disproportionately falling on racial minorities. The version is *Griggs* was more moderate, allowing for exceptions in cases of business necessity. It should also be noted that defenders of disparate-impact theory typically use it to explain discrimination against minorities. When a practice has a negative impact disproportionately falling on whites, such theorists typically see the practice as discriminatory only if there was a prejudicial intent behind it. In effect, these theorists switch to the intent theory, discussed in the following text. The switch is defended on the grounds that minorities need greater protection from the majority than the majority needs from itself.

37. *Washington v. Davis,* 426 U.S. 229 (1976).

38. During the 1980s, the Court further weakened the disparate-impact approach of *Griggs* by relieving companies of the burden of proving that their practices met the business necessity test. Instead, minority plaintiffs had to prove not only that the practices they challenged had a disparate racial impact, but also that the practices depended on illegitimate business goals. In 1991 Congress enacted a new civil rights law shifting the burden back to the companies, once plaintiffs had shown the existence of a disparate racial impact.

39. An interesting question, which will not be examined in this chapter, is whether this dual-track approach makes any sense.

40. J. L. A. Garcia, "The Heart of Racism," *Journal of Social Philosophy* 27:1 (Spring 1996), 26. Garcia's account of racism is consistent with the revised version of intent theory developed later in this chapter.

41. Among the other notable differences between the Black Power movement and CRT is that the latter has been more concerned with fighting against the racism that harms all "people of color," not simply blacks but Asians, Latinos, Native Americans, and others not socially regarded as white. In addition, CRT has been influenced by feminism to a degree that the Black Power movement never was, and it takes as a central concern the distinctive forms of prejudice that confront women of color.

42. Derrick A. Bell, *Faces at the Bottom of the Well: The Permanence of Racism* (Basic Books, 1992), chap. 9.

43. Dinesh D'Souza, *The End of Racism* (Free Press, 1995). D'Souza and other conservatives explain existing inequalities between blacks and whites in the United States as largely a product of cultural values within the black community that fail to place importance on education, self-restraint, an "honest" job, and the other prerequisites for a successful life in a modern capitalist system. Conservatives claim that blacks now have equal opportunity but that many fail to take advantage of it because they subscribe to cultural values that denigrate as "acting white" getting good grades in school and working hard at an honest job.

44. Richard Delgado, *The Coming Race War* (New York University Press, 1996), p. 46. The book is a series of dialogues among various characters holding different views. I am assuming that Delgado's views are expressed by the characters whose positions are closest to those of CRT.

45. *Ibid.*, p. 47.

46. Jury nullification is the practice of juries that vote to acquit defendants, even though they know that the defendant is guilty and that the prosecutor has proved the guilt beyond a reasonable doubt.

47. Paul Butler, "Racially Based Jury Nullification: Black Power in the Criminal Justice System," 105 *Yale Law Journal* 677 (1995) at 693.

48. *Ibid.*

49. *Ibid.*, 694.

50. *Ibid.*, 708.

51. *Ibid.*, 710.

52. Alexander M. Bickel, *The Morality of Consent* (Yale University Press, 1975), p. 133.

53. *Ibid.*, pp. 132–133.

54. Affirmative action policies have also taken gender into account and sought to include women in areas traditionally reserved for men. The focus of this chapter, however, is race.

55. 42 U.S.C. 2000d.

56. Among the effects of Proposition 209 has been a downward "cascading" of black and Latino applicants to the California university and college system. Applicants who would have been admitted to the top-tier schools under a race-conscious admissions policy have had to go to second-tier schools, and those who would have

been admitted to the second tier have had to go to the third tier. In addition, the number of Asian Americans accepted to top-tier schools has increased, reflecting the fact that they outperform all groups—whites included—on standardized tests and class rankings. See James Traub, "The Class of Prop 209," *New York Times,* May 2, 1999, sec. 6, p. 44.

57. The most comprehensive empirical study of the effects of race-conscious admissions programs is found in William G. Bowen and Derek Bok, *The Shape of the River* (Princeton, 1998). The book casts doubt on at least some of the claims asserting that such programs have been bad for racial minorities.

58. Individuals also have other rights that make some "tasks" inherently impermissible, for example, torture.

59. The Supreme Court has repeatedly held that the purpose of rectifying general societal discrimination is not a compelling interest that can justify a policy under the strict scrutiny test. The issue here, though, is not whether the purpose is compelling but whether it is relevant to the job of a university.

60. This argument appears to be what Justice Blackmun was driving at when he wrote in *Bakke,* "In order to get beyond racism, we must first take account of race."

DISCUSSION QUESTIONS

1. Law enforcement agencies in the United States have used the practice called "racial profiling" in their efforts to identify and apprehend criminals. A "profile" is a description of the kind of person believed to be disproportionately involved in a certain kind of criminal activity, such as drug smuggling or car theft. Police are more likely to consider individuals who fit a profile to be criminal suspects than those who do not fit. Accordingly, individuals who fit a profile are more likely to be stopped, questioned, searched, and arrested by the police.

Profiles can include a person's sex, age, manner of dress, and nationality. A racial profile is one that includes a person's race. And in recent years, the practice of racial profiling has come under increasing scrutiny and criticism.

Critics of the practice argue that it is fundamentally unfair because it taints an entire race with the suspicion of criminality. They point out that the very large majority of any race consists of law-abiding citizens. Racial profiling subjects these citizens to harassment and humiliation. It is a form of racism, the critics charge.

Defenders of the practice argue that as long as race is just one factor among others in a profile, then it is a legitimate and reasonable law enforcement tool. Evidence shows that race, along with other variables, is correlated with certain kinds of crimes. Racial profiling helps the police do their job by focusing on persons who are, as a matter of empirical fact, more likely to have committed the crimes in question. It is not racist but rational police practice, say the proponents.

Is racial profiling a legitimate law enforcement practice? As long as race is just one factor in the profile, can it be considered racist? Is it consistent to favor the use of race as a factor in admitting students to college and to reject it as a factor in a criminal profile?

2. Gay-rights activists sometimes draw a parallel between their movement and the earlier struggle of African Americans for civil rights. The activists argue that both the civil rights and the gay-rights movements seek to end unjust and systematic discrimination based on morally arbitrary characteristics. But others do not accept the analogy between the two movements. For example, during the debate over gays in the military, General Colin Powell explicitly rejected the notion that the exclusion of gays from the military was like the racial segregation that the military had practiced until after the end of World War II.

Is there a true analogy between the gay-rights and civil rights movements? How is discrimination based on sexual orientation like discrimination based on race? How is it different?

ADDITIONAL READING

Bell, Derrick. *Faces at the Bottom of the Well: The Permanence of Racism.* Basic Books, 1992.

———. "Civil Rights in 2004: Where Will We Be?" R. Fullinwider and C. Mills, eds. *The Moral Foundations of Civil Rights.* 1986. pp. 15–35.

Bickel, Alexander. *The Supreme Court and the Idea of Progress.* Yale University Press, 1978.

Bowen, William G., and Derek Bok. *The Shape of the River.* Princeton University Press, 1998.

Boxill, Bernard. *Blacks and Social Justice,* rev. ed. Rowman and Littlefield, 1992.

Cahn, Steven M. *The Affirmative Action Debate.* Routledge, 1995.

Carmichael, Stokely, and Charles V. Hamilton. *Black Power.* Vintage Books, 1967.

Cole, David. *No Equal Justice: Race and Class in the American Criminal Justice System.* New Press, 1999.

Crenshaw, Kimberle. "A Black Feminist Critique of Antidiscrimination Law and Politics." David Kairys, ed. *The Politics of Law,* 3d ed. Basic Books, 1998.

———. "Race, Reform, and Retrenchment." *Harvard Law Review* 101 (1988), 1331–1387.

———, et al. *Critical Race Theory.* New Press, 1995.

Davis, F. James. *Who Is Black?* Pennsylvania State University, 1991.

Delgado, Richard. *The Coming Race War.* New York University Press, 1996.

———. *Critical Race Theory: The Cutting Edge.* Temple University Press, 1995.

Garcia, J. L. A. "Current Conceptions of Racism: A Critique of Some Recent Social Philosophy." *Journal of Social Philosophy* 28:2 (Fall 1997), 5–42.

———. "The Heart of Racism." *Journal of Social Philosophy* 27:1 (Spring 1996), 5–45.

Higginbotham, A. Leon. *In the Matter of Color.* Oxford University Press, 1980.

Kennedy, Randall. *Race, Crime, and the Law.* New York: Pantheon, 1997.

Kull, Andrew. *The Color-Blind Constitution.* Harvard University Press, 1992.

Lopez, Ian F. Haney. *White by Law: The Legal Construction of Race.* New York University Press, 1996.

Rosenberg, Gerald N. *The Hollow Hope: Can Courts Bring About Social Change?* University of Chicago Press, 1991.

Spann, Girardeau. *Race Against the Court.* New York University Press, 1993.

Thernstrom, Stephan, and Abigail Thernstrom. *America in Black and White.* Simon and Schuster, 1997.

Tushnet, Mark V. *Making Civil Rights Law.* Oxford University Press, 1994.

9

※

Critical Legal Studies

THE CRITS: AN INTRODUCTION

Law, Power, and Hierarchy

At the center of the Western tradition in legal philosophy is the idea of the rule of law. For those philosophers who endorse it, the rule of law represents an essential and effective way to restrain and regulate the exercise of power, including the power of government. The rule of law insists that those who hold political power obey the rules, just as the rest of us are expected to do. It asserts that the power of government must not be wielded in an arbitrary or capricious way. It demands that judges decide all legal cases and controversies according to what the law requires, not according to their own notions of what is good public policy. These ideas have been central to the Western tradition because its thinkers have been so wary of the dangers of unrestricted and arbitrary power.

Modern philosophers have been especially concerned to endorse the rule of law. They see it as essential for the preservation of the central value of modern society: individual liberty. Restraining power by law makes it possible for all to enjoy equal and extensive individual liberty. Moreover, modern thinkers have stressed how power brings with it the desire for more and more power until the limits of legitimate power are exceeded. By setting limits to power, the rule of law can serve as an effective weapon against the growth of illegitimate power. Such is the dominant view among modern legal and political philosophers.

Nonetheless, some find fault with the idea of the rule of law. In Chapter 1, we examined the arguments of Hobbes and Austin that are aimed at showing that the idea rests on a confusion. Although some of the arguments make valid points, we saw that they do not ultimately discredit the idea of the rule of law.

Yet, the strongest challenge to the rule of law may come not from any of the great legal thinkers of the past but from a relatively recent movement in legal thinking, Critical Legal Studies (hereafter CLS). CLS emerged during the mid-1970s as an attack on mainstream ideas about law and legal institutions. The attack came from the perspective of radical left-wing politics and had as its ultimate aim the fundamental transformation of society.

Proponents of CLS—often called "crits"—argue that contemporary society is riddled by illegitimate hierarchies of power. A hierarchy is a relation in which one element is dominant and another subordinate. Where the elements are persons, it means that some persons have power over others. And such a hierarchy is illegitimate if that power cannot be justified, that is, if it is a matter of might, not right.

Crits say that the hierarchies of power that make up our society are illegitimate: the power of capitalist bosses over workers, of judges over litigants, of lawyers over their clients, of teachers over students, of adults over children, of whites over nonwhites, of men over women. All these relations are based largely on might rather than on right. And all of them should be dramatically reconstructed so as to create a more egalitarian society in which no one holds illegitimate power over anyone else.

In the view of crits, law has helped support and preserve the illegitimate hierarchies of society. It has served the interests of the powerful at the expense of the powerless. And the rule of law has turned out to be nothing more than a fiction. The idea of restraining power by law may sound good in theory, but in practice law turns out to be an instrument that the powerful use to maintain their dominant position in society.

Crits do not dispute the contention of modern philosophers that governments have a tendency to grab illegitimate power and that such a tendency must be combatted. But the crits contend that other centers of illegitimate power in society must also be combatted and that the usual focus on the dangers of tyrannical governments obscures the existence of tyranny in the way bosses treat their workers, whites treat nonwhites, teachers treat students, and so forth. Moreover, crits argue that it is a fundamental mistake to think that we should rely on the rule of law to combat illegitimate power, be it the "public" power of government or the "private" power of institutions like corporations.[1]

Against the Rule of Law: Politics, Morality, and Law

Crits deny the existence of the rule of law. The most aggressive arguments of the crits entail that the rule of law could never exist in any society. A more restrained argument is that it does not exist in ours and that there is good reason to think it could not be brought into existence in the kind of society we have. In either case, the strategy of relying on the rule of law to combat illegitimate power is misguided, in the view of crits.

According to crits, in order for the rule of law to exist, making decisions on the basis of positive law would have to be essentially different from making them on the basis of political or moral considerations. This does not mean that a legal decision in a case would always have to be different from the best moral or political decision. But it does mean that law must use a method of decision that is different from simply appealing to those political or moral considerations that are relevant to the facts of a certain case. The problem, say crits, is that there is no such method of decision: no distinctively legal method of deciding a case is available that is clearly different from a political or moral approach to the case. One prominent crit, Duncan Kennedy, puts the point plainly:

> Teachers teach nonsense when they persuade students that legal reasoning is distinct, as a method for reaching correct results, from ethical or political discourse in general. There is never a "correct legal solution" that is other than the correct ethical or political solution to that legal problem.[2]

Philosophers call the process of making a decision "practical reasoning." It is a form of "reasoning" insofar as it involves a process of thinking that aims to reach a conclusion based on certain considerations or reasons. It is "practical" insofar as the conclusion sought is a decision that concerns action rather than belief. Crits are arguing, in effect, that no distinct subcategory of practical reasoning can be legitimately called "legal reasoning." The kind of practical reasoning judges and lawyers do is no different from the kind anyone else does when making a moral or political decision.

The CLS attack on legal reasoning is not entirely novel. Early in the twentieth century, the movement known as legal realism also denied the existence of legal reasoning. Many of the realist claims have been picked up and elaborated on by crits. Yet, the realists never drew the logical conclusion of their attack on legal reasoning, namely, that the rule of law is a fiction. Crits have had no such hesitation.

The denial of legal reasoning goes directly against one of the prominent elements of mainstream legal philosophy. Mainstream theories hold that there is a method of legal reasoning that is distinct in important ways from political and moral deliberation. Shortly, we will examine a mainstream account of legal reasoning, an account arguing that such reasoning does indeed exist as a distinct form of practical reasoning. Then we will look at the assaults on the idea of legal reasoning, mounted first by the legal realists and then by the crits.

Before we turn to the topic of legal reasoning, a few remarks on the relation of CLS to both feminism and political conservatism are in order. First, let us look at feminism.

Crits, Feminists, and Critical Race Theorists

Clearly the ideas of CLS about contemporary society are very similar to those associated with Critical Race Theory (CRT) and the radical wing of feminism. All three approaches regard contemporary society as seriously illegitimate. All three claim that the illegitimacy involves the oppression of some in society by others. All argue that the law plays an important role in maintaining that oppression. Moreover, many radical feminists and Critical Race theorists endorse the CLS contention that the rule of law is a fiction that does not exist in our society. It should not be surprising, then, to find that much of the early work by radical feminist legal philosophers and CR theorists was carried out under the banner of CLS.

Nonetheless, important differences exist among CLS, CRT, and radical feminist legal philosophy. CRT revolves around the idea that whites systematically oppress nonwhites through law, politics, and informal social norms. Radical feminism revolves around the idea that men systematically oppress women in a similar way. CLS is committed to the idea that systematic oppression pervades our society, but is hesitant to accord any specific form of oppression—racial, gender, or otherwise—a privileged status.

Moreover, the three theories take somewhat different approaches in rejecting the liberal idea of the rule of law. For radical feminists, the rule of law is a fiction principally because the law is enacted, interpreted, and applied in a way that is biased in favor of the interests of men and against those of women. The law does not rule, in their view; men do. For CRT, the rule of law is a fiction because law is biased in favor of whites and against nonwhites. The law does not rule; whites do.

On the other hand, for CLS the rule of law is a fiction principally because legal reasoning is not essentially different from reasoning about moral and political questions. The law does not rule, in the view of crits; politics rules.

Crits agree that our politics is biased against women and nonwhites. And they endorse the idea that such biases destroy the pretension our society has to be operating under the rule of law. But for CLS, deeper theoretical reasons make the rule of law impossible, quite apart from the existence of systematic racism and sexism in our society.[3]

Crits and Conservatives

The CLS view of society as riddled by oppressive and illegitimate hierarchies sharply distinguishes it from political conservatism, which generally sees the fundamental institutions of society not as perfect but as basically fair and just. Conservatives scoff at the crits' idea that capitalist bosses oppress workers, men oppress women, teachers oppress students, adults oppress children, and whites oppress nonwhites. But it is logically possible to accept conservative political ideas and also endorse the crits' rejection of legal reasoning and the rule of law. This means that the crits' political views on society and how it should be transformed are logically detachable from their views on the rule of law and legal reasoning.

Yet, an important strategic connection is evident between the political and legal sides of CLS. Crits aim to delegitimize existing society: to convince people that our institutions and practices are basically governed by might, not right. Many people who think that society's institutions and practices are legitimate do so because they see that the law supports those institutions and practices, and they believe in the legitimacy of the law. By discrediting the ideas of legal reasoning and the rule of law, crits aim to delegitimize the law and thereby delegitimize our society's institutions and practices. Thus, a conservative could theoretically agree with the crits' claim that the rule of law is a fiction, but he would not use that claim in a political effort to delegitimize society. In contrast, for the crits, the main point of criticizing the ideas of the rule of law and legal reasoning is to persuade people of the fundamental illegitimacy of the society they inhabit.

LEGAL REASONING:
A MAINSTREAM ACCOUNT

Law and Authority

Legal decisions are decisions made on the basis of an appeal to authority; thus the concept of authority is crucial to understanding the nature of legal reasoning. In order to grasp the idea of authority that lies at the heart of legal reasoning, we need to keep in mind a few basic points.[4]

The functioning of any society requires that decisions be made and followed about everything from food and sex to life and death. Some decisions are, of course, left to individuals. And in a free society, many important decisions are up to the individual to make for him- or herself. But even in such a society, many decisions must not be left up to individuals; there are many matters on which decisions must made for everyone (or at least for some large class of persons within society). I can decide for myself whether to drive my car to the store today. But I should not be allowed to decide for myself which side of the road to drive on. For that, some decision must be made, not by each individual for him- or herself but by society for everyone.

To take a different sort of example: I can decide for myself whether to buy a General Motors car or a Honda, but I should not be allowed to decide whether to take your car without your permission. Again, society needs to make a decision that would take the matter out of the individual's hands.

If the society is in any way democratic, I will have some voice in the process by which society makes these kinds of decisions. But the decisions will be collective ones, not individual. They will be collective in two distinct senses: the decisions will be made (1) by some person or group regarded as representing society as a whole and (2) for society as a whole (or some substantial portion of it).

The positive law consists of general, authoritative decisions made for society as a whole (or some substantial portion of it) by some individual or group regarded as representing it. The decisions are general in that they concern kinds of actions rather than just one specific action. That is why laws can be formulated as rules or principles, such as "Motor vehicles shall be driven on the right side of the road." And the decisions are authoritative in that they preempt, at least to a certain extent, individual decision making: they take certain decisions out of the hands of the individual.

The individual may well have made the same decision, had it been up to her. Based on certain political or personal considerations, for example, she might have ended up doing the exact same thing. On the other hand, those considerations might seem to her to weigh against the decision embodied in the law. Nonetheless, the law's authority means that, even in such a case, the individual is to set aside those considerations and follow the decision of the law.

This does not mean that the law's authority is absolute. Certain kinds of reasons may be so compelling that the law's authority cannot demand that they be set aside. For example, if it is necessary to violate the law in order to protect the victims of grievous injustice, then the authority of law may be insufficiently strong to set aside such a consideration. Thus, the authority of law does not totally preempt individual decision making. Nonetheless, that authority does disqualify or exclude at least some kinds of practical considerations that might otherwise dictate actions contrary to the law. Those considerations must be set aside by the individual who is deciding what to do.

Law and Reason

Legal reasoning proceeds on the assumption that the authoritative decisions that make up the law are not arbitrary: there are reasons for the decisions. It is important to distinguish two very general types of reasons: motivational and justifying. A motivational reason helps explain why a person did something, while a justifying reason helps show that it was right or good. Legal reasoning assumes that there are justifying reasons, not merely motivational ones, for the decisions that make up the law. It does not assume that those justifying reasons are sufficient to defeat any possible counterreasons: as we have noted, the authority of the law is not absolute. But legal reasoning does assume that the decisions represented in the law have something to be said for them: they have some kind of a basis that helps to show them to be justified. Thus, where legal reasoning is called for, the law is a matter not of arbitrary authority but of reasoned authority.

This account establishes an important connection between legal reasoning and the rule of law. At the center of the idea of the rule of law is the distinction between arbitrary government and government under the rule of law. That distinction would collapse if the authoritative, general decisions of a government under the rule of law could not be supported by any justifying reasons, even weak ones. Such a government would not be fundamentally different from one controlled by the arbitrary whim of a despot. If there is to be a genuine contrast between arbitrary and constitutional government, then the rule of law will require that some justifying reasons lie behind the laws. And legal reasoning is the form of practical reasoning that interprets and applies the laws of a system that operates under the rule of law.[5]

Accordingly, in this mainstream account, one of the crucial aims of legal reasoning is to determine the justifying reasons behind the decisions represented by legal rules and doctrines. This is because the nature and scope of general decisions are determined, in part, by their justifying reasons.

For example, suppose that my university decides that students must withdraw from a course no later than seven weeks after the start of the semester if they do not wish the course to appear on their transcript. The reason is to give the students some time to determine whether a course will be worthwhile for them but not so much time that they can withdraw without penalty after having done a substantial amount of coursework. Now suppose that a snowstorm causes the cancellation of classes during the entire fourth week of the semester. In such a case, it would be reasonable to allow students an extra week to withdraw during that semester. The reason behind the rule about withdrawal dictates that the rule is justifiably qualified so as to take account of the lost week of classes. Similarly, legal reasoning interprets and applies legal rules in light of the justifying reasons behind them.

The fact that legal reasoning attends to the justifying reasons behind legal rules has important implications. For one, it means that legal reasoning is not always a matter of applying a legal rule as literally written, with no qualifications or exceptions. Legal reasoning itself will determine whether and when a rule should be literally applied. Depending on the reasons behind a rule, literal application may be reasonable or not.

For example, consider the provision of the Constitution that sets an age qualification for the presidency: a person must be at least thirty-five years old. One justifying reason for the rule is to help ensure that the president is of sufficient maturity and experience to hold such a high office. In light of that reason, it may seem that the rule should not be applied literally in all cases and that courts should allow an unusually mature thirty-year-old to be eligible for the presidency. But such reasoning would not take account of the fact that there is another reason behind the constitutional provision, namely, to make the qualifications for the presidency clear-cut, so that no reasonable disagreement is possible about who is eligible. In light of that reason, the provision should be literally applied in all cases. Failure to do so would run contrary to an important reason behind the rule.

In contrast, consider the First Amendment, which requires that Congress make no law abridging freedom of speech. There are many justifying reasons for the provision, first and foremost to ensure a healthy and functioning democratic form of government. In light of that reason, clearly the executive branch of government should not be permitted to stifle political dissent, even though a literal reading of the Free Speech Clause would apply only against Congress. Again, legal reasoning looks to the justifying reasons behind a legal rule in order to arrive at a reasonable conclusion concerning what the rule does or does not cover.

There is a second important implication of the fact that legal reasoning looks to justifying reasons. If some consideration is a justifying reason in one case, then it must be a justifying reason in all similar cases. Because of that, legal reasoning must be careful to ensure that its treatment of justifying reasons is consistent from case to case. For example, if we say that ensuring a healthy democracy is a reason behind the Free Speech Clause, we must acknowledge that reason just as much in a case in which the speaker is politically conservative as one in which the speaker is liberal. Or if we say that the need for clear-cut presidential qualifications is a reason behind the minimum-age rule, we must acknowledge that reason whether the would-be presidential candidate is a Republican or a Democrat or a Socialist or from any other political party.[6]

Reasoning: Legal and Practical

Legal reasoning is essentially a method of determining what authoritative decisions have been made for society and what they entail or require in a given case. The correct legal decision in a case is determined by what authoritative decisions have been made, which makes legal reasoning a distinctive form of practical reasoning. It is a form of practical reasoning in that it aims to arrive at some decision that concerns what is to be done rather than what is to be believed. It is distinctive in that the decision is made on the basis of the principle that matters should be decided according to the dictates of prior authoritative decisions. Legal reasoning seeks decisions that accord with previous decisions that preempt subsequent individual decision making.

Legal reasoning is not only based on a decision to follow prior, authoritative decisions; it also often involves clarifying or elucidating the authoritative decisions in order to determine what was decided and their implications for the matter at hand. The need for clarification and elucidation stems from the fact that the authoritative decisions embodied in law are general in nature. Every general decision, whether it is made by an individual for him- or herself or by society's representatives for everyone, raises questions about its precise scope and application.

The Doctrine of Precedent: *Stare Decisis*

We are now in position to see the significance of the traditional legal doctrine of *stare decisis,* or "following precedent." Most commentators suggest that it is important for precedent to be followed because the stability of society requires that the law not change too rapidly. This is true, but it is also crucial to recognize the connection between *stare decisis* and the authority of legal decisions. Precedents not only declare what, in the view of the judge, society's authoritative decisions require or entail. They also have their own authority: they are authoritative decisions about what society's authoritative decisions mean and entail. Judicial decisions are authoritative not simply for the litigants in a case and for other members of society in similar situations. *Stare decisis* means that they are authoritative for other judges ruling on similar cases in the future. As such, they preempt, at least to a certain extent, the decision making of judges in the future. An authoritative ruling having been made about some authoritative decision of society, judges in the future are preempted from considering the matter from scratch: the simple fact that they believe another ruling would have been better is by itself insufficient ground for them to rule differently in the future.

This does not mean that precedents must always be followed, no matter what. The authority of judicial precedents is no more absolute than the authority of the rules enacted by a legislature. In our system of law, the decision making of lower court judges is completely preempted by the decisions of higher courts. But for courts at the same level—or the same court on some later occasion—considerations of sufficient importance may justify overturning a precedent or at least sharply limiting the scope of its application. Thus, if a precedent is clearly wrong about some important legal matter, its authority may be insufficient to save it. But the burden is on the judge who would overturn a precedent to show that there are sufficiently compelling reasons to override the authority of a previous judicial ruling.

LEGAL REASONING: THE ATTACK BEGINS

Realism and Formalism

During the first few decades of the twentieth century, a movement in legal thought emerged in the United States that claimed to provide a more realistic picture of legal reasoning than the traditional one. This movement came to be known as *legal realism*.

The immediate target of realism was an approach often called *legal formalism*. According to the most extreme version of formalism, the law consists of a complete, clear, and consistent body of rules that dictates a single correct answer to any legal question. The job of the judge is to find the applicable rule for a case and then deduce by means of a syllogism the correct answer from the rule in conjunction with the facts of the case.[7]

The realists attacked this formalist picture as utterly false. They pointed out that judges do not arrive at their decisions via syllogistic reasoning. The processes of arriving at legal decisions, the realists argued, involved personal, moral, and political considerations not reflected in the formalist account.

Moreover, some of the more radical realists contended that the law itself was riddled by conflicts, vagueness, ambiguity, and gaps: it was far from the seamless body of rules and doctrines formalism assumed it was. Not even the traditional doctrine of *stare decisis* was without problems, according to the realists. Even the more moderate realists contended that the doctrine placed little or no constraints on the reasoning of judges: some way could almost always be found to get around precedents one did not like.

The realist attack on formalism was not merely an academic exercise. There was a crucial social and political dimension to the realist repudiation of the formalist picture of legal reasoning. During the period in which realism developed, the central social and political conflict of American life was between labor and capital. Wage workers and their bosses fought many battles, some bloody, over wages, working conditions, and control of production. As we saw in Chapter 4, the realists generally sided with labor in these battles. They believed that progress and the good of society would be best served by the victory of labor, and they sought to make the law into an instrument to promote such a victory.

In the view of the realists, the formalist account of legal reasoning was hindering the progress they sought. Judges deciding labor disputes would side time and again with the owners over the workers. And instead of acknowledging the political nature of their decisions, the judges would hide behind formalist rhetoric and pretend that correct legal reasoning compelled their rulings.

The realist attack on formalism had as its major motivation to expose these political decisions for what they were: not the inescapable conclusions of legal reasoning but the political choices of judges who had a preference for capital over labor. It was not that the realists opposed political decisions by judges. Rather, they opposed the pretense that judicial decisions were not political but rather the results of formalist legal reasoning. The realists thereby hoped to open the door to judicial decisions more in line with their ideas of where the country should be going politically.

The realists saw the law as a flexible instrument for promoting the general good of society. They saw society as undergoing a process of evolution and change, requiring new legal rules and new interpretations of old ones. In the eyes of realists, formalism was fundamentally flawed by an excessively rigid and hide-bound conception of the law. It blocked social progress and made the law unfit to meet the existing needs of society.

Indeterminacy

The most extreme versions of formalism are a very easy target, and realism would not be a particularly interesting theoretical approach if all it amounted to was a rejection of such extreme formalism. It is fairly obvious to any unbiased observer that the formalist picture of syllogistic legal reasoning based on a complete and consistent body of rules is, at best, a serious distortion. The true significance of legal realism lies in the fact that many of the arguments it made against extreme formalism apply even to much more moderate accounts of legal reasoning, such as the mainstream account given in the previous section.

For example, the realist contention that the law is riddled by conflicts, vagueness, ambiguity, and gaps suggests that there are few, if any, legal questions to which there is a single determinate answer. Legal reasoning is compatible with the existence of some degree of indeterminacy; that is, some absence of determinate answers to specific legal issues and questions. But if the law is mostly indeterminate—if most such issues and questions have no determinate answer—then the whole idea of legal reasoning begins to look very dubious, and the kind of mainstream account provided in the previous section begins to seem fundamentally misguided.

One of the key features of legal reasoning is that it is based on the assumption that the prior, authoritative decisions of society are to be followed. The reasoning itself is an effort to elucidate, clarify, and apply those authoritative decisions. But if the law is as indeterminate as some of the more radical realists suggest, then society's authoritative decisions really decide little or nothing. The issue or question that society supposedly settled with its decision is actually open, and each judge considers it afresh with every legal case. This situation makes legal reasoning, as mainstream accounts understand it, impossible. No reasoning regarding the law can proceed on the assumption that society's authoritative decisions are to be followed if those decisions are as empty as the more radical realists say.

If judges are not engaged in legal reasoning when they decide cases, then what are they doing? The radical realist answer is that they are making from scratch an authoritative political decision that the litigants in the case before them will be compelled to obey, unless the decision is overturned on appeal by a judge on a higher court. Notice that on this account, judges are not making the law, if by "law" one means authoritative, general decisions. For the judge's decision has authority only for the particular case, according to the radical realist account, and does not extend to any other case, no matter how similar it may seem. This goes contrary to the doctrine of *stare decisis,* which holds that the authority of judicial decisions extends to similar cases in the future. And the realists did not hesitate to attack directly *stare decisis.*

So Long, *Stare Decisis*

For both radical and moderate realists, one big problem with *stare decisis* stems from the fact that similarity is in the eyes of the beholder. Whether one sees two cases as similar will depend on much more than the objective facts of the cases. It will also depend, for example, on the moral and political views one holds. Thus, which cases one sees as precedents for a given case will depend on considerations that go beyond the law.

Moreover, even the more moderate realists argued that there is a great deal of leeway that judges have in deciding what a precedent has authoritatively settled. Precedents can be interpreted very broadly or very narrowly or somewhere in between, and there is no single, legally correct way of determining exactly what a precedent has decided.

Traditional accounts of legal reasoning tried to deal with the problem of determining what a precedent has decided by distinguishing between the holding in a case and the dictum. The holding is the essential legal grounds on which a judicial ruling in favor of the plaintiff or defendant is made and, together with the ruling, constitutes what has been authoritatively decided. The holding is what should be followed in future cases. In contrast, the dictum consists of anything in a judicial opinion that is not necessary to the ruling in the case. It is not part of the authoritative decision and need not be followed in future cases.

The realists, however, rejected this distinction between holding and dictum. They argued that judges had considerable leeway in deciding which part of a precedent was the holding and which the dictum. Even if the judge who wrote the precedent said that a certain part of his opinion was essential to the ruling and another part was "mere dictum," other judges deciding subsequent cases could redefine the holding and incorporate into it what was previously regarded as dictum.

In addition, the realists argued that in virtually every legal case, one can find precedents on either side of the issue. The doctrine that precedents should be followed does not help resolve a case when both sides can cite precedents to support the decision it wishes the court to make. So argued the realists.

An Example: Hardwick's Right to Privacy?

Some of the problems the realists saw in the doctrine of *stare decisis* are illustrated by the homosexual sodomy case, *Bowers v. Hardwick,* which the Supreme Court decided during the 1980s. Hardwick, a homosexual caught in the act in his home by police, was challenging the constitutionality of a

Georgia statute that criminalized sodomy.[8] The precedents he invoked included *Griswold v. Connecticut,* the case overturning a state law criminalizing the use of contraceptives, and *Roe v. Wade,* the famous case overturning a state law criminalizing abortion. Hardwick interpreted those precedents as establishing a fundamental right of sexual autonomy: consenting adults must be free to decide for themselves how to conduct their private sex lives. In short, the constitutional right of privacy, interpreted by the Court to cover contraception and abortion, also covered sodomy.

The majority of the Court rejected Hardwick's arguments and let the Georgia statute stand. They interpreted in a narrow way the precedents relating to sexual privacy. They said the precedents had nothing to do with homosexual relations; rather, the prior privacy cases concerned procreation and marriage. Moreover, the majority cited precedents acknowledging that government has the authority to prohibit what occurs within the privacy of the home, even when it is consensual. Thus, they pointed out that the possession of narcotics and firearms may be criminalized.

Justice Blackmun dissented, arguing that *Griswold* and *Roe* had everything to do with homosexuality, as they established that the Constitution protects from state interference the choices consenting adults make about how to conduct their intimate affairs. These intimate decisions are protected because they are so important to individuals and the way they define themselves. As for firearms and narcotics, Blackmun denied that they were analogous to homosexual activity: unlike guns and narcotics, no evidence cited in court suggested that such activity is physically dangerous.[9]

Legal realists would see in *Bowers* an illustration of their points about legal reasoning. They would say that it is apparent that there is no single, correct mode of legal reasoning in this case. One side reads the privacy cases narrowly, while the other reads them broadly. One side interprets precedents as supporting the idea that homosexual activity in the home is protected by the Constitution, while the other interprets them in the opposite manner. It is not that one side is legally right and the other wrong. There is no correct legal answer and no way of reasoning to any such answer. From a political or moral point of view, one side may have the superior argument. But from a legal point of view, there is simply no determinate answer to the question of which side should have won in the *Bowers* case. That is the realist way of understanding the case.

Clusters of Rules

For many legal cases, indeterminacy arises not so much because of the leeway judges have in interpreting precedent but rather because there is a cluster of competing legal rules relevant to the case. The judge's decision will hinge on which rule he chooses as the guiding one for the case. For example, consider *Hudnut,* the pornography case examined in Chapter 7.

Judge Easterbrook saw it fundamentally as a case about speech, and so the First Amendment's free speech principle was the guiding legal standard in his view. And in accordance with that principle, the judge struck down an ordinance restricting pornography. But another judge might have seen the case as Catharine MacKinnon urged: as a case about equal rights for women. For such a judge, the Fourteenth Amendment's equal protection principle would have been the guiding one, and the ordinance may well have survived. Again, the realist point is that it is a political choice as to how one views and decides the case. There is no correct legal answer and no correct mode of legal reasoning that will yield an answer in the case.

Justification and Motivation

Some of the critics of legal realism have pointed out that the realists tend to confuse questions of motivation with questions of justification. The former concern the psychological principles by which a judge (or some other party) arrives at a legal decision. The latter concern the logical and legal principles by which a judge (or some other party) shows that a certain decision is correct or incorrect.

Many critics admit that the realists are correct in claiming that unstated personal, political, and moral considerations play a role in the psychological process by which judges are motivated to think that a certain decision is the best one. But the critics insist that the logic of justifying a judicial decision is a different matter. For purposes of justification, judges must state the considerations that make a decision legally correct, and those considerations cannot include the judge's personal beliefs as such.

It is probably true that some realists confused the psychology of legal decision making with its logic. Nonetheless, key realist claims go to the question of justification. If the law is as indeterminate as the more radical realists suggest and if *stare decisis* is as empty as even the moderates say, then virtually no judicial decisions can be justified on the basis of legal reasoning. They might be justified on the basis of morality or politics. But the possibility of legal justification is excluded.

Reluctant Realists

One of the crucial implications of the realist attack on the idea of legal reasoning is that the rule of law does not exist. Instead of the rule of law, we have the rule of judges and other official decision makers. The realists were, however, reluctant to make explicit this implication of their view.

During the mid-1930s, when the influence of the realists ran high in the United States, Germany was being taken over by the Nazi Party, which exercised its power without legal restraint. Many legal and political thinkers in the United States argued that the rule of law was one of the crucial differences between us and the Nazi regime: we had the rule of law, while they had destroyed it.

Perhaps the realists were reluctant to make explicit their attack on the rule of law for fear of being associated with the Nazi regime. Such an association would have been wholly unwarranted, as the realists hardly endorsed the terror inflicted by the Nazis on Jews and others regarded as enemies. But opponents of realism did argue that it undermined the rule of law, and they pointed to Germany as an example of the horror to which that can lead.

Domesticating Realism

The legal realist movement died out after the close of World War II. Mainstream legal thinking was prepared to repudiate neither the idea of legal reasoning nor the principles of the rule of law. Accordingly, the more radical aspects of the movement were rejected as excesses. Yet, mainstream legal thought conceded that there was some truth to realism, especially in its idea that law could and should be seen as a flexible instrument to promote the general good of society.

Many mainstream thinkers conceded to the realist view that a certain amount of indeterminacy existed in the law: on some legal questions, society's authoritative decisions simply had no resolution, since the legal rules and precedents were too unclear or ambiguous or conflicting. On such questions, the law "ran out" and judges had no choice but to go beyond the law and legal reasoning and to make decisions based on moral or political considerations. The utilitarian criterion of the general good of society was typically regarded as the appropriate one for judges to use in such decisions.

Many mainstream thinkers argued that it was actually good that the law was not the seamless and comprehensive system of rules the most extreme formalists had seen it as. Legal rules needed to have some flexibility and adaptability built into them, so that judges could adjust them to changing social conditions. The fact that the law did not have a determinate answer to every legal question allowed judges to participate in its evolution and adaptation to the needs of society.

At the same time, mainstream thinkers insisted that the idea of legal reasoning did not have to be jettisoned. Although utilitarian (or some other moral or political) decision making was inevitable in some cases, in most cases traditional legal reasoning was called for, namely, determining what society had authoritatively decided about the issue at hand and deciding the case in accordance with that authoritative decision.

Only recently have the arguments and claims of the realists been revived. During the mid-1970s, a group of legal thinkers began to work out an understanding of law that drew upon the realist views and developed them in a new direction. This approach was Critical Legal Studies (CLS), and its proponents were the crits.

LEGAL REASONING: THE CRITS ATTACK

Law as a Patchwork

The crits accepted the realist indeterminacy arguments but developed them in a way that went beyond the realist analysis of law. The realists examined the legal rules and decisions that could be found in official documents: judicial rulings, statutes, and so forth. Because of vagueness, ambiguity, conflicts, and gaps within the body of these rules and decisions, realists argued, judges could decide for either side in virtually any case and support their decision on the basis of the existing rules. The crits agreed with this analysis but sought to understand the body of legal rules on a deeper level. In particular, they sought to explain why there were conflicts within the existing body of legal rules. Their explanation led the crits beyond the realist analysis.

The crits argued that underlying the body of authoritative decisions and rules were fundamentally incompatible moral and political viewpoints. The rules and decisions were in conflict because they were expressions of deeper views about right and wrong, good and bad, that were themselves in irreconcilable conflict. And the result was that the law was a patchwork quilt of rules and doctrines reflecting contradictory moral and political views.

Judges holding a certain moral or political view could and would focus on those parts of the law reflecting that view and decide the case accordingly. Judges holding a different view would focus on different parts of the law, or interpret the same parts differently, and come up with a contrary decision. Thus, crits explain the different judicial opinions in *Bowers v. Hardwick* in terms of the conflicting moral and political beliefs of the justices.

Moreover, the crits claim that none of the moral and political views reflected in the law are carried to their logical conclusions; rather, all are arbitrarily truncated or cut short. Again, *Bowers* illustrates the problem. Some of our law reflects the principle that government should not be permitted to interfere with what consenting adults choose to do in the privacy of their home, as long as they are not victimizing anyone else. Thus, the state cannot criminalize the use of contraceptives or the viewing of sexually explicit materials in private. But the principle is not carried to its logical conclusion: we do permit government to prohibit the possession and use of marijuana in the home. And the majority in *Bowers* used that fact to arbitrarily truncate the principle still further: we must allow states to prohibit private, consensual homosexual activity within the home, says the Court.

But if the majority opinion was arbitrary, according to the CLS analysis, Blackmun's dissenting view was no less arbitrary. For he would stop the state from prohibiting homosexual activity but would continue to allow it to outlaw the possession and use of drugs such as marijuana. Even Blackmun would be unwilling to take to its logical conclusion the principle that government ought to let consenting adults do whatever they choose in private, as long as they are not victimizing anyone else.

From the CLS perspective, the contradictory and arbitrary character of the law was only reinforced when, a decade after *Bowers,* the Court again faced the issue of homosexual rights. The state of Colorado had adopted by referendum a state constitutional amendment prohibiting the state or any locality within it from enacting laws against discrimination based on homosexual, lesbian, or bisexual orientation. Was such an amendment consistent with the U.S. Constitution?

In *Romer v. Evans,* the Court struck down the state's amendment as a violation of the Constitution's Equal Protection Clause. Referring to Colorado's amendment, the Court wrote that "laws of the kind now before us raise the inevitable inference that the disadvantage imposed is born of animosity toward the class of persons affected." In other words, depriving homosexuals of the possibility of civil rights protections is clearly the result of hatred toward them. And the Court proceeded to claim that the Equal Protection Clause means that "a bare desire to harm a politically unpopular group cannot constitute a *legitimate* governmental interest."[10]

It is unclear why the exact same reasoning would not lead to the invalidation of state laws criminalizing homosexual conduct, the very laws that the Court upheld in *Bowers*. Indeed, the apparent contradiction between *Bowers* and *Evans* was noted not only by crits but, for example, by Justice Scalia as well, who dissented in *Evans*. However, there is a key difference between the crits and Justice Scalia on this score. For Justice Scalia, the decision in *Evans* is a simple legal mistake and the logical coherence of the law can be restored by overturning it. For the crits, the decision exemplifies the law's pervasively arbitrary and contradictory nature.

Accordingly, crits argue that all areas of the law are characterized by a patchwork of conflicting and truncated principles. This patchwork quality is not limited to laws regarding sexual orientation or even to constitutional law as a whole. Throughout our entire system of public and private law we can find contradictory moral and political viewpoints struggling with one another. In the next section, we will examime the contradictory and arbitrarily truncated principles that characterize private law.

The Contradictions of Private Law

Consider the legal rules regarding an individual's duty to act in aid of another, when no contractual or statutory obligation is involved. The general common-law rule is that there is no duty to aid in such a situation. Yet, some rules specify exceptions to the general rule. If a person helped create a dangerous situation in which another now finds herself, there may be a legal duty to aid. Or if the two parties stand in what the law calls a "special relationship," there may be a duty to aid.

Crits make several important points about the private-law rules covering the duty to aid. First, the common-law rule of no duty reflects a certain moral viewpoint, while the exceptions reflect an opposing moral view. Second, neither of the opposing moral views is carried to its logical conclusion in the law: both are arbitrarily truncated. Third, the rules that specify exceptions are extremely elastic and can be made to cover just about any case. And fourth, the judge deciding a case involving the duty to aid can and will interpret the legal rules so as to reflect which moral viewpoint she finds preferable. Let us examine these four points.

Individualism and Altruism Crits contend that the no–duty rule reflects an "individualist" moral viewpoint, according to which there is a basic moral duty to refrain from acts that harm others but no such duty to take action to help them. Each adult is an individual who must succeed or fail in life based on his or her own efforts. Help from others should be expected only when one has something to offer them in return. Contracts in which equal partners benefit one another are consistent with the dignity of the individual. But a person degrades himself and treats others unreasonably when he expects to get something from them for nothing.

In opposition to such an individualist view, say the crits, the exceptions to the no-duty rule reflect an "altruist" moral viewpoint. According to that view, we should face the dangers and risks of life together, so that a person has a basic moral duty both to refrain from harming others and to act affirmatively to help them when they are in need. When one of us needs assistance that another can provide, she should provide it: after all, but for sheer luck, she may have been the one to need the help. It is neither degrading nor unreasonable to ask another to share her good fortune when one is in need and she can help out. It simply reflects the fact that the benefits and burdens of life are often visited upon persons in arbitrary ways.

Crits proceed to point out that both the altruist and individualist views are found in the law in arbitrarily truncated form. If the individualist view were carried to its logical conclusion, then there would be no exceptions to the common-law rule that there is no duty to aid another. And if the altruist view were carried to its logical conclusion, then the common-law rule would impose an affirmative duty to aid others. Instead, the private law consists of a patchwork of conflicting rules, reflecting incompatible but truncated moral viewpoints.

Exceptions to the Rule   The crits argue that the exceptions to the common law's no-duty rule are so elastic that they can be stretched to cover virtually any case. Consider *Buch v. Amory,* the tort case in which a boy was injured by a machine while on the property of a mill. The overseer knew that the boy was on mill property but, after telling him to leave, neglected to see to it that the boy left the property safely. The court held that the mill owners were not legally responsible for the injuries: it decided the case on the basis of the rule that there is no duty to act affirmatively to help another.

However, crits point out that one could just as well decide the case on the basis of one of the exceptions to that rule, namely, the counterrule that there may be a duty to aid if the defendant's actions helped create the dangerous situation in which the plaintiff was harmed. One could argue that the mill owners helped create the dangerous situation by constructing the mill in the first place and running dangerous equipment within it.

The other exception to the no-duty rule is equally if not more elastic, namely, the counterrule that there may be a duty to aid if the plaintiff and defendant stand in a "special legal relationship." Traditionally, special legal relationships were ones in which contract, custom, or statute imposed a duty on one party to aid another. Thus, lifeguards must save drowning swimmers in the area where they are working, since their contract calls for it. And parents have a duty to aid their own children because custom and statute impose that duty. But it is entirely possible to stretch the idea of a special legal relationship beyond such boundaries.

Consider *Tarasoff v. Regents of the University of California,* a case in which a patient told his university psychologist that he intended to kill a woman whom he, the patient, knew.[11] The woman, Tatiana Tarasoff, was not a patient of the psychologist or otherwise connected to him in any way. Yet, the court ruled that the direct special relationship between the psychologist and his patient created an indirect special relationship between the psychologist and Tarasoff.

Accordingly, the court found that the psychologist had a duty to warn Tarasoff of the threat against her life.

Crits argue that cases like *Tarasoff* illustrate the fact that judges decide cases involving the duty to aid on the basis of their own moral beliefs about whether the defendant should have acted to assist the plaintiff and that there is no other way for them to arrive at or justify such decisions. They choose to decide on the basis of the no–duty rule, if that rule better reflects their moral judgment about a case. They choose to decide on the basis of one of the exceptions to the no–duty rule, if that better reflects their moral judgment about a case. And the law itself fails to dictate which choice is correct.

According to crits, there are no legally correct or incorrect answers to these private-law cases. As in all other areas of law, there are conflicting legal rules, reflecting incompatible moral viewpoints. The judge must decide for herself which rule to use as the basis of decision.

The crits' analyses of law led them to endorse the conclusion that the legal realists had been so hesitant to embrace explicitly: the rule of law is a fiction. The law is too riddled with indeterminacy and conflict to rule. There is no distinctive method of legal reasoning to tell us what the law requires. And there is no single consistent set of requirements that the law imposes. There is, in short, no rule of law.[12]

LAW, LIBERTY, AND LIBERALISM

Liberalism and the Rule of Law

One of the principal viewpoints attacked by the crits is the political philosophy known as "liberalism." In the lexicon of philosophers and legal theorists, *liberalism* refers to an approach that takes individual liberty as a value of central importance. According to liberalism, society must be organized so that each individual has a wide area of freedom in which to decide for him- or herself how to live and that zone of freedom must be equal for all individuals.

Unlike premodern societies, in which there was a single set of shared values that virtually everyone accepted as objectively correct, in liberal society individuals are free to develop and pursue values very different from their neighbor's. And in the eyes of liberal thinkers, the law is key to establishing such a society. Equality under the rule of law is an indispensable condition for the existence and preservation of liberal society. A commitment to observing the rule of law makes possible a liberal society where freedom flourishes.[13] Individuals may disagree with one another over values, but if they agree to obey society's authoritative decisions, then they can live and work together in peace and freedom. That is the view of liberalism.

An important assumption behind liberalism is the mainstream idea that legal reasoning is a form of practical reasoning distinct from moral and political decision making. If individuals who hold conflicting values are to live together in peace and freedom under a system of authoritative rules they agree to obey, there must be some method of determining what those rules require, and that method must filter out the value disagreements that divide people.

The idea that such a method is possible is precisely the idea that legal reasoning is distinct from moral and political decision making. If there were no such method of reasoning, then the disagreements that individuals had with one another over values would generate disagreements over the meaning and application of the rules that they had agreed to obey. In that case, it would be futile to turn to the rule of law in order to establish peace and freedom. The agreement to obey the law would be practically meaningless, since each individual would decide what the law required in a way that reflected his or her own values.

Crits contend that such an agreement is meaningless, precisely because value disagreements invariably generate disagreements over the meaning and scope of society's authoritative rules. Moreover, the existence of disagreement over values invariably means that some persons will have good reason to refuse to enter an agreement to obey the rules, as no process for enacting legal rules and making authoritative decisions will prove acceptable to everyone.

Accordingly, crits argue that the rule of law cannot possibly work in a society in which individuals are free to develop and pursue their own, differing values. Peace and freedom cannot be achieved in liberal society by means of the rule of law.[14]

Unger and the Contradictions of Liberalism

Roberto Unger is the crit most famous for developing the preceding line of argument against liberalism, and many crits have endorsed his argument. Unger contends that there is no value-neutral process for enacting society's authoritative rules: any process will favor some values over others. Those persons whose values are not favored will have good reason to reject the process as unfair to them, and they will likely refuse to agree to obey the rules that are enacted. For example, Hardwick could legitimately complain that a political process that allows sodomy to be criminalized treats him and his values in a disrespectful and discriminatory manner. And he would have good reason to refuse an agreement to obey the results of such a process.

Moreover, Unger argues also that no value-neutral method is available for interpreting society's rules. Any approach to the interpretation of law will reflect certain values to the exclusion of others. For example, in the abortion debate, many of those on the pro-life side interpret the Constitution as requiring government to protect the life of the fetus, while those on the pro-choice side interpret it as requiring government to protect the choice of the pregnant woman. The two sides see in the very same words—the Due Process Clauses of the Fifth and Fourteenth Amendments—very different requirements, because they adhere to very different values.

Unger claims that the value disagreements that exist in liberal society are invariably reflected in disagreements over the meaning and application of society's authoritative rules and decisions. Liberalism holds that the members of liberal society can live in peace and freedom with one another if only they agree to obey the authoritative rules and decisions. But any such agreement must ultimately fail, because the members of liberal society cannot agree on what the rules mean and what the decisions have settled. As Unger puts it, "[N]o coherent theory of adjudication is possible within liberal political thought."[15]

Unger's attack on liberalism clearly goes hand in hand with the attack on legal reasoning examined in the previous section. Both attacks bring into question the widely held idea that the rule of law exists in our society. But Unger's attack goes further. If the attack on legal reasoning is correct, then the rule of law does not exist in our society. If the attack on liberalism is correct, then it could not even be brought into existence, as long as we remain committed to a free society.

THE MAINSTREAM VERSUS THE CRITS

Critics of the Crits

CLS has proved to be an extremely controversial approach to understanding the law. One dean at a prestigious law school even went so far as to suggest that crits are not fit to be on law school faculties. The problem in the eyes of such critics of the crits is that CLS fosters cynicism about and disrespect for the law. But the philosophical question is whether the CLS analyses are sound: do they reveal the law and legal reasoning for what they are?

Mainstream legal thinkers contend that the crits' view of law is severely distorted because they focus on the most controversial legal cases. Many cases never get to court because what the law requires is clear: society has made authoritative decisions that settle certain matters, and virtually everyone recognizes that. Many cases that do get to court are decided without much controversy or disagreement about the law among legal professionals.[16] And even when serious disagreement exists, judges and lawyers employ a method of reasoning that differs from practical reasoning about moral or political questions. They are practicing law, not politics or morality. So claims mainstream legal thinking.

These claims contain important truths, but they are not in themselves sufficient to rebut the arguments of realists and crits that indeterminacy is pervasive in our law and there is no distinctive method of legal reasoning to arrive at correct legal answers. The fact that in many cases judges generally agree on what the law is may not reflect the fact that the law has a determinate meaning. It may only reflect the fact that judges tend to share many moral and political views. Moreover, it is very plausible to suggest that judicial decisions necessarily take account of moral considerations in many cases. Is there some mainstream theory that can accommodate this plausible suggestion and still vindicate the idea that legal reasoning is distinct from moral and political decision making?

Dworkin and Legal Reasoning

Ronald Dworkin is the mainstream thinker whose theory provides perhaps the most interesting response to the claims of realists and crits.[17] It accommodates the notion that considerations stemming from moral and political principle are necessarily taken into account in many legal cases; yet it insists that legal reasoning is not reducible to moral or political decision making and that judicial decisions represent the legitimate exercise of power.

Dworkin contends that the law is not an arbitrary collection of decisions; rather, the authoritative decisions represented in legal rules and doctrines form a largely coherent whole that embodies a consistent set of moral and political principles.[18] Such principles provide the justifying reasons behind the authoritative decisions. And the job of legal reasoning is to interpret and apply legal rules in light of the strongest possible justifying reasons consistent with the authoritative decisions represented in the law.

Dworkin does not explicitly rely on the distinction between arbitrary and constitutional government to make his case, but he does appear to assume such a distinction. His position rests on a premise articulated in the mainstream account of legal reasoning examined earlier in this chapter, namely, that the existence of justifying reasons behind the law is necessary to maintain the distinction between government under the rule of law and arbitrary government. A government whose laws were purely arbitrary in the sense that no justifying reasons could be cited to support them would not be fundamentally different from a government controlled by the arbitrary whim of a despot. Our system of government is fundamentally different, in Dworkin's view, because there are justifying reasons behind the law, and the job of judges in rendering decisions is to apply the law in light of the strongest reasons that could justify it.

Indeed, for Dworkin, judicial decisions are not arbitrary exercises of power precisely because they are based on such justifying reasons. The decisions handed down by courts are not acts of might but of right, which we have at least a prima facie obligation to obey. And that obligation is rooted in the very nature of legal reasoning as practiced in our legal system and any other genuine system of constitutional government.

In Dworkin's view, legal reasoning requires the judge to examine the range of legal rules and doctrines potentially relevant to a given case. An ideal judge (whom Dworkin calls "Hercules") would be able to keep in mind every authoritative decision and determine what the strongest reasons were that justified those decisions when taken as a whole. Mortal judges will settle for something less, but they still must think of the law as embodying a coherent set of decisions behind which there are justifying reasons.

For Dworkin, the task of legal reasoning is not to determine what reasons those who made the authoritative decisions believed justified the decisions. Different legislators and judges may well have had different reasons in mind, and in any event legal reasoning is not a matter of psychological guesswork. The simple fact that some decision maker believed that some consideration provided a justifying reason for his decision cannot create a prima facie obligation to obey it, as it may in fact have had no justifying power.

Rather, the task of legal reasoning, for Dworkin, is to determine the best possible reasons that could be given to justify the authoritative decisions embodied in legal rules and doctrines. It does not matter whether the original decision makers thought about those reasons and acted on them.

Dworkin makes it clear that legal reasoning as he describes it requires one to make judgments of moral and political principle.[19] Such judgments are necessary in order to determine what the strongest possible justifying reasons are for the authoritative decisions embodied in the law.

For example, in Dworkin's view, the best possible justifying reasons behind the Supreme Court's decisions in its cases regarding contraception and abortion involve the moral principle that individuals have a right to make decisions about their own private, consensual sexual conduct without the interference of government. Dworkin does not hide the fact that it takes a moral judgment to arrive at the conclusion that this principle provides the strongest justifying reason for the decisions in question. Dworkin is prepared to defend that moral judgment.

Moreover, since the principle applies to homosexual conduct just as much as it does to the use of contraceptives and the termination of pregnancy, he is prepared to criticize *Bowers* as wrongly decided. In light of the precedents and the strongest principles that could justify them, the majority decision was indeed arbitrary, as the crits suggest. But Justice Blackmun's dissent was not arbitrary at all, in Dworkin's view, as it rested on the moral principle that provided the strongest justifying reason for the decisions made by the precedents.

Yet, for Dworkin, an important difference remains between legal reasoning and other forms of practical reasoning. Unlike reasoning about moral or political questions, legal reasoning must generally respect society's authoritative decisions and accept what those decisions have settled. Some judges may have moral doubts about what the privacy cases settled; for example, they may regard the use of contraceptives as immoral. But society has authoritatively settled the question of whether individuals should be free from government interference to use contraceptives, and judges must accept that decision even if they have moral qualms about it.

This point does not mean that judges can never regard any authoritative decision as a "mistake." It is legitimate for them to overturn or reverse a certain precedent, if they find that other precedents and authoritative decisions are best justified by principles that are incompatible with the precedent in question. Dworkin would argue that this is exactly how we should view the decision in *Bowers*. It is a decision that is completely out of line with the best principles underlying the relevant precedents, in Dworkin's view, and so should be overturned.

For Dworkin, then, legal reasoning is distinct from the forms of practical reasoning involved in moral or political decision making. Legal reasoning operates under the distinctive constraint embodied in the principle that legal decisions must be based on what society has authoritatively settled. To reject legal reasoning as a distinct form of practical reasoning would be to reopen afresh every social and political issue that came to court. Whether or not it would be better for society to do that, Dworkin insists that it is not part of the best account of the way our legal system works.

The Crits' Response

Crits can respond to Dworkin's theory by developing two distinct lines of argument. The first insists on the idea that the law is a patchwork quilt of rules that reflects incompatible and arbitrarily truncated moral and political principles. The second denies that legal reasoning is, in the final analysis, essentially different from moral or political decision making. Let us examine each in turn.

According to the first line of CLS argument, the authoritative decisions embodied in the law do not form a largely coherent whole, as Dworkin claims. The judge who looks for a consistent set of moral and political principles behind those decisions will find instead contradictory and arbitrarily truncated principles.

Some legal rules reflect individualist principles. Crits would cite as an example the consideration doctrine in contract law, which says that a promise does not give rise to a legal obligation unless something of value is given or promised in return for the promise. Thus, courts have often ruled that promises made without consideration cannot be enforced. But other legal rules will reflect altruist principles. Crits would cite the doctrine of reasonable reliance, which says that a person may be legally obligated to compensate someone to whom he made a promise, even if he did not receive consideration in return, if the promisee reasonably relied on the promise and suffered a loss as a result. Accordingly, courts have also found that promises made without consideration can be enforced, if the plaintiff suffered a loss as a result of reasonably relying on the promise.

Thus, society has authoritatively decided to adopt an individualist view of promises, but it has also authoritatively decided to adopt the contradictory altruist view of promises. This makes the law an incoherent patchwork, according to the crits, and a Dworkinian judge who looks for a consistent set of principles reflected in the law that governs promises will discover only contradiction and inconsistency. Crits claim that similar contradictions can be found throughout the law.

The second line of CLS argument against Dworkin claims that his way of distinguishing legal reasoning from other forms of practical reasoning fails. Crucial to his efforts to draw the distinction is the principle that legal reasoning must generally abide by society's past authoritative decisions. This principle allegedly constrains legal reasoning in a way that other forms of practical reasoning are not constrained. But crits will insist that the principle is toothless: it has no real bite and cannot constrain judges in a way that distinguishes legal from moral or political decision making.

The problem with the principle is that judges can, consistent with the principle, determine what has been authoritatively decided in a way that reflects their own moral and political viewpoints. Liberal judges can and will see their liberal principles reflected in those decisions, and conservative judges can and will see their conservative principles in them. And neither side will be wrong, because society's authoritative decisions reflect the range of political and moral views that form a significant part of our culture.

This problem is not solved by telling judges that they must look to the strongest justifying reasons that could be given for a decision. The strength attributed by a judge to a given reason will depend on that judge's moral and political views. For the conservative majority in *Bowers,* it was a strong reason to exclude homosexual sodomy from the protections of the right to privacy that the moral traditions of our society have historically condemned the practice. For the liberal Justice Blackmun, that reason counted for naught: the decisive consideration was that sodomy represented a choice made by consenting adults about how to conduct their intimate affairs. Thus the majority concluded that the precedents decided that only heterosexual activity was protected by the right of privacy, while Blackmun concluded that homosexual activity was also protected.

Notice that the crits are not arguing that judges turn away from the law when it does not contain a clear answer to their case and make their decisions purely on extralegal grounds. That argument was made both by realists and by many mainstream thinkers. The difference was that the realists thought the law "ran out" much more often than did the mainstreamers.

Dworkin criticizes both realists and many mainstreamers for failing to see that when the law does not have a clear answer, judges do not leave it behind but rather look for the strongest moral and political principles that could justify its authoritative decisions. In hard cases, judges do not turn away from the law but dig deeper into it. And the crits can agree with Dworkin on this important point. But they contend that when judges dig deeper what they see is a reflection of their own moral and political principles.

The two lines of CLS argument against Dworkin converge on the conclusion that he has failed to show that judicial decisions represent acts of right rather than might. He has not succeeded in demonstrating the legitimacy of judicial decision making. And for the crits, all efforts to establish that legitimacy will fail to the extent that they are based on the notion that legal reasoning is a form of practical reasoning distinct from moral and political decision making.

Competition and Contradiction: Dworkin Replies

Dworkin concedes that the CLS claim that the law is a contradictory patchwork cannot be dismissed out of hand. Yet, he contends that the crits have not succeeded in making the case for their patchwork thesis. One problem with their argument, he asserts, is that they fail to distinguish between contradictory principles and competing principles. Dworkin does not explain this distinction at any length, but what he seems to have in mind is the following.

Contradictory principles are incompatible with one another on any reasonable interpretation of them. Thus, "Keep absolutely every promise" and "Break absolutely every promise" are incompatible, however one reasonably construes them: one cannot accept and follow both of them. In contrast, competing principles are potentially incompatible with each other in some situations, but reasonable interpretation can render them compatible. Thus, "Keep your promises" and "Help those in serious need" are potentially incompatible in some situations but can be rendered consistent.

For example, suppose I have promised my sister to go to the movies with her one afternoon, but a friend of mine has a heart attack and needs me to drive him to the emergency room at that time. A potential conflict arises between the promise-keeping principle and the helping-those-in-need principle. Yet, the two principles can be reasonably interpreted so as to make them compatible by means of this auxiliary idea: in an emergency situation when someone's life is at stake, relatively insignificant promises may be broken if necessary to meet the emergency. This auxiliary idea helps us to tailor the scope of the two principles in a way that makes them compatible with one another.[20]

Accordingly, Dworkin's point against the crits is that they regard the different principles behind legal rules and doctrines as contradictory when in fact the principles can be reasonably interpreted so as to dissolve any potential incompatibilities. Underlying the doctrine of reasonable reliance is the principle that we have an obligation to those who suffer losses as a result of reasonably relying on our promises. Underlying the doctrine of consideration is the principle that individuals cannot legitimately demand that the law give them something for nothing.

Crits assume that the two principles are contradictory, when in fact they may only be competing principles whose scope can be reasonably defined with the help of auxiliary ideas so as to render them compatible with one another. Some cases of promises without consideration would be treated as unenforceable, but others would not be. One would need to look carefully at the facts in each case and judge them in terms of whether there was reliance, how reasonable it was, how great the loss suffered was, how great the burden would be on the promisor if held liable, and so forth. There may be no simple or mechanical way to make these judgments, but legal reasoning as Dworkin describes it does not purport to be a simple or mechanical task.

In Dworkin's view, then, the crits' claim that the law is a patchwork of rules that reflects incompatible and arbitrarily truncated principles rests on a confusion. What the crits call the arbitrary truncation of incompatible principles is actually the reasonable tailoring of different principles to the facts of different cases so as meld the principles into a coherent system of law.

The crits' second argument against Dworkin rests on the claim that no constraint is imposed on judges by the principle that judicial rulings must follow society's prior authoritative decisions: judges can, consistent with the principle, read their own moral and political values into those decisions.

Dworkin responds to this argument by pointing out that it succeeds only if society's authoritative decisions really settle little or nothing about how society is to operate. The decisions would need to be so vague or so ambiguous that any judge could take the decision as embodying his or her own values: the law would have to be like a giant Rorschach test, in which what one saw in its patterns was a reflection of what was in one's own mind.

Dworkin regards as wholly implausible such a view of law and of the authoritative decisions it embodies. Those decisions surely have some degree of ambiguity and vagueness: that is precisely why it is necessary for legal reasoning to seek the strongest justifying reasons that lie behind them in order to arrive at answers in hard cases. But there is little plausibility in the claim that society's authoritative decisions actually settle little or nothing.

Griswold settled that government may not outlaw the use of contraceptives by married people. *Roe* settled that government may not criminalize early-term abortions. The Civil Rights Act of 1964 settled that employers may not refuse to hire blacks on account of their race.

Dworkin would be among the first to concede that each of these authoritative decisions was unclear in certain respects. *Griswold* did not make clear whether government can outlaw the use of contraceptives by unmarried people. And so legal reasoning was needed to formulate the strongest justifying principle for what it did clearly decide and then to apply that principle to the case of unmarried people. *Roe* did not settle the question of whether government could require minors to obtain parental permission before obtaining an abortion. And so legal reasoning was again needed to formulate and apply justifying principles. The Civil Rights Act did not clearly settle whether employers could favor blacks in hiring as part of some affirmative action plan, and so legal reasoning was again called into play.

From a Dworkinian perspective, the crits' assumption that society's authoritative decisions settle little or nothing can be explained by the fact that they focus on those cases in which the decisions are unclear. As other mainstreamers have pointed out, the crits ignore the wide area in which matters have been clearly settled by society's authoritative decisions. This ambiguity leads crits to the implausible contention that legal reasoning is not constrained by the need to follow what those decisions have settled. And it ultimately leads to the crits' mistaken notion that legal reasoning is not essentially different from the forms of practical reasoning involved in moral and political decision making.

The Crits' Last Stand

There is one last line of argument that crits might raise against Dworkin. They might focus on the idea that justifying reasons lie behind the law. Dworkin and other mainstreamers assume that the existence of such justifying reasons is needed to preserve the distinction between government under the rule of law and arbitrary government. Unless there were reasons that could help to justify its laws, a "constitutional government" would not be fundamentally different from one in the grip of the arbitrary will of a despot. In claiming that we have the rule of law, Dworkin and other mainstreamers assume that behind our system of law, there are such justifying reasons.

But crits might reply by arguing that the justifying reasons behind our system of law are too weak to distinguish our system from arbitrary government. For them, the law supports the illegitimate hierarchies that pervade our society. While there may be something to be said in favor of some of our laws, on the whole very little can be said for them, too little to clearly distinguish our system from one in the grip of the arbitrary whim of some despot.

Dworkin and other mainstreamers could respond to this line of argument by pointing to clear differences between societies such as Nazi Germany, the former Soviet Union, and Communist China, on the one hand, and the United States and other Western liberal democracies, on the other. The Western liberal democracies are far more decent and humane than Nazi or Soviet or Chinese society, and some of the differences that make us more decent and humane can be reasonably explained by saying that we have the rule of law, while they did not. Our system of law may be vulnerable to very legitimate and sweeping criticism, but the justifying reasons behind our laws are, to put it mildly, far stronger than whatever justifying reasons one could come up with for Nazi or Soviet law. It would be implausible for the crits to insist there is any moral equivalence between the United States and, say, Nazi Germany or the Soviet Union. But they might argue that it is a mistake to account for the differences between us and the Nazis by saying that we have the rule of law and they did not. The crits say that the law does not rule—politics does. And so they might claim that the difference between us and the Nazis is that the Nazis had a brutal and barbaric form of politics, while ours is less so.

But Dworkin and his fellow mainstreamers will reply that our politics is less brutal and barbaric in part because the power of government and of other institutions in society is restrained by the rule of law, while under Nazism the party and the Fuhrer were above the law. The rule of law may not guarantee substantive justice, but the facts of human nature and society argue strongly for restraining human power by the rule of human law. Contemporary society may not fully embody the rule of law, but that is no reason to repudiate the rule of law or to declare it a fiction. Rather, it is reason to make a more concerted effort to live up to its principles.

SUMMARY

And so we return to the question that occupied us at the beginning of this book: What is the nature and value of the rule of law? The legal thinkers of the Western tradition have been discussing, analyzing, and arguing about this question and the philosophical issues that stem from it since the early days of our civilization. Their thinking and arguments about law have shaped the society we live in, the security we enjoy, and the freedoms we exercise. By learning about and critically examining what they have thought, we help carry that tradition forward. And perhaps we will also help change society for the better.

NOTES

1. Crits generally endorse the legal realist and feminist critiques of the public-private distinction. See Chapters 4 and 7.

2. Duncan Kennedy, "Legal Education as Training for Hierarchy," in *Politics of Law*,

D. Kairys, ed. (New York: Pantheon, 1982), p. 47.

3. Some CR theorists also argue that, though the rule of law is a fiction, the rhetoric of legal rights can play a more useful role than crits think in advancing racial

equality. CR theorists have also joined forces with radical feminists in arguing that oppression based on race and gender are intertwined in complex ways to which CLS has not paid sufficient attention.

4. The most sophisticated account of the concept of authority in the context of legal and political issues is given by Joseph Raz. The mainstream account of legal reasoning developed in this section relies on some of his important ideas. See his *Practical Reason and Norms,* 2d ed. (Princeton, NJ: Princeton University Press, 1990).

5. If this mainstream account of legal reasoning is sound, then we need to add a sixth principle to the five rule-of-law principles enumerated in Chapter 1: The general and authoritative rules by which government regulates society must be such that sufficiently strong justifying reasons can be cited in support of them.

6. The importance of consistency in the appeal to justifying reasons was emphasized in an influential essay by Herbert Wechsler. See his "Toward Neutral Principles of Constitutional Law," *Harvard Law Review* 73 (1959), 1.

7. A syllogism is a form of reasoning in which a conclusion is drawn from two premises that contain some common term. The two premises are usually called the "major" and "minor" premises. Consider: (a) All men are mortal and (b) Socrates is a man; therefore, (c) Socrates is mortal. *Man* is the common term; the major premise is (a), and the minor is (b). Extreme legal formalism holds that all legal reasoning can be put into the form of such a syllogism, with a legal rule as the major premise, the facts of the case as the minor premise, and the correct legal answer as the conclusion.

8. The police were initially looking to arrest Hardwick for failing to appear at a hearing after he had been given a ticket for public drunkenness. A housemate let the policeman into the house and directed him to Hardwick's bedroom. The district attorney declined to proceed with the sodomy charge against Hardwick unless further evidence developed, but Hardwick decided not to take any chances and went to court to have the antisodomy law declared unconstitutional.

9. What would Blackmun say about the dangers of the transmission of AIDS through homosexual conduct? Most likely, he would reply that unprotected heterosexual conduct can also transmit AIDS and that the relevant distinction here is not between homosexual and heterosexual conduct but rather between protected and unprotected sexual conduct.

10. *Romer v. Evans,* 517 U.S. 620 (1996) at 634.

11. *Tarasoff v. Regents of University of California,* 17 Cal. 3d 425, 551 P.2d 334 (1976).

12. In recent years, some prominent crits have drawn back from the conclusion that the rule of law does not exist. See Duncan Kennedy, *A Critique of Adjudication* (Cambridge: Harvard University Press, 1997), and Roberto Unger, *What Should Legal Analysis Become?* (London: Verso, 1996).

13. Most persons we would normally describe as "liberals" or "conservatives" endorse some version of the kind of liberalism discussed in this section. Few persons would claim we should return to premodern days when little individual liberty existed and a single set of values was regarded as binding on everyone. Conservatives typically emphasize the importance of the economic liberties of the market, while liberals stress personal liberties such as sexual freedom. The disagreements are not over whether a wide area of individual liberty should be legally protected but over which liberties are of central importance and how those liberties are to be understood.

14. Crits typically argue that liberal society goes too far in its emphasis on individual liberty. They contend that the values of community and solidarity have been unfortunately lost and advocate that such values be treated with renewed importance.

15. Roberto Unger, *Knowledge and Politics* (New York: Free Press, 1975), p. 98.

16. Disagreement over the facts of a case, rather than over the meaning of the law, will often be the basis for disagreements about the correct legal outcome.

17. Dworkin's general theory of law is discussed at greater length in Chapter 2 and his theory of constitutional interpretation in Chapter 3.

18. We will see later that, on Dworkin's account, the law does not need to be perfectly coherent, as he allows for the possibility that some authoritative decisions are "mistakes."

19. Dworkin distinguishes between arguments (or judgments) of principle and arguments of policy. The former concern the rights of individuals, while the latter concern the general good of society. He believes the former arguments are the ones relevant to decisions in legal cases, in which the judge must determine the rights of the litigants.

20. See Henry Richardson, "Specifying Norms as a Way to Resolve Concrete Ethical Problems," *Philosophy and Public Affairs* 19:4 (Fall 1990), 279–310.

DISCUSSION QUESTIONS

1. Is CLS right in claiming that contemporary society is radically flawed by illegitimate hierarchies of power and privilege? If so, would it really be possible for the legal system to have strong justifying reasons behind its rules and principles?

2. Is our law more accurately viewed as a messy patchwork of conflicting rules and principles or as a coherent system of norms that expresses an underlying philosophy?

ADDITIONAL READING

Altman, Andrew. *Critical Legal Studies: A Liberal Critique.* Princeton University Press, 1990.

Belliotti, Raymond. *Justifying Law.* Temple University Press, 1992.

Delgado, Richard, and Jean Stefancic. "Critical Race Theory: An Annotated Bibliography." *Virginia Law Review* 79 (1993), 461–516.

Edmundson, William. "Transparency and Indeterminacy in the Liberal Critique of Critical Legal Studies." *Seton Hall Law Review* 24 (1994), 557–602.

Fiss, Owen. "The Law Regained." *Cornell Law Review* 74 (1989), 245–255.

Fitzpatrick, Peter, and Alan Hunt, eds. *Critical Legal Studies.* Blackwell, 1987.

Greenawalt, Kent. *Law and Objectivity.* Oxford University Press, 1992.

Hutchinson, Alan, ed. *Critical Legal Studies.* Rowman and Littlefield, 1989.

Kairys, David. *The Politics of Law,* 3d ed. Basic Books, 1998.

Kelman, Mark. *A Guide to Critical Legal Studies.* Harvard University Press, 1987.

Kennedy, Duncan. *A Critique of Adjudication.* Harvard University Press, 1997.

———. "Form and Substance in Private-Law Adjudication." *Harvard Law Review* 89 (1976), 1685–1778.

Kennedy, Duncan, and Karl Klare. "A Bibliography of Critical Legal Studies." *Yale Law Journal* 94 (1984), 461–490.

Kress, Ken. "Legal Indeterminacy." *California Law Review* 77 (1989), 283–337.

Rumble, Wilfrid. *American Legal Realism.* Cornell University Press, 1968.

Solum, Lawrence. "On the Indeterminacy Crisis: Critiquing Critical Dogma." *University of Chicago Law Review* 54 (1987), 462–503.

"Symposium: Critical Legal Studies." *Stanford Law Review* 36:1–2 (January 1984).

Tushnet, Mark. *Red, White, and Blue: A Critical Analysis of Constitutional Law.* Harvard University Press, 1988.

Unger, Roberto. *The Critical Legal Studies Movement.* Harvard University Press, 1983.

———. *Knowledge and Politics.* Free Press, 1975.

———. *What Should Legal Analysis Become?* Verso, 1996.

Index